THE JOURNALIST'S PREDICAMENT

The Journalist's Predicament

Difficult Choices in a Declining Profession

Matthew Powers and Sandra Vera-Zambrano

Columbia University Press   New York

Columbia University Press
Publishers Since 1893
New York   Chichester, West Sussex
cup.columbia.edu
Copyright © 2023 Columbia University Press
All rights reserved

Library of Congress Cataloging-in-Publication Data
Names: Powers, Matthew, author. | Vera Zambrano, Sandra, author.
Title: The journalist's predicament : difficult choices in a declining profession / Matthew Powers and Sandra Vera-Zambrano.
Description: New York : Columbia University Press, [2023] | Includes bibliographical references and index.
Identifiers: LCCN 2023003315 (print) | LCCN 2023003316 (ebook) |
  ISBN 9780231207904 (hardback) | ISBN 9780231207911 (trade paperback) |
  ISBN 9780231557177 (ebook)
Subjects: LCSH: Journalism. | Journalists—Attitudes. | Journalists—Job stress.
Classification: LCC PN4797 .P66 2023 (print) | LCC PN4797 (ebook) |
  DDC 070.4—dc23/eng/20230425
LC record available at https://lccn.loc.gov/2023003315
LC ebook record available at https://lccn.loc.gov/2023003316

Cover design: Chang Jae Lee
Cover image: Shutterstock

The reporter has to be courageous, sharp as a hawk, mentally untiring, physically enduring. He comes in contact with everybody, from monarchs to beggars, from noblemen to nobodies. He sees the tragedy and comedy of human life, its cynicism and toadyism, its passionate struggle and feverish ambition, its sham and subterfuge, its lavish wealth and gasping poverty, its joy and sorrow, its good deeds and its most hideous crimes. His is a strange career, with its constant predicaments and anxieties. But it is an attractive, fascinating life to many, because of its wondrous change and kaleidoscopic variety.

—EDWIN SHUMAN, *STEPS INTO JOURNALISM*, 1894

Contents

Acknowledgments ix

INTRODUCTION
Why Would Anyone Be a Journalist? 1

CHAPTER ONE
The Genesis of the Journalist's Predicament 28

CHAPTER TWO
Living For—and Maybe Off—Journalism 54

CHAPTER THREE
At Their Best 86

CHAPTER FOUR
Conserve, Challenge, Accede 114

CHAPTER FIVE
Leaving Journalism 142

CONCLUSION 169

EPILOGUE
Is Journalism Dying? 191

Appendix A: Interviewing as Comprehension 197
Appendix B: Seattle and Toulouse as Regional Media 203
Appendix C: Tables and Data 209
Notes 227
Bibliography 265
Index 285

Acknowledgments

Thanks first and foremost to the journalists in Toulouse and Seattle that took the time to speak with us for this project. The diversity of their experiences—as well as their perceptions of them—provided insights into the reasons why journalism continues be an attractive career option, how individuals maintain their belief in the profession's worth amid conditions that often threaten to erode it, and the point at which some no longer find work in journalism deserving of their efforts. If the story we tell in this book is neither entirely cheerful nor wholly gloomy, it is because our primary aim has been to capture the kaleidoscopic range of responses we encountered. We hope that the individuals interviewed recognize the representations we offer of their experiences and that the larger predicament we describe in these pages resonates with those working as journalists elsewhere.

A grant from the University of Washington's Royalty Research Fund provided the resources necessary for initially getting the project off the ground. At that early stage, input from colleagues on both sides of the Atlantic helped us define and delimit the scope of our study. Thanks in particular to Pauline Amiel, Chris Anderson, Olivier Baisnée, Randy Beam, Lance Bennett, Franck Bousquet, Angèle Christin, Patricia Moy, Rasmus Kleis Nielsen, Nikos Smyrnaios, and Doug Underwood. As the project developed, we benefited from the feedback we received at conferences and symposia, as well as from journal reviewers and editors for articles that stemmed from this larger project. These comments helped us to slowly figure out what the larger story for the book could be. Just as importantly, their engagement furnished us with the sense that we were working on a topic that, without being central to most extant scholarly conversations about journalism, was nevertheless worthy of study.

Research assistants aided in the collection, transcription, and analysis of data throughout the years in which we worked on this project. They also helped track down sources, identify relevant literatures, and suggest ways the argument for this book could be streamlined. For this work in France, we thank Clémentine Berjaud, Aicha Bourad, Elise Cruzel, Frédéric Dessort, and Cyriac Gousset; in the United States, we thank Meagan Doll, KC Lynch, Rico Neumann, Polly Straub-Cook, Hai Wang, Rian Wanstreet, and Yunkang Yang. PhD students associated with University of Washington's Center for Journalism, Media and Democracy also offered comments and criticisms on the project at multiple points. Finally, Rossana Bouza entered the project in its final stages and formatted the entire manuscript with editorial aplomb.

Several colleagues gave feedback on various drafts of the book. Rodney Benson and Érik Neveu provided stimulating comments at multiple points that opened up new ways of grasping our research findings. They also warned us away from several early—and, in retrospect, misbegotten—frames for the larger project. Olivier Baisnée delivered his usual close readings, astute advice, and penetrating questions, which forced us several times to rethink what we thought we knew. Adrienne Russell read the entire manuscript, showed us that we had buried the lede, and suggested how to remedy the problem. John Tomasic listened as we (seemingly endlessly) rehearsed the book's main arguments and pointed out ways we might connect journalists' experiences in Toulouse and Seattle to those working in journalism elsewhere. Jerry Baldasty and Richard Kielbowicz lent their historical expertise in the comments and suggestions they provided on chapter 2.

At Columbia University Press, Philip Leventhal saw value in the book before we could fully articulate its contribution to him ourselves; for that, as well as his efficient editorial oversight, we are grateful. Several anonymous reviewers provided careful, generous, and probing comments, both on the proposal and the full manuscript. We are truly appreciative of their insights and engagement. Thanks also to Robert Demke for his careful copyediting and to Susan Pensak for overseeing the book's production. Any remaining errors, of course, are ours alone.

Thanks finally to those closest to us: Ekin, Pablo, and Marco. The work for this book sometimes tested their patience; we are grateful to finish without having exceeded its limits.

THE JOURNALIST'S PREDICAMENT

Introduction

Why Would Anyone Be a Journalist?

> The other day my esthetician told me that her eighteen-year-old daughter wants a career in journalism. "No way!" I cried out. "Tell her to become a lawyer or a doctor, not a journalist." The prestige is not what it used to be and in reality, we hardly make a living. . . . And yet, doing radio is what I like the most. I like being all alone in a studio where no one can see you but everyone can hear you. . . . You have to get everything across with your voice. . . . It's just incredible.
> —RADIO JOURNALIST, TOULOUSE, FRANCE

> I went into journalism firmly believing that it would be a safe middle-class lifestyle. I am foolishly married to another journalist who also thought this. My foolish daughter, having had so much fun at our dinner table talking about the news of the day, now wants to be a journalist. She's enrolled in journalism school. We are not doing very well in our family with getting the big message that this craft is in serious trouble. . . . And yet there is no other job in the world I would rather have. . . . As you can tell about me, I have a journalistic essence. I may not be the greatest reporter, and I do not have prizes. But it is something that I really feel is really wired into my soul.
> —RADIO JOURNALIST, SEATTLE, UNITED STATES

Separated by an ocean and a plethora of national particularities, the journalists quoted in the epigraphs nonetheless describe a common predicament. Their professional conditions are in various respects undesirable. The prestige is "not what it used to be"; the pay—never substantial to begin with—has stagnated at levels below the "safe middle-class lifestyle" they hoped for and expected; the "craft," for reasons seemingly so obvious that they pass by unarticulated, is "in serious trouble." Yet despite these somber sentiments, both journalists continue to feel powerfully attracted to the profession. Working in the solitude of a radio studio to find the right timbre in which to narrate news to an invisible audience is "just incredible." Garnering prizes, moreover, may not be one's lot in professional life but journalism is no mere job that these two dutifully clock in to and out of. Instead, it appears, to borrow words from the American poet Stanley Kunitz, as "a principle of being" from which they "struggle not to stray."[1]

The predicament these journalists describe entails material and symbolic dimensions. For them, the profession is frustrating in part because it fails to deliver anticipated or desired levels of job stability and material comfort. But journalism, like other cultural occupations,[2] is also experienced and evaluated in relation to the opportunities for self-expression it provides and the sense of self-fulfillment it promises. These dimensions can be evaluated in relation to each other; the French journalist's low pay is offset by the sense of self-fulfillment she experiences while narrating a radio program. But each dimension can also be evaluated in its own right. The failure of the American journalist to earn prizes or be considered a "great reporter" is counterbalanced by her deeper sense of attachment to the profession. Bringing these points together, *the journalist's predicament* can be characterized as the struggle to attain a personally acceptable balance among the overall material and symbolic rewards expected and obtained from the profession.

This predicament is both inherent in journalism and an amplified feature of life in contemporary news media. What is personally acceptable is always a matter of the expectations one holds and the negotiations one is willing to make on their behalf. A discordant relationship between the overall balance of material and symbolic rewards could therefore transpire even in journalism's more prosperous days. Yet the profession today is also characterized by upheavals that result in a broad diminution in the material and symbolic rewards on offer.[3] This diminution stems foremost from a heightened tension between the profession's distressed commercial underpinnings and its historically derived social functions.[4] With few exceptions, journalists' employers are seeing revenues decline drastically due to the rise of a novel information ecosystem that wreaks havoc on advertising budgets, intensifies competition for audience attention, and erodes previously stable business models. Most have responded by cutting costs and exploring new avenues to "monetize" their offerings. These developments bring opportunities for some, but for many they introduce some combination of job insecurity, wage stagnation, and deteriorating working conditions. Intensifying the challenges, journalists' public standing has diminished, and their role as chief mediators of public debate is challenged recurrently. Given such apparently insalubrious conditions, why would anyone be a journalist?

Addressing this question matters, and not only because of its implications for journalists' capacities to fulfill their social functions like speaking truth to power or informing citizens. In important ways, journalists are significant because of *who they are*, sociologically speaking. Knowing that they could almost certainly make more money outside of the news business, journalists maintain a relationship to work that foregrounds personal expression, promises self-fulfillment, and connects to broader social values. Through the lesser emphasis they place on material rewards, journalists also express, if only tacitly, a critical relationship to the primacy of economic considerations in social life. It is this orientation to work, and the social arrangements that support it, that the journalist's contemporary predicament brings into view. Their responses highlight efforts to deal with the growing intrusion of market considerations in many domains of social life. In this regard, the journalist's predicament is just one example of a much broader issue concerning many socially important professions like teaching, nursing, and caretaking that struggle to recruit and retain individuals to their ranks amid an increasing emphasis on market principles in professional life.

This book explores how journalists adjust themselves to this predicament and, when finding an acceptable balance of rewards, maintain their belief in the profession's worth. Belief that the profession is worth the struggles that the predicament presents is foundational. Journalism cannot exist without individuals who believe that the profession is worthy of their efforts. The persistence of this belief requires regular renewal; its loss instigates a crisis that is, literally, existential.[5] That this belief persists at all merits investigation, given the general diminution of material and symbolic rewards and the growing tension between the profession's commercial underpinnings and its long-standing social functions. Indeed, anything else that matters about journalism—including the extent to which it facilitates democratic life by performing its social functions—depends on journalists' capacities to retain this belief. How and for whom it persists, and when and for whom it dissolves, are considered here both as a topic in its own right, and as a starting point for addressing broader issues facing journalism in contemporary societies.

One can hardly claim that journalists are naively unaware of the predicament in which they find themselves. As the quotations at the chapter's outset make clear, the journalists believe their profession is worthy in spite of their experiences with its adverse conditions. Their belief therefore entails much more than an abstract faith in the importance of journalism. Instead, it resembles what Pierre Bourdieu has termed an *illusio*—i.e., a belief that the profession is worthy of *their* energies and *their* investments.[6] This belief that journalism is "worth the candle"[7] underwrites the sacrifices they make and the meanings they construct by being journalists. It also demands a commitment to the profession's stakes, including those that seem puzzling or senseless to those outside the profession (which can be glimpsed in magnified form in the foreign correspondent's willingness to risk death in order to report a story). Without the possibility of material or symbolic rewards, these commitments would make little sense. How journalists come to believe in, manage, and sometimes become disillusioned about the profession's worth is therefore the primary focus of this book.[8]

Interviews with journalists based in two cities—Toulouse, France, and Seattle, United States—form the book's empirical basis. Prior research suggests that the journalist's predicament is especially pronounced in locales outside the well-studied media capitals of Paris and New York due to the increased tensions their employers face between the profession's economic foundations and its social functions.[9] The interviews provide insights into the attractions that make an investment in journalism seem worthy, and explore what journalists expect from the profession in return. These data also uncover ways that journalists retain their belief in the profession's worth through works in which they take pride and ascribe meaning. Journalists discuss their doubts and frustrations in light of the discrepancies between the expected and the realized balance of material and symbolic rewards. They also describe adjustments that allow them to retain, at least for the time being, their conviction that the profession is worth their efforts. Completing the inquiry are interviews with journalists that have left journalism, which shed light on the point at which belief in the profession's worth becomes personally untenable.

These interviews show that it has become extremely difficult for journalists to find an equilibrium between the profession's commercial concerns and its most prestigious social functions. Few have conditions that afford them the time and resources necessary for doing the grandiose, explicitly civic vision of journalism inscribed in the profession's most hallowed ideals. The opportunities to produce long-form, in-depth, and well-composed reporting—whose provenance among regional journalists is of relatively recent vintage—are therefore decreasing. In their place, many describe doing poorly paid tasks that require great versatility. They endlessly feed websites and social media accounts that constantly need to appear "fresh." They use multimedia to report on topics that are assigned primarily for their potential to amuse and entertain rather than to inform or provoke thought. They spend more time sitting at their desks sifting through press releases than gathering original reports from the field. Given the nature of much of this work, it is hardly surprising that at least some find the balance of rewards unacceptable and exit the profession.

More surprising, and indicative of evolutions in the profession, are the *modes of adjustment* that many journalists make to remain in journalism. In a first mode, journalists develop ways of managing the disappointments associated with a profession increasingly riven by the tension between its commercial needs and its social functions. Sometimes, they rationalize the dissatisfying work they do by finding ways to occasionally take on assignments that remind them why they became journalists in the first place. Such efforts, they hope, will lead to a future in which they can more regularly do the types of journalism they actually find fulfilling; at least some of their peers have advanced in precisely this way. Other journalists manage their disappointment by deprioritizing their professional identities, downgrading their sense of journalism as a vocation to that of a mere job, seeking fulfillment instead in their lives outside of journalism (e.g., families, hobbies, social commitments). With each of these adjustments, journalists find a personally acceptable balance of rewards while leaving intact—that is to say, unchallenged—the definition of what constitutes the profession's most prestigious social functions.

Introduction 5

A second mode of adjustment redefines journalism's social functions to better adapt them to the profession's current commercial needs. Without explicitly rejecting journalism's most vaunted ideals, these journalists adopt a less grandiose and less explicitly civic vision for the profession. Rather than reporting on topics about which audiences are often uninterested or feel helpless to resolve, these journalists view themselves as practical advisers on people's everyday concerns. Whether those concerns pertain to lifestyle and leisure, consumer affairs, or politics, journalists aim above all to hold audience attention by giving them the information they want, when they want it, and in whatever format they want it. Correspondingly, the competencies they cultivate focus less on revealing uncomfortable facts and developing knowledgeable commentaries than on providing digestible information and soliciting audience participation. In their efforts to match the profession's established social functions with its current commercial needs, these journalists endeavor to establish *a new equilibrium* between the two, one in which the work of journalists is valued first and foremost—but never only or exclusively—for its potential to address the profession's commercial concerns.

These various adjustments—dealing as they do with individual expectations, hopes, desires, and meanings—appear deeply personal. But they also have social correlates, which become evident when looking at the responses in relation to a journalist's gender, social origins (e.g., parents' occupations), educational attainment, prior journalism experience, and location in the professional hierarchy. Thus, the relatively few journalists who have the time and resources necessary for long-form, in-depth reporting also tend to be men from liberal professional families who hold degrees from prestigious universities and have ample professional experience as beat reporters and editors. Conversely, many of those whose experiences stand in stark tension with the profession's most esteemed ideals tend to be women of working-class origins who hold degrees from nonprestigious universities and have less professional experience, often working as general assignment reporters or freelancers. These social correlates are not random; they reflect socially cultivated expectations of what to expect from a profession and how (and how much) to adapt in its pursuit. To be sure, these patterns are neither automatic nor immutable. Those who seek to redefine journalism's social functions in the hopes of professional ascent tend to be socially diverse, united and organized primarily by their educational experiences; those who depart from the profession are extremely heterogeneous. Outliers even occasionally defy these general patterns. But the balancing of material and symbolic rewards that is necessary for the reproduction of belief is always more than a matter of pure volition or individual psychology.

The cross-national design of the inquiry adds a comparative dimension to the analysis. The standard opposition between a French "journalism of ideas" and a more "information-oriented" American tradition does not simply reflect cultural differences; they instead are historically derived variations in the profession's social functions. While important and enduring, these functions pertain primarily to the most prestigious, and thus least representative, forms of journalism in both countries. Just as importantly, they exist alongside commercial functions that are broadly shared. The heightened tension between these functions, especially outside the media capitals of Paris and New York, and the difficulties many journalists experience in trying to reconcile them, are therefore largely similar across the two cases. At the same time, France and the United States provide distinctive legal, regulatory, and cultural settings in which journalists seek an overall balance in the material and symbolic rewards they seek from the profession. These differences make possible very divergent responses to a shared predicament. French journalists, especially those holding permanent job contracts, can and sometimes do downgrade the symbolic rewards they expect from the profession without risking a loss of their employment. American journalists, by contrast, invest heavily in the symbolic rewards the profession promises because labor regulations afford few protections. By highlighting the contexts in which these contrasting approaches take shape, the book provides further evidence that journalists' adaptations always entail more than questions of individual motivation.

The journalist's predicament is explored in Toulouse and Seattle, but it is unique neither to these cities nor to France and the United States. The specific forms this predicament assumes may vary across contexts, as might journalists' particular adjustments to them. The processes analyzed, however, reflect general issues in journalism, both as they relate to its current "crises" and its role in society more broadly. The heightened tension between the profession's commercial and social imperatives is present in most capitalist democracies. How it is addressed, and the extent to which journalists continue seeing the profession as worthy, have implications for the types of news that get produced. The case of journalism, moreover, presents in magnified form a predicament that can be observed in many other cultural occupations—and, beyond cultural work, vocations generally—and that therefore require similar adjustments. By shedding light on the meanings that permit the reproduction of belief, while attending to the multiple social inequalities in which they are inscribed, this book offers an answer to the question of why anyone, given the contemporary predicament, would be a journalist.

THE DIMINUTION OF MATERIAL AND SYMBOLIC REWARDS

The journalist's contemporary predicament—the effect of diminishing material and symbolic rewards on a journalist's belief that the profession remains worthy—stems from multiple upheavals in the profession. First, journalism's imperiled economic basis reduces the total number of jobs available, and creates less-than-ideal work conditions. Second, the rise of a novel information ecosystem loosens journalism's monopoly on the production and distribution of legitimate information and erodes the sense of importance that stemmed from that exclusivity. Third, growing levels of public distrust in and antipathy toward journalists challenge the sense of prestige and social worth associated with journalism. While these developments bring forth opportunities of which some take advantage, they also heighten the tension between the profession's commercial and social functions, reflecting a broader reduction in many of the long-standing material and symbolic rewards associated with journalism. The predicament journalists face therefore entails the necessity of finding ways to maintain their belief in the profession's worth amid these ongoing professional upheavals.

The profession's economic difficulties are well known. Newspapers, the primary employers of journalists in both France and the United States, have lost substantial revenues. Craigslist and Leboncoin.fr were only the initial sites to which classified advertising money migrated; then came platforms like Google and Facebook that direct audience attention, often away from newspapers, while also capturing a growing share of advertising.[10] Regional newspapers, which held near monopolies on their local advertising clients and readerships, have been especially hard hit by these developments, and new income streams come nowhere close to offsetting lost revenues.[11] Looking beyond newspapers, audiovisual and digital news organizations face substantial challenges of their own. For the former, audiences are aging and fragmenting; for the latter, reaching a state of economic stability is elusive and many digital news organizations fail.[12] Variation across media types and national settings no doubt exists: many magazines and news agencies in both countries continue to generate profits, and French news media are on the whole less dependent on advertising revenues than their American counterparts.[13] But looking at the forest rather than the trees yields a bleak overall picture in which journalism's economic foundations appear substantially reduced and, in some cases, existentially threatened.[14]

These economic difficulties translate directly into a reduction of the overall amount of economic rewards available to journalists. Fewer jobs are available. In France, the total number of journalists with a press card peaked in 2008 and has declined slightly since (from 37,303 in 2008 to 34,571 in 2019).[15] In the United States, total employment has dropped nearly a quarter in that same period, from 114,000 full-time journalists in 2008 to 85,000 in 2020.[16] Many of these jobs, moreover, are increasingly precarious. Journalists in France who either work as freelancers or hold short, fixed-term contracts are now estimated to constitute 40 percent of the total journalistic population.[17] In the United States, permanent contracts of undetermined duration are mostly unheard of, and the share of freelancers has grown and is projected to continue doing so; the length of the working day has also increased.[18] Finally, pay, especially in comparison to other jobs in the rapidly expanding "communication" sector, has stagnated and lagged inflation.[19] This is especially true for journalists operating outside of the media capitals of New York and Paris.[20]

News organizations have undertaken reforms in order to recapture lost audiences or find new ways to "monetize" their offerings.[21] For many journalists, this entails a quickened pace of production. Describing the American case, Dean Starkman suggests a "hamster wheel" model of journalism, in which speed and volume are increasingly demanded of journalists.[22] The need to "feed the beast" highlights the sense of a news "hole" that can never be filled, and that as a result forces news organizations to rely on third-party sources or journalists with limited knowledge of the subjects being covered.[23] This hamster wheel model is also notable for what it lacks: the time, resources, and topical expertise necessary to develop original reports that are associated with the profession's most esteemed social functions. These in-depth, time-taking stories—never so common anyway[24]—nonetheless served as important sources of self-fulfillment and meaning to individual journalists. Like a romantic relationship gone awry, many journalists find themselves struggling to reconcile their feelings toward a profession to which they feel deeply committed but whose everyday realities frustrate and sometimes call into question the very belief that their efforts are worthwhile.

These economic transformations have occurred in the context of an emerging information ecosystem that weakens the journalist's role as the primary intermediary of legitimate information.[25] The ecosystem metaphor refers to the diverse yet interdependent set of actors that shape contemporary information environments. In contrast to "low-choice" settings, in which audiences consume news in part because they have few alternatives, consumers can in principle receive information from a seemingly endless number of sources—politicians, celebrities, activists, civic groups, business associations, friends, and family—and often in formats better aligned with their own preferences.[26] For journalists, this development threatens the self-fulfillment drawn from being an author of history's "first rough draft." No longer engaging only with each other as "competitor-colleagues,"[27] journalists instead operate in a "multiaxial" information ecosystem in which their work is simply one of many potential options for audiences to consume,[28] where social and political elites sometimes exclude journalists that do not serve their own ends, and where audiences often ignore the work of journalists entirely.[29]

The journalist's predicament is further shaped by increasingly antagonistic feelings among many segments of the public toward journalists.[30] Right-wing social movements and political parties cultivate among their supporters a sense that journalists are "the enemy of the people" disseminating "fake news"; portmanteaus are crafted to deliver novel insults (e.g., *lamestream media, merdia, journalope, presstituée*).[31] Harassment of journalists has risen, partly due to journalists' visibility on social media platforms.[32] This hostility, moreover, is not solely the provenance of the political right. The *Gilets Jaunes* (Yellow Vests) movement in France has been notable in part for its antagonism toward the press;³³ the Occupy movement in America chafed at their perceived misrepresentation in the news and distrusted the corporate structures in which journalists worked.³⁴ Even those not directly attacking journalists express negative sentiments toward the press. In both France and the United States, polls show declining levels of (generic) trust in journalism and journalists.³⁵

These antagonistic sentiments threaten to further reduce the sense that journalism is worth journalists' efforts. While some might take pride in angering "both sides" of a debate, a sense of self-fulfillment seems fleeting when one is regularly bombarded with a stream of personal criticisms, invectives, and threats. It may also be difficult to generate, or regenerate, belief in the profession's worth when the public for which a journalist assumes she is working selects not on the basis of a self-understood social function (e.g., informing citizens, facilitating debate) but instead based on a prior political predisposition.³⁶ One need not be nostalgic about the past, or lacking in appreciation for the profession's advances away from deferential reportage and toward more critical fare,³⁷ to recognize that the respectability associated with being a journalist has in many ways declined.

At the same time, each year thousands of students in France and the United States enroll in journalism programs, pursue internships and, eventually, land jobs in the profession. If the profession has lost some of its prior luster, as suggested by enrollment stagnation or outright declines, it nonetheless retains its appeal to some. What's more, the very constraints that these upheavals induce also appear as opportunities for some: to find ways to "do more with less," to think of fresh ways to attract audiences, and to reconsider what is most essential to the profession. But no matter how attractive or opportune one finds journalism, or how worthy they believe the profession's mission to be, a journalist necessarily encounters these diminished rewards in their everyday work lives. Whether in the form of less stable jobs, longer hours, a loss of prestige, or an inability to do the work one likes, the journalist's predicament is an inescapable feature of contemporary journalistic life. Understanding how journalists manage this predicament thus entails asking how belief in the profession is managed and, sometimes, dissolves as a result of these upheavals.

JOURNALISTS' ADJUSTMENTS

Knowing how journalists (do or do not) keep their belief in the profession requires knowing what belief they hold in the first place. To be a journalist is, above all, to believe in a profession whose fundamental mission is to inform. This certainly includes informing in the definitional sense of discovering, distilling, and disseminating facts. It also involves informing in the etymological sense of giving shape to—literally, *putting in-form*—the chaos of everyday reality. This is the mission in which journalists believe; it underpins the extraordinary variety of journalistic work, ranging from sports and arts to economics and politics. This mission can be perceived as personally attractive, as it provides opportunities for self-expression and the possibility of self-fulfillment. But it also gathers weight through its connection to broader social values and functions. The journalist's mission to inform is thus also perceived as a way to address injustices and help society function better. How journalists maintain a belief in these functions in seemingly unfavorable circumstances is a central challenge confronting the profession.

Faced with journalism's multiple upheavals, journalists need to convince themselves that their belief in the profession remains worthy. It would be too burdensome to expect journalists to rise each morning and offer explicit justifications for their beliefs. Instead, this conviction is given life (again, or not) via practical sensibilities that structure what material and symbolic rewards appear possible and appropriate to expect from journalism.[38] The product of lengthy learning processes—as well as repeated social interactions—these sensibilities operate primarily in three ways.[39] First, particularly for journalists, they take some arrangements for granted, as happens when it "goes without saying" that journalism jobs confer smaller salaries than other jobs, thus lowering expectations regarding material rewards while often bolstering a sense of the symbolic rewards gained from the profession (e.g., the opportunity to do interesting work, to talk with strangers, to circulate in social circles that intersect with cultural, political, or economic elites). Second, they make virtue from necessities, as occurs when journalists emphasize the upsides of otherwise objectively difficult conditions (e.g., as seen in the very intense relationship to work that many maintain), thus balancing out the overall rewards they receive or expect to receive from journalism. Finally, they develop a "sense of one's place" that defines the overall rewards that one should, and should not, expect for someone like themselves in journalism (e.g., evident in the idea that one may not be the best reporter but nonetheless possesses a "journalistic essence").

The operation of these practical sensibilities can be seen as mechanisms that allow journalists to continue doing their work amid changing or difficult circumstances. Journalists retain their belief in the worthiness of the profession not necessarily by achieving its highest ideals or even by doing the journalism that attracted them in the first place. Instead, they do so by adjusting the overall balance of material and symbolic rewards they expect to attain so they align with their everyday realities. Whether this happens by taking things for granted, finding virtue in necessity, or having a sense of one's place, these adjustments are what enable a journalist's belief in the profession to persist. The effort is "worth the candle" only insofar as these rewards appear possible. When they no longer seem possible or worthwhile, it becomes increasingly likely that a journalist will consider leaving the profession.

These adjustments feel, and are, deeply personal. But they also have a social dimension. What a journalist considers a desirable and acceptable overall balance of rewards stems from sensibilities that are shaped from birth onward. Their family, schooling, and work experiences, as well as their gender and race, shape their sense of what is possible and probable to expect from journalism, what can and should be sacrificed in pursuit of a career, and what gives meaning to the work one does. Because these experiences arise socially but reside in the individual—like "a muscular physique or a suntan,"[40] they cannot be acquired secondhand—they can be thought of as social properties.[41]

These social properties are different across journalists and in some ways reflect idiosyncratic individual experiences. However, they are also embedded in hierarchies that are defined by holding more or less of a particular social property, or by holding more or less prestigious forms of a property (e.g., education, professional experience, money). How a journalist views and assesses the adjustments they make is impacted by their background and social properties. Thus, one can possess more educational experience (e.g., graduate education), as well as more prestigious education (e.g., degrees from elite universities). Adjustments can therefore also be viewed as indicators of social inequalities, revealing as they do differences in the ways that beliefs in the profession's worth are managed based on family origins, educational attainment, professional experience, and gender.[42] The fact that these adjustments appear primarily personal (i.e., the result of personality differences, tastes, preferences, or motivations) screens out their social dimensions (i.e., the outcome of unequal backgrounds). As a result, these inequalities can only be explored empirically to the extent that they are assumed theoretically.

Two final points. First, adjustments are dynamic. They can and do change over time, due to the accumulation of work experiences and developments in one's personal life. Such experiences present the possibility of modulating the adjustments that one makes in order to sustain their belief in journalism, resembling the "shifting involvements" between public and private action described by Albert O. Hirschman.[43] Expectations or sacrifices that appear acceptable at one point in time might seem unreasonable at another (e.g., due to the introduction of family obligations, it may no longer be sensible to work such long hours). This suggests that journalist's adjustments are never solely professional but mix their work and non-work lives. Moreover, there is no guarantee that expectations and desires will be realized. Situations can change, leaving those anticipations unexpectedly satisfied or, alternatively, frustrated. The heightened tension between journalism's economic basis and its social functions makes this especially so. It is thus possible, and necessary, to explore how belief in the profession does and does not get renewed over time, including to the point at which journalists leave the profession.

Second, adjustments *tend* to correspond to social properties. To the extent that journalists experience an "enchanted relation" to the profession,[44] it stems from the fact that they "find their place" in journalism without it appearing as derived solely from these social properties. The expectations they hold and the sacrifices they make appear primarily in personal terms. Highlighting the correspondences between journalists' expectations and their social properties—i.e., the tendency of men from liberal professional families holding prestigious education degrees to expect and attain different experiences in journalism than women from working-class families with less prestigious education—provides a prism onto the ways that social inequalities are produced and reproduced within journalism. Just as importantly, it does so without neglecting the meaning that *all* individuals garner from the profession, which is crucial to their continued belief in its worth.

This does not eliminate outliers who defy these patterns through adjustments that depart from these regularities. Such outliers include journalists whose career paths—whether ascending or descending—differ from what might be expected given the social properties they possess. Alternatively, outliers can follow from "misreadings" of one's potential, as happens when a journalist transposes conditions found elsewhere (Paris) onto their local settings (Toulouse). This can take the form of an intense personal investment in journalism that corresponds to the profession's social functions even when there is no immediate economic reward, such as when a freelancer does long-form reporting that does not get picked up by any news outlet. In all cases, these outliers are departures from regularities; they therefore provide an opportunity to understand how a journalist makes sense of their work in relation to the social properties they possess.

ANOTHER FRENCH/AMERICAN COMPARISON?

The present study joins other comparative studies of French and American journalism.[45] In both countries, journalism is a well-established liberal profession with roots in the nineteenth century; journalists tend to have higher levels of education than the general population. The contemporary discourse of upheaval in the profession is also broadly shared in both countries. These similarities provide an initial basis from which to begin constructing a meaningful comparison. At the same time, scholars typically stress important differences between the two countries. France and the United States are regularly conceptualized as representing what Rodney Benson terms "opposing ideal types with unique professional traditions, structural ecologies, and relations with the state and market."[46] These differences structure well-known distinctions between each country's best-known forms of journalism, with a French "opinion" model contrasted with an American devotion to "facts." Prior research thus highlights ways French-American comparisons can both build theory and test hypotheses.

But this scholarship also presents the risk that any further comparison, like the kind offered here, will merely restate prior observations and recapitulate extant conclusions. However, prior research is heavily concentrated on journalism as practiced by leading journalists at news organizations in the media capitals of Paris and New York (and, to a lesser degree, Washington, DC). While these journalists may be "agenda setters," they constitute an extremely small and highly unrepresentative proportion of the overall workforce. In France, roughly half of all journalists work outside of Paris, and many of those working in Paris are employed at specialized outlets or press agencies whose working conditions bear little resemblance to leading Parisian news outlets.[47] The situation in the United States is even more stark, with more than 80 percent of all journalists working outside of New York and Washington, DC.[48] Foregrounding the experiences of journalists at regional news media, otherwise largely excluded from prior comparative analyses, offers an opportunity to refine prior theorizations of journalism in both countries while exploring the journalist's predicament in settings that likely better reflect journalists' working conditions in other nonmedia capitals.

Given these considerations, the empirical material for this book is taken from original interviews with journalists in two cities, Toulouse (France) and Seattle (United States). The experiences of journalists in these cities are important in several ways. The economic and social viability of journalism in these settings is especially precarious, as older audiences perish and younger audiences flock to niche outlets or national news, or simply avoid news altogether.[49] How journalists do or do not maintain their belief in the profession's worth thus affords insights into the types of journalism that are most likely to be provided in these regional settings. Theoretically, journalists in these cities also occupy intermediate positions between journalists working at prestigious outlets in the media capitals of Paris and New York, on the one hand, and journalists working in smaller towns and villages, on the other. This bolsters the book's theoretical generalizability, as adjustments discovered in these relatively constrained middle strata are likely to exist across more sociodemographically diverse samples of journalists in both countries. Finally, journalists in these cities—precisely because they are not "agenda setters"—provide the opportunity to explore how previously described "national" differences manifest beyond a few leading news outlets in each country.

Toulouse and Seattle are comparably sized cities located on the geographic peripheries of their respective countries (southwestern France and the northwestern United States, respectively). They share similar industrial bases, as Toulouse is the historical home of Airbus, just as Seattle is to Boeing. Both cities are also significant technology hubs within their respective countries. Demographically, each boasts a population that tends to be more educated, younger, wealthier, more digitally connected, and more civically engaged than national averages. To be sure, these are not the only two mid-sized cities along which a French and American comparison could be constructed; neither should their use be implied to somehow "represent" all mid-sized cities in the two countries.[50] Selecting them, however, ensures equivalence across the cases so that any findings are likely to stem from the journalists studied and not from other confounding factors.

Within these two cities, interviews were held with a purposive sample of journalists. This included men and women journalists holding a range of job titles (e.g., freelance, general assignment, beat reporters, editors) with varying degrees of professional experience working for a range of news media (e.g., online, audiovisual, print). (For a description of the sample and methodological details, see the appendices.) Prior research suggests that differences in job titles and organizations are linked to differences in social origins.[51] By "sampling for range,"[52] the study explores how journalists from different social backgrounds, educational attainment, and professional experiences attempt to maintain their belief in the professions' worth. Interviews began in 2014 and continued into 2022, sometimes with the same journalist to illuminate how their views change over time. In total, interviews with seventy-one individual journalists were conducted (forty-one in Seattle, thirty in Toulouse).

Interviews asked journalists about their social backgrounds, educational experiences, and professional trajectories. Specific questions also explored journalists' attractions to, and expectations of, their careers in journalism; the work—both their own and their peers'—they admire and gain meaning from; and their perceptions of change in the profession over time. A subset of journalists who left journalism during the course of the study were also interviewed after their departure to gain insight

Introduction 17

into the factors precipitating their move, the sense they made of their departures, and the lives they pursued after leaving journalism. Throughout, the aim was to develop an understanding of journalists' beliefs and the adjustments they make in relation to those beliefs. The approach is both theoretical (i.e., based on testable assumptions about the importance of social properties in shaping dispositions and adjustments) and practical (i.e., an effort to grasp the overall circumstances of an individual journalist's life that renders her or his beliefs sensible to them). To avoid repetition across the chapters, descriptive data about social backgrounds, educational experiences, and professional trajectories are presented in the appendices.

Interpretation of the interview data was supplemented by prior scholarship on French and American journalism. This research provides insight into the historical struggles that crystallized journalism as a profession, and that continue to make it attractive today. It also identifies the various legal, regulatory, and cultural factors that shape how journalists attempt to realize an acceptable balance of symbolic and material rewards. By understanding the meaning of an idea or practice in its context, this approach uses comparison to examine the mechanisms that unify and differentiate the two cases.[53]

It is the nature of empirical results, whether qualitative or quantitative, to be limited in both time and geographic reach. Rather than emphasize the "generalizability" of the empirical findings, this book emphasizes the modes of adjustment that produce them: i.e., the ways that journalists manage their disappointments or redefine what constitutes a legitimate social function. Comparison of the sort attempted here thus aspires to be doubly useful: first, in providing insights on particular cases (journalists in Toulouse and Seattle specifically; France and the United States more generally); second, and more ambitiously, in formulating research questions and analytical approaches that can be applied to and explored in other empirical settings beyond those studied here.[54]

A SOCIOLOGY OF JOURNALISTS

Describing the "emerging news ecology," Michael Schudson writes that "this is the best of time for journalists, as long as they can survive on relatively little income; show themselves agile in gathering data, connections, ideas, and relationships online; and develop the psychological makeup to handle experimentation, innovation, and risk."[55] Everything that follows in this book can be read as an effort to specify the conditions that underpin such felicity, as well as those that generate its opposites: disappointment and disillusionment.[56] Foregrounding the adjustments journalists make to render an acceptable balance of material and symbolic rewards, it shows that what counts as sufficient income, appropriate online agility, and openness to change is neither universally shared nor solely the result of a developed psychological makeup. Instead, it also stems from socially cultivated dispositions that are themselves rooted in multiple inequalities related to gender, social origins, educational attainment, and professional experience.

In highlighting these dispositions, and the adjustments they engender, the book complements a well-established sociology of journalism with a much more muted *sociology of the journalists* that give life to the profession.[57] While closely related, the former foregrounds the functions the press fulfills, and the various determinants (economic, political, organizational, technological, and the like) that enable and constrain such performance. By contrast, the latter, at least as developed in these pages, addresses a question whose answer, given the journalist's contemporary predicament, can no longer be presumed: namely, why anyone would bother being a journalist. All the things that matter about the sociology of journalism—its capacity to inform citizens, act as a counterweight to political and economic elites, shape social solidarity, and so on—depend on such a question being resolved. It is a curiosity of contemporary scholarship, especially in the Anglophone world, that the issue is rarely even raised.

The approach offered here refrains, at least initially, from the normative registers of denunciation or praise that weigh so heavily in most discussions of the press as an institution. Journalism of course has social functions (e.g., to inform, to hold the powerful to account), and the institution can be organized in ways that facilitate or constrain those functions (e.g., in terms of its relationship to the market, state, other segments of civil society, its internal organization, and so on).[58] But journalists, regardless of the social functions they do or do not fulfill, are

Introduction 19

also social agents with dispositions, social backgrounds, and trajectories. Understanding these conditions of existence is also important: why they are journalists, how and in what they gain meaning from the profession, and how these meanings are stratified by social properties like gender, background, and education. These conditions, which necessarily highlight patterns of social stratification and thus inequality, are muted or screened out in much of the contemporary analyses of journalism as an institution. This is part of what a sociology of journalists can provide.

Paradoxically, this initial bracketing of normative language can also shed fresh analytical light on some of those very normative concerns. Amid journalism's many crises (of employment, legitimacy, and so on), few calls are repeated more regularly than the need to protect or rethink "quality" journalism. By this, scholars and journalists typically have in mind "public service" reporting that constitutes its historically derived social functions: the sort of journalism, in other words, that often makes the press "unlovable" to power-holders.[59] Highlighting journalists' conditions of existence shows which journalists (read: typically, white, male, educated, of high social origins) tend to benefit from such calls. When connected to a sociology of journalists, these calls for "quality journalism" highlight the need to consider the social conditions that make some journalists more or less likely to produce such news. Said otherwise, a sociology of journalists provides a reminder that the social functions of the press are not, and have never been, socially neutral.

At the same time, the approach offered here aims to make sense of the meanings that all journalists derive from their professional existence. These meanings are basic to their belief that the profession is worthy of their efforts. Some of these meanings are unlikely to resonate with readers' own normative visions for journalism. Certainly, the French reporter who admits to doing "crappy work" but remains in the profession because of its stable hours operates at some distance from journalism's social functions. And readers might debate the utility of redefining journalism's social functions, as some journalists in both cities do, so that they better conform to the profession's commercial needs. But can these efforts be understood without surrendering to narratives that blame journalists for failing to live up to their social functions, or that victimize journalists as the exploited workers of greedy management? That is the wager undertaken in this book.

In making this wager, this book begins from the assumption that professional journalists remain important. Admittedly, informing is hardly the sole provenance of journalists in a contemporary information ecosystem to which many contribute. Intentionally or incidentally misleading information is rife, but so too is reliable and useful information contributed by many who stake no claim to being journalists. Digital technologies, moreover, make it possible to automate many of the tasks previously accomplished by reporters and editors, and to collect massive amounts of data that would be impossible for a single reporter to evaluate. Yet journalists remain important agents in this emergent ecology nonetheless. Their audiences are diminished, but they generally remain far larger than those enjoyed by civil society groups or political parties. The skills they possess range from the verification of information to the narration of that information in an appealing way to audiences. While they no longer hold a monopoly on the production and distribution of legitimate information, it is difficult to imagine that their social functions could be assumed by any other set of social agents.

Journalists are worthy of study not only because of what they do but because of who they are. Like other cultural occupations, journalism attracts a broad range of individuals, mostly from middle- to upper-middle-class origins, who find the profession attractive less for the material comforts it provides than the symbolic rewards it promises.[60] Very few expect, or are willing, to work for free; however, it is difficult to find anyone going into journalism with the expectation of becoming wealthy. Instead, they emphasize work that is interesting and substantial, with an exciting lifestyle and the opportunities to build social relationships. This orientation to work, itself socially cultivated, expresses in some form a critical relationship toward the economic system, if only because of the lower value it assigns to material wealth, even as it participates in the reproduction of that system. This form of work is very clearly challenged by journalism's crumbling economic foundations. How journalists respond thus offers insight into how one group adapts itself to a profession that is increasingly riven by tensions between its commercial demands and its social functions.

CHAPTER OUTLINE

The book proceeds by exploring the genesis, management, and, for some, dissolution of the belief that journalism is worthy of one's investments. Chapter 1 sketches the historical emergence of the journalist's predicament. In both France and the United States, the rise of a commercial press in the nineteenth century corresponded with the emergence of an understanding of journalism that foregrounded the principle of informing. This principle, which took hold well beyond New York and Paris, emphasized both the definitional and the etymological senses of the term. In contrast to the partisan press that preceded it, journalists were expected to use empirical details (facts) to make sense of (give form to) the worlds on which they reported. New roles, like that of the reporter, and new techniques, like the interview, expanded the material and symbolic rewards available to journalists. As a result of these developments, journalism became attractive to many as an opportunity for social ascent; it also appealed, through the proximity to power it offered and the opportunities for self-expression it promised, as a source of self-fulfillment and a contribution to broader social values (e.g., keeping the powerful in check).

Even in this period of expansion and growth, journalists varied in the adjustments they made in relation to the principle of informing. In both France and the United States, an opposition between popular and elite orientations emerged, each proposing different understandings of what types of facts should be emphasized and what sense they made of the social world. While scholars typically emphasize this opposition as stemming from the commercial strategies of publishers, it can also generate insights into the social inequalities that underpin symbolic hierarchies in the profession. Those with less education and from lower social origins tended to align with a journalism that was denigrated for being sensationalist and irresponsible, while those with more education and from higher social origins generally represented work that was valorized for its seriousness and quality. What constituted seriousness and quality (and, thus, the profession's most prestigious social functions) varied cross-nationally. Elite French journalists used facts to aid in their interpretation of the world while American elite journalists emphasized empirical details as a way to reveal otherwise hidden dimensions of social life. In both countries, though, the principle of informing was at the heart of the profession.

Shifting to the present, chapter 2 explores journalists' beliefs in the profession's worth in light of the diminution of material and symbolic rewards associated with journalism today. Despite deep uncertainties concerning the profession's economic basis and social utility—concerns that loom large in regional media—journalists in Toulouse and Seattle describe the principle of informing as remaining attractive. The opportunity to tell stories, reveal information, understand the world, and give worth to diverse experiences makes journalists feel that the profession, while difficult, is nonetheless worth their efforts. These attractions, crucially, are polysemic; transformations in journalism education, itself under increasing economic pressure, channel two different readings of their meaning: one, more elite, tends to emphasize the profession's most prestigious social functions; a second, more popular, offers a more relaxed, less civic approach to journalism, a "communication journalism"[61] that can be easily transferred to other jobs should their bets as journalists not work out.

A relatively small number of journalists in each country expect to make a career doing the work associated with the profession's most prized social functions. They are talented and hard working; they also tend, as a group, to hold the most favorable social properties (social origins, educational attainment, and so on). Their experiences can be described as both "living for" and "living off" journalism. A far greater number of journalists, generally with less favorable social properties, emphasize the sacrifices they make—and expect to continue making—to remain in journalism. They "live for" journalism, hoping either to someday approximate its most distinguished ideals or to do work that corresponds to its less distinguished but increasingly important "communication" forms (e.g., solicit audience participation, provide digestible information). French labor protections mean that some journalists (typically women) with less favorable properties sacrifice professional ambition in favor of their nonprofessional lives, often foregrounding their role as mothers. These journalists "live off" but not "for" journalism. In the United States, weak labor protections mean journalists (both men and women) with less favorable properties sacrifice their nonprofessional lives (e.g., by moving, working long hours) for their professional careers. They live for journalism but worry whether they will ever live off it. In both countries, journalism's most esteemed social functions appear doubly fragile: difficult for many journalists to fulfill, and also decreasingly useful as a basis for social recruitment in the face of the profession's multiple uncertainties.

Chapter 3 explores the work that journalists most admire, both among their peers and from themselves. In both countries, journalists overwhelmingly tend to emphasize in-depth, long-form, and well-composed reporting that showcases the enduring weight of the profession's most esteemed social functions. While unrepresentative of their everyday routines and productions, these works reconnect many journalists to what initially attracted them to the profession. As such, they constitute a key source of meaning and a way for belief in the profession's worth, and the sacrifices one makes for it, to persist. At the same time, such works also construct symbolic hierarchies—i.e., practical judgments regarding what constitutes the "best" forms of journalism—and place themselves and their work within it. Not everyone does long-form, investigative reporting, but journalists in Toulouse and Seattle find some works in which they can take pride, either by translating the "best" forms of journalism (e.g., investigative reporting) into their local spaces or by finding worth in less prestigious works, which typically appeal to audiences without undermining professional commitments. Because these best works generally correspond to the social properties they possess, journalists' discussions of their best work also highlight the best they can do given the conditions they have.

Journalists' best works offer opportunities to refine comparative theorizing and question some normative discussions around "quality" journalism. The standard oppositions between a French "journalism of ideas" and a more "informational" American tradition are not general cultural tendencies. Rather, they capture the most prestigious journalistic styles and traditions in each country. Journalists working at regional media in both countries share much more in common, in part because they gather similar social properties that place them in more intermediate positions in the profession. Showing the relationship between these social properties and the symbolic hierarchies in which journalists believe also highlights the need for a sociology of journalists. Calling for quality journalism (i.e., journalism's most distinguished functions) is tempting.

But is it not also a hidden description of the people producing (and, logically by extension, consuming) the work?

Chapter 4 documents journalists' responses to the reduction of symbolic and material rewards. While economic constraints generate doubts about the viability of the profession for all, many journalists find ways to preserve their belief in the profession. For some, this entails an effort to conserve the overall balance of rewards, typically by ignoring the impacts of economic and technological transformations on their work, and seeking to approximate the profession's most esteemed social functions. Others challenge the overall balance of rewards by introducing novel forms of journalism (e.g., multimedia reporting, audience engagement), which they link to the profession's economic and redefined social functions. Still others accede to the overall balance of rewards, recognizing the status quo as most legitimate but also going along with transformations and professional redefinitions without feeling they will personally benefit from them.

Cross-nationally, French journalists, as a group, tend to undertake strategies of conservation, while their American counterparts are more likely to challenge the status quo. These strategies, which are often read voluntaristically as evidence of greater or lesser degrees of individual motivation, can also be viewed as the product of distinct regulatory contexts that facilitate different responses to broadly similar conditions. While journalists that challenge are more common in the United States, in both countries they tend as a group to be socially diverse, including men and women with diverse social origins, and professional experiences. Their educational attainment, in terms of both prestige and overall amount, distinguishes them as a group. As such, they are united in an attempt toward social ascension but are often highly uncertain whether their efforts will bear fruits.

Chapter 5 explores the point at which journalists' belief in the profession dissolves. What explains the timing and manner of these departures? In both Toulouse and Seattle, a period in which individuals question their relationship to the profession precedes such exits. Departures themselves are linked to "trigger events"[62] like professional conflicts or personal transformations. The individuals who leave journalism are extremely diverse socially, including both young and old, men and women, all of varying social origins and diverse levels of educational attainment. What unites them is a sense that their relationship to the profession is no longer worthwhile. While this suggests serious problems for retaining journalists, it also implies that the underlying belief in the profession as such remains strong, as no individual left because they thought the idea of using facts to tell stories was worthless. Finally, the chapter offers insight into the ways that journalists resocialize their professional identities after leaving journalism, typically in ways that reflect both their socially cultivated dispositions and the social properties at their disposal.

The conclusion situates the findings in relation to broader discussions about the role of journalists in society. The potential for journalists to do work that combines social and commercial functions is increasingly narrow. Transformations in journalism, therefore, can be read primarily as ways either to redefine social functions to better align them with the commercial needs, or to replace social functions with political ones, evident in the growth of partisan media in both countries. Yet if the landscape of media appears increasingly fluid, journalism in many ways remains structured by the desire for work that is substantial and meaningful. These desires, as the book shows, are increasingly frustrated, and often in ways that reflect very different conditions of possibility for individual journalists. Thus, if societies face risks from the rise of actors that aim to cynically exploit and manipulate audiences, this book highlights the threat that comes from the intrusion of market considerations in nearly all dimensions of journalistic work.

Taken together, the chapters that compose this book highlight the enduring weight of journalism's most esteemed social functions but also the growing pressure of commercial imperatives. The implications for journalists and for news consumers are neither wholly positive nor entirely negative. Long-form, in-depth, and well-composed works of journalism appear increasingly at risk but they have not disappeared, even at the regional news media in which they seem so fragile. If this kind of journalism is no longer economically profitable, such works nonetheless remain important. The profession's social functions, moreover, are also in the process of redefinition. If these redefined functions sometimes appear stunted, or unduly utilitarian in their fixation on addressing commercial concerns, they are still determined to find ways to make power-holders speak more clearly and to address citizens' everyday concerns. It would take a naive optimist or a cynical pessimist not to see this mixture of opportunities and constraints in contemporary journalism, even at the regional level.

For journalists, though, the contemporary predicament makes it increasingly difficult to achieve a personally acceptable balance of rewards. This finding is of course specific to the field of journalism and likely plays out differently among individual journalists in different cities. But the increased weight of commercial considerations generates an instability that can at times seem relentless for nearly everyone: in the degeneration of working conditions, the diminution of prestige, and the diminishing opportunities for work that affords self-fulfillment. Amid these upheavals, journalists must constantly find ways to adjust. Is the instability such developments usher in not also visible in a host of other vocations and social groups, themselves increasingly subject to market pressures that threaten their own historically derived social functions? Is there not an echo of the journalist's predicament to be found in the experiences of artists and musicians, teachers and professors, nurses and caregivers?

CHAPTER ONE

The Genesis of the Journalist's Predicament

Newspapers have existed since at least the seventeenth century; the position of journalist, however, is a more recent invention.[1] Early periodicals in both Western Europe and North America carried official state announcements, expressed views associated with political parties and movements, provided advertisements for goods and services, and served as sources of literary criticism and social satire.[2] Contributors to these publications, though, mostly pursued livelihoods and sought recognition in politics and the arts. To speak of newsroom employment in this time period would be anachronistic; correspondents, as the name implies, did not work for newspapers, and typically received little or no payment for their efforts. To the extent their writings garnered recognition at all, it derived from their expressions of literary wit and political engagement, not the "scoops" they broke or the information they revealed. Newspaper contributors no doubt faced predicaments in their lives, but these were not directly related to their newspaper activities, which offered few, if any, specific material or symbolic rewards. Instead, early newspapers were valuable primarily as means to accomplish political or literary aims. They did not generate a belief that the activities undertaken for newspapers were worthy or rewarding in their own right.

This changed dramatically in the latter half of the nineteenth century.[3] In France and the United States, seeking employment at newspapers—and, for some, magazines and news agencies—became a conceivable option within the space of possible jobs and careers. Compensation for one's contributions came to be expected; such work even appeared to some as a potential path for social ascension. Just as importantly, newspapers and news agencies became attractive on the basis of the symbolic opportunities they promised to new entrants. The work they did could be interesting and substantial, and supported by an exciting lifestyle with opportunities to build social relationships. No longer just an avenue into politics or literature, such work was increasingly conceived in connection to broader social concerns. Through the provision of news, the work of news making could be valued for promoting the common good, fighting injustice, taking on the powerful, and perhaps even improving society. Together, these developments made it possible for individuals both to seek returns from journalism and to believe that a career in it was worthy of their energies. Journalism as a modern profession was born. So, too, was the journalist's predicament.

As a modern profession, journalism was newly understood to have both commercial and social functions.[4] Rather than rely on government or partisan subventions (e.g., printing contracts, government advertisements), newspapers in the nineteenth century came increasingly to pursue revenues on the basis of attracting audiences and advertisers. By inducing new practices and absorbing older ones, this commercial basis also gave rise to an understanding of journalism's social functions that centered on the principle of informing. In both France and the United States, the need to entice readers brought about a fact-oriented approach to news that was applied, through the expansion of the beat system, to a growing number of topics and issues, well beyond the political or literary foci of their predecessors from a previous era. It was on the basis of these facts, sometimes presented with expressions of wit and political engagement borrowed from this earlier time, that journalists could believe their work served society by holding the powerful to account and, more broadly, giving shape to the chaos of everyday life. The novel commercial basis made a career in journalism possible; the social functions made it seem like a worthwhile pursuit.

The journalist's predicament arose as individuals sought a place for themselves among these dual functions. Some garnered a personally acceptable balance of rewards doing journalism that attracted audiences while being seen as socially useful. Others adjusted themselves to their circumstances by doing work that favored one of these functions over the other. This sometimes took the form of doing work that was broadly popular but derided by critics for sensationalism. Other times, it appeared as journalism that attracted few readers but prided itself on informed commentary and thoughtful debate. The diverse adjustments journalists made reflected in many ways the social properties they possessed. Those criticized for sensationalism or apolitical news tended to have limited education and prior professional experience; they also came from lower social origins than their peers working at upscale publications. By contrast, those praised for serious and socially useful journalism had higher levels of educational attainment, often came from upper-middle-class families, and were almost exclusively male. While these different forms of journalism stemmed from the commercial strategies of publishers, it was journalists who instantiated them.[5]

Exploring the journalist's predicament in light of the profession's new commercial and social functions refines comparative characterizations of French and American journalism. In contrast to French "opinion" opposing an American "fact-based" model,[6] the rise of a commercial press in fact shaped an extremely similar orientation to facts, which is most clearly visible when looking at popular newspapers, both within and beyond Paris and New York. These similarities stemmed from an effort to be as inclusive as possible by telling stories in ways that would appeal to a broad audience. Cross-national differences pertained to journalism's social functions, which were expressed most clearly in the most prestigious newspapers of the time. In those settings, the journalists with the most favorable social properties interpreted the principle of fact-based storytelling in light of distinctive national traditions. In France, the enduring influence of politics and literature saw facts as useful tools for interpreting the world. The influence of Progressive Era reforms in the United States, by contrast, utilized facts to reveal dimensions of social life that were otherwise hidden or obscured from public view.

Journalism's commercial and social functions did not merely coexist. Instead, they introduced a struggle over the legitimate definition of journalism that continues to the present day. The synthetic history provided here shows the centrality of facts in shaping this struggle, in both attracting and informing audiences in the nineteenth century. From the outset, this led to conflicts in terms of *which facts* and *which audiences* were deemed worth pursuing. Whether a particular employer's orientation seemed attractive or even acceptable depended very much on the socially cultivated expectations journalists held regarding their work. Since the profession's earliest days, journalists have endeavored to manage their predicament by finding ways to retain their belief in the profession while adapting themselves to the journalism their circumstances make possible for them to do.

THE BIRTH OF MODERN JOURNALISM

Twin developments in the latter part of the nineteenth century gave rise to modern journalism. In both France and the United States, the introduction of a commercial business model for news dramatically expanded career opportunities for journalists and enlisted them in an effort to reach audiences by providing lively, entertaining content. At the same time, journalists in the two countries also began to see themselves as members of a growing occupation, perhaps even a profession with important social functions. One important basis for their claim to this status revolved around the growing—if sometimes begrudging—acceptance of the principle that news should use empirical details (i.e., facts) to make sense of (i.e., give form to) the worlds about which they reported. These twin developments helped to make journalism an attractive career option, with journalism appearing to new entrants as a career in which one could, among other things, see the world, witness history, tell stories, and rub shoulders with the powerful.

This "new" journalism of the nineteenth century set itself in direct opposition to the partisan model that preceded it.[7] Whereas the partisan press was sustained primarily by political patronage, the new journalism explicitly understood itself as a commercial enterprise. This orientation—itself fueled by the growth of cities and industrialization—can be glimpsed in part through the changing profile of newspaper owners. Whereas prior owners tended to be linked to political parties, the new owners fashioned themselves first and foremost as businesspersons. William Randolph Hearst (*New York Journal*) and Moïse Polydore Millaud (*Le Petit Journal*), to take two major figures of the era, each put their inherited family wealth from mining and banking, respectively, to new uses in the media business.[8] Figures like Joseph Pulitzer (*New York*

World), Adolph Ochs (*New York Times*), Alfred Edwards (*Le Matin*), and Fernand Xau (*Le Journal*) all built substantial personal fortunes through their media holdings. Even those with partisan connections, like party-deputy Louis Andrieux (*Le Petit Parisien*), entered into journalism primarily with the hope of making money.

Developments in the media capitals of New York and Paris extended outward, with newspapers springing up as commercial enterprises throughout the United States and France more broadly. The trajectory of Alden Blethen captures this diffusion nicely in the American case. Originally from Maine, he got his start working on the business side of newspapers in Kansas City, Missouri. From there, he moved to Minneapolis, hoping to build his fortune by launching his own paper, *The Penny Press*. After seeing that effort fail, Blethen moved to Seattle and became co-owner of the *Seattle Times*, which had been founded just a few years prior (his descendants own and operate the paper to this day). In each city, he sought to mimic what he called "the magnificent successes of three cent and penny papers" elsewhere in the country, citing Pulitzer's *World* and, especially, Hearst's *Journal* as models.[9]

In France, the changing ownership of Toulouse's main daily newspaper highlights a similar commercial shift. Originally founded by left-leaning workers at a printing plant, *La Dépêche de Toulouse* changed hands several times in the latter part of the nineteenth century. In 1879, it was sold to a group based in Paris, which in turn sold it in 1881 to three businesspersons, all friends from the most prestigious high school in the region who hoped to make the paper a regional version of the *un sou* (five-cent) newspapers that had become so popular in Paris.[10] These successive owners did not remove the paper's leftist political orientations; they did, however, make clear that these orientations were useful as much to attract audiences as to change minds on political issues.[11] In this way, *La Dépêche* (literally, The Dispatch) differed dramatically from earlier newspapers in the region, whose very titles—*Le Journal de Toulouse, Journal Politique et Littéraire de Toulouse et de la Haute-Garonne*—foregrounded their political and literary orientations.

Wherever they were geographically located, owners were explicit about their commercial aims. When, for example, a Boston newspaper came under new ownership in the 1890s, the proprietor published an editorial stating: "This property has been bought for business purposes....

You cannot put that too strongly."[12] Even figures linked to the parties acknowledged this development. "In today's world newspapers are no longer created by political parties but by bankers. They create them to promote a deal," wrote Jules Simon, a former French prime minister, in the pages of *Le Matin* in 1884.[13] From this point forward, a core question for *all* news organizations would thus concern the degree to which—rather than whether—they would seek to increase revenues and optimize audience share.[14]

The commercialization of news expanded the overall number of newspapers, which bolstered the number of jobs for journalists. Between 1870 and 1900, the number of daily newspapers in the United States quadrupled. Major cities like New York experienced intense battles for audience loyalty, but the development extended well beyond those cities. As Paul Starr notes in his synthetic history of the period, the ratio of dailies to cities increased during the 1870-to-1900 period from 2.5 to 4.1.[15] At that same time in France, the print run of daily newspapers increased from 1.4 million in 1870 to nearly nine million by the turn of the century.[16] In Paris, *Le Petit Journal* was just one of the four "millionaire" newspapers—so called because each sold a million copies per day—founded during this period; the others were *Le Petit Parisien* (1876), *Le Journal* (1892), *Le Matin* (1884). This expansion can be seen in cities and towns well beyond Paris. Prior to 1860, there existed only fifty-seven non-Parisian newspapers. By 1885, this figure would increase to 250 unique titles.[17] By the early years of the twentieth century, newspaper circulation in both countries had reached heights that have never again been seen in either setting.[18]

Where earlier newspapers relied primarily on correspondents and were run often by a single person, newspapers in urban settings offered jobs to members of the rising middle classes.[19] One American trade publication estimated in 1889 that one hundred thousand individuals sought journalism jobs. Discussing this data, Randall Sumpter reports that this was "about 10,000 more than the number of people already employed in the field" and that newsroom employment had grown substantially.[20] In France, growing numbers moved to the cities in the hopes of finding work in journalism, eschewing previously common middle-class career paths in the military.[21] As Marc Martin puts it, these individuals "swapped the sword for the pen and the press" as journalism increasingly became the place "for young people in search of success."[22] By the 1890s, journalists in France and the United States could on average expect to earn wages comparable to those of secondary school teachers, but doing jobs that for the most part did not require similar levels of educational attainment.[23] Partly because of the material rewards it offered, journalism was increasingly seen as a path for social ascension.

In their jobs, journalists were tasked with engaging audiences by providing lively and entertaining content. Journalism textbooks in the United States and France were remarkably frank in emphasizing this entertainment function. "The paramount object," wrote Edwin Shuman in his 1894 handbook, *Steps Into Journalism*, "is to make an interesting story."[24] A turn-of-the-century manual for novice French journalists stressed that any event—whether a "run over dog" or a "fine crime"—could be transformed from a local occurrence to a news story of national interest.[25] This feature appealed to aspiring journalists, more than a few of whom were attracted to a sense of adventure and the potential entry into more prestigious literary careers that it offered.[26] Some of the important literary names of the era started as—and in some instances partially remained—journalists: in the United States, these included Stephen Crane, Theodore Dreiser, and Richard Harding Davis; in France, they featured Gaston Leroux, Guy de Maupassant, and Émile Zola.[27]

At the same time, journalism came increasingly to be seen as a profession in itself, not merely a passageway to a career in other fields.[28] E. L. Godkin, editor of the *Nation* and the *New York Evening Post*, took to describing journalism as a "calling."[29] Reviewing the American case more broadly, Michael Schudson notes that by the 1880s, journalism was "less strictly a job one drifted into, more and more a career one chose."[30] Christian Delporte describes a similar development in France, where journalism was no longer seen as a job for "enlightened amateurs" looking to make their mark in literature or politics, but rather as a vocation in its own right.[31] In both countries, associations for journalists sprang up throughout the latter half of the nineteenth century. In France, l'Association Syndicale Professionnelle des Journalistes Républicains Français (The Professional Trade Union Association of French Republican Journalists) was founded in 1881, and the Association des Journalistes Parisiens (Association of Parisian Journalists) came about just a few years later (1884). In the United States, press clubs arose in major cities around the same time. The Washington Correspondents' Club was started in 1867 and the New York Press Club in 1873. These more formal organizations were mimicked elsewhere. At the turn of the century, Seattle journalists created an informal "almost Press Club" that met on Saturday evenings at local watering holes after the final editions were sent to the printer.[32] Discussing the French case, Martin notes that such associations ensured, "first and foremost, the definition of journalists' identity in a period of great movement and of the rise of the ranks of the profession."[33] In particular, the Club de la Presse in Paris helped journalists to meet and form a body in a moment where they were not very well accepted.[34] These associations, as well as the more informal meetings in cafes and bars, were important sources for giving individuals a sense that journalism was a profession worthy of their pursuit.

A core aspect of this nascent professionalism was a growing acceptance of the principle that news should be based on facts. In his autobiography, Theodore Dreiser would recall his first impressions upon entering the *World*'s newsroom: "I looked about the great room . . . and saw posted on the walls at intervals printed cards which read: 'Accuracy, accuracy, accuracy! Who? What? Where? When? How? The Facts—The Color—The Facts!'"[35] Neither the printed cards nor the principles they conveyed were specific to Pulitzer's newspaper.[36] In Seattle, for example, Alden Blethen installed in the lobby a life-size bronze newsboy hawking a newspaper with a one-word, capitalized headline: TRUTH! As Schudson notes, American journalists in the late nineteenth century saw themselves "uncovering the economic and political facts of industrial life more boldly, more clearly, and more 'realistically' than anyone had done before."[37] This work was not only exciting; it also served as the basis for the profession's self-understanding of its social function. Journalists could now conceive of themselves as a "fourth estate" or "counter-power" by using facts to hold the powerful to account.[38]

The orientation to facts was also increasingly adopted among journalists in France. The so-called new journalists of the 1880s focused their work increasingly on "finding the scoop" before their colleagues; such scoops were, at their core, about "the unpublished and ignored details" of social life.[39] Thomas Ferenczi calls this "new journalism of inquiry and observation" a "turning point" in French journalism, and argues that the turn revolved primarily around "a greater attention to the facts," which emerged initially in the *fait divers*[40] of the large nonpolitical dailies and came eventually to be an accepted principle even among political journalists,[41] through what is known as the passage from *le petit reportage*, which was centered on the popular press, to *le grand reportage*, which was reserved for the elites.[42]

In both places, new roles and techniques aided the development of fact-centered reporting. The role of the reporter was created in this period. In contrast to the correspondents and salon chroniclers that preceded them, reporters saw their task as observing and documenting the social world around them.[43] The interview—initially an American invention—also came to be widely used in both countries as a way to generate news about the activities of political officials and other powerholders.[44] While these roles and techniques nowadays appear "extremely banal," they were then "experienced as a revolution."[45] They served not only as jobs and reporting tools but as a growing source of prestige and as the basis of the journalist's social function, especially vis-à-vis older models of partisan journalism. Writing in 1889, Hugues Le Roux noted that "the former columnist [represented by] the man of wit, of good words and random talk is dethroned by a writer less anxious to shine, but better informed of the subjects he deals with: the reporter."[46]

Older techniques were also adapted to fit these new understandings. Moral crusades, for example, had been in existence for at least a century; newspapers increasingly offered realistic documentation of the social ills upon which such crusades were based. They did so in part on the assumption that empirical details would better mobilize the public and ameliorate the problems described, while also boosting circulation.[47] "French journalists," Jean Chalaby writes, "crusaded to reform the penal system, to change the laws on prostitution or to prove the innocence of a prisoner.... For the journalists... the symbolic and financial profits of this discursive strategy were immense."[48] The description applies equally well to the United States, where journalists like Nellie Bly and Jacob Riis made their mark pioneering a journalism that documented the social conditions of factories and city slums.[49] In France, the same spirit also appears in figures like Avril de Sainte Croix—"reporteresse de la Fronde"—who described the conditions of prostitutes in the Saint Lazare prison. These roles and techniques further solidified the sense of the journalist as a professional who interacted with, and sometimes challenged, the powerful in society by providing audiences with factual information.

By the end of the nineteenth century, French and American journalists broadly subscribed to an understanding of the profession as rooted in fact-based storytelling. Bolstered by the growing commercial basis of news, this shared understanding served to attract new entrants who sought a life of excitement and adventure. Journalism, they believed, could potentially provide such a life through the material and symbolic rewards it offered. Using facts, moreover, to tell those stories underwrote their self-understanding of journalism as a distinctive and socially important occupation with its own strategies and techniques for gathering and distilling information. This shared understanding also generated debates regarding how these principles should be enacted in practice, with recurrent questions raised about which facts journalists should prioritize, which stories they ought to tell, and which audiences their work ought to serve. If the commercial basis of the press was now shared, journalists and their employers still envisioned different ways of attracting audiences and, in doing so, fulfilling their newly envisioned social functions.

A DOUBLE DIVISION

Both within and across national cases, divisions emerged regarding journalists' enactments of this belief in fact-based storytelling. In France and the United States, journalists working at popular newspapers appealed to popular classes by emphasizing accessible writing, often using facts to tell entertaining stories about urban life. Their counterparts at more upscale outlets adopted what they viewed as a more serious approach that aimed to satisfy the interests of upper-middle-class readers. Cross-nationally, journalists diverged in their understanding of what this more serious approach entailed. In the United States, it took the form of investigative journalism; in France, serious journalism was understood as using facts as a way to think about the world. While similar cross-national emphases stemmed from journalism's commercial bases, these contrasting approaches derived from nationally specific understandings of the social functions that journalists were expected to fulfill.

Journalists working at popular newspapers saw themselves as using facts to tell stories about urban life. In their efforts to reach popular audiences, publishers and editors exhorted reporters to explain events in terms that this desired readership could easily understand. At the *New York World*, Joseph Pulitzer mandated that his staff not write "over the heads of our readers,"[50] while Moïse Polydore Millaud took pride that his journalists at *Le Petit Journal* had "the courage to be stupid" by making their writing accessible.[51] Often remembered for their sensational and sometimes hyperbolic approaches to news, these publishers also demanded their journalists provide readers with empirical details.[52] As a result, French journalists writing *fait divers* provided extremely raw—and extravagantly displayed—reports of crime scenes. The 1869 trial and execution of serial killer Jean-Baptiste Troppman, for example, was covered extensively in papers like *Le Petit Journal*. Daily updates gave readers gory accounts of the killer's crime scenes.[53] Their counterparts in America's "yellow press" did much the same, with loud, attention-grabbing headlines (e.g., "Screaming for Mercy") hinting at the facts disclosed in news stories.[54]

Outside the media capitals of Paris and New York, newspapers generally followed this popular approach. In both Toulouse and Seattle, the titles that would become dominant pursued this pathway. *La Dépêche* outpaced its competitors by slashing its price, altering the paper's format to improve readability, and instituting reforms to ensure that local news would be covered in addition to reports on happenings in the capital and beyond. In the last two decades of the nineteenth century, the newspaper also developed what one historian terms a "playful side" by adding culture and, later, sports coverage to bolster circulation.[55] Alden Blethen's *Seattle Times* likewise promised readers it would be "lively and inexpensive" and provide "working men and women the opportunity to read the news of the world on the day it happened."[56] Its early editions featured a "distinctly 'yellow' shade of scandal-mongering" reminiscent of William Randolph Hearst's newspapers.[57] At the same time, they also contained reporting from the paper's own Washington, DC, bureau, which was conveyed alongside large photos and splashy graphics. Quickly outpacing rivals in a circulation war, it offered "titillation with a middle-class cast," according to one observer.[58] Through its success in building circulation, the *Times* forced the other two daily newspapers to "become more 'yellow' to remain competitive—looking bolder and brighter, featuring lively copy, emphasizing scandal, fraud and crime."[59]

Upscale news outlets, especially in New York and Paris, enacted a staider approach to their informing mission. When Adolph Ochs took over the *New York Times* in 1896, he expressly sought to make the paper serious by carrying accurate information that would be useful to an upper-middle-class readership. This included self-styled "dry" information like real estate transactions that business-minded readers would find useful.[60] Yet under Ochs's leadership, the *Times* did not avoid stories about crime, sex, and violence per se; rather, its journalists transformed such details into what they viewed as intelligent reports about social life. As one commentator has argued, such news appeared in the yellow press as "sensationalism" but as "sociology in the *Times*."[61] In France, Hippolyte de Villemessant contrasted the more literary writing featured in his newspaper (*Le Figaro*) with what he saw as platitudinous prose found in the popular press. Under his stewardship, *Le Figaro* expanded its upper-class audience. His success was very much rooted in his ability to use facts to entertain and inform this readership. One critic at the time called the newspaper "the great official intelligencer of Parisian scandals, listening at doors, winkling out secrets, whispering indiscretions, telling the upper-crust about the *demi-monde*, giving backstage intrigues the importance normally accorded to political events."[62]

Popular and upscale journalists differed not only in how they pursued their shared purpose; they also justified their approaches in relation to distinct interpretations of their social functions. The popular newspapers in both France and the United States saw their function as being inclusive of the largest possible audience. "Nothing is worth printing," Joseph Pulitzer declared in a cable to his editorial board, "that is not sure to be read by the masses, the many, not the few."[63] By contrast, the upscale journals emphasized the quality of their offerings. Émile Zola, for example, worried about the "information fever" that led journalists to give attention to the most mundane facts (e.g., crime, scandal). He advocated a journalism that used facts to "search for the truth . . . which makes it possible to show things as they are."[64] To the extent that *fait divers* should even be done, he argued, the assignment "should only be given to talented writers. . . . Only writers can ask social questions in *fait divers*."[65] This opposition between quality and inclusion was expressed even more intensely in the most upscale journals of the day. E. L. Godkin's *New York Evening Post* aimed, in his words, to avoid the "hollering and bellering and shouting platitudes like the *Herald* and *Times*."[66] While accepting the commercial basis of the press, such journalists eschewed larger audiences, preferring "a smaller one that was socially and politically more significant."[67] Étienne Bandy de Nalèche (*Le Journal des Débats*) made a similar trade-off between the press's commercial and social functions in France.

Cross-nationally, French and American journalists differed primarily in terms of the form that these more prestigious social functions assumed. In France, facts were seen as useful tools to aid in interpreting the world. This combined the novelty of new journalism (through the use of facts) with earlier forms of journalism like chronicles, polemics, and commentaries.[68] In highlighting a writer's quality of thought and expression, these earlier forms also evoked the enduring influence of literature and politics on journalism.[69] More prestigious newspapers turned toward a fact-centered approach only reluctantly, and with caveats about the dangers of "totally dry reportage" that in their view lacked sophistication.[70] Zola's famous articles on the Dreyfus affair—written after he had left journalism for a career as a writer—illustrate this combination nicely, using facts as a way to think about the world and denounce wrongdoing. Other leading figures, like Jean Jaurès, who got his start writing for newspapers in Toulouse, examined documents and testimonies to support their opinions on the issue. Commenting on the role played by these individuals, Thomas Ferenczi notes the combination of analysis and factuality as historically distinctive: "Certainly, [readers] do not miss the commentary and discursive argument [in these articles], but the role played by the texts and documents [i.e., the facts] is overwhelming."[71]

The enduring influence of politics and literature on journalism in France can be illustrated in part through the profiles of their upmarket publishers. While newspapers were attractive as a source of revenue, these figures nonetheless tended to have links—either by birth or through marriage—to the aristocracy. Hippolyte de Villemessant, editor and publisher of *Le Figaro*, was the son of an aristocratic mother; in his professional pursuits, he used her surname rather than that of his military father. Étienne Bandy de Nalèche, who oversaw *Le Journal des Débats*, entered into journalism through his marriage to the daughter of the newspaper owner, Count Henri de Vauréal. Their marriage was celebrated in Paris by the bishop of Versailles. The presence of such individuals did not immunize French journalism from the newly dominant commercial model. While *Le Figaro* by the 1890s belonged to the category of quality newspapers, it was known as much for its "society" and "gossip" pages as its political reporting.[72] Nonetheless, the presence of individuals from more cultural backgrounds undoubtedly contributed to the persistent importance of "ideas" in French journalism, as this model was linked to the aristocracy. What is more, the social organization of newspapers shaped the very oppositions between upscale and popular. When *Le Figaro* installed a new manager (Gaston Galmet) in 1902, he was tasked with modernizing the newspaper—a task that he carried out by looking for ways to expand the newspaper's readership among the former aristocracy.[73] In this sense, the enduring influence of politics and literature in the elite French press reflects the adjustments the aristocracy made to the press's newfound commercial basis.[74]

In the United States, prestigious journalism took the form of investigative reports that revealed social problems, especially those that power-holders preferred to keep hidden. Julius Chambers's investigation of Bloomingdale Asylum in 1872 is an early and classic example. By having himself committed, Chambers was able to verify and expose abuse of inmates. The great figures from that era are recalled for similar investigations: Lincoln Steffens's reporting on urban corruption, Ida Tarbell's exposé of Standard Oil, and Nellie Bly's own undercover reporting from an asylum for women. While these muckrakers, as many came to be known, saw themselves as part of an effort to reform society in a progressive direction, they largely did so without any necessary partisan link. The prestigious form in American journalism was in this sense, and unlike its French counterpart, a more complete invention in that it did not generally combine older genres and formats.[75] It was also more widely distributed across publications. Even amid the shouting headlines of Pulitzer's *World* and Hearst's *Journal*, readers could expect to find lengthy investigations that revealed information power-holders preferred to keep concealed (e.g., Nellie Bly worked at the *World*).

Unlike their French counterparts, the publishers and journalists associated with ascendant upscale newspapers maintained little relation to their partisan predecessors. Ochs (*New York Times*) was the son of immigrant parents; his father, himself the son of a diamond merchant, ran a dry goods store. He took pride in his self-made success and envisioned the *Times* as a newspaper targeted for the rising middle classes.[76] By emphasizing self-reliance, initiative, and personal work ethic, he echoed what Alexis de Tocqueville saw as the "equality of conditions" that differentiated American individualism from its European counterparts. Henry Villard came from an upper-class German family (his father was a Supreme Court justice in Munich); his purchase in 1881 of the *New York Evening Post* and the *Nation* came after he made substantial money in transportation, which allowed him to connect again with reporter friends he made working as a journalist during the Civil War.[77] While some of these friends had partisan links—earlier in his career Horace White was closely allied with Abraham Lincoln—the material links sustaining the partisan press died off during the latter part of the nineteenth century, as the government reduced and eventually eliminated various subventions like printing contracts and government advertisements.[78]

What would come to be seen as nationally distinctive journalism in France and the United States reflected one important form that journalism's social functions assumed. These distinctive forms also stood, and continue to stand, alongside sometimes less reputed—but cross-nationally very similar—manifestations. What's more, these social functions were never entirely nationally distinctive. French journalism has its own tradition of investigative reporting,[79] just as American journalism has its own history of literary and opinion-oriented writing.[80] Nonetheless, journalism prizes in both countries crystallize these distinctive and dominant understandings of journalism's social function. In France, Albert Londres would in the early twentieth century make his name reporting on wars. His efforts were admired not only for their attention to fact but also for his literary style and his denunciation of wrongdoings. In the United States, Joseph Pulitzer was a publisher, and the journalism he helped to consecrate was very much linked to muckraking and investigation. In this sense, the prizes are crystallizations of the social dynamics specific to the two cases.

FINDING A PLACE IN JOURNALISM

For journalists in both countries, a predicament arose as they sought a place for themselves among the profession's novel combination of commercial and social functions. In France and the United States, the extraordinary growth of journalism as a business opened up a range of new jobs; many people in the rising middle classes rushed to occupy them. At the same time, the clashing visions that publishers pursued in attracting audiences endowed journalists with unequal material and symbolic rewards. Individuals coming from the lower segments of the middle classes tended to find their place in the popular newspapers of the day, which generally paid less, provided minimal security, and often came under criticism for being sensational or apolitical but were nonetheless seen as exciting opportunities. Those coming to journalism from the upper-middle classes, by contrast, more often found employment in the more serious and sober upscale newspapers. Compared to their peers, they tended to be better paid and have more job stability and could take pride in doing work that they and their peers saw as the pinnacle of professional excellence. Nonetheless, so long as all journalists believed that journalism was worth their efforts, each generally found a place for themselves, despite the unequal returns each expected to receive.

Literature of the era nicely captures some of the ways a career in journalism might offer the means to a better life. Guy de Maupassant's *Bel Ami* (published in 1885), for example, tells the story of the charming but penniless Georges Duroy, who arrives in Paris determined to find a job in journalism—despite having no prior writing experience—and to make a name for himself. The novel proceeds in tracing his social ascent, which transpires alongside his rising stature in the field from reporter to, ultimately, editor-in-chief. In the United States, Richard Harding Davis's *Gallegher* (published in 1891) relays the story of an uneducated office boy at a Philadelphia newspaper whose street smarts give him a nose for crime news. The story culminates in Gallegher scoring a crucial scoop and being hired by the managing editor in the newsroom, thus giving him the opportunity to leave behind the "little house, where his mother and himself lived alone" on the outskirts of the city.

Such fictional accounts point to a real empirical trend: new entrants, inspired by the possibility of social ascendance, flooded into the field. In doing so, they occupied some of the new positions created through the field's expansion, which themselves corresponded with the new fact-based vision of journalism. The job of reporter, as the fictional examples suggest, corresponded directly to the new understanding of journalism as fact-based reporting.[81] Whereas editors had long been charged with deciding where news went, reporters went out and searched for information. And with the creation of news beats, reporters searched for many types of information, ranging from politics and crime to sports and fashion. Looking at trade publications from the era, Roberts Forde and Foss note the repeated invocation "of the news reporter who bravely and calmly ventured forth into an often-terrifying world to document it for his readers."[82]

This transformation brought new types of people into journalism as well. The number of women, while still a small proportion of all journalists, jumped substantially in the last twenty years of the nineteenth century.[83] Individuals from rural areas and small towns, too, increasingly saw journalism as an opportunity for social ascent.[84] Albert Londres was born to a coppersmith father in Vichy and initially worked as an accountant there before moving to Paris. The slight modification he made to his family name—to make it sound more like "London" than "laundry," which it initially meant—signaled his desire for social ascendance. To be sure, these individuals did not displace the dominant individuals preceding them in the field: well-educated men, often from well-heeled urban families, continued to hold the highest positions in journalism (e.g., editor-in-chief).[85] But the overall mix of social properties in the field shifted decisively. If the newspapers of the early nineteenth century were primarily the products of party or cultural elites, by the end of that century they more closely reflected the middle classes that increasingly consumed them. The new journalistic vision of fact-based reporting thus had a social basis in the shifting patterns of social recruitment that accompanied those changes.

Individuals hailing from the lower segments of these middle classes tended to find a place for themselves among the popular newspapers of the day. As newsroom employment in the United States boomed in the last decade of the nineteenth century, total pay in fact declined slightly.[86] New middle-class entrants accepting lower salaries than their peers at upscale newspapers likely accounted for this trend; women in particular took home half as much in salary as their male counterparts. Men and women alike also enjoyed few job protections. As Sumpter notes, many publishers of popular newspapers sought to control costs by hiring reporters that could be more or less "interchangeable" with one another and easily dismissed during slow news periods.[87] This cost control by publishers depended crucially on the willingness of at least some journalists to find these conditions acceptable, at least on a temporary basis.

These same journalists also tended to undertake less prestigious forms of work. Women, for example, were relegated to the society and gossip beats, and those that were not became "stunt" or "front page" girls by enduring physical challenges while doing reporting.[88] Such work was regularly derided at the time as being depoliticized or a form of "gutter journalism." Across gender lines, Gerald Baldasty notes that many of the stories produced by "the young and inexperienced" were not bylined.[89] The structure of pay, he reports, favored stories "of unusual interest or excitement."[90] While in principle this could cover a wide range of issues, in practice it tended to favor reporting that critics pilloried for sensationalism. He illustrates the point with the disappointed recollections of a reporter who was sent out to cover a drowning, only to find the imagined female victim had survived. "He cursed his fate. If she had drowned, he would have received six dollars for the story instead of two."[91] The very sensationalism against which social elites sometimes railed thus had a basis not merely in the system of beats or even the political economy of the field but also in the social conditions of journalistic production.[92]

In France, those doing the work of producing *fait divers* occupied a similar social position. While the overall amount of such news increased substantially in the nineteenth century, such items typically carried no byline, thus suggesting the relative lack of importance associated with the individuals doing such work.[93] Their work, moreover, was regularly criticized for being thoughtless, and lacking in writing ability. In his study on the topic, Kalifa writes that individuals doing *fait divers* were "the most despised workers of the newspaper."[94] The best-known figures associated with these "softer" news beats likewise suggest lower social origins than those previously writing for the press. Pierre Giffard, who pioneered coverage of sports (cycling, running, auto-racing), was born in a small town; his father was a notary (thus highlighting the entry of middle classes into journalism). After service in the military, Giffard moved to Paris to explore a career in journalism.

The case of Giffard highlights one reason why so many journalists, especially among the lower middle classes, found the balance of material and symbolic rewards at least temporarily acceptable. Even if the work a journalist undertook might be unsatisfying at a particular moment in time, one could nonetheless look at and take inspiration from real world cases of social and professional ascent. While presumably rare in statistical terms, such cases gave life to the belief that journalism was worth one's efforts and, crucially, that those efforts might one day pay off both materially (in the form of a higher salary) and symbolically (via increased recognition and social renown). A figure like Nellie Bly offers a similar example from the American context. Through her "stunt reporting," she was able to make a name for herself doing fact-based reporting. As Brooke Kroeger notes, the genre of stunt reporting offered women an opportunity to demonstrate they possessed the skills needed to undertake rigorous reporting linked to the profession's social functions.[95] It was in part through these atypical cases that the more typical and, frankly, disappointing returns were rendered acceptable.

Others found their place in journalism acceptable for different reasons. Some women reporters, for example, found journalism "less taxing than the traditional career choice of teacher."[96] Many stressed the excitement associated with the work, which underwrote a willingness, at least for a time, to emphasize symbolic returns over material ones. Rheta Childe Dorr worked as a freelancer from Seattle during the Klondike Gold Rush. In her memoirs (published in 1924), she recalled the "wonderful yarns" that she gathered during that period by talking to miners, walking the docks, and hanging around outfitting stores. This excitement could fade, as it did for Dorr, who struggled to find any stable employment after the rush subsided. As with any occupation, the reasons were complex and depended on the expectations one held of their work, as well as their relationship to one's personal life.

Those entering journalism from the upper-middle classes often faced a dramatically different set of conditions. Editors at the leading upscale newspapers in France and the United States boasted of hiring only college-educated men.[97] In both countries, the percent of the population with such degrees was extremely small (approximately 3 percent), and typically limited to those coming from wealthy or well-connected families. These experiences gave an appreciation for more intellectual ways of posing social problems that accorded with the more distinguished social functions attributed to journalism. Lincoln Steffens, one of the best-known journalists of his generation, was born into a wealthy California business family; one of the homes in which he was raised would eventually become the California governor's mansion. Before becoming a well-known muckraker, Steffens studied philosophy and history—first as an undergraduate at Berkeley, and later in classes throughout Western Europe. Explaining how he got his first beat reporting job, covering Wall Street, despite having no experience in either banking or business, he explained: "My universities had taught me to study," and this meant he could "read up" on the subject matter.[98] In a subsequent beat, he sought to place "some crime [news articles] in the *Post*" by finding a "political, a literary, way to write about robberies, murders, etc.," which he contrasted directly with the "sensational, conventional" approach to such news.[99]

Like Steffens, the renowned French journalist Gaston Leroux was born into a well-to-do family. From an early age, his father pushed for him to train in law, though Leroux harbored wishes to become a writer.[100] After completing a bachelor's degree in Normandy, he moved to Paris to take up his legal training. Following the death of his father, he began writing small items about legal issues. Recalling his initial forays into journalism, Leroux would say that such reporting seemed "the most solidly based in a quiet tradition" that entailed using his knowledge of the legal system to chronicle "what was happening" at the trial. At the same time, he landed on a "formula" for doing such reporting that would distinguish his work from the mere chronicles offered by his colleagues, and correspond nicely with the idea of using facts to interpret the world. "Leave the paperwork aside," he told an interviewer later in life, and "work with a single document, life! Day to day life. . . . Let my colleagues take care of what happened . . . yesterday, [I will] announce what will happen the next day."

Life was hardly friction-free for these and other journalists from upper-middle-class origins. Their family backgrounds did not automatically confer them with professional success, though they did provide familiarity with the worlds about which they reported and sometimes offered social contacts that helped careers get started. What's more, they had to adjust in order to secure a personally acceptable balance of rewards. Their predicament was different from that of their peers from lower social origins, but it was a predicament nonetheless. Steffens, for example, writes in his autobiography that he was "ecstatic" early in his

The Genesis of the Journalist's Predicament 47

career about having his pay halved so that he could participate more fully in his work as a reporter rather than a freelancer.[101] Other journalists, perhaps equally talented, had to ensure their work supported them economically. What the upper-middle-class entrants enjoyed were higher expectations of their careers, as well as more resources that positioned them to succeed in pursuing it. This hardly guaranteed a uniform response, as some favored symbolic rewards over material ones (and vice versa).

What united journalists from all these social backgrounds, though, was a belief in journalism as worthy of their efforts. Such a belief underwrote their willingness to struggle. For some, these struggles mostly involved freelance work for popular newspapers that were derided as commercial rags. For others, this entailed work that was lauded for being thoughtful and high-minded. These symbolic hierarchies were underpinned by social inequalities, but across all these cases belief in journalism was crucial. Even at the moment of the profession's modern birth, one can read memoirs and commentaries of those who exited the profession after losing this belief. William Salisbury offers one illustrative example. After working in journalism for nine years, he grew bitter about the work. Whether his account is interpreted as the disappointment of a true believer or the bitterness of one frustrated by the weight of the profession's commercial functions, his disillusionment is nonetheless clear. "I engaged in journalism with the belief that I was entering the noblest profession," Salisbury wrote in his account of his time in newsrooms. "I gave, and gladly gave, my physical and mental energies, my enthusiasms, my dreams; and as a result, I have only a head full of chaotic memories, and a weakened constitution from the irregular life I had to lead."[102]

JOURNALISM: AN ABSOLUTE GAMBLE

Writing in the early decades of the twentieth century, Max Weber characterized the journalist's life as "an absolute gamble in every respect and under conditions that test one's inner security in a way that scarcely occurs in any other situation."[103] The labor market promised jobs to aspiring journalists; popular representations suggested that those jobs would entail substantial work and the possibility of public renown. Most journalists, in Weber's view, knew that the reality, while attractive, was not always so glamorous. The pay was often subpar, and working conditions made it difficult to write "promptly and convincingly on all problems in life—whatever the 'market' happens to demand"—without becoming "absolutely shallow." Given these conditions, Weber argued that it was entirely unsurprising that so many struggled to handle this predicament, which has been described here as an effort to find a personally acceptable balance of material and symbolic rewards. Instead, what surprised him, and what struck him as worthy of further investigation, was that so many in fact attempted this work in spite of these obstacles.

Belief was crucial to making this gamble seem worthy. In both France and the United States, journalism came to be seen as an occupation in which one could invest one's energies and efforts. This depended on the possibility of attaining, or at least anticipating attaining, material and symbolic rewards from being a journalist. In contrast to their partisan predecessors, journalists in the nineteenth century could imagine getting paid to inform audiences, both in the sense of distilling facts and in the broader sense of giving form to the chaos of everyday social life. These expectations in turn depended on transformations in the profession, whose novel combination of commercial and social functions made these rewards seem both possible and attractive. Returns on these investments, however, were never guaranteed. One could fail to find an acceptable balance of rewards; many likely did. It was in this sense that Weber highlighted the journalist's life as an "absolute gamble."

Yet the gamble that journalists took was never a simple game of chance, offering equal possibilities of success or failure to all. With its relatively porous boundaries, journalism in the nineteenth century admitted individuals from a relatively wide variety of social backgrounds with substantial differences in social origins, educational attainment, and professional trajectories. This was genuinely different from the partisan press that preceded it, which relied overwhelmingly on political and cultural elites as correspondents. The different socially cultivated expectations, toward both work and life, that this new class of journalists held shaped the ways they dealt with their predicament. What constituted acceptable working conditions, a sufficient salary, and a reasonable and fulfilling work load was always in important ways a result of one's socialization. As a result, the different expectations that journalists held helped to make the very unequal possibilities of material and symbolic rewards that journalists faced acceptable. In this sense, the very real democratization of journalism in the nineteenth century proceeded not by eliminating hierarchies but by internalizing them within the profession.

If the nineteenth century can be seen as the genesis of the journalist's predicament, it is also the period that gave birth to modern journalism criticism.[104] Terms like *yellow journalism* and *sensationalism* trace back to this period. They arose due to the novel combination of commercial and social functions that the press undertook in its attempts to inform readers. Some newspapers aimed to make money by including the widest audience possible. The flashy headlines and nonpolitical topics they utilized toward this end were defended not only on the basis of making money, though that was clearly an aim, but also as an effort to be as inclusive as possible. Other newspapers endeavored not to ignore these commercial concerns but to tailor them to more educated audiences. The dry information they contained and the "thoughtful" essays they published were defended on the basis of excellence rather than inclusion. This division, between two different principles of legitimation, continues into the present.

While publishers developed these different approaches, it was journalists who carried them out in practice. A journalist's personally acceptable balance of material and symbolic rewards was thus layered on top of the profession's novel commercial and social functions. Those criticized for sensationalism or doing apolitical and soft news tended overwhelmingly to have limited education and experience and to come from lower social origins than their peers. By contrast, those praised for serious and socially useful journalism generally had higher levels of educational attainment, often came from upper-middle class families, and were almost exclusively male. These various realizations of the profession's functions were, and are, subject to condemnation and praise. By highlighting the social properties associated with the journalists producing this work, it can also be recalled that the profession's novel social functions were never socially neutral. They favored those with some properties more than others, even while ignoring the social inequalities that subtended different social functions.

Exceptions to these patterns undoubtedly existed. In the United States, for example, one of the most prominent muckrakers of the time (Nellie Bly) was a woman of rural working-class social origins.[105] Clearly talented and extraordinarily industrious, her ascent in journalism was atypical for someone holding the social properties she did. Rather than refute the importance of a sociological analysis, however, her trajectory (as well as those of others like her) invites examination of the social conditions that permitted and, in important ways, limited her ascent. Her early career was structured entirely by writing about "women's topics," which was the only point of entry for her into journalism. Her frustration with the format led her to New York, where she believed there might be more opportunities. After numerous rejections, primarily on the basis of gender, she secured an assignment at Pulitzer's *World* to report undercover on conditions at a woman's asylum. What had been the basis of her exclusion previously (gender) became the entry point into the story that would launch her to fame, as only women were permitted access to the asylum. At the same time, in important ways her ascent remained limited, as the investigations she did generally were published in the popular newspapers and innovated on the stunt reporting that was itself highly gendered. The staid pages of the serious press, whose journalists criticized such stunts as mere sensationalism, remained off-limits even for her. Bly's trajectory can thus be seen as atypical, in that she ascended far more than most of her peers with similar profiles. But it was nonetheless still very much rooted in the social dynamics of her era.

Highlighting the journalist's predicament in relation to the press's newfound commercial and social functions refines comparative analyses of journalism. The typical opposition between a French "journalism of ideas" and an American "journalism of facts" elides much of the shared history between the two cases. These commonalities stemmed from the rise of a commercial model of journalism in both places. This model induced practices and values that were extraordinarily similar in both places, and for similar reasons: publishers sought to provide audiences with fact-based news that would entice them to purchase their newspapers. Certainly, the specifics regarding what French and American (and other) audiences find enticing vary. But the commercial principle underpinning them is identical across both cases. This was true in the nineteenth century, and for cases well beyond just France and the United States.[106] It remains true today.

Rather than invalidate prior scholarship that finds enduring differences between French and American journalism, highlighting commercial and social functions circumscribes this conclusion more carefully. In both countries, the most enduring oppositions—between fact and opinion, or politics and information—reflect the ways that the most dominant journalists adapted to the commercial logic of journalism in the nineteenth century. In France, the commercial model initially took root among the emergent popular press, as early nineteenth-century newspapers existed primarily for upper classes. It is in the *fait divers* that fact-based reporting emerges through what historians term *petit reportage*. The upper-class Parisian press initially resisted these fact-based principles, seeing them as uninteresting and dry, as lacking in the sophistication necessary for thinking about the world, which was in their view the sine qua non of journalism's social function. They turned to them only reluctantly and, crucially, by reinterpreting them in light of the ideas-based journalism that preceded it. What came to be known as *grand reportage*—the highest form of journalism in France—was the result of this reinterpretation. Its creation reflects the capacity of better-resourced journalists (read: more educated, coming from higher social origins) to assert their supremacy, even as their prior forms of journalism came to be devalued. As a group, this can be interpreted as their effort to find an acceptable balance of rewards in journalism.

In the United States, the strength of the rising middle classes and businesspersons was far stronger than in France. Even the prestigious or upscale newspapers were from the start very clear about their commercial orientation, rejecting the very model of quality—using facts to think about the world—that came to define prestigious journalism in France. Writing in the nineteenth century, for example, no less prestigious a figure in American journalism than Lincoln Steffens wrote, "if it were something to think about that he [the reader] wanted, the best commodity to offer for sale might be editorials, essays and important facts. But the commercial journalist, after studying and testing the market, is convinced that his customers prefer something to talk about."[107] At the same time, the American emphasis on investigation reflects the Progressive Era influence of reformers on social institutions. Journalists, particularly those at the most upscale newspapers, felt themselves to be part of this movement. For those with resources, they could even envision themselves using facts, often painstakingly gathered, to challenge power-holders. As such, it helped underwrite the sense in which journalism could contribute to the broader common good.

This chapter's historical synthesis highlights the genesis of the journalist's predicament, but the usual caveats about such analyses apply. The historical record is not a neutral accounting of the past. Instead, it reflects the perspectives of a particular class of agents, usually those most dominant at a specific period in time. This is certainly true in journalism of the nineteenth century, where the lowest-status reporters often did not even attach their names to the works they did, and where the majority of memoirs come from successful journalists. As a result, inferences are the best that can be offered in many instances regarding what attracted so many of these individuals to journalism, and what they expected from it in return. While this aims to make sense of their meanings, it also risks "making them speak as silent people" by using their absence from the historical record to prove a preestablished theoretical point.[108] Grasping those attractions and expectations across a wide range of journalists therefore necessitates a shift to the present. This provides the possibility to speak with individuals facing the predicament today, and for whom a life in journalism remains very much a gamble, though for different reasons than those of their nineteenth-century predecessors, as journalism's eroding (rather than expanding) commercial basis appears to threaten the profession's long-standing, historically derived social functions.

CHAPTER TWO

Living For—and Maybe Off—Journalism

Darren was attracted to journalism as a way to reconcile his talent for writing with his passion for sports.[1] During primary school in the rural town where he was raised, he was "the only kid in class who could make my poetry rhyme."[2] His time outside the classroom was mostly spent playing basketball. He loved the game but recognized early on that he "wasn't that good at it." By the time he got to high school, Darren had come to terms with the fact that he stood no chance of becoming a professional athlete. "How then," he remembers asking himself, "do I get into the NBA without actually playing basketball?" As someone who "religiously" read the sports section of the newspaper, he wondered whether journalism might be a way to "marry" his passions and talents. What could be better, he thought, than "having someone pay me to watch sports and then write about it?"

At the regional public university, Darren studied journalism and took whatever freelance sports assignments he could reporting on local high school teams. From conversations with peers and mentors, he knew that sports journalism was "very much a ladder game. You have to start at the bottom and work your way up." It did not bother him, therefore, that after graduation he had to move across the country and live in a small, unfamiliar town for his first job. He worked a lot ("eighty to one hundred hours a week") and made little money (roughly twenty eight thousand dollars annually). But he loved the job, even though he sometimes worried how long he could work such long hours while getting so little pay in return. At times, he admits, he even wondered whether it would be better to get a job outside of journalism. At that moment, though, he focused on the pleasures of his work. Someone was paying him, however meagerly, to do exactly the work he had wanted to do since he was a teenager: to watch sports and write about it.

Darren's experiences offer an initial entry point for a contemporary analysis of why anyone would be a journalist. Two features of his otherwise idiosyncratic case can be applied to the journalist's predicament more broadly. First, Darren finds journalism to be an attractive profession for the opportunities for self-expression it provides and the sense of self-fulfillment it promises. Certainly, not everyone wants to do sports journalism;[3] however, the profession's primary appeals are polysemic enough that a diverse range of individuals can read their own talents, interests, and passions onto them. These attractions, which also vary in intensity among journalists, are crucial because they underwrite the belief that a career in journalism is worth pursuing. Such a belief is especially important given the profession's current economic conditions, which entail for nearly every journalist the acceptance of lesser material rewards than what is possible in cognate fields like public relations, marketing, or advertising. The first half of this chapter therefore explores what journalists in Seattle and Toulouse find attractive about their chosen profession.

Second, Darren maintains this belief by adjusting his career expectations to his particular conditions of professional possibility. His own adjustment—common among journalists in both Seattle and Toulouse—entails "living for" journalism. It foregrounds the personal sacrifices he has made and expects to continue making to keep his dream of a career in journalism alive. Some others, in France but not the United States, see the profession not primarily as a source of excitement but rather as a guarantee of modest pay and regular hours that provide an acceptable personal life. "Living off" journalism is worth their modest efforts for the modest rewards it provides them in return. Still others—these constitute the fortunate few in both places—find meaningful work doing at a local level what they love about journalism at their respective national levels. They expect to continue securing a personally acceptable balance of rewards in the cities of Toulouse and Seattle, but mostly not by ascending to Paris or New York. Through these adjustments, journalists reproduce their belief that journalism, or more specifically the journalism they do, is worth their efforts. The diversity of these adjustments, and the social properties that underpin them, are therefore explored in the second part of the chapter.

These adjustments are often framed in the language of individual motivation or volition. Those who live for journalism are lauded for their passion and selflessness; those living off are pilloried for their cynicism and resignation; those who live for and off are taken as evidence of a meritocratic system that rewards the most deserving and talented. This chapter instead emphasizes the social properties and national contexts that structure the expectations that journalists hold, the possibilities they deem conceivable, and the adjustments they make in their pursuit. Like Darren, journalists in both Toulouse and Seattle that hold less favorable social properties (i.e., lower social origins, less professional experience, and often less prestigious educational attainment) tend to make a virtue of their difficult conditions. Whether in earnings, time, or personal life, they sacrifice in the present for the possibility of more satisfying work in the future. By contrast, those with more favorable social properties (i.e., higher social origins, more professional experience, and often more prestigious educational attainment) likewise struggle to find a place in journalism; however, many of them expect work satisfaction to be a present reality, not just a future possibility.

Cross-nationally, differences appear regarding the form that specific adjustments entail. In France, labor regulations make it relatively difficult—and expensive—for news organizations to lay off employees holding permanent contracts. This means that some journalists (often but not exclusively women) with less favorable properties sacrifice professional ambition in favor of their nonprofessional lives, while those holding more favorable properties are able to refuse work they find unsatisfying or unappealing. In the United States, weak labor protections mean that nearly all journalists, regardless of the social properties they hold, sacrifice their nonprofessional lives (e.g., by moving cities, working long hours) to make their careers in journalism possible. They can never solely "live off" journalism because the regulatory context in which they labor makes it relatively easy for their employers to terminate their contracts.

The adjustments that journalists make, and the beliefs those adjustments serve to maintain, relate to the profession's commercial and social functions in several ways. Some of those who "live for" journalism aspire to do work regularly associated with the profession's most acclaimed social functions: to monitor power-holders, to stand up against corruption, and to use facts to denounce injustices. Others, like Darren, "live for" a less civic vision of the profession and do work that corresponds more closely to the profession's commercial functions. Still others "live off" a profession that, with its emphasis on regular updates and productivity, growingly resembles—in their view—a factory more than a newsroom. For all, deteriorating economic conditions make it difficult to do the work that attracted them to the profession originally. In this sense, the fulfillment of both the commercial and the social functions of the contemporary press is predicated in part on the capacity of many journalists to manage the disappointments they feel between what attracted them to the profession and the experiences that characterize their everyday existence.

Seen from this perspective, journalism's most esteemed social functions appear particularly fragile. Their fulfillment relies on at least some journalists making sacrifices that seem difficult to sustain over time. At some point, one tends to ask whether it is worthwhile to work such long hours for so few rewards, all while struggling to produce journalism for which there appears to be, at least in Seattle and Toulouse, limited demand. In this context, it hardly seems surprising that a less civic vision of the press, like Darren's, is also expressed by a growing number of journalists. If one cannot reasonably expect to fulfill the profession's most hallowed social functions, they can at least find it enticing to have an exciting job that corresponds to the news media's commercial needs. This vision, channeled in part by journalism schools as an effort to address their own declining or stagnating enrollments, also bets that if the professional gambit in journalism does not work out—if the balance of rewards is no longer deemed personally acceptable—they will have skills that can be readily transferred to other jobs with better terms and conditions. Journalism's most esteemed social functions are thus doubly fragile: difficult for many journalists to fulfill, and also decreasingly useful as a basis for social recruitment.

But journalism's most esteemed social functions are not only fragile. They are also highly exclusive. In both Toulouse and Seattle, the journalists who expect to attain an acceptable balance of rewards doing this work tend to be men, typically from families of liberal professionals (e.g., lawyers, professors, doctors). Journalism for them is hardly a stroll in the park. They have made very real sacrifices to do the work they do; their talents and skills are not illusory. But they also generally faced conditions that were more propitious than many of their peers. The sacrifices they made—the low pay they took doing internships with prestigious news outlets, the risky moves they made abandoning stable but unsatisfying jobs for more intellectually fulfilling ones—were possible in part because of support that was not available to other journalists. To be sure, the civic vision of journalism they hold corresponds almost perfectly with many of the normative ideals ascribed to the press. But what does it mean when journalism's most civically valued functions are also its most socially exclusive?

A POLYSEMIC PROFESSION

Existing scholarship—often utilizing surveys and drawing on the language of motivations—shows that individual attractions to journalism are "diverse and varied."[4] Some journalists emphasize the opportunity for creativity that they perceive the profession as affording them. Such creativity includes personal expression through writing, photography, and various forms of multimedia production.[5] Without excluding this attraction, others see journalism as an exciting career to explore one's passions and curiosities. These passions are sometimes focused on specific thematic foci, like Darren's fondness for sports. Other times, they deal more broadly with the way journalism enables a sociable lifestyle: a job where one spends one's day talking with strangers, learning their stories, and sharing those stories with audiences. Still others describe journalism as attractive because of the social function they perceive it as performing in society. This includes the "watchdog" role expected of journalists in many liberal democracies, but also encompasses more developmental orientations found in countries around the world.[6]

The diversity of the attractions stems not solely from their variety but also their polysemic nature. The issues about which one is passionate; the forms that creative expression takes; the lifestyle that one anticipates—all these can be interpreted and adapted to fit a very broad range of ways to be a journalist. They therefore apply not only to the dream of being France's next Edwy Plenel or America's next Woodward and Bernstein, though the passion for politics and investigations is certainly an attraction and aspiration for some.[7] They also take shape in more modest or practical aspirations: to be the sort of journalist that provides information about daily life, leisure, and consumption; that finds pleasure and excitement in writing news that amuses and distracts; that favors above all work that, in this view, actually interests audiences, and that often bears little relation to the investigations and political reporting done by their most esteemed colleagues; that is a "journalist of communication" in the language offered by Colette Brin, Jean Charron, and Jean de Bonville.[8]

This polysemy is productive. It both engenders the belief that journalism is worthy of their efforts and provides the ideals to which individual journalists subsequently adjust themselves. Darren, to return to the example discussed at the chapter's outset, very clearly believes that journalism, at least for now, is worth his efforts and sacrifices. But this belief has very little, if anything, to do with the profession's primary social functions. He does not assign any particular social import to sports reporting. Such work is fun and exciting to him personally, and it offers a way for his news organization to attract audiences. His "gamble," to revisit Max Weber's phrasing from the prior chapter, may or may not pay off for him personally. But at no point does his narrative touch upon anything related to journalism's role in democratic societies. He is not, and will not be, disappointed by his failure to approximate any particular social function; it is not an expectation he has of the profession at all.

Journalism schools serve as one important setting where these polysemic attractions are organized and channeled. Through the courses they provide, the skills they emphasize, and the attitudes they cultivate, educational institutions perform the "organized socialization" that structures the profession's preferred readings of itself.[9] In both France and the United States, journalism schools have long foregrounded skills-based training (e.g., reporting, interviewing, presentation) over "content" knowledge."[10] This model has been criticized for failing to provide subject specialization that would allow journalists to better understand the social worlds they cover.[11] Some schools, typically the most elite, have responded by offering coursework aimed at training journalists to be better equipped to perform the profession's long-declared social functions.[12] Nearly all schools, though, have developed curricula devoted to skills—attracting audiences, valorizing entrepreneurialism, and understanding business management—that highlight journalism's commercial functions and market those skills as "transferrable" to other communication professions.[13] In doing so, journalism schools have retained the older sense of a social function (i.e., journalists exist to serve democracy by informing citizens) while also more explicitly training students in the profession's current commercial needs by making those issues their own professional concerns.

These transformations in journalism education, which function partly as a shifting strategy of social recruitment,[14] provide the primary readings that attractions can assume. In one reading, journalism is an exciting job because it affords the opportunity to use facts to conduct investigations that will hold the powerful to account or develop a fresh understanding of the social world. It is a demanding vision, in every sense of the term, requiring skills, commitment, and knowledge. A second reading, however, suggests a more relaxed, less civic version of the profession. In this version, journalism is an attractive career because it allows one to be a storyteller who meets with interesting people and uses creative skills to communicate those findings to audiences. Not only is this vision of journalism less explicitly civic in nature; it also fuels belief in part because the skills gained are assumed to be transferable. If a job in journalism does not work out, one can always find a job in a communication sector that pays more and affords better hours.

Journalists since the nineteenth century have been attracted to a profession that seems exciting, that affords the opportunity for self-expression and a sense of self-fulfillment.[15] But the specific meanings a journalist associates with these ideals are not static. They reflect what a journalist feels they can bring to journalism at a specific moment in time (in terms of skills, interests, passions), and what journalism can provide them in return (in terms of material and symbolic rewards). Rather than list a set of attractions and ask journalists which ones they identify with, the in-depth interviews utilized here invited respondents to describe the sources of attraction and provided an opportunity to understand what those attractions mean to each journalist individually. In doing so, it captured the polysemy associated with broad attractions, which serve as the basis of the socially cultivated expectations that journalists come to hold of their own careers.

Journalists in both Toulouse and Seattle commonly referenced four attractions to journalism: telling stories, revealing information, understanding the world, and giving voice. While not exhaustive, these attractions each usefully illustrate the polysemy of the profession, as each is interpreted in ways that express more or less civic, enchanted, or intense commitments to the profession, while also emphasizing different skills and abilities. Just as importantly, each attraction gives rise to the belief that journalism is a profession worthy of their efforts. Without them, journalists would have little reason to see the profession as worthwhile, especially given how difficult the labor market has become in journalism. In both cities, then, journalism is able to engender belief among journalists by offering attractions that can be interpreted and adapted to fit a diverse range of individuals and interests.

Telling Stories

Growing up in Eastern Europe, Alexandra never dreamed of becoming a journalist. While she loved writing, the profession was "an elite career" that seemed impossible for someone like her to break into.[16] "Back home, you don't just get into writing or journalism," she said. When her family immigrated to the United States, she enrolled at a local public university with "very little idea of what I wanted to do." A magazine journalism class convinced her that, contrary to her earlier assumptions, journalism was "an actual career track that I would really love." In that class, she did an article about a mountain climbing accident that left two students dead. For it, she interviewed one of the survivors and read reports about the accident. "I really liked the storytelling aspect of it and just the whole process of journalism, of interviewing people and telling their story." Writing the article, she recalled, entailed "weaving in facts and also weaving in . . . the human experience" for readers. Thinking back about the story, she recalled that while the subject matter was "tough," it was also the point at which she recalls thinking to herself, "Oh yeah, I'm going to do this for a living."

Nearly all journalists echoed this attraction to telling stories for a living. Like Alexandra, many emphasized the personal gratifications associated with this storytelling. "It is a job where we are not bored," explained one journalist, "where we meet different people every day, we tell stories about new things [that] we learn every day."[17] While this journalist acknowledged that the stereotype is "a bit cartoonish," she nevertheless loved having a job that allows her to tell stories one day "about a farmer dealing with drought" and the "next day we are at the Airbus headquarters with big bosses." As someone who traveled as a child with her parents, she saw journalism as a job that would provide her with a sense of adventure and meaning. "I didn't want to be bored. . . . I didn't see myself at all being in an office doing the same things and repetitive tasks all the time." This view was echoed by another journalist, who followed her father's footsteps into the profession. "I like this opportunity that was offered to meet people, to tell their stories."[18] It's a "really cool job," she explained, to "get paid to talk to people" even though that money would "never be a lot."

The idea of journalism as storytelling expresses a sense of curiosity and open-mindedness about the world, and can be applied to an extremely diverse range of topics and formats. "I am a very curious person and I like to know what is going on in the world," as one person put it.[19] But this curiosity can encompass everything from high school sports reporting for a local newspaper to long-form magazine reporting on social issues. Across all these topics and formats, journalists saw themselves as possessing a set of skills that make them "a good match" for a job that emphasizes storytelling. Many emphasized a disposition toward writing, and a realization that journalism was a profession that allowed for the development and deployment of that skill. "I liked to write a lot," explained one person about his attraction to journalism, and to "tell people about the events" that he had observed.[20] Others highlighted a perceived skill at narration, of "crafting someone's story so audiences can understand it."[21] Summing up these attractions, which nicely captures the idea of journalism as storytelling, one person said: "I really enjoyed writing and I really enjoyed talking to people about things that moved them and learning things and turning around and telling other people."[22] To her, she said, those elements are "just what journalism is, in a nutshell."

Revealing Information

"I loved the scoop!"[23] These were the first words, which describe an exclusive news story,[24] that came from one journalist when asked what attracted him to journalism. Working as a journalism student on the college newspaper, he experienced "the thrill" on several occasions of being "the first" to report a piece of news, sometimes even covering a story before professional news media did. Looking back on those experiences several decades later, he thinks that maybe the exclusive information he reported was "not so important, it's not like we exposed corruption or anything." But he found "the hustle" required in getting a scoop attractive. "You have to find ways to get information that no one else has." Chasing this information, even if it was not always so important, seemed to him from the outset like a "cool way to make a living. I love[d] it."

Like storytelling, many journalists in both Toulouse and Seattle described bringing information into public view as an attractive aspect of the profession. Some linked this attraction explicitly to broad social values, like holding the powerful to account. One journalist described her attraction upon learning that journalists exist to investigate "the industrialists, the politicians," and those who "believe they are allowed [to do] anything."[25] She loved the idea that "we are there to tell them, 'no, it's the taxpayer's money, the taxpayer [should be] informed.'" For her, the "real job" of a journalist was and is to "seek information that no one has or that we want." Similarly, an American journalist called himself a "Watergate baby." He was in high school during the time in which Carl Bernstein and Bob Woodward became famous for their reporting that helped lead to the resignation of President Richard Nixon. "Reporters were the heroes," he said, noting that their heroism drew from their ability to bring information into public view that otherwise remained unknown or obscure. "It was very enticing and interesting." He worked at the school newspaper and loved it, especially any story that permitted him to reveal information. "Once I had a taste of it, I wanted to do it. . . . I jumped at the opportunity."

Not everyone linked their attractions to social values so explicitly. Some echoed the idea of a "scoop" being exciting; the term is used regularly among journalists in both France and the United States. For them, revealing information is important not necessarily because it exposes something about an important social issue per se. Rather, it provides them a way to "be in the know" and learn information, only some of which is related to politics, that others are not aware of. "I've always been kind of nosy. I like finding out if gossip is true," said one journalist.[26] She always felt like reporters "knew what was happening before anyone else did," and that "really fit my personality well." This sentiment was echoed by a variety of journalists, from those reporting on city hall to those covering lifestyle issues, sports, and other forms of entertainment. For all, revealing information is exciting because it allows them not only to report "on" the social worlds they do but, in some sense, to be "of" them: for example, to stand on the sidelines rather than in the stands of sporting events and to have backstage access at cultural events rather than waiting in the crowds.

Regardless of the link between revealing information and broader social values, all respondents emphasized broad dispositional orientations to "persistence" and "hard work." This could be applied equally to the work of investigative reporters and multimedia journalists who cover general news topics. Thus, one current investigative reporter described a university experience that involved a lot of "mind-numbingly tedious" work shifting through reams of data and conducting interviews.[27] But he found the work "pretty fascinating" and was attracted to it, because he realized that if he just "stuck to it" he could gather information that no one else had access to. But those same traits of persistence and hard work applied equally to reporters who had to ask "tough" questions to a range of social actors, only some of whom would be power-holders.

Understanding the World

If nearly all journalists were attracted to telling stories and revealing information, some envisioned those stories and that information to be more exclusively tied to a social value or function. Journalism for them was attractive not only for the personal rewards it provided in terms of an exciting and meaningful life; it was also experienced partly as a form of selflessness because what they found attractive about journalism was the opportunity it afforded to understand the world. This attraction was less common in the sample, and most directly tied to the civic meanings associated with journalism. While less common, it also fueled a strong, and often intense, sense of belief about the worthiness of the profession.

Some, for example, highlighted the "witnessing" role that journalists play in world events, which was valued not only for being exciting but also for helping audiences to understand important events. One person recalled listening to live BBC reports of the First Gulf War as a child. "I just thought it was the most interesting thing in the world, because it was just one reporter . . . dictating what they were learning and what was happening," he said.[28] "It just seemed like . . . an interesting way to spend a life to have this, you know, kind of privileged spot to watch the world." Another reporter noted that "September 11 . . . marked me. . . . I said to myself, they [journalists] are there, they see people, they interview people, they do analyses. It's really interesting. . . . That always stuck with me."[29] Still another talked about watching news reports of Mount St. Helens's eruption in 1980. "I very distinctly remember coming home and turning on the late news and watching the coverage of this thing," he said. "It was a pretty impactful moment of thinking, 'I want to be those guys who kind of race into [the event]' and 'deliver your story.'"[30]

Others highlighted the social role of journalists in shaping public debate as attractive, largely echoing normative accounts that underscore this role.[31] One person said he loved the idea, which he traced back to his university days, that journalists "bring to life a democratic debate" by being "the link between the one who has information and the one who does not." This role affords personal pleasures, as it "confronts points of view." But it also serves, in his view, a key social role by "giving all the keys of reading to the readers so they can form an idea for themselves in a debate."[32] Another noted frustration during his time as a journalism student with what he perceived as mainstream news media's failure to shape a wide-ranging public debate in the lead-up to the second Iraq war. His attraction to journalism was shaped by his idea that "they [mainstream outlets] were not doing a great job" in facilitating this debate and he was "going to do it better!"[33] Others said that journalism was attractive because journalists "give information" that "keeps the public debate alive."[34]

Still others saw journalism as an opportunity to shed light on the diversity of the social world. One journalist identified as an immigrant and said that reading the news was a way for him to both connect from a young age with his new country and stay abreast of developments in his old one. "I came to this country without knowing English," he explained. "I read a lot and I became interested in newspapers at an early age." In newspapers, he was able to see "how others live" and follow others' life stories. "I enjoyed reading them [the stories]. So I just kept doing it."[35] Another described how newspapers gave her a "sense of perspective" from a young age. "I thought I had problems," she explained, "but then I would read about kids in Pakistan whose whole village just got wiped out." She "did not understand" these issues as a child. Nonetheless, she thought to herself: "Holy crap. I am so glad that somebody is reporting from here so that somebody who can help will help. I guess I wanted to be a journalist forever after that because I love the idea" that understanding the world "will help to change it for the better" over time.[36]

The dispositions and skills associated with a journalist that endeavors to understand the world demand more than just skillful writing, hard work, curiosity, and open-mindedness. Bearing witness to history entails a willingness to be present in potentially unsafe situations (e.g., war settings, disaster zones, school shootings). Facilitating debate assumes a capacity for thinking quickly and processing information from a range of perspectives. It also requires a willingness to be the public "link" that connects different points of view, but is often criticized for its role. Making sense of others' lives requires a sense of social empathy, an interest and disposition toward learning about the life circumstances of individuals and groups that are different from oneself. These dispositions and skills do not cancel out or even necessarily compete with those associated with journalism of storytelling. But they do suggest a stronger sense of belief (visible in the willingness to put oneself in harm's way), and a demanding but also enchanted vision of the profession that is attractive in part because of its connection to broader social values and functions.

Giving Voice

A final attraction mentioned by some journalists in both samples centered on giving voice. One journalist, for example, said that the appeal of journalism for her was the ability to "give more voice to people" and specifically to "approach people in environments that do not have much voice and [to] provide new speeches that we do not often hear." She specifically described immigrants, who in her view experienced difficulties "integrating into French society."[37] She saw journalism as a forum that could aid in their successful social integration. Her view was echoed by an American colleague, who grew up in a house with a social worker for a mother and a labor organizer for a father. His parents "instilled in me an idea that people's stories have value and... by telling each other's stories we lend, we enhance our humanity in some way."[38] The aspect of telling stories, specifically of those less privileged in society, "always just kind of appealed to me, and journalism always seemed like... kind of how you do that."

By giving voice, especially to the marginalized, these respondents described an attraction to journalism at least partly rooted in a vision of social justice. One journalist, for example, was a theater major in college and gained exposure to journalism "by happenstance" at a part-time job in a radio station. "I've always been one to take on the good fight," she said, and through her exposure to journalism on the radio station, "I just realized this [journalism] was the way to do it."[39] Looking back, she realizes that, while she might have been "somewhat naive," she "believed very strongly that people that don't have a voice... need people to stand up for them." By standing up for them, she said, journalists ensure that "the things that need to be spoken out loud" and subsequently addressed are.

The idea of giving voice frequently intersected with the notion of journalism as storytelling, and thus required many of the same skills. One person talked about a graduate school class she took during a period when she wasn't sure whether to return to journalism or pursue another profession. The class—based in a divinity school—had a "very strong communication use for social justice" component.[40] In one class, the professor talked about "how the way our communities tell their stories change the way they act... We can be part of that process of storytelling." And "I don't know why but there was something in my brain that said, 'it's kind of what a journalist does!' It gives people the opportunity to tell their stories and either choose a topic that moves us forward or moves us backward."

WHERE PASSIONS FIND THEIR PRICE

Journalists hope to find meaningful work that corresponds with their original attractions; however, their expectations of doing so are far more mixed. Adverse economic conditions in the profession lead many to expect they must work hard but not "count on stable employment, full-time jobs, or indeed life-long journalistic careers."[41] At least some anticipate doing work that is not meaningful to them and may even stand in contrast with what initially attracted them to the profession.[42] In interviews with journalism students in the United Kingdom, for example, Jackson and colleagues note that a "recurring theme" was not only that "getting into journalism was going to be difficult"[43] but also that "in the short term they were prepared to compromise their ambitions, even if it meant working in journalistic sectors that they were highly critical of."[44] More broadly, journalists confront a broad diminution in the material and symbolic rewards available to those seeking a career in journalism. Fewer jobs, less stability, and diminished prestige coexist uneasily alongside increased demands, longer hours, and constant reskilling.

This is the context in which journalists adjust what attracted them to the profession with what they feel able to expect from a career in it. If they share broadly similar, if polysemic, attractions to the profession, they do not necessarily converge in what they consider a personally acceptable balance of material and symbolic rewards. One person's exciting job opportunity can appear to another as boring or unappealing. The sports fanatic neither desires nor pursues a job covering local politics. Just as importantly, the rewards they anticipate attaining from a career in journalism can also vary. These differential expectations make it seem reasonable (or not) for a given journalist to, among other things, work long hours, move far away from family, or take a job with lesser pay. In doing so, journalists' passions (i.e., what attracted them to journalism) find their price (i.e., in their personally acceptable balance of material and symbolic rewards).

These patterns of adjustment are not entirely random. In important ways, they reflect socially cultivated expectations regarding work. Those with less favorable social properties tend to emphasize the sacrifices they make in the hopes of a better future. These individuals, often but not exclusively women, tend to include those from middle- or working-class social origins; typically work as freelancers or general assignment reporters; and on average have university degrees from less prestigious schools. By contrast, those with more favorable social properties expect work satisfaction to be not just a future possibility but also a present reality. As a group, they skew heavily male, and tend to come from more professional families.

The adjustments also occur in nation-states that make some adjustments more or less possible. In France, legal regulations stipulate that any employee who is fired is entitled to compensation from the employer. For journalists, this payment amounts to more than one month of salary for each year worked with the firm. Furthermore, organizations with more than fifty employees who wish to engage in layoffs are required to develop "Employment Protection Schemes" (*Plan de Sauvegarde de l'Emploi*). These schemes require employers to identify alternatives to layoffs, typically by providing an equivalent position elsewhere in the company or by offering the possibility of early retirement to those who might otherwise be made redundant. At least some French journalists are able to "live off" journalism in part because labor regulations create this possibility.[45]

This French regime contrasts with the comparatively weaker labor protections in the United States. While journalists' unions have grown in recent years,[46] labor negotiations are typically devolved to employers and union representatives. In this scenario—and given the lack of financial support from the state[47]—layoffs are often viewed as "inevitable" and unions aim to make the process more transparent, for example, by providing advanced notice to impacted journalists.[48] This makes the category of "living off" more or less unavailable to journalists in the United States.

These regulations reflect a longer history of labor struggle that resonates today in how workers draw "symbolic boundaries" between their work and their personal lives.[49] In France, greater job stability makes it possible and socially valid to draw firm boundaries between the two; journalists living off journalism therefore emphasize their ability to work thirty-five hours per week and retain a meaningful family life. By contrast, the lack of job stability in the United States corresponds with a discourse of meritocracy, in which hard work is assumed to open career doors. Even if a journalist could "live off" journalism, it would be difficult to elicit such a discourse in the American context.

Living For Journalism

Amanda's story embodies the idea of living for journalism. She got "sucked in" by the profession while at university, where she fell in love with learning how to interview people and tell their stories.[50] The reporting she read in her classes also fed her sense of adventure. Having grown up in a small town—her mother was a city clerk—she loved the idea of working a job that might allow her to travel and see the world. While she never endeavored to be a political reporter, she loved the idea that journalism was a way for her to talk with people, learn their stories, and share those stories with a broader audience. Seeing her name in print, she admitted, was also a nice boost to her ego.

After graduating from university, Amanda worked for a brief period at a production company doing sports and entertainment programming. The job was decent but not especially exciting—and excitement was one of the things that had attracted her to journalism in the first place. Most days, she wasn't interviewing people or writing stories. She was not seeing much of the world, either; the position was located in the same town where she had attended university. She wondered if perhaps a career outside of journalism might satisfy her more. Looking at job postings one week, a position as a flight attendant caught her eye; she applied for it, was hired, and for several years left journalism to work in the airline industry.

Initially, working as a flight attendant was exciting. Amanda was traveling more than she had ever in her life: not only outside of the rural state in which she was born, but also around the world. The working conditions were also a substantial step up from her job at the sports and entertainment programming company. "Great benefits, union job," she noted. Within just a few years, she had traveled to more places around the world than she had ever thought possible. What's more, her salary made it feasible to really enjoy the places she visited: to have nice dinners, to take tours, to really "see the sites."

Despite these adventures and excitement, Amanda felt unsatisfied. "I just wasn't passionate about it [the airline industry]," she said. "I wasn't intellectually challenged. I was bored." She found herself longing to do journalism again. "I just missed writing and talking to people, having a job that I like going to every day." She recognized that her desires seem "crazy when you look at the paychecks and benefits" in journalism and compare them to the conditions that she had in the airline industry. But, foreshadowing her next step, "I love what I do [in journalism]."

Amanda left her job as a flight attendant and took up a position at a rural newspaper. For two years, she worked as a community reporter, writing seven to ten stories per week. The hours were long and the pay was low, but she was happy to be back in journalism. From there, she landed a job at a suburban daily located just outside of Seattle. The pay was marginally better and the job was a step up in career terms, seeing how she was given slightly more time to report and write her stories. But her willingness to accept the balance of rewards she has now seems fragile. Sometimes, she admits, she thinks about how much better the working conditions in the airline industry were. "Everybody [in journalism] thinks that it's totally fine to work twelve hours and put down eight [hours] on your time card, when you are making twenty-seven thousand dollars a year in the first place." In spite of these conditions, though, she considered herself "lucky" to have a job as a journalist, doing work that she found more satisfying than being a flight attendant.

At the center of Amanda's account is her passion for journalism. More than anything else, she expects journalism to be interesting and exciting. The sort of job, as she says, that she wakes up in the morning excited to go to. She is well aware of—in fact, she emphasizes—the sacrifices that she has made and anticipates continuing to make to pursue this passion. The long hours, low pay, and nonexistent job security are all adjustments; she didn't have to make them when she was working in the airline industry. But she sees these adjustments as acceptable as they made it possible to get back into journalism. She hopes that her career will bring more stability and higher wages; perhaps she will even get to write some of the "long stories" that some of the journalists she most admires get to produce. But she does not necessarily expect this to be the case. She trades those assurances, for the moment at least, for a life in journalism.

Other respondents described similar expectations of and sacrifices taken for the opportunity to explore a life in journalism. Pierre, a freelancer in Toulouse, studied mathematics at a nonprestigious university and expected to follow in his parents' footsteps by becoming a teacher upon graduating. After graduation, though, he realized fairly quickly that he didn't enjoy teaching. This led him to seek out alternative careers. In the late 1990s, amid the dot-com boom, he got into building websites.

During that time, he worked on a few sites that were linked to news companies. "That's how I discovered this job of a journalist," he said.[51] Investigative reporting, in particular, fascinated him: the ability to spend time looking into and really understanding social problems. He did not immediately get into journalism, but he traces his passion for the profession back to this time, while emphasizing the happenstance of it all: "It was absolutely not premeditated. I had no idea I was going to be a journalist."

At the time of his interview, Pierre had been working as a freelance journalist for more than a decade. His path had not been an easy one. Sometimes, he experiences long periods where assignments are few and far between. While he is regularly expected to propose topics and subjects to editors at local publications, no guarantee exists that any of those pitches will be accepted. He notes that the work involved in researching stories is unpaid. Moreover, the "meager income" he makes when one of his articles is picked up also means that he has to supplement his journalism with work as a math tutor, the job for which he was initially trained but did not feel passionate for. "I must complete it [the tutorials] if I want to live." Such work serves to "stabilize myself with jobs on the side that allow me to continue doing freelance work." He realizes that sometimes this life involves "struggling and hard times." But he loves the work nonetheless.

Some who described themselves as living for journalism work hope for future security but acknowledge they have not yet achieved it. One talked about a job early in his career at a television station in Alaska, which he took shortly after graduating from a regional public university. The news company there was a "great station with good people" working at it. "At [that] point in my career, I just wanted to be a reporter who ... gets to do really good stories. And this station had it."[52] While the location wasn't ideal and the pay was not great, he stayed for four years so that he could do "really good stories." Despite this work, he nonetheless found it difficult to get a job in a larger market. He decided to transfer to a different outlet where he might get more visibility and thereby increase his chances of professional advancement. This brought him to South Bend, Indiana, "which is like the Detroit of Indiana. It is not an exciting place. I did not really want to live there." He was, however, willing to live there in the hopes that he could get his work noticed in larger television markets.

Perhaps unsurprisingly, some respondents who described themselves as living for journalism have relatively limited professional experience. Several students, fresh out of journalism school, started an online news site in Toulouse. "We had exactly the same vision," one of them explained, "and it's not trivial because there are as many visions of journalism as there are journalists."[53] The opportunity, in their view, was to do news "the right way"—i.e., how it was taught to them in school, including long investigations on topics of public importance. "For me, it is a downright passion." They worked long hours ("endless days") and struggled to secure funding that could provide enough resources to keep the site going, let alone pay them nominal salaries. At least one of them emphasized that his passion for investigative journalism meant that he would rather shutter the website than do journalism in which he didn't believe (e.g., soft news, sensationalist coverage). "I would rather give up than sell my soul to the devil."[54]

Other younger journalists, who had not started a news enterprise of their own, also described the sacrifices they made to pursue a journalism career. A journalist in the American sample who had grown up on a farm described herself as "incredibly fortunate" to have a radio station "take a big chance" on her by giving her an internship after graduating from a regional public university.[55] She had to work as a barista to get by financially, but she didn't mind as it allowed her to live in a large city for the first time in her life. "I was working sixty hours a week and trying to figure it out." Eventually, she was able to find a part-time copy-editing job, which supplied her with the money to "pay my student loans and pay my rent" while also keeping time for her to explore a journalism career. "I was working technically as a freelancer but actually I had two jobs." She explained that she had done freelance work for more than twenty news organizations over the past several years.

This passion and its associated uncertainty are not restricted to the young. It appears across journalists of all ages in the sample, especially those holding freelance positions or working at nondominant news outlets. A freelance journalist with fifteen years of experience explained that she took up work outside of her journalism as a press officer for a local festival "because really I am in search of stability and for the moment in Toulouse that does not exist."[56] The magazine for which she does most of her work did not offer her a permanent contract, and this was disappointing. Sometimes she feels "fed up with freelancing." At the same time, "I love this job" even though doing it in Toulouse is "complicated."

A seeming paradox of those who live for journalism is that some, especially those in the United States, expect to do work that is in tension with their attractions. Claire, a television reporter in Seattle, expected that a lot of her reporting wouldn't "be the highest use of my brain space" because she was assigned a lot of general assignment, spot news.[57] She hoped that eventually she would get to do more "substantial" reporting on topics like climate change. For the moment, though, she felt "OK" about her position because "I can still use my skill set and I don't have to sit at a desk." Amanda's perspective mirrored this view. The longer-form reporting that she'd like to do might not be about a topic like climate change per se. "I'd just like to have more time to really tell a story well," she says. But she'd like the time nonetheless, even though she does not expect to get it anytime soon. It is frustrating, she explains, but "on the whole" she would still rather do the work in journalism that she does than go back to the airline industry.

Whether doing work that accords with their attractions or stands in tension with them, those who live for journalism make a virtue of the difficult conditions in which they find themselves. The hours may be long and the pay may be poor, but it is better to do the work in which one believes than it is to "sell one's soul to the devil." The work might not always be satisfying, and may sometimes stand in direct tension with the very ideals that attracted one to journalism initially. But it's still a preferable way to make a living in light of the potential alternative careers one might pursue. In living for journalism, these journalists foreground the sacrifices they make in order to render personally acceptable the rewards that the profession confers upon them.

Living Off Journalism

Michel works on a permanent contract at a radio station. The contract constituted a significant advance for him in terms of wages and job security. Previously, he had worked as a freelancer. "The schedules changed every week," he explained of his freelancing work, and this made it "hard to organize [his work life] as the manager sent them [the work schedules] at the last moment."[58] The permanent contract he now holds gives him a stable schedule and predictable pay. "It's a day's work, and it's paid," he says. Quickly, he adds that the pay is "not a lot."

Michel doesn't especially love the work he does now. Each working day, he arrives at the radio station early in the morning. "I start at 4 or 5 AM, and I finish at noon." He spends his time producing a series of news flashes that can be put on air. For the most part, he creates these flashes by reading local news reports. He does almost no original reporting. "I don't have the time to dig well" and do reports that are better researched. The lack of time is something he mentions at several points in the interview. He says that he doesn't have "the time to deepen the subjects, to question more people, to cross-check the points of view." While he loves journalism that digs deeply, "this is not the case in radio, where we really work day to day. When we have a subject to do, its [deadline] is in an hour."

In addition to the lack of time, Michel also notes that his ability to select what stories to work on is limited. He is "not interested in *fait divers*" but his managers often ask him to do news flashes about them. "I adapt, of course," he says, "but I am not interested in these kinds of news items." He tries to give them less time in the news—his own small act of resistance—but even then, he acknowledges that "sometimes you have two minutes [to fill]" and the *fait divers* is "the only thing you've been working on." News about social movements and criminal justice "interest[s] me more" but management prefers that he spend more time on lighter topics. The news flashes are short, plus, he says, "We can't end [the news segment] with a murder story and say 'good day everyone!'"

Michel finds himself in a situation in which he lives off of journalism. His wages, while modest, are regular and his hours are stable. He does not love the work that he does—frankly, he finds some aspects of it trivial. Moreover, he regularly describes himself accepting changes to accommodate management demands ("I adapt, of course"). While he shares some of the same civic attractions to journalism as his peers do, he doesn't expect to approximate any of them in his own work. If the stable working conditions changed or the pay substantially decreased, it seems plausible to venture, he might even explore a career outside of journalism.

This expectation—to live off but not really for journalism—appears only among our respondents in the French sample. This set of journalists no longer expected much from journalism in the way of excitement, interest, or job satisfaction. One described her radio station as a place dedicated to the production of large amounts of breaking news content. "We produce massive amounts of flashes. . . . I myself record six flashes per hour."[59] Another talked about doing work for a magazine that paid well but was professionally unsatisfying. "It's lifestyle" news, she explained, about "the good addresses" rather than social issues that might, in her view, be worthy of public debate.[60] Still another noted that the news she produces daily is derivative, conceiving her work as less a journalist than a "relay" between original reporting done elsewhere and audiences. "To be very honest, we only relay the local press. It is not a job of researching information. It is a job of relaying information."[61] Still another talked about her job as "outsourcing information to groups that are dragging us down" as a profession.[62]

Several journalists compared their work to that of a factory. One described her newsroom as a "flash factory." For her the metaphor could be applied in the sense both that the work could be mindless but also that the investment required could be limited. "It's true that it's a factory but since it's a factory, we really do thirty-five hours [of work], like at a factory."[63] Moreover, she notes, "the atmosphere is very nice, the people are very nice. It's very livable." But at the end of the day, "it's still a factory and we really do thirty-five hours [of work]. We get twenty-five days off [for vacation]. It's really basic."[64] While not substantial, the pay is sufficient for her, and often better than prior journalism jobs. "I'm paid well, I now realize," explained one person.[65] She knows this because in prior job she was "paid a lot less" to do the same amount of work. "It's a comfort to know that we are going to finish" our work at the same time each day. "Few journalists have schedules like that."

Several respondents in Toulouse described their refusal to maintain a press card—despite being legally entitled to hold one—as a way to acknowledge this labor status. "I refuse to have it. . . . I don't see the point of having it," said one journalist. In her current position, none of her work actually utilizes the card: "I'm on the desk, I never go out, I don't need to do interviews. . . . I don't need to be accredited for anything [I do on a daily basis]."[66] When asked to explain her decision, she said that the card is above all a symbol. Therefore, "it's also a symbol to refuse it." In her view, this act of refusal is a way for her to express disapproval of the work her news organization does. "We take journalism to a place that I do not like." And at any rate, she said, "I can take my tax allowance without having the card. . . . it is enough to have a journalist's contract to make a tax allowance." Others called the press card "useless" apart from providing free entry into French museums.[67]

Others highlighted the relative freedom that stable jobs afforded them. One freelancer with two long-term relationships at news organizations described the setup as convenient. "I feel good that I work from home on my terms. It's good that I can do other things on the side." The pay was not great, but it was regular. The job thus gave her a "freedom" even though that freedom "costs me a bit because it is expensive in the sense that my salary is limited."[68] While she wasn't especially happy about her work, she did describe herself as being "happy with this freedom." She would only change for a different job in journalism if it offered "a big contract." It's not worth leaving for a newspaper job, which would pay no better. Indeed, she said that a substantial increase in salary would be the only motivation to take a different job. "Otherwise, it is useful. I prefer to stay in my current position, by far." A reporter with a permanent contract noted that she liked the predictability that comes with her job. When she was a freelancer, she was on call "on weekends, emergencies, . . . the holidays, Christmas, the new year. You have to be there."[69]

Respondents who live off journalism expressed awareness that alternative steps could have been taken, and that such steps might have made their work more interesting or satisfying. One journalist explained that she knew she could enjoy much better working conditions if she sought to get a better job in Paris. Such work would give her "time to write, time to think, and especially [time] to have opportunities for development that we will never have here."[70] If she wanted to get her own program or opportunities to write, "I would have to move. You have to go to Paris." However, "it's a choice not to go to Paris. It's a personal choice, in fact, to work in Toulouse, to live in Toulouse." While a journalism career in Paris might be more exciting and fulfilling from a professional perspective, it would be "too much for me. I want to keep a balance with my private life, so it's a good compromise." Nonetheless, it's not "always easy" to accept the compromise "because you don't do the job you dreamed of."

While not always easy to accept, respondents typically found ways to compromise. Michel noted that while he would "love having the time to do more interviewing," he was "grateful" for his position, as it removed the uncertainty associated with freelancing, which he had done previously.[71] What's more, working in journalism affords him an opportunity that his parents (a building painter and nursery assistant, respectively) and his long-time partner (a baker) don't have: "an office, a computer, and I sit." In reconciling himself—at least temporarily—to the particularities of the job, his negotiation finds virtue ("at least I sit") in the necessities of his situation.

Having Both: Living For and Living Off Journalism

Ryan started out working in television. It had been a dream since childhood. "As a kid, I would line up three TVs and watch all three networks if something big was happening."[72] By the time he got into the news business—after attending a prestigious university—television news was "the equivalent of being on a down escalator." Especially local television, where he worked, "had hit its peak in terms of getting the most eyeballs and being the most innovative." In his first few years, he saw local stations across the United States being bought up by large corporate owners. "The pay and benefits were declining." The future looked dim. "I was looking at where this was going and thinking, this doesn't look like a business or an industry that is heading toward new heights or even survival."

He began to freelance for radio and television. While television provided an income, radio—especially public radio—opened his eyes to new professional possibilities. Early on, he did a few stories about educational reform. In contrast to television assignments, "I had time to tell these stories" when he worked for public radio. He traveled to California for a convention. "I didn't have to turn the story around that day." He went to a state school board meeting in Central Washington and profiled a student member of the board. "I didn't have to race back and get the story on air. I could think about it. I could pull these pieces together and do something that was more substantial" and given more airtime. He loved it; doing this work mirrored at a local level the national news he enjoyed consuming. "I thought, 'Wow, I like this opportunity to be a little more reflective and thoughtful and have more time, both to produce the story and more time on air to tell the story.'"

Eventually, he found more stable work as a general assignment reporter for a radio station. The job was better than his experience in television—he had more time to produce stories—but he never felt able to really dig into a topic fully. Working as a general assignment reporter, he explained, was "a little bit like being an emergency room doctor. You know, [it is] shift work. It's always different, always new. Constantly changing. You go home and somebody else comes on shift and you don't have to worry about it. But after a while, you might actually like to see a case through."[73]

Within a few years, a job opened up for the statehouse reporter position. Ryan jumped at the opportunity. "It's a great job." He took it fifteen years ago, "and I haven't really looked back." He has the time to really dig into policy issues and get to know them well. "I get to follow something through. Own it." He loves being able to do "long interviews" and have "one-on-one access to decision makers, policy makers, agency heads, party chairs. People who are one or two degrees separated from actual policy." He feels respected by peers, sources, and audiences for the work he does.

Several years into his beat assignment, Ryan even got the opportunity to return to television. A colleague invited him to do a weekly public affairs program. "I still like TV. I think it has value. I like getting to do it on my own terms," he says. In contrast to his early television experience, the show gives him the opportunity to have live conversations with key political figures. "I get the governor usually once or twice a year. I get the AG [Attorney General] a lot." Facial recognition is "the one thing you lose when you go from TV to radio." Having the program changes people's perceptions of him at the state capitol. "You walk the halls of the capitol and people know who you are."

Ryan's story nicely illustrates someone who expects to live for and also off journalism. His passion for the craft is undiminished; he loves the work that he does. Even with all the changes in journalism—"there are so few of us left at the state capitol," he notes—he has never enjoyed his work more. Yet he also enjoys a relatively stable job and commands the respect of his peers, sources, and audience. Unlike his early television days, he has the time needed to do his work. Having been on the beat for fifteen years, he also has built up a network of sources that constantly provide information and story ideas. His knowledge of the policy process has grown, too.

Not everyone experiences the same type of ascendant trajectory. Some come to live for and off journalism after failing at other endeavors. One journalist in France went into journalism only after failing at the legal career his parents had chosen for him. "I was bad at that level [graduate] of study."[74] During his graduate studies, he had done some work at a community radio station. He enjoyed the ability to express himself that radio afforded, and he told his father—a lawyer—that he wanted to see if he could make a career in radio. If he was going to do something with radio, he recalls his father saying, he should "at least be a journalist."

With some prodding from his family, he switched tracks and enrolled in a graduate school for journalism. He still wasn't a great student, he says, but he found that doing journalism appealed to him. His family approved of the career, and that was important to him, and he liked the idea of being able to write for a living (and then read his writings on air).[75] After graduating, he moved to Paris and worked for a private radio station where found a "very comfortable position." He earned some recognition in Paris because he talked about the economy from a leftist point of view on a right-oriented station. He was proud to have "made [my] way in Paris, having money, recognition ... and my father would listen to [me] on the radio."

After seven years in Paris, his boss proposed that he move to another city and do general assignment reporting. He accepted because he would have a higher salary. The new job allowed him to keep his "upper Parisian income" despite the "very low cost of living" in the new city. Shortly into the job, he realized he hated, truly despised, doing general assignments and breaking news. "I was frustrated ... and tired." The job impacted his private life. "You never fully sleep. . . . One night out of two someone calls you at any time and tells you to go to an event, even on weekends." He felt that management didn't care at all about the journalism he did. "The only thing you needed was productivity. The accent was on quantity, never the quality. You are nothing but an executant." By his own description, he "burned out" and "cracked" under the pressure of his job.

Concerned about his well-being, his parents proposed that he move to Toulouse, where they lived, and where he and his family (his wife and young daughter) could be near loved ones. They did. Upon moving back, he met with some old journalist friends, all of whom wanted to do something new and different. The idea they landed on was to launch a magazine based on investigative "slow" journalism. This allowed him to focus on his true passion: writing. The magazine position doesn't earn him a lot of money, but it's enough for him and his family to live on and to live well together. "I have my nights. I sleep. I am no longer woken up by my editorial staff." Just as importantly, the job is one he can take pleasure in doing again. "My pride is immeasurable because it is the most beautiful work of journalism that I have ever done." Moreover, he says, he loves having control of his work process. "You choose the speakers, you write your text," which contrasts with the frustration he experienced at his earlier jobs, where even on good stories you walked away saying, "If only I had one more day" to work on them.

These respondents are the fortunate few. As the preceding narratives suggest, they achieve their position in part through hard work and personal struggle. It is hardly a friction-free life, and at various points they might have simply given up and left journalism for a different career. At the same time, these respondents also possess more favorable social properties, broadly understood, that make them more likely to match their passions and their careers. The French respondent, for example, came from a family of liberal professionals. After failing in law, journalism was an acceptable liberal profession. He didn't have to make a lot of money per se; he had to have a career of which he and the people around him could be proud.

These fortunate few talked about specific moments where their expectation of what a journalism career is led them to make specific choices. One respondent, for example, said that she applied for (and got) an internship at a major national newsmagazine after graduating from a prestigious university. "I wanted to up my game and my credibility. I wanted to do more serious reporting."[76] This experience enabled her to "participate in larger investigative projects that I was proud of. I was able to publish a piece in the magazine, which won an award." After that, she secured a job at a prominent alternative weekly on the East Coast. "I'd always wanted to write for an alt weekly, because in the past it had served as a pipeline for crafting great writers doing really good reporting." New management came in shortly thereafter, and much of the staff was laid off. For money, she took a job at an online news site, where she had to post three stories per day. Not only was the pace difficult to maintain; it also conflicted with her idea of journalism. "I'd always wanted to write longer reported features. I was able to do that a couple of times but given the workload it wasn't happening." She saw a job at a Seattle weekly newspaper. "I'd always wanted to work here." The editor had won a Pulitzer "for this amazing piece that I totally worship. . . . I loved his work, and I just wanted to work with him and learn from him." It might not pay as much as she might like, but it offered stable pay and the possibility of an upward career trajectory.

These respondents were not unique in their desire for more satisfying work. Many of the individuals classified as "living for" journalism expressed similar sentiments. What differentiates these respondents is the fact that they found a position, and had the conditions, that actually support their civic vision of what journalists should be. One journalist talked about leaving a full-time position to freelance so that she could "move myself from doing that kind of really hard-core daily turnabout kind of journalism to doing more thoughtful features." She considered herself fortunate to find a job at a weekly newspaper in a suburb of Seattle that allowed her to do this work for decades. After that, "this wonderful job" opened up for her at the city's main daily newspaper. "It was just perfect for me and that is where I am now."

The clearest signal that these respondents can live both for and off of journalism is their ability to refuse specific tasks while also enjoying the thrust of the job they do. In France, for example, several reporters talked about refusing specific assignments because it contradicted their idea of what it meant to be a good journalist. "I absolutely refuse to be a specialist in anything," one person said. While his emphasis on general news was unusual in this group, his capacity to refuse was typical. "I am a local information generalist, which means that I refuse, unlike many of my colleagues, to lock myself in certain areas."[77]

A FRAGILE SOCIAL FUNCTION

Despite the difficulties facing journalism, the profession nonetheless remains attractive to many. Not everyone is captivated for the same reasons; the strength of their enchantments also varies. But the profession's allures are polysemic enough that a wide range of individuals is able to envision themselves as journalists. This vision is a central basis of the belief that journalism is a worthy site of struggle for an acceptable balance of material and symbolic rewards. Absent this conviction, it would be hard to understand why anyone would bother with journalism, especially given the diminished rewards it furnishes.

Journalists in France and the United States are sometimes assumed to be attracted to journalism for opposing reasons.[78] While Zola's "J'accuse" and the muckrakers' investigations certainly represent different historical traditions, journalists in Toulouse and Seattle describe broadly similar attractions. Partly, this stems from the profession's noted polysemy, which allows for different interpretations of similar attractions. It also likely derives from the research settings, as the further away one gets from the media capitals of Paris and New York, the less journalists see themselves in relation to those dominant visions. ("It's a choice not to go to Paris," to recall the words of one French informant cited earlier.) At the same time, these similarities also reflect real overlap in the attractions themselves. In both places, journalists see the profession as attractive for the lifestyle and opportunities for self-expression it promises. French journalists seek not only to express their opinions or denounce the powerful, but to use facts and tell stories. Their American counterparts see journalism as an opportunity to reveal information but also to tell stories and sometimes even to give voice to those who are marginalized socially. Highlighting these similarities points to one limit of this traditional opposition between French and American journalists.[79]

The main cross-national differences among journalists are found less in what attracts them to journalism and more in the adjustments they make in pursuing those attractions. French labor laws, themselves the result of a long history of labor struggle, make possible forms of adjustment—chiefly, "living off" journalism—that are not conceivable in the American space. The comparatively weaker labor protections in the United States make layoffs a very realistic possibility. Journalists must "live for" their profession not only as a matter of passion but also as a requirement for their continued employment. The recent history of newsroom employment in Toulouse and Seattle shows that these different adjustments are linked to very different realities. Since 2008, journalists in Seattle have experienced job losses at roughly 6.5 times the rate observed in Toulouse.[80]

But even these substantial differences cannot obscure the shared and growing fragility of journalism's most prestigious social functions. In both Toulouse and Seattle, these social functions are fragile in the sense that they are based on adjustments that appear delicate and vulnerable. Rather than attain stable employment for established news outlets, some pursue this work by founding websites that are economically tenuous; others undertake freelance work that pays so poorly that side jobs are necessary to pay one's monthly bills. Many holding jobs at news outlets find themselves tasked with work that stands in tension with what attracted them to the profession; more than one person said they did the work they really like "off the clock" and "on their own time."[81] They hope someday for a job that will align more closely with those ideals, but that outcome is far from certain. In this sense, journalism's social function is fulfilled partly to the extent that these journalists find ways to manage the disappointment that arises between what they love about the profession and the actual situation they find themselves working in.

Journalism's social functions are also fragile in the sense that they appear weakened as a basis of recruitment into the profession. For many journalists, the most esteemed social functions are not primarily what attracts them to journalism. They are not disappointed that they do not report on the politics at City Hall or the latest malfeasances of political or business elites. They aspire instead to provide information about daily life, leisure, and consumption. Others may read social functions into their efforts, but these are not the initial basis of their own self-understandings. They can, of course, still be disappointed with their experiences; they still struggle to secure a personally acceptable balance of material and symbolic rewards. But the disappointments they feel are not liable to bear any clear relationship to their role informing citizens or fostering democratic government.

The fortunate few whose work mirrors the social functions that initially attracted them provide one important source of journalism in both Toulouse and Seattle. They produce essential reporting from the halls of power; they offer long-form reports and analyses that shed light on each city's social world; they offer a forum that describes issues of broad public concern. But if this news is civically important, it is also socially exclusive. The relationship between the two is not random. The civic functions that are most symbolically lauded also require social properties that are not equally distributed across the journalistic population. The often poorly paid internships one can afford to take; the social contacts that those experiences build up and that are parlayed into job opportunities; the family support that makes it possible to take a satisfying but poorly remunerated position; even the very idea that journalism ought to have a civic purpose—all these desires and expectations reflect not only an individual's motivation but also the specific conditions that make them more or less possible in part because they are more or less conceivable to an individual journalist.

Whether they live for or off journalism, all journalists undertake adjustments aimed at securing a personally acceptable balance of rewards. These adjustments in turn raise further questions about how journalists deal with the contemporary predicament in which they find themselves. Apart from hoping for a better professional future, how do those journalists that live for journalism manage the disappointments that come from doing work that stands in tension with their self-understood raison d'être? Is there anything they do in the present, infrequently perhaps, that serves to renew their belief that their efforts are worthwhile? And for those fortunate few that live for and off journalism, is their very definition of professional excellence under threat as growing numbers of journalists join the profession less for its civic aims and social functions than for the fact that the opportunities it affords accord closely with the profession's commercial needs? Or is it possible that journalists who sidestep the profession's social functions are simply refusing opportunities that have already been denied to them and that they might, under different conditions, in fact find appealing?

CHAPTER THREE

At Their Best

By definition, a journalist's "best work"—defined here as the work in which an individual takes the most pride—is unrepresentative. It assumes its meaning not by typifying one's ordinary efforts, but by standing apart from them. Describing best work, the interdependencies, constraints, and contingencies that often frustrate journalists instead seem to work in their favor. The source calls back on time and shares exclusive and exciting information; the editor affords more space to work on an assignment about which the reporter is simultaneously passionate and knowledgeable; the journalist finds herself by chance getting a scoop simply by being in the right place at the right time. As a representation of journalists' routines, best work is undoubtedly misleading, perhaps even false. But can these atypical productions nonetheless be mobilized to shed light on the maintenance and management of journalists' beliefs that the profession is worth their efforts?

Such is the wager of this chapter; two propositions underpin the bet. First, in relation to their more ordinary productions, a journalist's best work can be grasped as an opportunity to explore the meanings that are crucial to maintaining belief that the profession is worthy. The very real sacrifices and negotiations entailed in "living for" journalism would seem like puzzling acts of self-abnegation were it not for the presence of such works. Being anomalous is in fact what renders them subjectively meaningful, revealing the symbolic hierarchy—the "good" work that stands out among the more ordinary productions—in which they believe.[1] Reconnecting journalists to their initial attractions to journalism, such works allow for belief in the profession's worth, its perceived hierarchies, and one's sacrifices and negotiations in it to persist. This is especially true for those individuals whose ordinary routines are occupied by work that diverges sharply from their initial attractions. But even those with more favorable material conditions experience frustrations and disappointments, discrepancies between what they do and what attracted them to journalism. For all, then, best work offers one source of meaning that supports journalists to be able to remain in the profession.

But a journalist's best work is not solely a source of meaning. It also provides evidence of an individual's location in a broader hierarchy of professional excellence. To do one's best work is not to dissolve the interdependencies, constraints, and contingencies that characterize ordinary routines. Rather, it is to approximate professional ideals as well as one can within them. This implies a need to grasp this hierarchy of professional excellence and understand how journalists evaluate themselves in relation to it. Doing so sheds light on the extent to which contemporary upheavals reorder the profession's principles of excellence toward more commercially profitable news or, conversely, whether the normative weight of journalism's historically derived social functions retains its force. Just as importantly, it also provides an opportunity to explore the adjustments that journalists make to adapt their best work to their specific conditions of possibility. Even at their best, not everyone has equal opportunities to reach the heights of the professional hierarchy, however it is defined. That their efforts are meaningful reflects their ability to adapt their beliefs in the profession's worth to fit their personal circumstances, even if those differences are rooted in very different social properties and dispositions that make such work more or less possible to a given journalist.

With these propositions in mind, the chapter proceeds in three parts. First, prior journalism scholarship's utilization of "best work" data is revisited. Deployed primarily in surveys administered to journalists in the United States, data from the question has typically been used to explore its potential association with professional roles.[2] Finding little evidence to support a relationship between the two, the prompt has, with limited but important exceptions, generally been cast aside in more recent survey work.³ Rather than jettisoned, best work data, it is suggested, might instead be profitably marshaled to understand how journalists maintain and manage their belief in a profession worthy of their efforts. This requires grasping the perceived hierarchy of professional excellence in which best work takes on its meaning, and for which adjustments are made.⁴

In the second part, this perceived hierarchy of professional excellence is explored by asking respondents to discuss the journalists and journalism they admire. Even if the names and works they cite are highly diverse, and sometimes only loosely connected to historically privileged domains of reporting like politics—thus signaling the growing importance of commercial criteria in shaping contemporary definitions of professional excellence—journalists in both Toulouse and Seattle emphasize similar principles of professional excellence. Journalism's long-esteemed social functions dominate these responses. Respondents discuss in-depth reporting, typically produced by nationally prominent journalists and news organizations, that "moves the needle" on issues by going beyond the claims offered by officials. They praise work that astonishes audiences by breaking news, which they distinguish from reporting that merely relays extant information. They appreciate stories that are well-crafted and showcase a refined aesthetic sensibility. Beneath differences, though, lay a cross-nationally shared model of professional excellence that privileges work that is in-depth, long-form, and well-composed.

In the final and most lengthy part of the chapter, journalists' best works are discussed as practical adjustments to this hierarchy of excellence. Some describe their best work as approximating these ideals reasonably well in their local spaces. The needles they aim to move and the audiences they hope to shock are in Toulouse and Seattle rather than their respective national stages. These respondents express pride in work that either reveals information that power-holders prefer to keep hidden or uses particular cases to think about social phenomena more broadly. The form is termed *discovering*, the latter *edifying*. Cross-nationally, the prevalence of each varies, highlighting the relative weight accorded to specific social functions in each country. Discovering is more common among—but hardly exclusive to—journalists in the United States, underscoring the historical attachment to original reporting associated with watchdog ideals. By contrast, edifying is more typical of journalists in France, where the "exposition of ideas" through engaging prose is more accentuated, although it is not absent from the American counterparts.[5]

Other respondents acknowledge a more sizable adjustment between their best work and the work they most admire. In both Toulouse and Seattle, these respondents describe efforts to translate complex issues into intelligible language for audiences or to give worth to individuals, especially those perceived as holding little social power. These efforts are labeled *decoding* and *dignifying*, respectively. This group of respondents acknowledge—with greater and lesser degrees of regret—distance between their best work and journalism's dominant ideals, even as they ascribe meaning to their work. Their work, they argue, informs audiences about important topics without sensationalizing the subjects of news coverage. These responses are found in equal measure in both France and the United States, a sign of the weight of commercial concerns in both countries, which manifest for journalists as a need to attract audiences without abandoning their professional ideals.

Each of these forms of best work can be viewed as adjustments based on one's social conditions of possibility. It would be too easy—and, in important ways, misleading—to read the results as stemming solely from differences in talent, skills, and effort. Instead, these symbolic differences correspond with social inequalities. Like the fortunate few that live for and off journalism, those with the most favorable social properties tend to describe work that translates the most admired forms of journalism to their local settings. Those with less favorable properties describe work that is oriented in important ways to journalism's commercial functions. It is in this sense, finally, that best work—otherwise fundamentally unrepresentative of regular practices—nonetheless turns out to be a useful tool for making sense of how journalists manage their beliefs in the profession. Nearly everyone finds a way to maintain their beliefs, and find meaning from being a journalist, but usually in ways that reinforce extant social and symbolic inequalities.

WHAT TYPE OF DATA IS A JOURNALIST'S BEST WORK?

The use of best work as a source of data in journalism scholarship has a curious history. It seems to have first been used in the American

Journalist Survey, pioneered by John Johnstone and colleagues[6] and developed and carried out subsequently by G. Cleveland Wilhoit, David Weaver, Lars Willnat, and colleagues.[7] Beginning in the 1980s, Weaver and Wilhoit asked respondents to identify and discuss a recent example of what they considered to be their "best work."[8] In a survey otherwise consisting primarily of fixed-answer questions, the openness of the prompt—the opportunity it afforded journalists to speak in their own words—was unusual. Yet the results seemingly generated few insights with respect to their theoretical interests in journalistic roles, with the authors reporting at best modest associations between the professional roles a journalist favored and the topics chosen or rationales given for one's best work.[9] Perhaps because of these disappointing results, the Worlds of Journalism survey, which otherwise draws substantially from its American predecessor, did not include any question about journalists' best works in its questionnaire.[10] Even the most recent wave of the American Journalist Survey seems to have dropped the question from the survey.[11]

If the essence of folly entails asking the same question and expecting different results, best work would seem a data point better off jettisoned. Perhaps, though, a different set of theoretical principles can be used to realize a profit. What if the best work data is useful not as a correlate of professional roles but as a source of meaning? Like the inspired lecture that reinvigorates a frustrated professor, a journalist's best work has the potential to reunite individuals with their initial attractions to the profession. Through their connection to work they perceive as better and more valuable, it reminds them of what makes the profession worthwhile. Instead of being a sampling bias, its unrepresentativeness—its *extra*ordinariness—can be understood as enabling individuals to downplay or rationalize, at least temporarily, the everyday struggles and frustrations that might otherwise dampen and diminish one's belief in the worthiness of journalism as a profession.[12]

This perspective has implications for how the responses are analyzed. Rather than categorize best work primarily in terms of its topical focus, the labels describing these productions aim to parsimoniously capture what individual journalists express pride in and find subjectively meaningful. Certainly, some topics are cited more frequently than others, reflecting a well-documented hierarchy of professional beats that corresponds to journalism's historically derived social functions.[13]

But journalists discussing the same topic often express different sources of pride, and these imply distinct relationships to standards of excellence. The politics reporter, for example, can take pride in revealing hidden information, which entails a confrontation with power-holders that is historically valued; or she can place value on the effort entailed in explaining complex legislative issues, which translates the work of power-holders to a broader audience. The social relevance of these different actions can certainly be debated;[14] the hypothesis advanced here is simply that these different expressions of pride are likely to be subtended by differing social conditions of possibility. This implies a necessary interpretive labor on the part of the researcher, whose initial aim is above all in the pithy description of such pride, which underpins the belief that journalism remains a worthwhile profession.

But one's best work is also a doubly-relational data point: first, with respect to a journalist's ordinary work, which discussion of their best work affords insights into; second, with regard to the work they most admire in the profession more broadly. These latter responses highlight a hierarchy of professional excellence.[15] Because not all journalists or forms of journalism are equally admired, the responses to this question can be seen as elucidating what counts as the most legitimate form of journalism. Journalists' own relationships to this hierarchy are likely to be socially differentiated, with some embracing these standards and seeking to approximate them as much as possible, while others may acknowledge them but not see them as directly related to their professional realities. However, because the journalists and journalism they admire hold the monopoly of the legitimate definition of journalism, they are unlikely to be altogether ignored. In this way, responses about those most admired figures and forms of journalism highlight the hierarchy of professional excellence to which they must adjust.

For decades, analysts in both France and the United States have warned that the growing weight of economic pressures might warp definitions of journalistic excellence.[16] One important line of sociological reasoning in this scholarship hypothesizes that economic pressures will lead to different patterns of social recruitment into the profession.[17] In contrast to an earlier generation of journalists attracted by the thrills of reporting on Watergate or the sinking of the Rainbow Warrior, more recent entrants appear less interested in politics, especially its institutional forms, and more curious to work on topics that focus on social issues, broadly understood. This has been interpreted as evidence of at least a partial shift toward commercial criteria in shaping definitions of excellence, as the most admired stories are important not strictly for their political importance but for their capacity to attract audiences.[18] But to what extent does the work that journalists most admire jettison these historical commitments or instead integrate them into a new model of professional excellence?

Whatever their definition of excellence is, journalists' best work can be seen as adjustments to their profession's symbolic hierarchies. Such work not only renews one's belief in the value of the profession; it also positions journalists at a specific segment within the profession's symbolic hierarchy. The modesty with which some respondents begin their best work answers is one indicator of such positioning. ("It's not really an incredible story but . . ."). Their practical knowledge of, and belief in, the field—its symbolic hierarchies and their place in it—make these adjustments possible. Even if *their* best work is not *the profession's* best work, it is nonetheless meaningful to them. That these evaluations appear largely symbolic or resulting primarily from individual talent or hard work is partly what makes the social inequalities that correspond to them so pervasive. In this way, best work serves as a mechanism that allows individuals to reproduce their belief in the profession by doing "as best they can" in relation to the profession's symbolic hierarchy.

JOURNALISTS AND JOURNALISM WORTHY OF ADMIRATION

"I listen to *France Info* every morning," one journalist explained. "I can't live without it."[19] This person's perspective was in no way unique.[20] Asked to describe work they admire, journalists in both Toulouse and Seattle overwhelmingly named nationally recognized news organizations and the journalists that work at them. The most admired journalists in the United States were ones that are employed for the *New Yorker, New York Times,* and *Washington Post.* "All the normal ones," as one person put it when listing these titles.[21] Their counterparts in France likewise work for a relatively small number of overwhelmingly Paris-based news organizations, like *Le Monde, France Info,* and *Le Monde Diplomatique.* In both countries, but especially in France, these outlets tend to garner the greatest number of journalism prizes. While none faces the financial stresses typical of regional or local media, these publications are also not the most economically prosperous, in terms of either audience size or profits. This offers a first indication of the relative permanence of a professional hierarchy that prioritizes journalism's long-standing social functions.

This hierarchy of journalists and news outlets is replicated across media types. Those working in television reference investigative or documentary news programs like *60 Minutes* and *Complément d'enquête*; journalists working in radio discuss their admiration of programs like *Planet Money* and *Secret d'Info*. When respondents identified online-only organizations, they almost exclusively highlighted high-profile journalists whose reputations were made in legacy media, particularly the print press. Mentions of Paris-based *Mediapart* and *Rue89* dominated the French sample. The former was founded and continues to be run by Edwy Plenel, former editor-in-chief of *Le Monde* and one of France's best-known investigative reporters; the latter was formed by a group of leading journalists from *Libération*.[22] The American sample was likewise dominated by a small number of sites, most especially *ProPublica*, which Paul Steiger, the former managing editor of the *Wall Street Journal*, initially managed and whose early staff comprised Pulitzer Prize–winning reporters from some of the country's leading daily newspapers.[23] The *Marshall Project*, which focuses on criminal justice issues, was also brought up by respondents; its two editors (first Bill Keller, followed by Susan Chira) both previously held prominent management positions at the *New York Times*.[24] In both countries, these sites are located in the media capitals of Paris and New York, respectively, thus highlighting the enduring influence of "agenda-setting" news media.

Respondents expressed near-universal admiration for journalists whose reporting produced in-depth investigations on topics they deemed publicly important. Specific topics sometimes focused on government accountability, but also included reports on negligent business practices and racial discrimination in education, as well as reports that attracted large audiences, like those linked to the category of "true crime," which "make the most mundane things really interesting and captivating."[25] Respondents expressed admiration for the way such reports go beyond the claims of power-holders to get at the underlying "truth" of the matter. "I always admire those who continue pushing the buttons and try to get the quote beyond the public information officer," as one American journalist put it while talking about reporting done at the *New York Times*.[26] A French journalist expressed her admiration for Edwy Plenel as someone who "doesn't back down" and through his refusal to do so "gives hope to the profession [of journalism]."[27]

Respondents also routinely expressed appreciation for work they viewed as holding high aesthetic value. French journalists regularly invoked *la belle plume* (literally, the beautiful feather, which is used as a term to describe a great writer) as a reason for admiring a particular journalist. "He wrote really very, very well with a style all his own," one reporter said about Antoine Blondin, a deceased writer known and regarded for his sports writing. "He really gave life [to what he observed]."[28] This evaluation also appeared in audio-visual media, with one respondent praising a pair of television reporters: "They inform and they inform well. They have a very beautiful voice."[29] American respondents likewise lauded specific individuals in similar terms. The author of a twenty-eight-thousand-word report about child homelessness published in the *New York Times* was deemed "an amazing and beautiful writer."[30] A journalist working in radio expressed her appreciation for the "creative approach to storytelling" taken by journalists on the public radio program *This American Life*.[31]

Additionally, respondents praised journalists who through their reporting and presentation shed new light or offered a fresh angle on a topic. One American journalist, for example, discussed a column written long ago by New York City–based Jimmy Breslin about John F. Kennedy's funeral. Rather than "write about the stuff of the memorial" as most other journalists did, Breslin focused on a "gravedigger who was to deal with the aftermath."[32] Another respondent described her admiration for Edna Buchanan's reporting on the police beat in Florida. "She had a knack for really making the most mundane things really interesting and captivating."[33] A French journalist praised a now-deceased war reporter for avoiding stereotypical frames regarding war reportage. "His choices of angles are always well thought out."[34] In both cities, the referencing of deceased journalists (Breslin and Blondin, among others) offers an additional indicator of the enduring weight of journalism's historically derived social functions in evaluations of professional excellence.

In-depth. Well-composed. Novel angles. Respondents consistently highlighted these as being the journalism they admired most. As the preceding examples suggest, respondents often looked to nationally recognized peers and news organizations when identifying such work. Journalists working in Toulouse or Seattle that are mentioned tend to be those that most closely align with the dominant values that national outlets are thought to possess. One respondent, for example, praised the work of two journalists who investigated allegations of child abuse and sexual molestation against the then-Seattle mayor. "That would have been a pretty hard story to report," he explained. "Old allegations. A vociferous defense on the part of the mayor. . . . To persevere through that. . . . [i]t needed to be done but the process [of reporting] cannot have been fun."[35] The founder of an online-only news site similarly praised one of its contributing writers for "in-depth reporting" and "highly creative writing."[36] A reporter working at the state capitol was lauded because "he knows about things that other people weren't really watching."[37]

Whether the references are local or national, respondents tended to emphasize professional criteria over commercial concerns. This serves as yet another indicator of the weight of the profession's social functions. But the growing influence of commercial considerations on journalism does not leave professional definitions of excellence entirely untouched. A number of respondents not only described their admiration of works that are in-depth, well-composed, and filled with novel angles; they also like works that capture a broad audience, which generate "buzz" and turn "really boring or really obscure" stories "into really interesting and fascinating stories that people actually want to read."[38] These perspectives suggest that while the hierarchy of journalistic excellence remains relatively stable, it might also be shifting slightly—slowly or quickly, it is difficult to discern—toward commercial concerns.

In discussing the journalism that they admire, many respondents emphasized what they perceived as the ideal conditions that enabled its production. One American journalist, for example, said that he read "a lot of the *New Yorker,*" which he viewed as "an ideal world."[39] Its articles feature "the sort of writing I would like to do—long-form reporting that you can spend a month [working] on." A French journalist echoed this sentiment, noting that the country's leading investigative reporters "take time to get to the bottom" of whatever issue they are investigating.[40] The respondent who admired the *New York Times* series on a homeless girl noted not only that the reporter was "an incredible narrative journalist" but also that she "spent a long time with this girl."[41] Clearly, then, journalists are aware that the potential to produce the profession's best work is linked to holding conditions favorable to its production.

And yet mentions of these conditions existed alongside an emphasis on the talents and efforts of individual journalists. The journalists that respondents admired were characterized as "super dogged," "tireless," and "unflappable."[42] An "old school, muckraking-type journalist" was the description accorded another. "It's like, man, this guy is really. . . . this [reporting] is his life."[43] Still another was admired for his security to "only publish when he has something really good."[44] Yet others were admired for their talents as writers, which was seen as setting them apart from their peers. One respondent, for example, described several journalists as "naturally gifted writers."[45] This implies that the best conditions are reserved for those that possess the most intrinsic talent. But there are also social properties, less often noted, that make the highest heights of this hierarchy more or less reachable for particular journalists.

JOURNALISTS' BEST WORKS

Discover: A Struggle with Power Holders

Some journalists described their best work as investigative efforts to pry open information that others, especially those perceived as holding power, prefer to keep hidden. This work nicely corresponds to the dominant ideals so widely admired by journalists in their discussion of journalists and journalism they admire. The label "discover" highlights the centrality of a power struggle aimed at revealing—literally, *dis-covering*—hidden or obscure information. As the subsequent examples suggest, it appeared more frequently among journalists in Seattle than in Toulouse, highlighting the enduring primacy of watchdog ideals in the United States. With limited exceptions, in both settings the journalists who described this work tended to be beat reporters and editors with ample professional experience, often holding degrees from prestigious universities; as a group, they skew male and tend to come from liberal professional families.[46]

A reporter working the aerospace beat nicely illustrated the "discover" label in his response. Asked about his best work, he replied immediately that, over the years, "I broke a lot of stuff Boeing didn't want known."[47] Several examples were provided; in each, the reporter took pride in his ability to report news that Boeing did not want reported in the public domain. On publishing the details of a speech given at an off-the-record executive retreat, he noted that Boeing executives were "outraged that we had done so because it was supposed to be a private meeting." On publishing an article about production delays and cost overruns on one of its new airplanes, he explained that doing so "caused a lot of confrontation within the company." These works allowed him to go to company representatives and confront them with facts they preferred to keep out of public sight. These confrontations almost perfectly capture the idea of the journalist as a watchdog: "When I get something . . . that I know they're not going to like, then I'll go to them and present it to them . . . and say, 'Look, I have this information. It looks bad . . . Now, what are you going to tell me?'"

Several other journalists echoed this struggle with power-holders over the legitimate definition of a social issue. A television reporter, for example, discussed a story that highlighted the Veterans Administration's failure to provide benefits to individuals who became gravely ill from consuming contaminated drinking water at a military base. The reporting "created a lot of fuss inside the beltway"—i.e., within the main corridors of political power in the United States, where politicians and policymakers were forced to address the issue.[48] "Anything I can do as a journalist to shine a light and make people sit up and say, 'Hey, we've got to do better than this.' That, I'm very proud to be associated with." Several journalists similarly employed language about being "troublemakers" to power-holders. A city hall reporter, for example, expressed pride about reporting that led to getting "kicked out" of the office of a City Council member.[49]

In emphasizing power struggles, journalists also expressed pride in developing contacts to whom they could turn for information. An online reporter, for example, talked about a story he did on the atypically high levels of turnover in the Seattle mayor's office. Looking through publicly accessible email records, which he obtained for a "totally unrelated" story, he noticed one employee's emails to the mayor's leadership team "about things this person [the employee] thought were not right."⁵⁰ The reporter got in touch with the person and was able to arrange a meeting in which the employee "talked about who was leaving and the reasons why and connected me with other employees in the office." With that information in hand, the reporter was able to return to publicly available documents to show how "abnormal" the turnover in the mayor's office was. Reflecting on the case, he said that it allowed him to do "what you are supposed to do as a journalist" by fostering "relationships with people, so people can trust you . . . and talk with you on sensitive issues that could in theory get them in trouble in order to reveal stories that other people" don't want revealed.⁵¹

As that quotation suggests, the struggle with power-holders is valued in large part for its ability to generate revelations, especially regarding information that power-holders would prefer to keep hidden. A journalist in Toulouse, for example, talked about a story regarding a financial crime. "I am happy when I manage to reveal something hidden," he explained.⁵² In that particular case, "the most difficult information to have was also the most interesting," and he was proud to have uncovered it. A journalist in Seattle likewise expressed pride in an hour-long radio special he did about suicides in state prisons. He noted that prisons constitute "a big book of business" for the state of Washington. "Most of what happens [in prisons] is behind closed doors. . . . You don't really see it." As a result, "it's easy for scrutiny not to happen."⁵³ Another journalist in the French sample expressed pride in revealing that an important public figure was under police investigation. "I got the real information that nobody else had. . . . For me, that's what journalism is."⁵⁴

The journalist's emphasis on what "journalism is" echoes comments made by others. For those who described their best work as an act of discovery, there was little to no tension between the profession's dominant ideals and their individual ability to approximate it. Several reported that their best work reflected what, in their view, journalism at its best is supposed to do; these respondents also tended to be recipients of journalism prizes, usually regional but in a few cases national. Furthermore, journalists often discussed their best work in relation to competitors who failed, in their view, to challenge power-holders. The aerospace reporter, for example, noted that he drew "big lines" between his work and the writing done by paid aviation bloggers. Whereas he saw his work as revealing information Boeing didn't want known, these bloggers "are just in the pocket of airlines.... They are not going to reveal anything Boeing does not want revealed."[55] Sounding exasperated, he explained that he does not "want to be in the same room with other blogger people. They shouldn't be there. They are not journalists.... It just annoys the hell out of me that they are given any credibility at all."

Journalists' responses often foregrounded the social rather than commercial impact of their best work in terms of actions taken by the subjects of their stories. The aerospace reporter, for example, expressed pride multiple times in getting Boeing to undertake actions that, in his view, the company would not otherwise have taken. The television journalist who reported on failures at the Veterans Administration made a similar point. Other journalists, when asked broadly about feedback received on their reporting, pointed to input from their sources. The reporter who wrote about high degrees of turnover in city hall, for example, responded to a question about feedback by saying: "Ed Murray [then-mayor of Seattle] himself called my office."[56] When journalists did reference audiences directly, they tended to focus not on its size but instead on the reasons they assumed that audiences found the story interesting. These reasons aligned nicely with the core tenets of the "discover" label. The aerospace reporter, for example, said that his reporting is the "sort of thing that people like to read because they know they are not getting a press release."[57]

Edify: Using Cases to Broaden Understanding

A second set of respondents described their best work as efforts to use particular cases to cast light on larger issues. Like the "discover" label described earlier, this work—with its emphasis on long-form, in-depth coverage—nicely corresponds to some of the dominant ideals admired by journalists in their discussion of journalists and journalism they admire. The label "edify" highlights the emphasis these journalists place on using particular cases to build up or construct a broader understanding of some aspect of the social world. This form of best work appears more frequently in the French sample than the American, and cross-national differences exist in terms of how journalists conceive of the social engagement that stems from such work. Like those who discover, this group generally skews male, and tends to comprise those who hold the most favorable social properties of all journalists in the sample (in terms of education, professional experience, and position, as well as social origins).

Two journalists working in Toulouse illustrate the edifying orientation nicely. One talked about his report on the ten-year anniversary of riots in several French cities. He visited areas where rioting had occurred and interviewed individuals and civic leaders to see how they sought to address some of the issues raised in the intervening years; he also looked at government policy to see how efforts at "urban renewal ... moves in the districts."[58] He contrasted his work against the *fait divers* that often cover the same topic. "If the paper [news article] had been in the hands of *fait divers* people," he explained, "there would have been a completely different story" that emphasized sensationalist imagery. His work instead intentionally focused on what he perceived as the "larger issues" like government policies that shed light—and gave, in his view, a fresh angle—on the underlying roots of the riots and their lingering social effects.

Another journalist in Toulouse cited his coverage of a murder trial as an experience that "marked me professionally."[59] Rival journalists covered the trial "day and night" giving audiences a blow-by-blow of court proceedings. By contrast, he sought to do reporting that used the accused murderer's trial as a way to explore the entire legal process through which individuals are tried in France. To do this, he could "not be satisfied listening to the proceedings" but instead met people (e.g., lawyers, prosecutors, witnesses) outside the courtroom; he also visited the alleged murder scene. In doing so, he sought to show the complex interplay between the various individuals involved in this particular case and the larger judicial system in which it functioned. In his view, the effort was a "remarkable journalistic exercise" that allowed him to offer a novel angle on a topic that was widely covered by most news organizations.

While less common, several journalists in Seattle also described their best work in ways that could be interpreted as edifying. One reporter discussed a narrative feature she had done about a mother on the verge of homelessness. Despite having a government voucher that directly subsidizes the landlord, the mother was still unable to secure housing. "I really liked it because I love to do those kinds of stories that are able to tell a larger story through one person's life."[60] For the reporter, "it's a way of making it very real for people and also you are bringing a narrative in, getting people involved emotionally, but you are also talking about a much larger issue." In that particular story, she continued, "I talked about a whole array of issues including recent shifts in homeless policy and the way the nonprofits were handling homeless people, and problems with the system, and the way the federal government was dealing with this subsidy program and all sorts of larger issues that could be told through one person's life."

Another reporter talked about a story she did on sex workers in the city of Seattle. A local prosecuting attorney was considering legislation that would decrease penalties for sex workers while increasing punishments for their clients. "He and a number of other local politicians were framing this as a do-gooder, antitrafficking policy."[61] But, she said, "a lot of it was ... couched in completely flawed research. And in fact, there were local sex workers who were saying, 'hey, this actually endangers us.'" Nonetheless, "local politicians and the prosecuting attorney refused to listen to them in any capacity. And they kept touting this really, really flawed research." In her reporting, she didn't take a side on it; rather, "I just kind of dived into the question of what does the research actually say about these types of policies, and kind of—I don't know, just dug into their numbers and found they were completely false, and interviewed a lot of sex workers, and got a bunch of perspectives in there, and I felt really good about that."

Journalists in both countries discussed "edifying" work as a form of socially engaged journalism. Explaining why they took pride in these works, many noted that they had not revealed new facts per se—as those who "discover" did—but rather used particular cases, often already known, to illustrate social tendencies that are otherwise forgotten or obscured. A journalist in Toulouse, for example, talked about a story he did on a couple that had once been active members of (one of) France's far-right political parties. The story quoted the couple denouncing racist statements and sentiments that had existed in the party. What was interesting to the reporter was not showing the somehow-expected relationship between far-right militants and racism. Instead, his idea was to show that historically the French have been "less Republican" than "they think they are." Taking the story of the couple as an epiphenomenon, he explained, he was showing "things we don't necessarily think of French society." Drawing a contrast between the 1968 protests that challenged a conservative social order with the right-wing collaborationist regime of the Second World War, he said: "We think of progressive, revolutionary France. When we say French society, we think of 1968 but we often forget Vichy. And France is that too."[62]

While journalists in both Toulouse and Seattle highlighted social engagement as a source of pride, the meaning of such engagement varied cross-nationally. As the example just given suggests, French journalists were more likely to view engagement as speaking on behalf of particular social groups or formations, like the Republican social order. American journalists, by contrast, tended to frame engagement in more general terms. The reporter who expressed pride in her story about homelessness, for example, noted that "it was great to see her [the mother] being helped" and that there was "an outpouring of support" from readers.[63] Such support, in her view, showed the "kindness of the local community." Even the reporter who did the story about sex workers emphasized that she wasn't looking to "take sides" on the issue, but instead "get a bunch of perspectives" and bring to bear the available research so that readers could understand the issue better.[64]

Whatever their other differences, all journalists describing their best work as edifying acts took pride in approximating the profession's dominant ideals. One journalist remarked that the story he did was important to him because it played a role in "feeding the public debate." By the time the reader gets to the end of his story, he felt, they should be able to see that he shed light on the important issues. "It's a job satisfaction, when you're [doing] this job [i.e., this type of reporting]."[65] An American journalist, after summarizing her best work, said that she was "very glad to be able to do that in a story" for her organization, as "that was part of why they hired me . . . to bring this kind of story."[66] In doing so, she articulated a reasonably close fit between the work she admires and the work she is able to do in her job.

Decode: Translating the Powerful

A third set of respondents described their best work as efforts to translate complex topics into intelligible language that could be easily understood by audiences. Unlike discovering and edifying forms of journalism, this type of best work explicitly highlights the value of reaching audiences. This response is given the label "decode" to emphasize the pride that journalists express in converting—rather than necessarily challenging—the words of power-holders in the process. This form of best work appears in both samples, and its meaning is largely constant across the two countries. Journalists express both pride and modesty in discussing such stories, noting that while they view such work as "important," they recognize it does not approximate the profession's dominant ideals in quite the ways that stories labeled as "discover" and "edify" do. Their social properties are correspondingly also modest, as they tend to include general assignment and freelancer reporters, overwhelmingly those with nonprestigious educational attainment, and tending as a group to be more mixed in both gender and social origins.

A journalist in Seattle illustrated the main features of decoding when discussing a news item she had done about legislation in the state of Oregon. Popular perception had it that the newly passed legislation would "give everybody . . . access to free community college."[67] On social media, she saw people writing comments like "'I'm going to quit my job. Because of this [bill], I can focus on my studies.'" Reading through the bill, though, she saw its parameters restricted eligibility to individuals who had graduated high school in the past six months. Her story, she explained, translated the bill's content for an audience that would not read the original legislation, and thus corrected popular misperceptions. "People are not looking at the language of the bill to find out if it works for them." Highlighting her work as a journalist, she emphasized her efforts to decode: "It was not communicated to them well. I felt it was my job to explain it and it was good that I could tell people that."

Journalists in Toulouse expressed similar pride in distilling topics in simple language for audiences. One talked about a story concerning gender inequality she did for a youth magazine. Her satisfaction centered not on her ability to make youth aware of the problem per se; rather, she emphasized the effort it took her to make "big statistics" understandable to the publication's target audience.[68] Another journalist described a story she did about working conditions for employees at *Charlie Hebdo*, the Parisian weekly that was attacked by gunmen in 2015. "What I like [to do]," she explained, "is to try to understand" and, emphasizing for effect, "dissect and vulgarize" the issues for a wider audience.[69]

Journalists operating neighborhood-style blogs highlighted their role in helping audiences understand what is happening. One explained that he took pride in helping readers know what led to changes in the neighborhood. Noting that the neighborhood "has changed pretty rapidly" in recent years, he believed this led to "a lot of alienation for residents" who did not understand what was happening.[70] "In a real sense, you don't own the city." His work, he said, "helps people" understand "the change a bit better . . . at least they know what's coming and we can explain some of the money or . . . decisions behind it better." Another journalist highlighted the way her blog explained the decisions already made by city officials. Several years ago, she noted, the City Police Department got a contract with Homeland Security to "put up surveillance cameras" in that neighborhood. "The details of the contract were something that was buried, five layers down in public documents. So, it was not like they were hiding it, but it wasn't obvious."[71] She read through the contract and summarized it for her readers.

Some journalists noted that their efforts to decode enabled them to reach large or new audiences. One journalist, for example, described a story that explained the significance of a new sports record, which he "managed to disseminate in many different newspapers and in particular big newspapers."[72] The article, he also noted, was eventually translated and published in three different countries and published by a magazine with a global circulation of 4.5 million. Another journalist talked about a multimedia gallery she did that explored what makes some hotels become known as haunted. "It did super well on social [media] and I . . . rewrote the copy on Twitter and Facebook several times to share it out. . . . Each time, it has attracted a huge reach and got a ton of [audience] shares."[73] These and other journalists argued that their work in translating ensured that otherwise abstruse or uninteresting topics would "resonate" with readers. Said differently, it was their successful decoding that allowed them to more widely disseminate their work.

Journalists describing their work as acts of decoding complex issues often began their answers modestly, suggesting a distance between their own best work and the profession's dominant ideals. One reporter talked about reporting she did about regulations of dairy manure on farms. "It wasn't some big exposé," she began, noting that she didn't discover the problem on her own.[74] Nor did her work aim to hold any particular social actor accountable for their actions. "I try not to demonize anybody in this regard." Instead, she wanted to explain the different perspectives—farmers, regulators, environmentalists, health advocates—on this complex issue to audiences in straightforward terms. The story, in her view, had "social consequence" because many farms around the country confront similar issues, and legal action taken in one state could be found elsewhere.

This relationship between modesty and meaning was made even more explicit by a reporter talking about a story he did explaining a ballot measure in an upcoming campaign. "It is not really a remarkable story in the sense that it broke news or was shocking in any way, or moved the needle necessarily on some policy," he explained. "But I thought it was an important story because the ballot measure has a lot in it."[75] What's more, the measure was "confusing but important." His story explained "what was in the ballot measure, and why it matters, and provided different perspectives on it in a certain digestible way." Summarizing his work, he noted that while it may not be the most shocking or impactful, it nonetheless "feels like an important piece of public service informational journalism. I am proud of that."

If those who "discover" conceive of themselves as challenging power, those who "decode" instead emphasize their work as facilitators. A reporter talked about a story he did about a group of children being kept in the hospital because they required ventilators to breathe. The situation was not optimal for the children and their families, he explained; additionally, "it's also not a cost savings for the state."[76] The problem was already identified by some state officials and legal advocates; the reporter saw his job as explaining to audiences "the hard work they [legal advocates and state officials] were already doing." Reflecting on the story, he argued that "it's just kind of a really dumb problem where the solution would actually save the state money." His reporting on the topic, he explained, helped audiences to understand why the issue was happening and "will help make the state just do something a little smarter."

Decode responses also differ in terms of the journalism they dislike. For the most part, these journalists did not criticize work that fails to reveal issues that power-holders prefer to remain hidden. Instead, they expressed distaste for work that fails to engage in the labor of translating complex issues. Several journalists mentioned news articles that merely regurgitate press releases, with one reporter calling them "derivative" and "cheap," and warning about the use of automated technologies that provide such services: "We [journalists] have to stand well away from that."[77] Broadcast journalists criticized news reporters that merely present banal information, and in doing so fail to tackle complex issues and explain them to audiences. A reporter, for example, discussed colleagues that broadcast for "two hours before the press conference and they have nothing to say; it has no interest, journalistically speaking."[78] She and her colleagues "laugh at them quite regularly"; furthermore, "their place, I do not want [it]." Instead, it can be conceived as an adjustment to align their best work within the professional hierarchy of excellence while infusing it with meaning.

Beyond press releases, journalists that described their best work as acts of decoding disliked reporting that failed to recognize the complexity of issues. This failure strikes at the heart of decoding, as failure to acknowledge complexity removes the need for a journalist who can decode it for audiences. A reporter on the crime beat said he dislikes stories "that are just lopsided [even though] they are complicated stories."[79] He emphasized that he had no problem with advocacy journalism per se. "We all [see] things through our personal prism. . . . I recognize that." Instead, the problem he saw was reporting that "just lacks any nuance" and fails to "recognize that things are sometimes more complex."

Dignify: Giving Worth to Individuals

A final set of respondents described their best work as efforts to give worth to individuals, especially those perceived as holding little social power. Unlike edifying forms of journalism, these responses place comparatively little emphasis on how individual stories can inform broader understandings. Instead, they take pride in work that entertains audiences without sensationalizing the subjects being covered.[80] The label "dignify" highlights these efforts to confer value upon story subjects. Like decoding, this form of best work appears in both samples and its meaning is largely constant across them; the social properties of these respondents are also very similar to those who decode. Moreover, and again like their decoding peers, respondents articulate both pride and modesty in discussing these stories, noting that they entertain without sensationalizing while also often acknowledging that their work does not approximate the profession's dominant ideals.

A Toulouse journalist's response nicely captures some of the main features of "dignifying." She described a popular profile she had done about an obese man who lost weight and subsequently founded a civic organization dedicated to weight loss. The journalist mentioned prior sensational news reports that focused on the fact he had not left his apartment for two years, and that firefighters had to break down his door to remove him from his apartment. By contrast, "I contacted him. I went to his place. We talked for a while. I tried to ask him about his journey."[81] Describing the story, she explicitly noted her effort to ensure the man's worth. "I painted his portrait to describe his situation as best as possible without falling into the pathos, caricatured side, 'Look at the obese.'" Contrasting her report with the "false empathy" that in her view is often shown on television reporting of such issues, she said: "I have the impression of having treated the subject in a correct way, without stigmatizing the person."

Other journalists expressed similar pride in giving worth to story subjects on popular stories. One reporter talked about a profile she did on an Iraqi boy who had been adopted by a local family in Washington State. The boy was blinded by a gunshot wound at age two, and the reporter was not the first to tell his story. "I have seen other reporters cover him and call him disfigured and stuff like that. And I just thought that was completely [*voice trails off*]. You do not say that."[82] She was proud to highlight the child's unique skills. "He is really amazing. He is super independent. He does echolocation . . . so he can tell where he is going." Another journalist discussed a radio series he helped start. Called "Ask A . . ." the program invites audience members to ask individuals from a specific community about their experiences (e.g., Muslim, transgender, immigrant). "The whole thrust" of the series, he explained, is "tell me your story. I'm talking to you as a person. . . . Why do you believe what you believe?"[83]

As these examples suggest, many of these stories deal with populations perceived by journalists as being socially vulnerable. A journalist in Toulouse, for example, talked with pride about a "series of reports on homeless people" he had done in the past year. He recalled saying to one person at the end of their interview, "You don't have to answer, but I'm asking you anyway. How did you get here? What was your life [like before]?"[84] Contrasting his approach with what he viewed as sensational peers, he said: "There's no voyeurism, if you don't want to answer." Through his reporting, he felt that he was able to show people who this person was. In similar fashion, a Seattle journalist described a story he did about one family's first day back to school after a school shooting in which several people were killed. The idea was "me being in their house when they are having breakfast, when they are leaving to go to school, and when they drop her [the daughter] off [at] school."[85] For him, the pride consisted in part of being "the only" journalist able to give worth to this moment, despite many other journalists being in town to cover the story. "This was probably going to be an important moment for hundreds of families in that school. But I did not think . . . anyone else was going to have that moment."

Respondents regularly noted that their best work resonated with audiences, and they linked this success to the fact of giving worth to individuals and communities otherwise marginalized or ignored in the news. "One of the complaints we've heard in the past is 'I don't hear myself on the radio.'"[86] Therefore for this journalist, programs like "Ask A . . ." bring new voices to radio in a dignified and respectful way. What's more, he argued, audiences appreciate such programming because it exposes them to "voices you hadn't heard before" and might be interested in. Another discussed a historical story about an immigrant family, which in his view "resonated with readers" by effectively capturing a universal aspect of human life.[87]

Respondents in this label expressed strong distaste for journalism that sensationalizes the topics on which they work. One reporter, for example, talked about disliking "sordid details" that are sometimes included in crime news coverage he consumes. He acknowledges that while crime stories are not his preferred subject to cover, he does sometimes have to cover them. When doing so, he tries to find a way to cover them that is respectful to the deceased, the families involved, and the audience more broadly. "If I have to say someone was found dead, I will only say that one person was found dead. I will not say that this person was found by the neighbor at 'x' o'clock."[88] He contrasted his approach with "the local dailies' crime stories," which tend to be "extremely well detailed, and that's not something I like." Doing so, he believes, "offends the listener. . . . I try to say something different, . . . something people will feel concerned about beyond the gossip."

Respondents simultaneously took pride in these works while also recognizing that it was different from—and, in some ways, distant to—the dominant ideals of the profession. A reporter, for example, talked about a story he did on a man who had died and left eight hundred thousand dollars to the United States government. "It interested me to find more about the man and so on. Why would someone do that?"[89] Going through the man's documents (provided to the reporter by his attorney) and talking with neighbors, he was able to construct his life story as a World War II refugee. "I found as much as I could [about the man] and put together various bits." Summing it up, he noted that the work was not a long-form investigative reporter. "It wasn't a story about some big exposé," as he put it. Nonetheless, it was a source of pride for him to tell "a story about the human condition."

JOURNALISTS AT THEIR BEST

For most journalists, the best work they do is adjusted to the conditions they have. Those who work as freelancers and general assignment reporters—who also tend to include more women, many of whom disproportionately come from lower social origins, and have less prestigious education as well as professional experience—have the conditions to decode and dignify, but generally not to edify and discover. Their discussions of both their own best work and that of their peers generally show that they know a more "legitimate" journalism exists. Just as importantly, they also demonstrate awareness that they do not possess the conditions, at least at the moment, to do that work. In this sense, it is accurate to say they "refuse what is anyway denied" to them.[90] But their best works are in no way meaningless. Instead, they serve to reinvigorate belief in the profession by having their extraordinary productions make their more ordinary struggles seem worthwhile. Moreover, what counts as extraordinary is itself variable, with some journalists recognizing the highest echelons of professional excellence without particularly seeing it as something for "someone like them" to do. By bolstering the sense of self-fulfillment from journalism, best works help journalists with less favorable social properties to find, at least for the moment, a personally acceptable balance of rewards in the profession.

Those whose best works more closely approximate the profession's highest ideals undoubtedly work extremely hard to develop their talents and skills. They also face frustrations in their ordinary work lives. Partly, their capacity to do best work that discovers and edifies may reflect their greater time in the field, as those who hold beat positions and editorial posts tend to have more professional experience. But these conditions also correspond with socially cultivated expectations, which help make it possible for their best works to reach the highest echelons of the professional hierarchy. Thus, a journalist in Seattle from a family of liberal professionals and a degree from a prestigious university acknowledged that she is "not quite as much at the end of the tiger's tail" as many of her colleagues, which she "personally could never do." If a story she is working on is not ready to be aired, she knows it can wait. She only airs stories "when they are ready," comparing it to making soup. "You know, [like] when it's soup [that is ready], you eat it."[91]

If the relationship between one's social properties and best work is patterned, it is hardly mechanical. While not common, some journalists do work that does not seem well adjusted to their conditions. They describe best works that accord with the principles of discovery when their social properties suggest they might instead be likely to decode. This is less surprising than it might at first appear. The hierarchy of professional excellence is one that journalists learn, either in school or on the job. Why wouldn't at least some aim to approximate its heights? The balance of rewards that constitutes the basis of the journalist's predicament is always about what is *personally* acceptable. In both cities, those who do work that stands in tension with their conditions raise questions about the durability of such efforts, and the beliefs that underpin them. How long does one find it acceptable to work without pay and on weekends to do the work they really enjoy, especially if that work does not translate into professional ascension? At what point do nonwork obligations require one to scale back? Misalignment is not impossible; it is fragile. It is likely because people know this practically that such misalignments remain relatively rare.

A freelance journalist in Toulouse demonstrates this seeming misalignment in a heightened form. Living for journalism but hardly off it, he described his best work as an act of discovering information. Side jobs, which entail work that he does not enjoy and is not part of his journalism, are necessary to enable him to do this work. His income from his journalistic activities is on its own insufficient for paying his monthly rent. Even the work that he considers his best production struggled to find a buyer among local news media in the city. His efforts demonstrate that it is possible to do such work even as they show how implausible it may be for the rewards received to appear personally acceptable to many other journalists. This particular freelancer struggles to pay his rent; he lives for, and in some sense almost only for, journalism, as he has no partner or immediate family. For how many other journalists would this be acceptable?

The example of this seeming outlier highlights a cross-national dimension of the best work data. While the most prestigious forms of journalism in Toulouse and Seattle *tend* to be different, they are not exclusively so. Some French journalists, like this freelancer, describe their best works as acts of discovery; some of their American counterparts do work that corresponds nicely to the work described here as edifying. These findings serve as a reminder that the regular opposition between a literary or political "French" journalism and a fact-based, watchdog "American" press has limits, even if it effectively captures the dominant social functions associated with the press in both countries. In both countries, the dominant social functions represent differences in the balance of power among competing forces in crucial periods of journalism's formation as a modern profession. But these social functions have always commingled with other notions of what journalism is or should be. Cross-national differences are thus found in the relative weight accorded to specific functions.

Moreover, the standard opposition between French and American journalism glosses over the substantial similarities that stem from the profession's shared commercial roots, and the pull they exert on contemporary journalists. In Toulouse and Seattle, many journalists describe best work as acts of decoding or dignifying. These descriptions are virtually identical across the two contexts. In both places, the effort is to find a way to do "good work" while more directly acknowledging the commercial bases of the press. These commercial influences are undoubtedly strong; the diversity of topics that journalists admire suggests the growing influence of such forces in potentially reshaping the profession's hierarchy of excellence. But if *all* these journalists cared about was expanding audiences, they could certainly find ways to expand their reach by sensationalizing rather than dignifying or decoding. Their efforts thus highlight the enduring social functions that give the profession its normative weight, and the belief that the journalist's predicament is a worthy one.

Whatever the specific form a journalist's best work assumes, all generally tend to emphasize the work and talent necessary for producing journalism that approximates the heights of the professional hierarchy. This emphasis is not naive; those who decode and dignify discuss work they admire by highlighting the conditions that journalists have, and that they see as enabling such work. At the same time, their discussion of such work inevitably also focuses on the skills and talents of those who do such work. Highlighting these traits also makes their production appear potentially achievable, even to those possessing less favorable social properties. This possibility, even if rare, is an important source of meaning, fueling as it does the belief that a different future is possible. But the focus on skills and talents can also be read as one way in which differences in social properties are transformed into differences in social achievement. Skills and talents appear individual; with enough work and luck, anyone can develop them. Social properties, by contrast, reflect very unequal conditions across journalists; one cannot wish away where they come from.

Best work, because it is irregular, can only go so far in sustaining one's belief that the profession is worthwhile. Certainly, it can make up for the frustrations one experiences on a more regular basis; more than one journalist made this point specifically while discussing their examples. But best work is not a stable solution to the journalist's predicament. This is especially true in the context of contemporary journalism, as the economic, technological, and social transformations reduce the overall amount of material and symbolic rewards on offer to journalists. If occasional forays into best work provide a sense of meaning, a more routine and quotidian analysis is also necessary to understand how journalists respond to these transformations and seek a personally acceptable balance of rewards, given the contemporary predicament in which they find themselves.

CHAPTER FOUR

Conserve, Challenge, Accede

Consider three journalists.

Daniel, a longtime beat reporter for the main daily newspaper, recognizes that audiences increasingly expect to receive their news in a digital format. He worries that this capacity to self-select news they do—and, as is increasingly the case, do not—consume will be hazardous for both the business of journalism and the functioning of society. But, he admits, these transformations have to date mostly left his day-to-day work life unaffected. He uses social media a bit; mostly, though, he focuses on doing "big page one" stories as regularly as possible. This work, which he has honed over decades, garners him the respect and recognition of his peers; several of his long-form stories have won prizes, both regionally and nationally. As a regional news reporter, he does not earn a lot. He could earn more doing public relations—some of his colleagues have left their beats to work for the very institutions they once covered—but the thought never seriously enters his mind, and anyway he lives comfortably enough off the salary that his job provides him. The balance of material and symbolic rewards he has worked so hard to attain is acceptable to him. To the greatest extent possible, he wants to conserve a version of journalism that allows him to continue attaining these rewards.

Thomas, a television reporter at one of the main commercial stations in town, has seen firsthand how precarious journalism jobs can be. His first job after graduating from journalism school lasted just six months; his employer went bankrupt and laid off the entire staff. The experience taught him that having *a* career in journalism, let alone a successful one, required more than just telling good stories; he would also have to find ways to make himself less readily dispensable to employers. Jobs for multimedia journalists (MMJs), he noticed, were becoming increasingly common. In an effort to hold down labor costs, news stations wanted to have one person do the work previously handled by two people. This type of job would change his work substantially, and some of his peers suggested that these MMJs could never produce stories whose quality would rival those done by two-person crews. But he did not mind the idea of working alone; it might even give him more control over his reporting. At the very least, he was willing to give it a try. By seeking opportunity in the profession's technological transformations and economic constraints, he hopes to challenge the idea that good journalism cannot be done by MMJs. He wants not only the material rewards—better pay, more stable work—associated with career advancement; he seeks recognition and respect for the tasks he undertakes, too.

Finally, Juliette, a radio journalist for a commercial news station, finds herself increasingly asked to do work she dislikes or feels unprepared to do. Her editors, hoping to bolster their listenership, ask her to report on topics—"ten ways to make your house more beautiful!"—that strike her as more sensational than serious. They also ask her to augment her audio reporting with videos that can be posted online. She could refuse these requests, as her job is reasonably well insulated from layoffs, but she complies nonetheless. The assignments will not bring her any extra money; certainly, they confer no prestige or sense of self-fulfillment. But they do preserve for her the possibility that her editors might from time to time allow her to take on work that she actually enjoys. As a mother, she also knows that doing these tasks will incline her managers toward permitting her to leave work in the evenings so that she can be with her children. Without abandoning her own ideas of what counts as good journalism, she finds herself acceding to whatever types of work are requested by her superiors. The balance of rewards she has is personally tolerable, and she does not want to risk losing them.

The upheavals in the profession that these three journalists perceive are the same; their adjustments to them, quite different.[1] Whether from experience or observation, they recognize that the economic basis of journalism is deeply distressed; that prior ways of generating revenues have been rendered unstable, even in some cases obsolete; and that new business models are needed. They acknowledge, moreover, that whatever form these new models take, the work of journalists is and will continue to be produced, circulated, and consumed in a digital news environment in which their offerings are just one of many available to audiences. But some, like Daniel, aim primarily to *conserve* a balance of rewards that is personally acceptable largely by ignoring technological transformations and economic constraints that they see as threatening. Others, like Thomas, see these upheavals as opportunities to do journalism differently, often with digital technologies, and, in doing so, to *challenge* the balance of rewards by seeking greater material and symbolic returns for their efforts. Finally, like Juliette, still others *accede* to whatever work is requested of them for fear of losing the balance of rewards they attain, and hope to continue attaining.

Each of these adjustments is a gamble, in two senses: first, with respect to the form that journalism will take; second, regarding the rewards a journalist expects or hopes to attain from their work in the profession. Those who conserve hope that the historical weight of journalism's social functions will preserve their extant balance of rewards; however, they recognize that the profession's commercial woes make the form of journalism this balance entails increasingly difficult to sustain. Those who challenge aspire to do journalism that will address the profession's commercial problems, but acknowledge that they do not know whether their efforts will yield a personally acceptable balance of material and symbolic rewards, or whether their efforts will ameliorate their profession's commercial woes. Those who accede aim to not lose the rewards they already have by going along with managerial requests and instructions, but realize this often involves work that stands in tension with their very reasons for being journalists. Because neither the shape of journalism nor a journalist's place in it is singular or settled, none of these gambles is guaranteed to pay off.

But if individual outcomes are uncertain, broader assessments of their implications can nonetheless be offered. The first concerns the socially cultivated nature of journalists' responses to their professional upheavals. Those who conserve have the most to lose should the profession devalue or alter its commitment to journalism's more esteemed social functions. They also tend to hold the social properties historically associated with models of excellence in regional journalism: predominantly men from professional families, typically with ample professional experience as beat reporters and editors, working at dominant news outlets. Those who challenge are more socially diverse: mixed in gender, social origins and professional titles as well as experience. Compared to their peers, this group of journalists displays very high volumes of educational attainment (either via prestigious undergraduate programs or postgraduate work in professional training programs), thus highlighting the role schools play in facilitating the profession's adaptation to journalism's commercial concerns. Finally, those who accede see themselves as having little, if anything, to gain in these upheavals; for them, journalism has been, and, they hope, will continue to be, a source of modest rewards. This group skews female and often comes from lower social origins; they also tend to be made up of mostly freelancers and general assignment reporters working for nondominant news outlets.

A second assessment relates to the cross-national dimension of the analysis. Both the salience and meaning of the three responses—conserve, challenge, accede—vary across the two contexts. Journalists in Toulouse are more likely to either conserve or accede, due to labor regulations that make losing a job difficult as well as the capacity of incumbent organizations to minimize the emergence of new journalistic organizations. Those who conserve are therefore able to largely tune out management concerns; those who challenge tie themselves to cost-cutting measures only when seeking to enhance their employability with dominant news organizations; and those that accede growingly experience their profession as a "mere job" rather than a profession. By contrast, journalists in Seattle are much more likely to challenge, as weak labor protections make the profession's commercial concerns a concern for all journalists, and heavy market exposure for all media creates opportunities for some but risks for all. Journalists that conserve therefore emphasize the social functions that they hope will support their continued relevance; those that challenge use technology as a way to reduce costs and bring in new revenues regardless of where they work; and those that accede find themselves working longer hours and being asked to perform more tasks.

A third and final assessment concerns the effects of these developments on the relationship between journalism's social and commercial functions. The possibility of news organizations simultaneously satisfying these two functions has become increasingly difficult. Especially at the regional level, these organizations and the journalists that work with and for them face a stark choice between, on the one hand, prestigious social functions, like long-form, in-depth, and well-written reporting, that retain their normative weight but struggle to profit commercially and, on the other hand, a commercial function that seeks to capture audiences and, by extension, revenues, but often by producing news that bears limited relation to these historically privileged forms of journalism. Journalists' varied adjustments to these professional upheavals can thus be read as attempts to establish a new equilibrium among these social and commercial functions. Rather than disappear, journalism's most distinguished social functions are becoming highly restricted to a small number of socially well-resourced journalists. They are also being redefined, often by becoming more consumer-oriented, by journalists seeking to address the profession's commercial woes without losing their belief that the profession, and the adjustments they make for it, remain worthy of their efforts.

A NEW EQUILIBRIUM

One way to read the history of technology in journalism concerns its role in shaping a new equilibrium between the profession's social and commercial functions.[2] In the broadest possible sense, technologies—the printing press, photography, radio, television—promise not only to deliver a new experience of the news; they also pledge to reach new, often previously excluded, audiences. Historically, this inclusion could entail a governmental logic, with media being used, depending on the circumstance and one's perspective on it, to either propagandize or educate citizens.[3] At least in Western Europe and North America, this inclusion growingly entails instead a clear commercial logic, in that technologies are typically promised to bolster revenues to those news media that capture such audiences.[4] At the same time, these technologies also contain a social dimension, with each new development providing an opportunity for journalists to reevaluate, and sometimes challenge or defend, what "counts" as a legitimate social function of journalism.[5] Far from fixed, the balance between these commercial and social functions and the specific meanings they assume is a point of ongoing struggle and contestation.[6]

Digital technologies are a central context in which these contemporary struggles over journalism's commercial and social functions occur.[7] Whether looking at the introduction of online publishing or the rise of social media, platform intermediaries, and digital analytics, these technologies give rise to two questions. The first concerns the economic costs and opportunities associated with their introduction: how much money it requires to utilize these tools, how these costs compare to prior ones, and how, in what ways, and for whom revenues can be realized from the utilization of these technologies.[8] The second concerns the types of journalism these tools make possible: the extent to which they facilitate a return to older, often more highly esteemed styles of journalism;[9] or, conversely, whether they introduce novel modes of journalism, which are sometimes praised for their novelty and other times criticized for the problems they are perceived to exacerbate.[10] How these two questions are answered shapes the equilibrium that gets formed regarding the profession's commercial and social functions.

The very weakness of contemporary journalism's commercial model makes economic concerns basic, even central to journalists. Despite their very different responses, the vignettes provided for Daniel, Thomas, and Juliette converge in their recognition that their profession finds itself in difficult, perhaps even dire, economic straits. However much one might wish it, going back to a predigital world is not possible; not even Daniel, who claims to personally ignore most of the technologies that his peers use, suggests this is an option. At the same time, it remains uncertain to each of these journalists to what extent a stable commercial basis for journalistic work can be established at the regional level. In beginning from the premise that journalism needs to secure the economic means necessary for survival, these journalists gesture toward the establishment of a new equilibrium between the profession's commercial and social functions, in which the pull of commercial considerations exert themselves ever more strongly, if unevenly, across members of the profession.

This commercial pull can be seen clearly in the acceptance, shared by nearly all journalists in both Toulouse and Seattle, that a digital future is inevitable. It is not simply that almost everyone agrees that they "cannot ignore the Internet," as one freelancer put it.[11] Rather, it is the economic rationale that very clearly underpins this perception. Asked to explain why the Internet and its associated tools "cannot be ignored," a newspaper journalist responded that it is "just becoming increasingly clear ... that young people are not getting news ... from a [print] paper and looking through it." Instead, "they are getting their news through feeds and through social media."[12] These commonplace observations give rise to differing reactions, sometimes celebratory ("I drank the Kool Aid! I'm super excited to do all kinds of media")[13] and other times critical ("It's problematic for all kinds of reasons ... people are only getting the information that they think they're interested in rather than discovering stuff they could be interested in but they don't even know about it, which of course you can find if you have the paper in hand").[14] Either way, they inform a very broadly shared sense among journalists that the profession needs to evolve to address these developments. As one person put it: "We need to find ways to reach young people where they are" and with journalism that appeals to them.[15]

In this professional evolution, commercial concerns serve as a starting point. With rare but important exceptions, journalists in Toulouse and Seattle mostly did not begin with the journalism they wanted to do and proceed to see if that would be economically attractive. (The few that did were generally considered by peers to be unrealistic, even naive). Instead, they began with what "new revenue models" and "new products" would support their work and proceeded from there. This was especially clear among journalists forming "startup" organizations, which typically positioned themselves first and foremost in commercial terms by emphasizing services that would attract readers and capture advertisers. Commercial concerns, though, could also be discerned readily among journalists working at established news organizations, as evidenced by one longtime radio journalist in Seattle, laser-focused on ensuring that journalistic offers (regardless of their content) would match the changing consumption habits of audiences. "What happens when the AM/FM dial goes away on the car radio," he asked. "What happens when we have self-driving cars and you can now watch YouTube in the car? What about the person on the bus who might be streaming and listening to something with ear buds ... is it over the air radio? Internet radio? A podcast?"[16]

In imagining or experimenting with new products, many journalists logically see audiences primarily, but not exclusively, as consumers. If an older and less fashionable model of a journalist adopts a posture akin to a teacher who informs and educates, even when the student is uninterested, the contemporary journalist sees herself more as an adviser, and sometimes even a close friend. This "journalist of communication" understands above all that she must hold the audience member's attention,[17] and that this task is especially difficult to do when news consumers have so many choices.[18] Technology in this regard is useful not in and of itself, but to the extent that it will help one "connect to audiences effectively," as one radio reporter in Seattle put it.[19] Because so much weight is placed on holding attention, should it be so surprising that at least some journalists see their audiences more in terms of their lifestyles and consumer choices than as common actors in a civic relationship?[20]

Older journalistic values, like immediacy, can also be interpreted in light of the growing pull of commercial concerns. If journalists have long taken pride in being the first to report a news item, this orientation—sometimes bordering on the obsessive—is increasingly a value in itself.[21] Thus, editors aim to keep a website "fresh" by constantly providing new information. Even if the substantive changes appear superficial, they nonetheless make a news site appear different and new to a returning audience member. This orientation toward immediacy—"update, update, update" is a web editor's "unwritten mantra"[22]—risks violating other journalistic principles, through the hazards it entertains of publishing information not fully verified or poorly understood. Government reports on employment figures or inflation data, for example, can be initially subject to a negative interpretation, only to have that view reversed after digesting the report and consulting with subject-matter experts.

But even if commercial concerns are primary, it is a mistake to see journalism's social functions as nonexistent. In some ways, it makes more sense to describe them as undergoing a process of redefinition. This redefinition can be glimpsed in developments like "solutions journalism," which has grown in popularity, especially at the regional level, in both France and the United States.[23] This approach to journalism articulates the social function of the journalist expressly in relation to the profession's commercial concerns. People avoid news, advocates of solutions journalism argue, because journalists spend so much time informing them about topics on which they either are uninterested or feel helpless to resolve.[24] If journalists aimed instead to assist audiences to act as enlightened consumers of goods and social services, then the journalist can assume the role of an "adviser" or "advocate" for his audience.[25] This redefinition does not eliminate or even necessarily marginalize historically prestigious beats, like politics. Instead, it shifts the journalist's emphasis away from revealing discomforting facts or offering enlightened commentary and toward a role in which they press political officials to speak clearly and find concrete solutions to the problems faced by everyday individuals.[26]

In other ways, social functions evolve by becoming inscribed in new professional competencies. From their education onward, journalists are increasingly expected not only to report and write but also to develop skills that permit the production and diffusion of their work across multiple media formats: video, photography, graphic design and editing, podcasts.[27] This turn toward multimedia has a clear commercial aim, in that it aims to reach audiences in whatever formats they prefer. But it also is conceived, and is stressed in university and professional training programs, as a way to tell stories more effectively than is possible in a single format. Thus, "immersive journalism," which offers a "360 degree view" of the world, is conceived as potentially "enhancing empathy";[28] social media are seen as opportunities to solicit participation from the public, not merely an exercise in personal and organizational branding;[29] maps, games, info-graphics, and quizzes are ways to make complex information more digestible and abstract topics more interesting, not just strategies for attracting users to a website.[30] The adaptation of journalism curricula to emphasize these competencies is one additional way in which schools aim to adjust student profiles to the new equilibrium between social and commercial functions.[31]

In still other ways, journalism's social functions persist through a more straightforward defense of their traditional forms. If *all* that mattered were commercial considerations, it would be difficult to explain the persistence of costly, and often time-consuming, reports that typically generate limited audience response but that can accrue a range of social benefits.[32] Long-form, in-depth, well-composed reporting is likely reduced as an overall proportion of regional journalism content, but it has hardly vanished. Its symbolic import remains visible in journalists' acknowledgments that such reporting remains the touchstone of professional excellence. These forms even inspire movements among journalists that aim to "go back to basics," using web technologies, for instance, to do a more rigorous job verifying the news and evaluating the veracity of politician's public statements.[33] In some instances, it even appears to imply a partial rejection of newer digital technologies in favor of a "slow journalism" that reinvigorates narrative, explanatory, and sometimes mobilized journalism.[34]

The problem, therefore, is not that these older social functions are extinct. Instead, it revolves in part around the fact that the equilibrium that once supported their production has withered away. That equilibrium, itself not eternal but rooted in a historically specific period, was based on the possibility that social and commercial functions could go hand in hand, that one could do the journalism they felt was socially important and expect commercial returns for doing so. Except for a few news outlets, mostly at the national level, this is no longer the case in either France or the United States—and, for that matter, for many other countries in Western Europe and North America. For most journalists at most news outlets, the choices are often clear-cut. On the one hand, there is the possibility of regaining a commercial footing by producing a journalism that adapts its social functions to fit these economic needs, but that risks reducing audiences to consumers rather than citizens and turning journalists into undifferentiated "information workers."[35] On the other hand, the normative weight of journalism's historical functions retains the potential for a journalism that critically engages its sources, spends time developing a novel angle and understanding of a social issue. But the path toward this sort of work is increasingly narrow, with fewer opportunities for journalists to pursue it. Through their responses to the new technologies that shape their everyday contexts, journalists find ways to adjust themselves to this new equilibrium.

CONSERVING BY IGNORING

"I find that working conditions have changed a lot, mostly for the younger," said one journalist in Toulouse when asked whether technological transformations impacted her work.[36] "The problem," she continued, is "that there is pressure for them ['the younger'] to work faster."

This statement acknowledges the constraints that news organizations and journalists confront as a result of such transformations while also articulating one's own position as an exception to those pressures. The journalist followed up by noting that she did not feel especially impacted by these same changes. "I love what I do, and I am the boss anyway!"

Others articulated a similar sense of exemption from the economic and technological transformations facing journalists. "I don't think [technological changes] changed a lot of what I have done," a veteran beat reporter in Seattle explained. Just as importantly, he still finds himself oriented to the work—long-form, in-depth reporting—that he had long done. "I still produce the same things, I still look for the big stories and so in my mind I'm thinking Sunday front page."[37] He acknowledged that his managers do not want him talking in terms of the "front page" because the report will be presented online. "But it doesn't really matter to me whatever you want to call it," he said. A Sunday front-page article means "a big long feature piece with information you can't get anywhere else.... That can be online or [it] can be in the Sunday print paper. It doesn't matter [what you call it]. It is the same work to me."

Some of these journalists acknowledged that perhaps they ought to do more, especially with social media technologies. "I want to start using Facebook again to share my stories," said the beat reporter for a print newspaper in Seattle. On Twitter, he said, "I sometimes tweet to someone if it makes sense, if he asks a specific question or just for fun. But I often do not."[38] The reason for not doing more, he explained, was that he did not want to "get caught up in a thread that would take my time away from doing *actual reporting*." This feeling was echoed by a counterpart in Toulouse, for whom the distribution of labor lessened his personal need to use social media. "I should do more," he confessed in response to a question about his own use of digital technologies, "but the truth is that I have an assistant who works for the online stuff, website, social media.... She also handles the Facebook page of the program."[39]

Still others noted a sense of good fortune in their ability to mostly ignore the constraints imposed by technological transformations and the economic pressures that come with them. Asked about her workday, a television reporter working in the investigations unit explained that it's "probably more typical in my unit than [others] because [they] never know what's going to, you know, be flung.... I'm not quite as much at the end of the tiger's tail as those folks tend to be."⁴⁰ Thinking about this for a moment, she said, "I have to say, I'm pretty lucky where I am at.... We're pretty well able to go and do what we need to do." In contrast to colleagues who had to meet difficult deadlines and produce for multiple platforms, she just "puts it on the air when it's ready."

A few journalists simply denied the utility of digital technology altogether. "Who needs [digital] social media when you have human social media relations?" responded one journalist when asked whether he maintained a social media account.⁴¹ More commonly, respondents acknowledged utilizing digital technologies, albeit in a limited fashion that supported their existing work. "I do use my phone to take notes sometimes, to record audio interviews [and] take pictures once in a while. That's it," one journalist explained.⁴² Another explained his limited use of Twitter. "I am not using it to network.... I don't do anything else except post my stories and little things about them in a link."⁴³ This corresponded with another who claimed to post to social media only on rare occasions. "In five years, I must have tweeted thirty times total."⁴⁴ Still another explained that he used online web searches rather than going to the library or archives for research. In his view, this actually diminished his personal workload. "The digital has helped us a lot," he said. "We lose less time [producing news].... It has actually diminished the workload, if we're being honest."⁴⁵

In ignoring the personal impacts of technological transformations and the economic pressures they induce, these respondents sought to conserve the dominant ideals of their profession, as well as their own balance of rewards that are based on them. One journalist, for example, expressed concern about new forms of storytelling that focused more on form than content. "I deeply regret that journalism fundamentals [*fondements*] are being discussed instead of being preserved," he said.⁴⁶ His priority, he explained, was the careful discovery of information. "I consider that the core of my profession is the research for information. I do it in a pretty crafty [*artisanale*] way. I like proximity, human relations, [and] dialogues." Another respondent expressed a similar view. "The kind of journalism I like," he said, "is the one based on asking and answering questions."⁴⁷ He continued by making a distinction between two types of journalists, one that "tends to copy press releases" due to demand for news content, and another that says, "OK. We have the press release. Let's verify and then ask questions about it." He contrasted the latter approach, with which he identified, with the former. "We do journalism and not communication because we do more than just transmit information. We ask questions.... We have this idea of making people discover.... It takes longer to prepare, but it is worthy."

For those journalists that use digital technologies in a limited way, they often expressed skepticism about their potential to fulfill extant ideals. "We use the Internet to find some inspiration to contact some people," one respondent said, "but we don't trust it."[48] She thought of herself as "old fashioned" in this regard. "We do everything the old way even if we're talking about multimedia." In her view, "what really matters" when a story or edition is completed is that she can take pride in delivering well-told, thoughtful stories. "I have always loved the nice writing ... the beautiful pictures, the beautiful page layouts, so there is always the same old satisfaction."

Several expressed criticisms of their colleagues' use of digital media. One noted that he uses Twitter to follow "police personnel and wire services."[49] By contrast, "I have little interest in the tweets by my fellow news people." Asked to explain why, he replied, he offered a defense of reporting that reveals information not already known. "They just keep repeating what I already know. There is very little new stuff. I am interested in something that is new and not part of the echo chamber." Much of the social media conversation, he concluded, "is not as important as the actual story." Another respondent expressed similar critiques. "I don't like what my colleagues do," he said.[50] "By that I mean taking information from an agency wire and then diluting it, molding it to the newspaper's format." By contrast, "I like being the producer of information."

In making these criticisms, this set of journalists seeks to conserve the social functions that they see as being at stake at this moment in journalism. This was expressed in a particularly clear way by the aerospace reporter in Seattle from chapter 3 who criticized the rise of "aviation bloggers," who take money from aviation companies and post content praising airlines services. For him, this development diminishes the potential for revealing information that the airlines themselves do not want published. The unique role of reporters, in his view, is precisely to provide this type of uncomfortable but socially important information. His being "annoyed" at their presence is therefore not precisely a sense of personal jealousness vis-à-vis new entrants; rather, it is an expression of concern about the de-differentiation between two visions of journalism. This is why he emphasizes that "they [the bloggers] are *not in the same category as me*."[51]

The social properties that enable and encourage a conservative stance toward technology are in many regards similar cross-nationally: skewing male and tending toward beat reporters and editors with ample experience working at dominant news outlets. But labor regulations make the prevalence of such responses more common in Toulouse. As also noted in chapter 2, the longer one works for a news organization, the more expensive it becomes for the company to fire them. Many established journalists recognized that their peers with fewer years of professional experience "struggle more than us" and were more vulnerable to layoffs.[52] As one journalist who has worked in journalism for thirty-five years put it: "Why do they [*La Dépêche du Midi*] keep me? Because it would be too expensive for them to fire me."[53] Just as important, journalists recognized that management was unlikely to tell them what to do. One longtime reporter described himself as a "free electron" that did whatever he liked. "Nobody imposes anything on me. If necessary, they propose, they suggest," he explained.[54] But ultimately, he decided whether to go along. Still another described an informal system among experienced reporters called "No initiative, no hassle" (*Pas d'initiative, pas d'emmerde*). "You do what you are expected to do and . . . they leave you alone. . . . You can lay back."[55] Such job protections create a situation in which some journalists thus had little incentive to do anything but defend the existing professional ideals, and from which their material rewards were stable and symbolic rewards were personally sufficient.

Journalists in Seattle, and the United States more generally, do not enjoy similar labor protections.[56] Their ability to ignore comes instead primarily from the symbolic prestige they have already accrued, highlighting the enduring weight, at least for now and for some, of the profession's most esteemed social functions. The journalists who respond to transformations by seeking to conserve older forms of journalism typically tended to work on prestigious beats and produce the work that accorded most closely with the dominant vision of investigative, long-form journalism. Respondents typically recognized this fact, noting that they felt fortunate to be in a position that afforded them the opportunity to produce journalism that aligned more closely with their ideals of the profession. "We don't have a leash on us," one investigative reporter explained. In contrast to colleagues who spend much time doing work assigned to them, "we're pretty well able to go and do what we need to do. We don't have to do pre-slotted time."[57] Even still, several journalists expressed their ability primarily as a result of their individual work. "I don't really have any constraint," one long time reporter explained.[58] "I am a big boy and I am not going to write inaccurate stuff, or slander, or do anything bad. It is trust. You [i.e., I] earned that trust."

CHALLENGING BY INVESTING

"Technology for me is . . . just thinking about different ways to tell stories."[59] This statement reflects a perception, shared among this set of respondents, that technology provides an opportunity to do new types of journalism, often aligned with their organization's commercial needs.[60] Another respondent described his role as being the person who uses technology "to take the lead in looking for new story forms. . . . Maybe that looks like a quiz . . . maybe that's video . . . you name it. . . . I am supposed to be trying to figure out how to use it."[61] Within specific media formats, respondents stressed different possibilities. A journalist working in radio, for example, noted that on radio "you're not able to pack in as many details" and contrasted this with online, where he not only provides more information but packages it in novel formats.[62] Regardless of medium, all respondents articulated a strong sense of opportunity made possible via digital technologies. As one person put it: "It's like there's so much hunger for new types of coverage, new types of stories, new types of writers. There are so many new audiences."[63]

For these journalists, transformations provided opportunities in which they could invest with the hope of boosting their material and symbolic rewards. For some, this took the form of specific jobs that relied on particular technologies. Several television reporters, like Thomas, talked about becoming "MMJs" (multimedia journalists), who record and produce their own video rather than be part of a traditional "two-person" crew (cameraperson, news reporter). As one person described it: "you are fully a reporter who is expected to do that part of the job, and fully a photographer who can shoot and edit and do everything."[64] Such a job is possible, she argued, because of transformations in technology. Another journalist expressly noted how the MMJ job helped him move into larger television markets. Prior to doing that work, he had only held jobs in small cities and was "having difficulties getting out and moving up in the business."[65] Despite "all my efforts," he recalled, "I could not get a job in a bigger market." Looking at job postings, though, he realized that "stations increasingly are hiring multimedia journalists or solo video journalists to work in their newsrooms. And ... they wanted people who do that well." The job was therefore a path for him to get to a larger market. He took it.

Other jobs, like developing a podcast, using data visualization tools, building databases, or working as a community engagement editor, are similarly exciting for the rewards they promise. Given the growing scarcity of journalism jobs with a permanent contract in France, the ability to use technologies, which organizations value as a way to attract audiences, provides the opportunity for job security. As one journalist in Toulouse put it: "They [the company] hired me under a permanent contract precisely because I had web skills which many people in the newsroom didn't."[66] The "main difference," between him and his peers, he explained, "was that I knew how to use the public databases and produce information; I knew how to film, how to edit, take pictures, and do interactive maps." These skills were attractive to the publication; the job was attractive to the journalist.

Still others saw possibility in forming their own online news sites. One founder in Seattle talked with excitement about forming his startup. People were "freaking out about the 'death of newspapers.' ... The theme was 'no one is reading newspapers anymore' and 'newspapers are going out of business.'"[67] Having run a popular blog for a print newspaper, he realized that he could use the web to do types of reporting not possible at a weekly newspaper. "I had really [come to] enjoy that type of reporting, the quick turnaround, the ability to break news. ... I really enjoyed that!" In his view, "the two things coalesced"—that is, the perception of a crisis in print journalism provided him with an opportunity to engage in a new venture doing the sorts of journalism he wanted to pursue.

The prevalence of education among journalists who challenge cannot be overstated. Nearly everyone in this category holds either an advanced degree or a degree from a prestigious university. For those who returned to school, the decision was a conscious investment in one's future. A journalist in Toulouse, for example, described "making a diagnosis of my possible evolutions in the profession."[68] The forecast was not promising. She realized that she was, metaphorically speaking, running toward a wall and about to smash her face [*casserait la gueule*] into it. "I realized I was heading for a disaster and needed some training courses about something that would go along with the evolutions of the profession." A reporter in Seattle explained his decision to pursue a graduate degree in his forties while working full-time in similar terms:

> In your forties you're supposed to be kind of at the top of your game. You're supposed to be—you have experience but you still have relative youth and you should be sitting pretty. And I'm looking around thinking, the world has changed a lot and I need a new set of skills. I need to hit the refresh button. I need to keep up with the times. If I want to keep doing what I'm doing I need to do something. And, so, this is about arming myself with—you know, I'll never be a digital native by virtue of my birthdate. So what else can I do except go back to school? . . . So yeah, I just thought, wow, instead of suddenly being like I've arrived in my forties and now I've got job stability and security and I know it all, it's like, oh, my gosh, look at how much has changed since 2007. I'm looking at the job descriptions for journalism even. And I need to retool, refresh, and get something digital on my résumé and in my portfolio.[69]

As these examples suggest, the decision to invest in technological skill is closely linked to economic transformations in journalism. Some respondents specifically discussed their skills as aligning with cost-cutting measures taken by their organizations. A solo video journalist, for example, explained that while newsroom staffing had fallen, programming demands had risen as a result of digital platforms as well as the cancelation of syndicated programs by television stations. As she put it: "If you are not going to hire more people then that's where that solo video journalism thing came from. You can hire more people by splitting crews, essentially. It gets cheaper if you pay for one."[70] Other times, these investments were linked to the prospects of future revenues. One radio reporter, given her own podcast, explained that it was part of an experiment by her station to "build listenership instead of losing younger audiences."[71] Still other times, these investments were seen as ways to enable journalists—especially those forming their own startups—to make a living. One founder of an online startup explained that he and his colleagues wanted the site to raise money so that they could travel for their reporting. "It didn't work terribly well, but we scraped enough money to do it."

All these respondents emphasized their belief that these investments challenged traditional definitions of how "good journalism" gets produced. A multimedia journalist working for a television station, for example, said that he was motivated to "prove" that it is possible to produce useful journalism through such an arrangement. "You can tell great stories by yourself," he said, "better than a lot of two-person crews can do. I wanted to prove that because I know that it is true."[72] Asked to expand, he explained: "I have total control over all aspects of the story—how it looks, how it feels, if I am using still pictures, or just every little detail [that] matters to me, every frame of the story matters to me." Another noted that by becoming a solo journalist, she was able to exercise greater control over the types of stories she covered. While many colleagues questioned the ability of a single person to do a good story on their own, she saw an opportunity to do the reporting she wanted to do. "It became very obvious to me that the story that I wanted to do, . . . that kind of out-of-the-box story, . . . those were the ones that you got to do . . . by yourself," she explained. "And if you were going to do breaking news, which I hated doing, you would work with a photographer."[73]

For most of these journalists, schools and training play an important role in teaching not only the skills but also the dispositions necessary for adjusting to the profession's increasingly commercial orientation. Multimedia skills are taught as a way to tell stories more effectively; staying current with new technologies necessitates being adaptable and learning quickly; all these efforts are promised as a way to ensure the possibility of professional mobility in an otherwise inauspicious set of conditions. At the same time, these programs also teach journalists about the social values of this work, that it is participatory and engaged, which could be contrasted with that of their "stodgy" peers who refuse to do such work. It is at least in part on the basis of these reformulated social functions that these journalists seek an acceptable balance of material and symbolic rewards.

While those who challenge often emphasize the profession's commercial functions, some important exceptions to this pattern exist. In Toulouse, for example, several recent graduates from a journalism school formed an online news site. Prior to launching, they operated a blog for the website of a print newspaper. In the course of doing so, they felt there was an opening for an online site that provided on-the-ground news coverage of local politics. With local elections coming up, they decided to form the site so they could "cover the municipal elections our way" and in ways that reflected a more Parisian form of political journalism.[74] Their inaugural statement on the website expressed the opportunity they perceived: "While some predict the end of the press, we rather see the beginning of another golden age of journalism."[75] In their view, "in a world where information travels fast" due to digital technologies, the work of the journalist is "more than ever necessary." They did no market research, and struggled to even find adequate funding. In discussions with other journalists, the site was often referenced as a laudable but naive misreading of journalism's economic basis in Toulouse. Even if the reporting they did was socially valuable, it was extremely difficult to generate advertising revenues, in part because of the strength of local incumbents.

Another set of journalists in France described investments that had nothing do with digital technology at all. For them, transformations in technology provided an opportunity to "do something different" by opening a magazine with no associated web presence. Three journalists collaborated in this endeavor; all had ample professional experience, and were highly regarded as professionals. One was a television journalist who previously worked in Paris, and moved to Toulouse after "burning out" from his work there. The others were former journalists at *La Dépêche*, one of whom worked in the magazine division. These journalists saw an opportunity for a new magazine to do good journalism rather than "immediate" or breaking news. Their magazine, therefore, focused on providing human interest reporting aimed at appealing to young, urban readers.[76]

What differentiates these strategies of investment in Toulouse is each's relationship to the dominant, commercial outlet, *La Dépêche*, and the rules of the field it enforced. Those who invested in technology highlighted skills that the dominant employer viewed as potentially useful as it transitioned to online platforms. Those who did not invest in technology developed a product—a print magazine, in this case—in which the newspaper was uninterested; the dominant outlet, therefore, would not be a competitor. In this regard, it is significant that *La Dépêche* had a print magazine but discontinued it to free up resources for digital productions. One of the journalists involved in forming a startup magazine stressed that they knew *La Dépêche* would not seek to compete with them for magazine audiences.[77] It is in this sense, too, that an online startup focused on local city news that would compete with *La Dépêche* is a misreading, as it remains a strong competitor for the very news they were hoping to produce.

In Seattle, by contrast, the overall weight of commercial concerns is even more keenly felt. The prevalence of "challenging" as a response to technological transformations is therefore proportionally greater than in Toulouse. School training, moreover, directly emphasizes the need for aspiring journalists to embrace multiplatform, interactive, and entrepreneurial forms of journalism. Very few, if any, journalists see a way to invest that ignores technology completely. Instead, they generally aim to find ways to develop new competencies that address commercial and social functions, and redescribe their social functions to better align with the profession's commercial needs. Doing so, they hope, will bring about an acceptable balance of rewards for themselves, but they realize this is not guaranteed.

ACCEDING BY GOING ALONG

In both cities, a third set of journalists described technological developments as facts to be accepted, if sometimes begrudgingly. Discussing social media, one journalist in Toulouse acknowledged that "we need to pay attention."[78] Such tools, she admitted, are "really time-consuming" and "we spend a lot of time tweeting, retweeting, following." In her view, digital technologies have created a "never-ending story," which contrasts with news items that previously were written once for the print newspaper. She described these developments as something to be endured. "It is really time-consuming, but [we] cannot escape from it." A reporter in

Seattle similarly talked about "all these little things" that he has to take care of when working on a story, mentioning specifically social media but also various story components (e.g., video, images) that were either not possible previously or delegated to someone else in the newsroom (e.g., photographer). Asked about his feelings toward these developments, he shrugged. "It's just a different world," he said. "And you have to accept [it]."[79]

Respondents noted that new technologies, coupled with economic difficulties, led them to a temporal intensification of their workdays. "I think what has really changed is the speed with which we are expected to do our job," explained one journalist in Seattle.[80] "Our job has become increasingly accelerated with respect to instantly collect[ing] and shar[ing] information, which puts a lot of stress on reporters." She stressed that "the tenets of journalism still apply," but also that journalists "have to be faster." She noted the "speed and convenience" of digital technologies but said that it comes with "a lot of pressure" from management to "put up your post on Facebook, tweet on Twitter, contribute to the website, and deliver the newscast." A journalist working in radio contrasted her workday in the past with her current one:

> Five years ago . . . I would have been expected to file a single news feature of about six-minute length. Now I am also supposed to produce an additional spot news report, . . . a promotional item, . . . a web post. And often there will be some other feature. I will in addition have to file for photography. . . . So the list of deliverables has gone like this [upward hand gesture to indicate increase] for a single project compared to the old [way of working].[81]

More generally, journalists in both cities talked about enduring low pay and sometimes precarious employment. "When you are a journalist, you are poor," said one.[82] Journalists also noted the meager salaries, even for those who held full-time jobs. Those who worked as freelancers described an even more difficult economic situation. A journalist who worked as a freelancer remarked that she found "fewer offers, fewer possibilities" to locate news outlets interested in her work. "I do my best to keep what I have now. If I lose one collaboration, I will suffer."[83] Because it is now "financially more complicated," she has to "be more flexible" in terms of what she writes about and for whom she writes. This was echoed by a freelancer who noted, "the faster you can do work, the more money you are going to make."[84] Still another noted that the problem is the oscillation between "empty periods" in which you have no work, and thus no pay, and busy periods "where you are totally overwhelmed." To be a freelancer, in her view, "you have to learn how to deal with both [situations]."[85]

How journalists endured economic and technological transformations varied cross-nationally. In Seattle, a common theme among some journalists was the lengthening workday. For example, one general assignment reporter who had worked in Seattle journalism for over forty years discussed changes to his workday over time. In the past, he said, reporters came in during the mornings, "spent all day on the phone, or reading stuff, . . . and then getting an idea . . . [about] how it all comes together. And you would write your story at four o'clock and go [home] in the evening."[86] Now, he says, it's not always easy to leave work behind when going home in the evening. "You're taking the bus home. That should be the time you decompress and walk in the door with a . . . clear head." But "it's not always that easy to do—because you have access, you're still checking things." Like many of his counterparts, he described this change as something he needed to accept would happen.

The willingness among Seattle journalists to endure longer work hours stemmed from the perception among journalists of job instability, itself rooted in the precarity of the profession's commercial basis. This perception has a clear basis in reality, given that in the prior decade, the number of paid journalism jobs in the city had been cut by more than half.[87] That perception led some journalists to accept rather than challenge their employers' requests. As one person put it: "If you ever see layoffs at a newsroom . . . it typically [happens to] the people who did not want to change."[88] Therefore, "it is important to be able to adapt to change." Others did not describe layoffs directly. Instead, when asked what they would like to see change in their work conditions, they simply expressed a desire to return to prior work conditions (i.e., before enduring these changes). As one person put it: "I guess if we can get back to where we were. We call that the Golden Age of the 1980s and 1990s, where [newsrooms had] lots of staff, good pay, lots of opportunities, travel. . . . That would be nice to have."[89]

In Toulouse, journalists described being assigned tasks that were devalued because their association with journalism was perceived as attenuated or absent. A journalist at a local radio station said she was given an iPhone and told to do some video and photography for the station's website. By her own account, she was not especially skilled with these tools, and producing video and images for the station's site was not valued by newsroom staff. Management, moreover, offered no training in using these tools. Nonetheless, they perceived her as being capable of learning, partly due to her relative youth as compared to many of her colleagues. "In the newsroom, some established journalists disagreed [with doing these tasks], or didn't accept because they didn't know how to use technology. . . . I did."[90] In other newsrooms, journalists with limited professional experience described even more devalued tasks, like being asked to manage the social media websites of their more established colleagues, which in their view had a closer relationship to marketing than to professional journalism.[91]

Relative to the American sample, and with the exception of freelancers, Toulouse journalists reported feeling stable in their jobs, due largely to labor regulations that limit the number of hours worked and make firing employees difficult. In this context, getting a job is difficult—the number of positions remains limited—but keeping one is not. Those who were asked to do different, or even more, tasks were therefore less concerned about losing their jobs or extending their workday. Instead, what concerned them was the transformation of their work life to the status of a mere job rather than a vocation. As one person put it: "My work is not very satisfying, but I work thirty-five hours per week. It's not what you would call . . . thrilling but I do seven hours per day and then leave. It is [a] great comfort to know the time you finish."[92] Another journalist contrasted herself with colleagues in their forties "who would not have accepted these conditions ten years ago."[93] In years past, she claimed: "We used to have great reporters [in Toulouse] with true living conditions, labor conditions, payment. . . . They used to work as Parisians." By contrast, "we ended up accepting almost anything." When asked why, she replied: "There are no jobs . . . and the idea is to have a job. If you want to stay in Toulouse, you need to tune yourself into 'humility mode.'"

Whatever cross-national differences may exist, journalists in both Toulouse and Seattle that accede sometimes feel themselves sacrificing the social functions in which they still believe for commercial concerns. "When you write six articles per hour," one journalist said, "you screw up [*vous faites de la merde*] from time to time." Sometimes, she continued, "it is even ... scandalous. It is badly structured, badly written, ... all because you have to work really fast."[94] Others noted that their work fell far short of the in-depth work they admired in other journalists. A journalist who does a newsletter explained that "you are ... doing a lot of stories but those stories are not going to be as in-depth or as good or as well-written [as] all journalists mostly try to do because of the sheer volume you are expected to produce though."[95] Reflecting on her own approach, she said: "You might just as well get a couple of paragraphs out so you can start the next thing. This pressure can impact the quality of your work for sure." Still another talked about some of the work that "gobbles up his time" even though he doesn't consider it "news":

> There is some web production stuff that I do [and] that my colleagues also do, where we'll manage the home page and create some—I mean they're slideshows, basically—it's photo galleries that either are topical or ... we have some success with historical galleries—galleries of historical photos—or sometimes they can be a little silly, sometimes they are a little.... they—they're different kind of content than what would have been associated with a print paper. And I don't mean to denigrate them, it's just ... they're not—they're not news and they're not, like.... they're not really reported, they're just a way of presenting photos to people in a way they seem to like on our site, so. And that—the web production and that kind of thing gobbles up about half my time.[96]

In noting the gap between their own work and what they would like to do, journalists affirm the profession's long-standing social functions even as they show awareness of its commercial needs. Several noted that they would like "more time" to be able to pursue the type of work that they most admire. "I wish I did have more time to actually report," one journalist said. "I think what I am doing most ... is kind of aggregating content.... I honestly do not have a lot of time out in the field to conduct interviews just because the social [media management] has taken up so much of my time."[97] A colleague said something very similar: "The whole trick right now is deciding how to spend our energy.... I of course would love to sit around and spend weeks on a... story and spend a lot of time tinkering with it. It's not realistic for my position right now."[98] In doing this, they affirm the dominant ideals that they do not have the conditions to approximate.

Finally, many journalists who endure nonetheless describe themselves as "being lucky" to have a job. "Honestly," said one journalist, "I do feel pretty lucky and very fortunate to have the job that I do," especially given the reduction in jobs due to budget cuts. "Is this where I envision myself? Not really."[99] Another noted her frustration with the pay and long hours. Asked why she didn't seek compensation for the extra hours worked, she replied: "People are willing to work around the clock just to have a job in journalism. We are lucky to have a job."[100] A colleague in Toulouse said that the profession was "devastated nowadays" and that finding a permanent job was "very rare." Therefore, "if you have one, you must take care of it."[101] And yet some still note the tug of journalistic ideals in keeping them going: "I am disappointed about our income, and how the profession is treated, but I don't really have a choice. For me, journalism is a way to fulfill my curiosity and my will to discover new things or places that regular people don't even think about. My income... that's something else. If I don't accept it, well... I would do something else."[102]

A COMMERCIAL PULL

Journalists' widespread uptake and use of digital technologies are often treated, by both scholars and journalists alike, as an incontrovertible fact of contemporary professional life, and for good reasons. Social media, multimedia, audience analytics, online and mobile publishing, platform intermediaries: all these technologies and more are increasingly basic to the working lives of many journalists. They are implemented both because of a more generalized use of digital technologies across society broadly, and more specifically as a potential way to address the commercial problems that the profession faces. Whether their use will in fact yield a workable economic solution at the regional level, and if so for whom, is far from certain. But it is a measure of their influence that almost no one doubts their importance and centrality.

Yet descriptions of the technologies used by journalists often also double as prescriptions for their use. In describing new competencies and redefining extant social functions, they open up the possibility for some ways of doing journalism while making others less likely. In both Toulouse and Seattle, the eroding commercial bases of journalism pull journalists toward the forms of journalism that appear best positioned to address these concerns in some fashion. This does not occur without countertendencies and even occasional opposition. The profession's most esteemed social functions persist, both as a real possibility for some to pursue and as an ideal to guide some of those who, for the time being, do not. It would be too glib and also too sweeping to claim their extinction. But the fulfillment of those more esteemed functions appears as a diminished proportion of the career possibilities for many journalists with the rise of digital technologies, and they are increasingly held to exist in stark opposition to the profession's commercial functions.

While this commercial pull and the effects it exerts on journalists are not inevitable, it is very much socially situated. If some journalists perceive themselves as "free electrons" able largely to ignore the technologies and economic constraints that surround the profession, this is at least in part because of the social conditions, themselves partly specific to national contexts, that afford them this freedom. In seeking to conserve the balance of material and symbolic rewards they already possess, the lack of interest they display regarding these transformations can also be interpreted as a form of interest:[103] for the preservation of older social functions and their relationship to them, which they recognize are becoming outdated and misaligned with the profession's contemporary conditions. It is a sign of the weight of these functions, most of which originated more than a century ago, that at least some journalists can continue to live off them. It is a sign of their unequal availability that the journalists with the most favorable social properties are most likely to adopt such a position in relation to the profession's upheavals.

The growing commercial pull provides favorable conditions for some journalists to challenge the balance of rewards by advocating a form of journalism better adapted to the profession's needs. In both France and the United States, journalism schools, themselves subject to commercial pressures of their own, instill or fortify the dispositions oriented to this approach to work; they also train the new competencies and teach the redefined social functions that allow this work to feel worthwhile to those that undertake it. Partly because the recruitment to these programs has expanded in recent years to include a wider range of social background,[104] the social properties of these journalists are also themselves quite diverse. That economic rewards are most readily available to those who challenge seems clear enough in both Toulouse and Seattle. The journalists undertaking these approaches tended also to be the ones that garnered more secure jobs or career promotions than their peers. The symbolic rewards appear less clear-cut, with more than a few complaining that their colleagues often did not respect or appreciate the work that they did, instead assigning the journalism they did as being of a second-rate quality at best. Whether their challenges are absorbed by the profession will depend in part on the capacity of journalists to secure a balance of rewards that is personally acceptable across this socially diverse group.

Those that accede respond to increased commercial pressures by seeking above all not to lose the modest rewards they already hold. This tendency to accept is associated with journalists from lower social origins and from less distinguished educational backgrounds, which inculcate dispositions of gratitude and acceptance. At least one gets to be a journalist, even if they cannot really change the conditions that seem unfavorable to the very sorts of work that attracted them to the profession initially. But accession is hardly a relation of straightforward servility. Rather, it reflects a practical calculation about where to place their investments. It is not random, therefore, that so many journalists who accede, especially in Toulouse, where the threat of job loss is comparatively limited, describe growing investments in their personal lives: as partners, parents, and friends. These relationships, which occur entirely outside the purview of one's professional life, help to render a personally acceptable balance of rewards that one attains as a journalist.

Journalists' responses to the technological transformations and economic constraints they confront are thus shaped by their social conditions, but they are not mechanically dictated by them. As social agents, journalists may possess social properties that are more or less inclined toward certain responses, but they must actually respond to them nonetheless. The presence of journalists whose responses are viewed by their peers as naive—to recall the case of a news startup in Toulouse committed to investigative reporting—suggest the potential for reactions poorly adjusted to their social conditions. Such responses, which seem destined to failure in economic terms from their outset, highlight the enduring possibility, if not the high likelihood, for journalists to challenge by seeking to secure a greater balance of material and symbolic rewards through a reconnection to the profession's most esteemed social functions.

In their different ways, each response is a gamble rooted in journalists' shared perceptions of their profession's contemporary upheavals. With each response comes the possibility of success. A journalist's bet may pay off, allowing one to attain a personally acceptable balance of rewards and offering an example to other journalists that the profession remains viable in part because it is worthwhile. Some can in fact conserve their rewards, finding ways to continue producing the journalism they love while remaining more or less unscathed by the profession's challenges. Some challengers do actually succeed not only in securing better material rewards but in garnering the recognition of peers and a sense of self-fulfillment for themselves. And some people who accede find themselves able to do work they actually like often enough to make the tasks they dislike tolerable.

But the bets may also fail. The sense of disappointment, sometimes expressing a sense of bitterness that borders on disillusionment, is not difficult to detect in some of these journalists. It is visible in the journalist that wishes to conserve but bemoans the evolutions of the profession that dilute the importance of long-form, deeply researched, and well-composed reporting; it is present in the MMJ that takes on new responsibilities but feels underappreciated by her colleagues or remains unable to advance professionally; and it surfaces in the freelancer that takes on tasks she dislikes yet somehow still finds fewer and fewer opportunities to engage in journalism that feels meaningful to her. This shared possibility of unsuccessful gambles across all responses gives the belief that the profession is worthy of one's efforts a perpetually provisional status. The adjustments that journalists make help to reproduce their belief that journalism is worthwhile. In finding a personally acceptable balance, they make life as a journalist possible. Until, for some, they do not.

CHAPTER FIVE

Leaving Journalism

The fact that some journalists leave the profession is hardly surprising. Indeed, one of journalism educators' long-standing "open secrets" is that many of those who study to be journalists do not remain in the profession for long.[1] Some journalism students never go into journalism at all, instead utilizing the skills learned in school to get jobs in public relations, marketing, or communication more broadly. Yet if securing an acceptable balance of rewards has always been difficult in a profession that pays little and demands much, it is all the more trying in the current period of professional upheaval. Given the overall diminution of material and symbolic returns, and the difficulties so many journalists encounter simply by being journalists, at what point and under what conditions does any one journalist make his or her exit?

Posing this question provides the opportunity to explore the dissolution of belief that the game remains "worth the candle." Two possibilities exist, each with distinctive implications for understanding the contemporary "crisis" in journalism. In one, journalists might question the worthiness of the profession itself. Given that journalism's most prestigious ideal (long-form, in-depth reporting) often seems to land on deaf ears and effect limited change, it seems possible to entertain the hypothesis that at least some journalists might find the utility of the profession wanting.[2] Why write stories when no one reads them? Why do long-form reporting when it changes the minds of no one who consumes it? This would imply a very deep crisis for the profession, akin to those experienced in the worlds of politics (e.g., seen in the loss of faith in communist parties among its former militants) or religion (e.g., visible in the priesthood and religious orders), where faith in the very utility of those activities and pursuits has come under question.

In another possibility, journalists might instead question *their* relationship to the profession. In this scenario, journalism remains worthy; there is no truck with the profession's historically derived social functions to inform and to educate, or perhaps even its redefined functions to advise and amuse. Instead, the loss of belief would stem primarily from the sense that it was no longer worthy of one's individual efforts. The causes for this disbelief might be multiple: too much time and not enough money, certainly; but also perhaps simply evolutions in one's life that makes working in journalism less well adjusted to one's individual circumstances. Or, conversely, it might stem from transformations in the profession that make it difficult for one to do the journalism in which she or he most believes. This would imply a troubling plight to retain individuals in the profession; it would clearly indicate a failure to garner a personally acceptable balance of rewards. But it would also suggest a profession still capable of fostering (and frustrating) powerful desires and attractions.

With those considerations in mind, this chapter explores individuals who have left journalism in Toulouse and Seattle. Departure is conceptualized as the cessation of journalism as an individual's primary work activity at the time of the interview. While each exit is unique, and a very wide range of journalists leaves the profession, collectively departures evince two key commonalities. First, they are preceded by a period in which individuals question their relationship to the profession, and consider whether their investments in it remain worthwhile. Second, departures are linked to what Sophie Denave has called "trigger events."[3] Such events appear in one's professional or personal life in myriad ways (e.g., as new job opportunities, the birth of children, the onset of health problems); crucially, they "modify the course of existence by altering the field of possibilities."[4] As such, they constitute the "when" of professional exits, even though they cannot be considered the direct causal source of it.

Yet if many journalists exit, variation in the manner these departures assume and the sense people make of their former professional identities stem in part from the social properties they possess. For some, departures are organized with a sense of choice. They are conceived above all as opportunities to do something new or different; the background understanding is that they could have decided otherwise. This allows for a degree of selectivity in the process: a preference for the "right job" or even the refusal to work altogether. Their journalistic identities are relatively easily reinvested in their new work, and those who leave the labor force feel they could reactivate their journalistic identity in the future should they choose to do so. As a group, these individuals tend to be professionally successful, with ample experience working as beat reporters or editors. However, they are split along gender and national lines, with men emphasizing work and women tending to prioritize family considerations, and French journalists utilizing labor regulations to negotiate favorable severance packages whereas American journalists, due to the less generous welfare protections, tend to prioritize salaries in their new careers as a way to "make up for lost time."

For others, departures are organized with a sense of necessity. These individuals feel themselves devalued in their journalistic work; their skills do not translate easily. They therefore seek out anything that secures their material needs. For these individuals, they do not feel themselves as having the luxury to be selective. They also struggle to reinvest their professional identities, which leads them to relegate journalism to an aspect of their past. As a group, these individuals tend to be less professionally successful, with lesser experience in journalism and typically holding positions as general assignment reporters or freelancers. They, too, are split along gender lines, with men emphasizing work and women prioritizing family. Cross-national differences are less stark in this group, though, as the labor regulations that serve as resources to better-established French journalists are not available to those without permanent contracts.

What, then, do these departures imply for journalism and journalists' belief in it? It is not a crisis of faith in the profession's social functions per se. Whatever their reasons for leaving are, journalists largely do not question the importance of a profession that uses facts to inform audiences about events in the world. Instead, they describe evolutions—either in their own lives or in the profession itself—that alter their relationship to journalism and, with that evolution, their belief that a career in the news is worth their efforts. They still believe journalism is worthy; they just do not believe in the journalism they do on a regular basis. Or, less dramatically, they still believe that journalism is worthy; they just no longer see their lives as fitting into the needs of the profession. This shows how difficult it is for journalists to retain their belief due at least in part to the diminution of material and symbolic rewards that characterize the profession. But it may also hold the potential for professional renewal, as it shows the enduring attractions of journalism and the beliefs that, more or less unchallenged, underpin them.

MAKING SENSE OF JOURNALISTS' EXITS

Extant scholarship generally follows one of two approaches in understanding professional exits from journalism. A first begins from the experience of job loss.[5] This perspective affords key insights into where individuals go after leaving the profession and how they make sense of the experience of job loss and career change. By starting from job loss, though, this view lends an implicit understanding of professional exit as someone else's choice, usually one's employer. Undoubtedly, layoffs—especially in more liberal labor markets, which as a rule offer few job protections to employees—push some individuals out of journalism. However, many individuals leave the profession without being fired, via so-called voluntary exits. Moreover, some journalists that are made redundant seek to remain in the profession by applying to other jobs or embarking on a freelance career.[6] Making sense of journalists' exits, especially in comparative perspective, thus requires capturing the broader array of individuals who leave journalism.

Research that begins with individuals who have left the profession takes up exactly this task.[7] By including both those who are fired and those who depart "voluntarily," this approach captures "the full and nuanced spectrum of journalistic exit."[8] In doing so, this scholarship highlights a number of factors that influence decisions to exit. Most commonly, these include poor working conditions, difficulty balancing work with one's personal life, and a sense that opportunities for better remuneration and conditions exist outside of journalism. While these factors certainly explain the samples to which they correspond, they are also shared by a great many journalists who do *not* depart from the profession.[9] Indeed, if these factors were the unique reasons for leaving journalism, it seems reasonable to suspect that very few journalists would remain. Thus, making sense of exits also requires an explanation of when those factors turn into a departure from the profession.

Rather than conceive of dissatisfaction as a causal reason for exit per se, it can be conceptualized as a factor leading individuals to question whether the profession is worthy of their investments. Because journalism is sustained in important ways by the presence of individuals willing to make sacrifices, "disillusionment"—as Daniel Nölleke, Phoebe Maares, and Folker Hanusch term it[10]—is a crucial precondition for professional exit.[11] While questioning one's relation to journalism does not inevitably lead to departure, it does afford insight into the nature of that disillusionment, and whether it takes the form of disbelief in the profession itself or instead in one's relationship to the profession. Moreover, at least in the cities of Toulouse and Seattle, there is no case in which a period of questioning one's relation to the profession does not precede departure from it. This chapter therefore follows the work of Henrik Örnebring and Cecilia Möller, who note that for many former journalists the "main question was not *if* one should leave the profession, but *when*."[12]

The literature on exits from journalism is rife with references to events or situations that precipitate departures. Fights with management or colleagues constitute the "last straw" that makes things untenable; a job opportunity in another sector is "too good to pass up"; a personal transformation makes working in the news less attractive. Drawing on Denave, these occurrences can be conceptualized as "trigger events."[13] Such events are moments of rupture; they constitute the "when" of journalists' exits. Importantly, it is not the inherent features or qualities of these events that lead to exits, as not every fight or job offer leads to a departure. Instead, it is their interaction in particular contexts that makes them the "final straw" of a longer series of frustrations, disappointments, or personal transformations. Therefore, trigger events make sense only in light of prior individual experiences of dissatisfaction. In relation to journalists, the concept usefully draws attention to the context in which an exit occurs without attributing to it any direct causal efficacy.

Trigger events are also useful conceptual tools for dating the decision to exit from journalism and, along with it, the tensions an individual previously sought to manage. Through such events, it thus becomes possible to see when constraints that were previously imposed or negotiated—long hours, unpleasant work relationships—suddenly dissipate. This can be seen in individuals who describe themselves as having struggled for long periods of time, only to declare a sense of "freedom" or "opportunity" upon leaving journalism. Crucially, this new sense of possibility belongs not just to those who depart for more attractive jobs elsewhere; they are also evident in many of those who are fired or whose contracts are not renewed, but who nevertheless report "a new window" opening as a result of their reconfigured circumstances. While such statements may stem from an effort to subjectively make the best of objectively unattractive circumstances, they also provide evidence of the removal of constraints that attend a trigger event. Bringing these points together, the concept thus enables the identification and empirical description of a key, and often missing, part of the mechanism that undergirds the process of professional exit.

ORGANIZING EXITS, RESOCIALIZING PROFESSIONAL IDENTITIES

With the decision to depart from journalism taken, exits must then be organized. Empirically, these vary in a host of ways: some pursue and attain jobs that provide a sense of meaning and purpose; others end up in positions they perceive as mere work that provides them with their material sustenance; still others leave the workforce entirely. If these differences reflect the particularities and idiosyncrasies of individual lives, they no doubt also owe a debt to the social properties that make different types of exits possible. The expectation of a job that has meaning and purpose; the willingness to accept a "mere" job; even the decision to leave the workforce so as to better tend to one's family or personal duties—each of these reflects both the socially cultivated dispositions and social determinants that make some exits appear more plausible to some combinations of social properties than others.

Many of these social properties and social determinants that are decisive in the organization of journalists' exits mirror those described in previous chapters. Social origins, educational background, and professional status all shape different orientations to and expectations of work. It is thus not surprising, but nonetheless analytically important, that professionally successful journalists coordinate their departures using social networks that provide different professional opportunities than their less esteemed counterparts. And the labor regulations and social welfare programs that make possible different possibilities for negotiating one's career as a journalist likewise condition cross-nationally distinctive manners of managing one's exit. The presence of regulations constitutes a resource that can be utilized while preparing for the "next step" after journalism, while the relative strength of social welfare programs can make basic considerations like salary more or less important.

One social property, however, takes on a particular importance in exploring the organization of journalists' exits: gender. Scholars have long shown that a gendered division of labor persists in part through the different social expectations placed on and assumed by women and men.[14] While women are less excluded from newsrooms on the explicit basis of gender than in the past, their participation in the workforce does not proceed along strictly equal grounds with their male counterparts. Whereas men continue, for better or worse, to be expected to prioritize work, both as a source of meaning and as a way of providing for their families, women tend to face a strong expectation that they find a way to balance their work and family demands. This is especially true of mothers, who form an important number of the individuals who leave journalism in the sample presented here. To be sure, these tendencies in no way exclude alternative arrangements. Some men stay home while women work and some people never have children, thus reducing, if not eliminating, concerns about a family-work balance. But the general empirical pattern suggests that family considerations weigh more heavily on women than men, and that this leads to gender-based variation in the organization of one's professional life after journalism.

These social properties also shape the ways that identities get resocialized. As Jean-Baptiste Legavre notes, journalists who leave the profession, in addition to securing a new identity (PR professional, mother, etc.), need to resocialize their prior one.[15] This resocialization can be more or less difficult, with some former journalists securing work that allows for the reintegration of aspects of that identity they still cherish (e.g., a sense of working for the public good, using technology to develop innovative forms of storytelling), while others distance themselves from aspects of that identity that are difficult to reconcile with their current jobs (e.g., the deemphasis on challenging power that is found among some who go on to work in corporate public relations). Still others might simply draw a rupture between their past as a journalist and whatever work they engage in at the present. In whatever form these resocializations take, they also shed light on the extent to which belief in the profession's utility and purpose is retained, even among those who have left journalism.

BELIEFS IN QUESTION

Among those who leave journalism, nearly all described periods prior to their departures in which they increasingly called into question their relationship to the profession. For some, this questioning arose as a result of increased knowledge of the field and their relationship to it, which attenuated the material and symbolic rewards that they could anticipate attaining. A journalist in Seattle, for example, related her experiences at several publications, each of which successively shaped her understanding of the limited and in her view unappealing career paths available to her. An online publication where she worked had been downsized substantially and prioritized "sexy headlines at the expense of us telling stories."[16] A subsequent job at a daily newspaper entailed difficult hours ("shift scheduling," which required her to work either early mornings or late evenings) and low pay. She could write "little news briefs" only if "the shift was slow." After failing to land a promising job at a radio station, she knew that her options were limited. "The media market in Seattle is pretty small . . . and I didn't want to move [outside the city] for a new job." Without knowing what to do next, she described a "reckoning" in which she was slowly forced to acknowledge to herself, "Maybe I don't want to do this anymore. Maybe I'm tired of this."

A journalist in Toulouse described a highly similar period of questioning. When she first arrived in Toulouse, she dreamed of working at another station in the city that had "great journalists" with great working conditions.[17] But that station had gone bankrupt and her employer was one of the few remaining outlets in town. She knew that if she wanted to advance professionally, she would have to move to Paris. "If you want to present a good program, if you want to write a good column, ... you have to move. You have to go to Paris in fact." But she preferred to remain in Toulouse for personal reasons, as that is where her partner and children were located. During her first interview for this project, which was conducted years prior, she acknowledged that her options were either doing "low end journalism" at her current employer, or leaving the profession entirely. The situation, she admitted then, was "not very optimistic" and she had no illusion that things would improve. She questioned her relationship to the profession and openly speculated that the returns she gained might become unaccepted (e.g., asking whether she could be satisfied doing "low-end journalism" for her "whole life"). Nonetheless, she saw herself as having a clear understanding of what was—and was not—possible for her professionally.

Others talked about transformations in the profession, particularly those driven by commercial concerns, that raised questions about their individual place in it. A Seattle journalist in a high-level management position could see that the daily newspaper where he worked was, financially, "on life support" and had been for well over a decade. Layoffs were necessary for the organization's survival, and he did not question their necessity, but he hated doing them. "It's horrible. You don't go to [journalism] school to learn how to do that."[18] One particularly "soul-sucking" instance came when he had to lay off someone "to save seventy or eighty thousand dollars" in the newsroom budget. This was, in his experience, "the first person we ever laid off that didn't do anything wrong. All the others that were part of the reduction, they had flaws in their game. He didn't. He cared deeply. He did really good work." Moments like this exacted a personal toll, and also made him question whether he could remain in journalism when it existed in this form. "For the first time ever, I was having anxiety . . . I started taking medicine for anxiety. It wasn't good." He realized: "I couldn't keep doing this forever."

Similarly, a Toulouse-based journalist described how he began "to resent the pressure from the web, social media, [and] Chartbeat" that he experienced in his work.[19] Reporters and editors in his organization increasingly were asked to focus on "what makes the buzz" and captures audience attention, regardless of a story's journalistic merit. "It annoys me. It pleases me less and less," he explained. When asked what specifically annoyed him, his emphasis lay entirely on commercial transformations in the profession that he viewed as reducing or trivializing its social functions. Describing the endless efforts to pursue audiences at whatever cost, he remarked: "that's not journalism. Not in my mind." A counterpart in Seattle expressed comparable concerns. Not only was she increasingly finding herself asked "to tweet every hour," she was also asked to do Facebook live events with very little on-the-ground reporting. "It was like, okay, do you guys want me to go with a photographer and actually interview people . . . or . . . [shrugs]. . . . That [kind of work] saddened me."[20] Still another described frustration with feeling like she simply could not do good journalism as an MMJ, where she had too little time to ever put together a story. "Every day, almost always, I felt like I had shortchanged the viewer on what was really going on because I barely understood what I was talking about; sometimes I really didn't [know]."[21] For these and similar journalists, the profession had "changed" and the work they did no longer corresponded to the work they hoped to do as journalists.

Finally, some described investments in other activities that reshuffled their priorities and led to a corresponding disinvestment in their professional activities. For many, these investments were linked to family life. One female journalist described how having young children made her less willing to work longer hours. "Once you start having kids, it starts becoming more important to not miss my son's soccer games."[22] Another, also female, journalist said that while she would have liked to remain in journalism, it came to seem less and less feasible as she started a family; her knowledge of the state of employment, and her chances for it, made this issue very clear in her mind. "Having become a parent," she had to start thinking about "what kind of job could offer some financial and employment stability in the coming decade. And it definitely didn't look like a journalism job in Seattle."[23] Still another described a desire to be closer to family, especially aging parents that lived hours away from her newsroom job. Moving back to San Francisco was "always the end goal" even if commercial transformations in the profession helped accelerate her timeline more than anticipated.[24]

Others made investments in hobbies that had grown over time. One person, for example, told us that she and her husband had begun a small winery, which had grown over time and increasingly occupied their waking hours. "It just kind of started as a hobby and then it grew, and grew, and grew, and grew."[25] As the winery grew, coordinating her professional work with it became "trickier and trickier." While starting a business was unusual among the journalists interviewed, all those who invested in other activities described a growing disinvestment in their journalistic careers. Another talked about renovating an Airstream with her partner to jumpstart their dream of living in the countryside. Increasingly, they spent more and more time together talking about buying property or land, and "maybe build[ing] a homestead."[26]

Whatever forms their questioning took, journalists in Toulouse and Seattle almost never questioned the profession of journalism itself. For them, the profession remained worthy; it was the economic and, to a lesser degree, social context in which it existed that had become untenable and led them to question their commitments. Thus, a television journalist in Seattle explained that she entered journalism "to tell a story and tell it impartially."[27] With increasing frequency, though, "I would be doing a live shot and somebody would scream, 'Fake News!' at me. And I was reporting on the weather!" She felt like fewer and fewer people cared about a "fair and balanced" approach to news, which was exactly the understanding of the profession she believed so strongly in. Others described getting run down doing stories that "required no complex thinking."[28] While there was "nothing wrong" with covering stories like a pizza shop's decision to discontinue the use of plastic bottles, it was "not the highest use of my brain space." These types of assignments led her to worry progressively about "how many of those can you do before you're like—is this why I got into it [journalism]?" Before any of these journalists ever left the profession, they felt in many ways as if the profession had already abandoned them.

TRIGGERING EVENTS

The diminution of belief does not, on its own, lead to an exit. It is when that diminished belief is coupled with a "triggering event" that individuals leave journalism.[29] For some, these events are more or less predictable points that allow individuals to reflect on their professional status. Several journalists, for example, described points at which their contracts had expired as triggers for their departure from journalism. A journalist in Seattle told us about "the very, very difficult decision" she made to not renew her contract.[30] Her manager had tried to create a "work-life balance" for her. As the mother of two young children, she didn't have to work early mornings or late evenings. Still, her job kept her away from important events in her children's lives, and she didn't want to keep missing them. "The news director created a job for me, worked with my schedule, and did everything." But "after three years, it was still at this point where it was just too much for my work-life balance." Another journalist's contract was not renewed, which was a "gut punch" because "I'd always had my contract renewed."[31] But it also forced her to acknowledge that comparable jobs at other news stations were scarce, and that she might have to exit. Suddenly, she recalls asking herself: "What do I want to do? Do I want to continue doing this?" Looking back, she now sees that as a moment that enabled her to pursue new professional vistas. "I know it's so cliché, but when one door closes another one opens."

Others were less sanguine. A journalist in Toulouse explained that he had to leave journalism once his freelancing contracts had dried up. "It took me a long time to leave journalism," he said.[32] For years, he struggled to get items placed with news agencies. More recently, though, it had become nearly impossible to find a buyer for his work. As a bachelor, he had always felt all right getting by on very little money; he only had to support himself. However, with the contracts drying up, he no longer had a way to even pay his monthly rent. It was at that moment, he explained, that he realized that he needed to make a change.

Some journalists whose contracts ended knew they could still get work but realized that the rewards were no longer worth their efforts. "I would have wanted to stay in journalism if there had been positions that paid well enough. . . . But those positions are few and far between."[33] Most news organizations were "contracting, not expanding." And the jobs that were opening up were, "to be frank, more appropriate for recent graduates with entry level or pay somewhere around forty thousand dollars a year." While this journalist could get those jobs, she couldn't accept the low pay. One organization did offer a job with higher pay as an editor; however, the newsroom was in the midst of a massive downsizing and "they were looking for someone that could manage that process." She had no interest in being the person who oversaw that effort. Online news sites, for their part, had opportunities. But they have "no security attached to them at all." If a "good opportunity" had "come my way, I absolutely would have taken it." However, "I also did not have any illusions that [it] was going to happen."

Others described professional conflicts that precipitated their departure. A former Toulouse-based journalist said prior to leaving he had taken a new position at the daily newspaper at which he had long worked. For the new job, which initially seemed to be a substantial promotion, he needed to live outside the city. To make sure he could return on the weekends to see his family, he negotiated a supplemental payment and a company car. The additional wages, however, never appeared in his checks. When he inquired with management, he was told that the supplemental payment could only be used for journalists who worked and lived in Toulouse. He was already unhappy working outside the city in which he lived, and he did not particularly like his new colleagues or the journalism they were doing. "If those are the conditions," he said to his boss, "I'm going back to Toulouse."[34] The company, however, did not have any position for him in Toulouse. What's more, because his company offered the best salaries of any media company in Toulouse, he knew that he could not hope to replicate his standard of living at another news organization.

A former Seattle journalist talked about a conflict that led to her departure from journalism. For years, she had dreamed of living in the countryside. She hated city traffic and living in a "tiny little place crammed in between other people's tiny little places."[35] She went to her bosses with a proposal. What if they reclassified her job in a way that would allow her to work from the countryside? It would give her more time to do better work on some of the environmental issues she was already covering; what's more, as a multimedia journalist (MMJ), she already produced everything on her own, so there would be no impact on photographers and cameramen at the company. She was happy to test the arrangement in a "trial run" of three months, after which the station could reassess whether it was working. Management rejected her proposal outright: "they thought it was just a crazy proposition" because television stations at the time were "still very focused on the money-making schema of broadcast" and therefore not investing much money into digital. Already frustrated by the intense production schedule associated with being an MMJ, she knew that she could not stay in her job. And because her job was at one of the main stations in town, she also knew she could not get a better or comparable position elsewhere. She knew the situation "was not going to change" for the better. "It was like, it's just time [to leave]."

Others talked about external opportunities that triggered their departure from journalism. The journalist working in management at the daily newspaper, described earlier, had thought about leaving the profession for several years due to the personal toll it was taking on him. His "decent" salary, however, made it difficult to find a personally acceptable job in Seattle. One day, he received a call from the CEO of a public service utility, who years earlier had worked on the business side of the daily newspaper. His organization had an opening for an editor of publishing operations. Did he know anyone who might be interested in the job? "I might be interested," he said.[36] The pay was good; the benefits, "amazing." And rather than fire people, he would also get a sizable budget to hire people and give them annual bonuses. He loved everything about the prospective job, and he also recognized that the timing was "perfect." He probably would not have taken the position earlier in his career, or if his news organization were operating under better economic conditions. "It was a chance for me to do something in normal hours and to have a life, essentially."

Those not working in management positions also described external opportunities, which followed lengthy periods of dissatisfaction and served to trigger their departures. A French radio journalist "hated" the environment in her newsroom. People didn't help one another and it felt like a "factory."[37] She was presented by a former colleague with the opportunity to do a podcast for a local company; initially, she did it on her own time and this allowed her to make some extra money on the side. After a while, though, she began to realize that she could make podcasting her full-time job. She could make more money and "be my own boss." Because her children were older, she could also justify working on nights and weekends occasionally. She loved podcasting from the first, but also realized that she could not have taken the job when her kids were younger. At that point, she really needed the fixed schedule that the radio station—however unsatisfying she found it professionally—afforded her.

Finally, some described nonprofessional events as triggers for their departure. A former print reporter said that he was "very sad to leave" the profession; however, the city had become "really expensive really fast, I needed to make some more money."[38] He and his partner had, in recent years, had two children and bought a house. "I had responsibilities and I couldn't stay there. To make that much money, I needed to go somewhere else." Another wanted to return to her hometown to take care of and live near an aging parent. No journalism jobs were available to her in that area, however; she had been "shuffling along" in journalism for several years.[39] Her decision to return home helped to usher her out of a profession that she felt she had been holding on to for too long. Still another described his personal experience with cancer, which exacted a physical toll and made it difficult for him to do his job as a photographer and cameraman. "Physically, I just couldn't do the job" anymore. "Your camera weighs twenty-five pounds; your tripod weighs twenty-five pounds." What's more, he could see that "I didn't want to be doing this when I was fifty."[40] Without knowing exactly what he would do next, he left his job at the television station where he had worked for years.

VARIETIES OF EXITS

A Sense of Choice

"I wanted to do something different," one former American journalist who left his job as a top newsroom manager said, "but I wanted to be sure it had meaning and value."[41] This emphasis on finding the "right" job was common among professionally successful journalists, especially those who held management positions in newsrooms. They wanted to find work "with purpose" and to feel as if the skills they had developed in journalism were not being wasted. For this reason, they generally rejected the idea of taking jobs doing work that seemed antithetical to this identity: almost none of these people took jobs in sales or advertising. Much more commonly, they took communication jobs for industries or organizations (e.g., nonprofits, civically oriented startups, social enterprise businesses) whose missions generally aligned with their own worldviews (i.e., socially liberal, often prioritizing social purpose over economic profit).

The newsroom manager who left to take an editorial position for a public utility illustrates these themes nicely. Undoubtedly, the work appealed for material reasons, with a nice salary and benefits package, and reasonable hours that would allow him to spend more time with family. But his attraction to the job was also shaped in important ways by the extent to which it allowed him to convert his journalistic identity in this new space. The utility, which publishes monthly magazines for consumers, reminded him of "a newsroom from the nineties"—he made the analogy multiple times throughout the interview—where "everyone is fat and happy but nothing ever changes." He saw himself as being able to lead his colleagues through a transition ("to innovate in an industry that is traditional and conservative") by "breaking down silos" and finding new ways "to serve" their audiences. Having done a lot of prior work getting foundations to support regional journalism, he also saw opportunities to partner with foundations to provide coverage on issues of mutual interest.

Even better, he conceives of all this work as fundamentally connected to the values that underpinned his work as a journalist. He sees the utility as a "community representative." The issues it touches on are a "public service." Because they are flush with resources, he can send his staff to cover events directly; in fact, he sent someone to report on the implications of a hurricane to utilities shortly after he took up the job. Doing this type of work is "important to me. I need that sense of service." There may be topics and issues that are outside his purview; he knows that he can't investigate utilities themselves. However, this is not a problem, partly because the utilities are not motivated by profit and thus strike him as less problematic than for-profit corporations. He thinks of himself as a "recovered journalist" but several times in the interview called the work he does "just a different kind of journalism"—still, in its core values and orientation, journalism. "We're serving the greater good," he says, noting too that since he took the job the magazine has also become an industry leader, recognized for excellence with multiple awards.

For this former journalist, the transition away from the newsroom is surprisingly painless. Initially, he admits, he had "survivor's guilt" that stemmed from being able to leave journalism so easily for a job that offered great satisfaction. "Everyone thinks that when you leave [journalism], you do something that you don't feel good about, but you just do it because you need a change." For years, as he half-seriously contemplated making a change from his newspaper job, he thought that would indeed be his experience. "Doing communications for somebody and not really loving it," in his words. But that, emphatically, was not what happened for him. "I'm having the time of my life."

While the extent of his enthusiasm was atypical, the themes he sounded resonated with the experiences of other professionally successful journalists, especially men. A former journalist in Toulouse left his comfortable position at the daily newspaper. He knew he was fortunate to hold that job—he had the coveted permanent contract—but felt himself to be "restless" professionally.[42] For a while, he had talked with a few of his colleagues about doing something "new" and "different." When the Nuit Debout protests began in 2016, he became an active participant, and through them found a way to express some of his dissatisfaction with the state of politics in the country. After that experience, he knew that he couldn't simply return to the newsroom. Because of his contract, he could negotiate his departure from the newspaper on favorable terms, receiving approximately one year of his salary as his severance package. With two colleagues, he began an enterprise that teaches communication skills (e.g., how to make a podcast, write a newsletter, publish a blog). Together, they earn slightly less than they did as journalists. "We are not yet at the point [of income] where we left" but he's happy. At any rate, he explains, his departure was not principally motivated by money. Rather, he wanted to do work that aligned with his political beliefs, and also be more relaxed, to have his weekends to himself and not be always on his phone for work reasons.

For many of the professionally successful women who leave, their decision often revolves around a feeling they are "missing" or "not doing enough" in their roles as mothers and wives. They organize their exits with the primary aim of being "better" parents and partners in mind. Some leave the workforce entirely; others find jobs that are more amenable to an improved balance between their professional and personal lives. Because of their success, most feel like they can return to journalism in the future should they desire; however, many question whether the overall balance of rewards could ever be personally acceptable to them. Their choice, then, is one in which they prioritize their nonprofessional identities over their professional ones.

The television journalist who decided not to renew her contract because of the difficulties she experienced trying to balance her work and professional lives provides a useful illustration of these themes. The profession had changed and television in particular had become more personality-driven. While this was frustrating for her, she nonetheless had a good position and management was willing to work with her to address her work-life balance concerns. For her, though, the breaking point was simply that she "wanted to be there for my kids."[43] She had put her children in daycare and hired nannies. While these measures worked as temporary solutions, they never felt satisfactory. At the end of the day, she often felt like she was not being the mother that she wanted and expected herself to be. "I was just thinking that at one point or another, I needed to make that break and figure out what I wanted to do with my family."

This decision was "very, very difficult" for her to make. She loved being a journalist. She still has "regular sort of sob sessions with my friends who have left journalism." Among them, she considers herself "probably the only one who still misses it wholeheartedly." While she still thinks of herself in professional terms first and foremost as a journalist, she does not question her decision to put family first at this point in her life. She can work jobs that provide more manageable hours and flexible schedules. And while "it doesn't feel like the right time to go back," she strongly believes that she could get a job in journalism again should she want to. "I've always done everything I can to maintain very strong ethics and beliefs, and very good relationships with everyone I've worked with." So, "if I decided after stepping back and kind of getting out of the pool, if I wanted to get back, that would be an option."

Not all professionally successful women felt their new work to be so distinct from journalism, and several in fact found ways to convert their identities into new jobs. A former reporter, for example, left the industry because she needed to make more money and have job stability that would support her family financially while allowing her to be more present with her children. She had offers for other journalism jobs; they just were no longer acceptable to her as a mother with children. Initially she had some trepidation looking at communication jobs. Such jobs paid more money, to be sure; however, she had this idea that "I would have to apply my media skills and knowledge to something that I felt kind of ambivalent about. . . . I was afraid it would feel sleazy. Or just disappointing."[44] Happily, she secured a job doing communication strategy for a

Leaving Journalism 159

Muslim organization that fights Islamophobia. She "liked the idea of being able to use some of those journalism tools and some of this media experience and really use it" to promote social justice. And to "help train a community to use those tools that unfortunately are often kind of turned against them [so that they can] empower themselves."

The orientation to family was especially prominent among recent mothers. However, well-established female journalists also described their professional departures strongly in terms of not only professional but also family considerations. A journalist in Toulouse, for example, was editor at a magazine that shut down for business reasons. This was extremely disappointing for her, as she really enjoyed the work she did at the magazine. Because of her recognizability among other journalists, though, she had little trouble finding a job at another news outlet in the city. The problem for her, though, was that the new job was uninteresting; she could think of nothing that she had done in it for the past year that she was particularly proud of. She was already approaching the retirement age; having a contract meant that she could negotiate a severance that would allow her to retire early. This would allow her to move from the city and to her family home on the coast. Being there would make it easier for her kids to visit her more regularly than they otherwise would.

Family considerations were not absent from the rationales that professionally successful men invoked. Several talked about wanting to have "more time" to spend with their families, especially in the evening and on the weekends, which were often occupied by professional commitments when they worked as journalists. More often, though, family issues arose when discussing salary needs, with many describing the need to ensure that the salary of their new job could provide for their family. None, however, ever described leaving as being motivated primarily for family reasons. Instead, their efforts focused first and foremost on trying to find new professional opportunities that would allow them to retain their sense of identity built through their careers as successful journalists.

Permanent contracts, embedded as they are in French labor laws, function as resources that can be utilized in organizing an exit. All professionally successful journalists in Toulouse held such contracts; therefore, they all used them to negotiate severance packages that afforded them the space to do work that appealed to them, often by more closely approximating the things they liked most about journalism. Their American counterparts could turn to no similar resource. In contrast to their French colleagues, they often described higher salaries as one of the reasons for leaving. "I wanted more money," said one person, "and I felt like I was worth it."[45] His statement was unusual in its frankness, but others described similar considerations regarding salary in managing their exits (e.g., not leaving until they could find a job that would pay them sufficiently). Professionally successful French journalists invoked money less frequently and generally accorded it less weight, instead describing themselves as motivated principally by a desire to be in control of their work lives.

A Sense of Necessity

For others, the search for life and work after journalism could hardly be more different. Those who sought jobs tended to find the experience to be protracted and labored. Those who left the workforce sought an arrangement that would keep the family going, not allow them to be "better mothers" per se. Nearly all struggled to translate the skills they had into something that could be useful in a nonjournalism environment. What they liked most about their professional identity as journalists was often less central, and sometimes irrelevant, for these new positions. Their difficulties in finding work shaped an orientation to the job search that emphasized finding *a* job rather than some perfect match. The principled rejection of jobs in advertising or marketing that characterized more professionally successful men is absent among these job seekers. For many, journalism has become part of their past, something that they still cherish and in certain ways miss, but that to them largely feels distant from the skills used for their current jobs.

The photographer and cameraman whose experience with cancer reorganized his priorities touches upon several of these themes. After leaving his job, he stayed at home with his two young kids for a year while his wife worked. Initially, he was "excited to quit."[46] Quickly, though, not having a job "really fucked with my sense of purpose. Whatever you do, it's tied to your self-image." While he loved his kids, "being a stay-at-home dad was not my thing." Not only was taking care of the children harder than he thought it would be; it also made him feel like he was not doing anything productive with his life. Whenever he would meet someone socially and they would ask him what his job was, he would feel a sense of shame when giving his response.

After a year at home, he set out to find a job. The task was not easy. His health made it infeasible and undesirable to get a job doing camerawork for a nonnews organization. Therefore, he sent applications for "anything in general communications, media relations, or PR because I thought I could relate my previous career experience to it." As a photographer and cameraman on a television crew, he not only handled the visual aspects of a shoot; he was also in charge of the logistics, planning, and production of all stories. While in principle this seemed like it could be really valuable to prospective employers, in practice he had a very difficult time convincing anyone to take his application seriously. Most hiring committees asked him the same question: Did he have any experience in public relations? The answer was always no.

Compounding the problem were the difficulties he encountered in the job interviews required for these types of positions. Television photographers and cameramen "don't really interview" for jobs. Instead, they have tapes that highlight their previous work, and references that speak to their ability to work well with others. He had never sat for a long, formal interview, and never had to take a two-hour writing exam "where you write a press release and a blog post on some complicated subject." His self-assessment of those performances was withering. "I was so bad. There were so many jobs where they probably would have loved to hire me until I opened my mouth and sounded like an idiot." Even the formality of the interview—"wearing a tie for the first time, sitting across from three people holding clipboards"—was a struggle. "It was terrible."

Eventually, he landed an entry-level job at the local transit agency doing "real time communications." If there was a car accident, he would send out an alert for riders to seek alternative routes. Even getting that job was difficult. "My interview was so bad I can't believe they hired me." The work itself was not exciting, and he did not feel like he used many of the skills that were so important in his journalism career. What's more, he missed the fun and excitement of working on a television crew. "Racing to the scene, shooting the shit with the other news crews"; he loved the camaraderie of television news and also its everyday social dimensions: "going with everyone to whatever the best sandwich place was" in the town they were visiting on a given day. But his current job is a job, and one that he can take a measure of pride in. "Public transit is something everyone can relate to. Everyone has a story about [their experiences with it]."

A longtime freelance journalist in Toulouse adopted a similar orientation to finding "any" job. As financial problems arose for him, he began to search online for a job that would bring him enough money to pay his rent. An advertisement for a headhunter position was attractive primarily because it offered an advance on his salary, thus providing him with the money necessary to cover his expenses. At that point, he explained, he was in such dire straits that he was looking only for a solution to "keep my head above water."[47] The headhunting position provided him with an initial solution to his problem. Some of his professional skills as a journalist were attractive to the employer: he was good at interviewing people, which was useful to a firm looking to recruit potential employees. He also knew "everyone" in the city because of his journalistic activities. But on a daily basis, the position felt very distant from his professional identity as a journalist.

A subsequent job formally prohibited him from engaging in any journalistic activities. While the headhunter position was a solution, he knew it could only be temporary. At a social event, he saw the former director of a local university. Engaging him in conversation, he admitted that things were terrible (*Je suis dans la merde*). The director told him about a new opening for a communication person at his university that he would be "perfect" for. The contract he received formally prohibits him from doing any published journalism under his own name. While the salary solved his economic problems, it also banished his professional identity. He found this disappointing, but also promised himself that he would "find a way" to continue doing some of the work that appealed most to him about journalism. Perhaps, he said, he could do long-form storytelling as a documentarian, which is not formally prohibited in his contract.

Many women described a similar sense of "necessity" shaping their search for work after journalism. A television journalist in Seattle whose contract was not renewed started immediately applying to a range of corporate communication jobs because those seemed to be the "best fit" for someone with her skills. While she was a finalist for one job, she did not ultimately land the position. The whole job search process was "like a rollercoaster," where she would get excited about the possibility of getting a job that would allow her to keep using some of her journalism skills, only to be let down when she did not score these positions. At some point, she recalled thinking to herself, "My gosh, am I ever going to get anything? Because you're just waiting and hoping someone's going to email you back."

Seeking advice from friends and former colleagues who had left journalism, she talked with someone who had ended up working in pharmaceutical sales. While the substance of the work was quite different from journalism, her friend explained, it was appealing to her because "you get paid for your performance and you can dictate your own schedule."[48] The woman understood what her friend found appealing; she found it attractive too. As the mother of two small children, she liked the idea of better pay and having a flexible schedule, even if she had never really thought of a sales position as a job option. That would afford her both the resources needed to help provide for her children while also ensuring that she actually had time to spend with them. A few days before the interview, a client found out she was a former journalist and asked her whether she might go back someday. She doesn't think so, she said. Right now, "I am truly my own boss. I dictate my own schedule and I'm able to tailor it to be able to accommodate getting my work done but also bring my kids to soccer."

This orientation to finding a job that would allow the family to keep going was common among these journalists in both cities. The mother of two children worked on children's projects for a local magazine. The job was unattractive and initially she thought she could reboot her career by doing some freelance work on journalism that interested her. That did not work out, though, both because it took too much time to do that work and because it delivered too little in terms of monetary rewards. She began doing some part-time work instead as a press attaché for a government agency. Her rationale for taking up this work was very explicit. She took this work "because we have to live" and the money it provided would help her do that. When she eventually left journalism, she took a full-time job doing exactly this work.

Those who are not in long-term relationships or mothers took a roughly similar approach to finding "any job" that would help pay the bills. For those who had lesser family responsibilities, though, they tended to stress some ways in which they could convert their professional identity into something meaningful. A former journalist in Seattle, for example, "really wanted" to go into the nonprofit sector because the "mission of the nonprofit sector seemed better aligned" with the "public service mission" and ideals of journalism.[49] However, this orientation to the nonprofit world, she admitted, was very broad. She did not have any specific thematic focus that she felt predisposed to, and she felt like she could have been happy in many different sectors of the nonprofit world.

Cross-nationally, the experiences of these journalists are highly similar. This stems primarily from the fact that labor regulations in France tend to protect incumbents, which favors those holding higher positions in the field. Those in lower or less-established positions, by contrast, cannot negotiate their exits with employers; as the case of the freelancer implies, many have no formal or sole employer at all. As a result, former journalists in both countries describe themselves as relying on their abilities and social connections to get their jobs. This was discussed less as a point of pride and more as a forced necessity. They had to get better at doing interviews, especially if they were "just terrible" in their early experiences. They could not afford, sometimes literally, the luxury of seeking out a job with "purpose" or meaning.

Which is not to say that the jobs these former journalists found were meaningless. In their search for alimentary work, these journalists often described meaning in the fact of having a job, regardless of its specific tasks and purpose. This was very clearly the case in the photographer who loves his children but hated being a full-time stay-at-home father. But it was also more broadly true among individuals whose skills in journalism had been devalued, and who thus often had to let go of the aspects of their professional identity that they valued the most. They could work in communication jobs or in public relations, and feel skilled and sometimes even good about being the best writer on the staff, or about having a more refined sense of how to pitch stories to their former colleagues. Generally, though, they experienced these professional transitions painfully, and often with a sense of regret or nostalgia for a world in which their skills retained both meaning for them and value for their employers.

RECONSIDERING THE CRISIS IN JOURNALISM

In one sense, leaving journalism is the most egalitarian event in journalists' careers. From the top editor at a daily newspaper to the most precariously employed freelancer, anyone can leave. The mechanisms leading to their exits, moreover, are also broadly similar, with a period of questioning one's relationship to the profession followed by a trigger event that pushes them out of the field. If these mechanisms can induce painful periods of self-doubt and questioning, they are also experienced by most as an opportunity of some sort: to find work that affords better conditions, to reimagine what sort of professional identity they value, to reconsider the overall relationship between their work and personal life. This reflects not only an effort to make a virtue of the difficult relationship they maintain to journalism; it also highlights professional transitions as new beginnings in one's life.

While anyone can leave journalism, the forms these exits take underscore the very unequal types of new beginnings available to former journalists. This inequality is rooted in very deeply internalized social expectations regarding, among other things, the gendered division of labor in society. The tendency of men to prioritize work and women to emphasize family considerations reflects and enacts this broader division. While these priorities appear as the product of individual choice, their very gendered patterning points to the ways in which inequalities are reproduced through such choices. The fact that they can be perceived as merely individual preferences, moreover, is one of the ways in which those inequalities can be made so durable, even if the form those inequalities take changes over time (e.g., from direct exclusion from the workforce on the basis of gender to unequal opportunities to pursue careers in relation to one's personal life).

These gendered divisions in the organization of exits interact with other social properties, which make the resocialization of the professional identity more or less difficult as a result. Professionally successful men, typically coming from higher social origins and more prestigious education, can thus rely on social networks to help find meaningful jobs, while their more devalued male counterparts find themselves searching for any job that will cover their material sustenance. Women, for their part, are divided in terms of the extent to which their shared orientation toward family is shaded by an effort to "be better" in their personal lives (common among the professionally successful) or an attempt to find a work-life solution that will merely keep the family going. The extent to which these departures are experienced as painful struggles stems in part from these differences in social properties. This should not be taken to imply that departures for the professionally successful are somehow friction-free; it should, however, serve as a reminder that the individually held and deeply felt experiences of these transitions are in important ways socially generated, in ways that reflect very different conditions of possibility.

France and the United States provide distinctive national contexts that enable and constrain distinctive modes for managing a professional exit. Rather than offer an essentialized culturalist trope about a less-market-oriented French worker and a more economically motivated American counterpart, these differences can be attributed in large part to labor regulations and social welfare systems that make these orientations more or less salient. At the same time, it is worth noting that labor regulations and welfare nets do not protect all workers equally. In both countries, those holding the most precarious jobs tend also to be afforded the fewest resources with which to negotiate their exits. Thus, if French workers holding the coveted permanent contract can use those contracts to create a favorable severance package for themselves, their counterparts with temporary contracts or doing freelance work have no similar resource. The comparative impulse to highlight national differences can thus profit from asking for whom those national differences are most available.

These exits, by their sheer number and the diversity of individuals involved in them, inevitably raise questions about the nature of the crisis in contemporary journalism. It would be Pollyannaish to claim that all is well in the profession, given the high levels of attrition that seem to occur among journalists. Over-time data on these figures are hard to come by; whether journalists leave in greater numbers or sooner in their careers than they once did is not a settled question.[50] But if one considers the fact that, on the one hand, journalism schools continue to churn out graduates at rates not entirely dissimilar from the past while, on the other hand, the profession's employment continues to shrink, it seems reasonable to surmise a genuine crisis of retention and a potentially looming crisis of recruitment. This is not a minor issue, given that the institution of journalism requires the existence of journalists who are willing to struggle within it for an acceptable balance of material and economic rewards.

It may well be that a crisis of recruitment leads to a deeper crisis, one characterized by the diminution of belief in journalism itself. Some of the conditions for such an occurrence can be discerned in the present. Journalists find their work often ignored by the very audiences they claim to serve. Moreover, their efforts to inform audiences are often encountered by readers, viewers, and listeners unmoved by facts or dispassionate analysis. If at least some journalists were to leave the profession because of these developments—out of a sense that the very idea of contemporary journalism was no longer possible—that would highlight a deep crisis indeed.

But what's surprising, and worthy of reflection, is the fact that so many journalists, despite these conditions, nonetheless still find journalism to be an attractive profession. This belief that the game itself remains worthy persists even among those who leave journalism itself behind as a professional identity. Professional exits, in the cases analyzed here, are characterized primarily by a dissolution of the belief in one's relationship to journalism, and almost never in the ideal of journalism itself. This suggests the power of journalism as a profession to continue to generate attractions, even if those attractions are so often frustrating (and thus frustrated) for those who follow them. But it also carries with it a warning. It is not that belief in journalism has diminished and that this leads to exit. Rather, it is that in many cases journalism itself has changed and shifted its social functions in ways that no longer generate the belief that *that* game—the one characterized by chasing audiences and clicks, by producing and updating constantly, by rarely having the time to think and reflect—is worthy of one's efforts.

Conclusion

In a 1994 essay titled, "L'emprise du journalisme,"[1] Pierre Bourdieu described the effects of intensifying commercial pressures on journalism. In their efforts to attract audiences, journalists increasingly favored scoops over analysis, the sensational over the substantive, and instant "made for TV" takes over in-depth reporting. This change, in Bourdieu's analysis, was brought about not primarily because of the medium of technology per se, which was not novel in the 1990s. Rather, a newly commercialized television sector—crystallized by the recent privatization of France's largest television channel—shaped these increasingly intense battles for audiences among nearly all news providers. In these changes, analysis, substance, and in-depth information were not jettisoned outright; however, the equilibrium between the profession's social and commercial functions shifted decisively. This new arrangement made it increasingly difficult for journalists to do work aligned with the profession's older social functions. By extension, it also tended to favor those individuals and institutions in other fields most aligned with the needs of an increasingly commercialized press.

Three decades on, the intensification of commercial concerns proceeds apace. Very few news outlets in either France or the United States are not touched by the need to develop a new business model to support journalism. These business models, however, are never just about business.[2] They also shape the principles that constitute what does and does not count as legitimate journalism. As the commercial crisis of the press grows stronger, journalism that promises to address these commercial concerns comes to be increasingly valued by those in the profession. The strategies deployed toward these ends are varied, and they do not necessarily exclude social functions. One can advocate solutions journalism on the grounds that it will attract audiences while also empowering them in their everyday lives, just as one can propose multimedia journalists (MMJs) as a way to reduce labor costs but also reinvigorate the practice of professional storytelling. Still, the variety of strategies and their intermingling with social considerations should not distract from the overwhelming primacy of commercial concerns that unite them, and the narrowing of opportunities to produce less profitable but nonetheless socially important forms of journalism like in-depth investigative reporting.

The intensity of commercial concerns amplifies the contemporary predicament that journalists face. By reducing the material and symbolic rewards on offer, it helps to establish conditions that make it ever more difficult for journalists to retain their belief that the profession is worthy of their efforts. Even those holding reasonably stable jobs find the world around them in a state of seemingly constant change, and not often in ways that seem personally beneficial. Resembling the "slippery slope" that, according to Hartmut Rosa, characterizes contemporary social life more generally, they worry that loss or disadvantage begets those who fail to keep up with the times, even as the times are less amenable to the investigations and reflections that for many make being a journalist a worthwhile endeavor.[3] For those with less stable jobs, the situation appears even more dire. The possibility of employment security is fleeting; the need to adapt is constant; there is the sense that it "goes without saying" that journalism is and will continue to be a job that one does as much for passion as for material security. That all this transpires amid a general environment in which audiences tend to scorn or ignore journalists is itself at least partly related to these commercial concerns, encouraging as they do forms of journalism—swift and superficial, stilted and stunted—that can be so readily disliked or disregarded.

In attempting to resolve this predicament, two journalisms can be discerned. A first leaves intact an older definition of journalism that privileges long-form, in-depth, and well-composed work as the profession's highest ideals. The opportunities to produce such journalism are limited, especially for journalists working in regional media. Therefore, most achieve a personally acceptable balance of rewards by finding ways to manage the disappointment that stems from the gap between these ideals and their everyday realities. They accept the dissatisfying work they do in the present and hope for the possibility of doing more satisfying work in the future. Or they make investments outside their professional lives, downgrading journalism to the status of a mere job that is acceptable because it fits, for now, into their broader life situations. Or they rationalize the often-menial tasks associated with their everyday work by highlighting the occasional work they do that more closely approximates their ideals. Whatever specific form the management of disappointment takes, it highlights the enduring counterweight of the profession's most esteemed social functions as well as the effects of the profession's intensifying commercial orientation on its realization.

A second journalism proposes to redefine the profession's social functions so as to better align them with its commercial needs. Rather than educators with a civic mission, these journalists assume the role of adviser in daily life. They offer suggestions on what to consume and how to spend one's leisure time; they find ways to amuse and entertain an audience with many demands for its attention. Less interested in the revelation of hidden facts or the cultivation of elite debates, these journalists instead focus on distilling what is already known and exploring ways to get audiences involved in the news-making process. Social concerns are rarely absent from these efforts but they are neither the primary focus nor the starting point. In prioritizing commercial considerations, and finding ways to adapt social functions to fit them, these journalists endeavor to establish a new equilibrium between the profession's commercial and social elements.

By definition, whether (and for how long) these two journalisms engender a balance of rewards depends on what a journalist considers personally acceptable. For this reason, there is no single objective measure that can be used to predict departure from the profession. It always depends on the necessarily subjective assessment of whether or not the investment remains worthwhile. Even if all external signs suggest the plausibility of exit—low pay, poor conditions, worsening prospects—one can, like a dinner party guest that overstays his welcome, remain in journalism well after one's primary nourishment has been attained. Conversely, one can leave even when their prospects seem newly brightened. Some journalists depart the profession just as they stand on the cusp of a promotion, after they win a substantial prize, or even upon receiving the coveted contract for which they worked so long and hard. This subjective dimension makes the journalist's predicament dynamic, a gamble that is useful to explore in part because of the opportunity it affords to see the different ways journalists maintain, reproduce, or dissolve their belief in the profession's worth.

While deeply personal, the management of this predicament is never merely a question of individual will or motivation. The expectations journalists have of journalism and their orientations to its upheavals are also socially cultivated. It is an old story, and not at all specific to journalism, that the individuals with the most favorable properties tend to be those that find their place doing work that most closely approximates a profession's most esteemed social functions.[4] Conversely, those with the least favorable properties tend to be those with the greatest disposition to adapt, to find virtue even in situations and circumstances from which they seem disinclined to benefit personally. Rather than a simple story of motivation, the journalist's predicament provides a prism onto the processes by which individual social conditions are turned into narratives of individual motivation.[5] This acknowledgment should hardly deny the work involved for all journalists managing their predicaments. But it does offer a prism onto the ways in which social inequalities are reproduced in professional spaces. It is precisely the fact that this reproduction happens while appearing largely unrelated to the social inequalities that underpin them that makes them so pervasive (i.e., by appearing as individual preferences and tastes).

To be sure, social origins are not fate. Some journalists' management of their predicament permits either ascent or descent in ways that defy the social properties they inherit and cultivate. But these movements are always done in relation to the complex of social properties that one possesses, and never in their total absence or suspension. An analogy to sports in this regard is apt. The unlikely success of the underdog comes by working with and against one's own inherent limits: the lesser height or physical ability that requires creative adaptation and entails anything but a golden ticket in which their success is ordained from the outset.

Exploring the relationship between social properties and journalists' management of their predicament allows, in this sense, for an appreciation of the diversity of the individual cases explored and the ways each journalist manages the hand they are dealt.

Social properties are also not static. What journalism schools, to take one property examined in the preceding pages, inculcate has changed over time. They teach not only the basic skills (e.g., reporting, writing) necessary for pursuing work in journalism. Increasingly, they also aim to inculcate an "innovative" mind-set or "entrepreneurial" spirit willing to take on the profession's commercial concerns, rather than point to a partition separating the two. This is done also by encouraging exploration of the social functions that aspiring journalists could aim to fulfill: the participatory "solutions" and engaged forms of journalism that increasingly constitute the profession's new equilibrium between its social and commercial functions. That this attitude cuts across a wide range of other social properties—gender, social origins, professional experiences, and job titles—is one signal of just how important these schools have become in shaping this orientation. And, also, how different the experience of journalism school is today than it was just a few decades prior.

The journalist's predicament has been explored in these pages through the experiences of those working at regional media in France and the United States. Commonly framed as opposing ideal types, journalists in Toulouse and Seattle in fact share a common predicament that stems from a similar pattern of diminution in the material and symbolic rewards available, even as their responses vary in part because of the legal, regulatory, and cultural contexts in which they transpire. Journalists working in other "media systems" in Western Europe and North America are therefore likely to face a similar predicament and to evince historically influenced reactions to them.[6] The commercial pressures no doubt vary in intensity across locales, as do the historically derived social functions that the press assumes. But the journalist's contemporary predicament is very broadly shared, even in countries well beyond the Western European and North American settings studied here.

For this reason, the style of comparison utilized here follows David Morley's well-known claim that "theory travels best."[7] This is so not because empirical specifics of the two cases do not matter or are somehow irrelevant to the accumulation of knowledge. Rather, it is precisely because empirical details are so context-specific that any effort to establish cumulative empirical knowledge through the standardization of methodological measures runs the risk—of which comparative scholars can be more or less aware—of misapprehending those empirical particularities.[8] The journalist's predicament is therefore offered as an analytical construct that can be utilized to ask similar questions in other empirical settings, as is its theoretical emphasis on the social properties that shape the ways that predicament is perceived, rendered sensible, and responded to by journalists. Similarly, the results that it emphasizes (e.g., the management of disappointment, the establishment of a new equilibrium between commercial and social functions) highlight the mechanisms that produce journalist's responses to their shared predicament. The utility of this book, therefore, can be measured less in the straightforward replication of its empirical results per se and more in the extent to which the questions it raises and the tools it uses to answer them can prove useful for other research projects, within and beyond the empirical settings examined here.

Yet if the work here offers questions that other researchers might find useful, and tools for thinking about the problems they engender, it no doubt also raises questions that the present work does not answer. From these limits, necessarily inherent to empirical research, other paths that might be followed and explored subsequently can also be glimpsed. In this sense, the two journalisms that journalists pursue can be seen not only as the result of efforts to secure personally acceptable rewards. They also raise, if only by implication, broader questions about the role of journalists, and therefore also of journalism, in society. Such questions resonate deeply today in a profession where the word *crisis* no longer appears as an apoplectic exaggeration or a dyspeptic mood but instead as something approximating a quotidian, if imprecise, description.

WHAT ARE JOURNALISTS (AND JOURNALISM) FOR?

If the question is old, it is not timeless.[9] In both Western Europe and North America, it assumed its modern form in the nineteenth century. Over the course of that century, the profession came to take on its dual commercial and social functions. Journalists were expected not only to express literary opinions or political ideas, the social functions that defined an earlier period of party-supported or aristocratic newspapers. They also came to understand and accept that the organizations they worked in and for had become, to borrow Max Weber's characterization, "necessarily . . . capitalist, business enterprise[s]."[10] As such, the success or failure of individual organizations rode on their capacity to generate sufficient revenues. This new commercial function, which varied in intensity across organizations and countries, led to a redefinition of the profession's social purpose that was assumed to better align with this commercial orientation. The rise of fact-based storytelling, which happened more or less simultaneously in France and the United States, was the result of this merger. Political and literary expression survived in part by being absorbed into this fact-based understanding of the profession's social function.

The merging of these social and commercial functions has always been an unstable alliance. The recurrent debates they provoke about the profession's role in society offer evidence of this instability.[11] From the nineteenth century onward, journalists have regularly been criticized for favoring news that serves the commercial considerations to the detriment of social ones.[12] Whether referencing journalists working for William Randolph Hearst, Gannett, or private equity firms, critics of this stripe argue that the sensational and the slipshod are outstripping the serious and sober news necessary for an informed citizenry. At the same time, a separate line of criticism holds that journalists, perhaps by being too protected from market pressures, tend toward elitism and a focus on issues far removed from the lives of a majority of citizens. Their obsessive focus on politics and the judgments of their peers; their inattention to or misrepresentation of socially marginalized groups; their lack of interest in listening to their own critics—all these are taken as signs of an inward profession too autonomous from commercial pressures that, counterintuitively, might serve as a mechanism for professional reflection and renewal.[13]

Contemporary debates can in one sense be seen as an intensification of these well-established concerns. The difficulty that most news organizations encounter in their efforts to generate revenues only makes commercial concerns all the more pressing. In fact, efforts to satisfy them sometimes appear to elide journalism's social functions altogether. This is the sense in which criticism of hedge fund owners—increasingly common among regional news media in the United States—assumes its importance, with this new class of proprietors displaying no obvious, or even passing, interest in anything other than their financial bottom lines.[14] In France, free urban dailies give this problem a different form, with some newspapers simply suspending publication during times when urban readership is scarce due to summer holidays.[15] If these types of cases and examples capture public attention, it stems in part from the way they threaten to detach journalism's social functions from the profession as it pursues its commercial needs. Such a pursuit is clearly a problem for journalists who seek employment and meaning from a career in journalism. But it is also concerning to anyone interested in the existence of the profession as anything more than a "capitalist, business enterprise."

This decoupling between journalism's social and commercial functions appears increasingly as the order of the day. Few are the journalists or news organizations that can manage to do work that simultaneously achieves both. The news organizations that do tend increasingly to be "national" (i.e., based primarily in New York, Washington, DC, or Paris), with audiences that pay in part for work that is long-form, in-depth and well-composed.[16] In regional media, partly because their most elite audiences prefer consuming those national publications, the choice for journalists and management is an increasingly stark one. While it might be professionally attractive to provide work associated with the profession's historically derived social functions, it is not often a winning commercial strategy. The redefinition of journalism's social functions aims to adapt the profession to its commercial situation. To varying degrees, noncommercial forms of support (public subsidies, tax breaks, philanthropy) offer a modicum of insulation from these pressures;[17] different modalities of ownership also vary in the extent to which symbolic rewards (e.g., prizes) might serve as a counterweight to commercial concerns.[18] But overall it is not an exaggeration to note that it is increasingly difficult for most journalists to fulfill many of the functions that are marshaled in response to the question of their profession's raison d'être: to hold the powerful to account, to inform citizens, to promote dialogue and critical conversation.

Shifting patterns of social recruitment serve to stabilize, at least temporarily, this unstable alliance between commercial and social functions. As the profession focuses increasingly on business matters, it evolves in part by attracting individuals that find or create meaning in journalism's redefined social functions. In both France and the United States, journalism schools have reduced entry requirements and altered curricula so as to encourage applications from those with less favorable social properties. Entrance exams in France, for instance, have been reformatted to emphasize an applicant's motivations for being a journalist, rather than their writing skills or level of cultural knowledge. This move aims explicitly to expand recruitment to students historically excluded from journalism schools, especially at the newer private schools of journalism and industry-related academies like Prisma.[19] In the United States, many programs have begun to market that the journalism skills they teach are useful in a wide variety of "communication" occupations.[20] This shift happens at a moment when enrollment is generally falling and when the parents of many students, particularly those from more professional backgrounds, question journalism as a sensible career choice for their children. In both countries (and presumably others), it is therefore a strategy of downgrading that allows the profession to realize this new equilibrium between social and commercial functions.

But this strategy likely has built-in limits. Journalism, particularly as it is practiced among regional media, remains in many ways a middle- to upper-middle-class profession. The skills it requires and the relationship to work that it demands are not universally distributed across the population. Some skills, to be sure, might be deemphasized to facilitate this strategy of downgrading; this is one way of interpreting the decreased emphasis on writing and the increased focus on multimedia facility increasingly taught, sometimes begrudgingly, in journalism programs. Similarly, the development of a less civically oriented journalism likely appeals in part to students less taken by politics, less interested in investigations, and more attracted to storytelling and the idea of being "useful" to audiences. Nonetheless, the idea that work ought to serve a source of multiple rewards is socially cultivated. For journalism, it has historically revolved around a trade-off between lesser material rewards and greater opportunities to do work that seems interesting and substantial, which offers an exciting lifestyle and opportunities for status, prestige, and self-fulfillment. Without knowing where exactly any line can be drawn, it seems logical to sense that the present strategy invites an eventual crisis of recruitment, which stems at its core from the fact that the journalist's predicament might no longer seem to be worth the efforts of a sufficient number of individuals. It also serves as a reminder that the question of what journalism is for always depends in part on who is willing to be a journalist.

Several additional implications follow from these points. One pertains to the rise of increasingly partisan forms of journalism in Western Europe and North America. On both continents, it is for some organizations clearly a profitable strategy to offer news and analysis that speaks to audiences as partisans rather than citizens. If this polarization has many nonmedia causes and origins, it nonetheless seems true that the journalists that work for these organizations generally garner less satisfaction from work associated with the profession's social functions (e.g., holding the powerful qua powerful to account, rather than as partisan opponents). Correspondingly, their work treats audiences less as citizens and more as partisans (e.g., establishing a sense of "us" and "them"); aspects of this can even be discerned in regional media, with at least some journalists increasingly rejecting "impartial" approaches to news and embracing values (e.g., multiculturalism) that, whatever one thinks of them, are clearly not equally appreciated across party lines. Partisanship in news is itself hardly new, of course; in a basic sense, it constitutes the historical norm. But today's journalistic partisanship is new in that it aims to satisfy journalism's commercial needs not by merging in some way with its social functions, but instead by replacing social concerns with political ones. This happens at least in part because merging those social and commercial functions has become so difficult within the profession.

Second, and in some tension with the previous point, the unstable alliance also feeds into new social roles for journalists. If long-form, in-depth reporting has for many news outlets become too costly to produce and too sparse in the economic rewards it returns, then journalists can instead become part of a network of information providers that provide citizens with facts and data that enable them to monitor the functioning of their democracies. Their work is composed not with the expectation that audiences will follow every decision or action of elected officials and institutions in the model of the "dutiful citizen" highlighted by Michael Schudson.[21] Rather, it is based on the understanding that audiences possess a floating but nonetheless real form of "monitorial" attention that can be triggered when shown behaviors or facts that register as problematic or scandalous.[22] The prevalence of a journalistic tendency toward "decoding" complex topics by distilling them as simply as possible is one signal of this redefinition; so too is the effort to deliver news in whatever technological format best suits their audiences. Whether this can be a commercially viable strategy, especially outside of media capitals, remains to be seen. But certainly, the social role of journalists implicit in this model is well adapted to the lives of audiences whose attention is, to put it lightly, increasingly oversolicited.

Third, the unstable alliance concentrates the works best aligned with journalism's most esteemed social functions in audiences possessing high volumes of cultural capital. Hyperbolic claims about the end of journalism are premature not because older models are dying away; they are. Rather, they are overblown precisely because they deny the existence of the extraordinary flowering witnessed in recent years of books and websites that provide exactly the sort of long-form, in-depth, and well-composed reporting that generates the highest regard among journalists. Sometimes, these works are related more or less directly to standard issues of democratic governance: the works of Stéphane Foucart and Sylvestre Huet on public health and pollution in France are certainly examples in this vein. But other times these works are nourishing not because they necessarily serve any direct democratic purpose (in the narrow sense of checking and balancing institutions) but because they offer a glimpse into otherwise hidden social worlds and provide the opportunity to think differently about those worlds. The immersive reporting of Ted Conover and the comics journalism of Joe Sacco offer two examples of this tendency from the American case. What unites all of them is the social properties of their audiences, well educated (though not always financially prosperous) and generally coming from professional classes.

Observing these developments, one would have to be pessimistically cynical or naively optimistic not to see both opportunities and risks in the contemporary moment. Today's long-form reporting certainly combines a depth of analysis with an attention to subjectivity that rivals any of its historical predecessors (e.g., muckraking, new journalism). How institutions are checked and balanced has evolved in the contemporary news ecosystem, with journalists providing not only facts but also context to help audiences make sense of the day's events. Even partisan forms of journalism can challenge some of the profession's staider tendencies (e.g., toward ritualized forms of "balance" that confuse and induce apathy in audiences). But blind spots and problems also proliferate, regarding which questions can be raised. To what extent, for instance, can "contextual" or long-form journalism capture the interest and attention of popular, rather than more elite and educated, audiences? If the news ecology permits greater fact checking, does it also not intensify the contributions of public relations personnel, who are often better resourced and thus seemingly well situated to shape news? And doesn't partisan journalism in many of its most prominent guises in fact promote the demonization of some social groups and marginalize the potential for a broader sense of social solidarity?

These opportunities and risks arise from the tensions found in journalism's unstable alliance between its commercial and its social functions. While the forms this alliance assumes are particular to journalism, the tensions appear throughout media, broadly understood as a site of cultural production (e.g., film, television, music, books).[23] Across all, media are conceived as being analytically and normatively important primarily for the relationship they maintain—affirming and reproducing, questioning and challenging, depending on one's perspective—to a broader democratic capitalist social order. What, then, are the principles that underpin this relationship between media and this order? And is this order, as some have recently suggested, withering away and being replaced with a media environment and social universe better characterized by fluidity and disorder, or sometimes even a sense of chaos?

MEDIA AND SOCIAL ORDER

Like questions regarding journalism's purpose, the democratic capitalist social order is also historically rooted. In the eighteenth century, it entailed revolutions in the deepest principles, and therefore the very foundations, of social life. In both France and the United States, the judgment of "the people," rather than the divine, came to be viewed as the legitimate basis for appointing rulers.[24] This change interacted with longer-term transformations across Western Europe and North America in social and economic organization, most obviously with the rise of capitalism, which entailed using markets to allocate resources, distribute goods, and generate profits.[25] These transformations, guided by the rising middle classes' "interest in utility and service," aimed at the management of spaces and populations, and its mechanisms "imposed a profound reorganization of the systems of perception and of the order of the social world."[26]

Three developments that arose in this new social order and its schemes of perception are especially pertinent for a discussion of journalists and media more broadly. A first pertains to the creation of professions. If newspapers existed prior to the rise of this social order, it was only through the imposition of this order that journalists and other cultural producers could by the nineteenth century expect remuneration for their services. This payment was possible because of the newfound economic viability of profit-oriented news organizations, and the rise of industrial capitalism was in this respect crucial. Its technological advances made printing cheaper, and its division of labor induced growing numbers of goods to be produced outside the household, thereby enlarging the market for newspaper advertising. Second, the possibility of journalism as a career path also rested upon the perception that this work was socially beneficial. Unlike the monarchical regimes that preceded it, the political dimension of this order—because, in it, power resided with "the people" and "the nation"—could be questioned. Journalists therefore could legitimately claim to speak *as citizens* and *on behalf of* citizens in order to hold the powerful to account and to, as the saying goes, "question authority." Third, this order replaced earlier hierarchies of "estates" and "ranks" with new principles of differentiation. One's legitimacy for being a journalist thus depended not on their inherited social status but instead on the recognition of their skills, talents, and passions.

These developments made modern journalism more or less perfectly adapted to the democratic capitalist order in which it arose. Economically oriented, it used advertising to provide a forum through which businesses could reach consumers, while also becoming an arena of business opportunity in its own right. Socially beneficial, it articulated ideals of journalism as a counterpower, using facts to function as a "fourth estate" that monitors the powerful, and as a civic arena of deliberation and debate on important issues of the day. Meritocratically based, it provided the broad and rising middle classes with a potential occupation, one in which they could expect to succeed or fail based on their capacities and efforts rather than their inherited status. The broader democratic capitalist social order structured and gave meaning to journalism's commercial and social tensions.

This relationship between journalism and a democratic capitalist order is increasingly questioned. Platforms and digital intermediaries like Google and Facebook cater to advertisers far more effectively, in terms of both reach and cost, than news organizations ever could, thus undermining its economic basis. Media owners for their part still seek, and sometimes gain, profits from their media enterprises but the broad overall financial picture of the industry, particularly the newspapers that served as the largest employer of journalists, is one of structural decline. Professional ideals also seem poorly adapted to a media environment in which audiences can choose options that most closely approximate their beliefs and preferences. In this context, Silvio Waisbord argues that "journalistic notions of truth-telling grounded in facticity and reason are questioned or simply ignored."[27] Without denying the capacity of journalists to produce news that challenges power-holders, its social benefit appears dampened under such conditions. These developments in turn make it difficult for at least some would-be journalists to believe that the profession generates a personally acceptable balance of material and symbolic rewards, thus providing one reason why the profession is decreasingly attractive, especially to individuals from liberal professional families.

The issue is further complicated by arguments that the democratic capitalist social order itself is in the process of transformation. Claims regarding the impending death of capitalism seem premature;[28] however, the ways in which capitalism is organized has changed and can no doubt change further. The ascendant place of finance in contemporary capitalism has a tendency, among other things, to reduce the noncommercial basis of the industries it enters. For a profession like journalism, this threatens the very possibility of an equilibrium, however slanted, between its commercial and its social aims.[29] And while it seems similarly hasty to claim an end to democracy, the loss of faith in authoritative social institutions is real, as are organized efforts to suppress participation, disempower citizens, and fracture the bases for social solidarity.[30] This, too, weakens contemporary journalism, by making the forms associated with its social functions increasingly threatened, sometimes outright in attacks on the press but just as often by stripping away the authority of journalists to vet political claims according to factual evidence.

But one need not deny the specificity or intensity of the present challenges in order to profit from a perspective that foregrounds journalism's enduring connections to a democratic capitalist order. The belief that journalism remains a path worth pursuing is one point that can be made in this regard. Journalists' very different reasons for entering the profession converge in the tensions embedded in a democratic capitalist order. The diverse rationales they provide are thus encircled by the principles of this larger order: that if they are skilled and persistent enough, they stand a reasonable chance of doing well in their careers; that if they explain issues well enough, audiences will come to better understand them; that if they show injustice clearly and forcefully enough, the world will change for the better; that if they innovate deeply enough, a new business model can be found. Never naively held, these beliefs persist in conditions that seem likely to exhaust them, offering as they do seemingly so many reasons *not* to be a journalist. This is one sense of what social order, at its most basic level, entails: it does not question its most foundational principles.[31]

Belief in these principles allows journalists from different social backgrounds to find their place in (or, when departing, outside of) the profession but in ways that generally reflect their very different conditions of possibility. Thus, to recall an example from chapter 5, the journalist from working-class origins who is the first in his family to hold an office job finds his professional advancement limited—further education, he acknowledges, would be needed—because being an "eternal student" would be unfair to his partner. While he loves journalism that takes the time to "cross different points of view," his position requires quick turnarounds, often on topics like crime news that are explicitly aimed at capturing audience attention. He does not question this editorial policy or the commercial concerns that drive it; he adapts himself by doing the reporting while finding ways to avoid the "sordid details" that would distract, rather than aid, the audience in understanding the events. His job is personally acceptable to him, at least for now, and in no small part because he has "an office, a computer, I sit," in contrast to family members working in factories that stand all day.

It is through these practical, often quotidian, adjustments that journalists reproduce their belief in the social order's deepest principles while generally accepting the social inequalities that attend it as differences in personal tastes. A preference for "more thoughtful" reporting in contrast to "the hardcore daily turnaround" of daily newspapers is thus seen primarily as a personal choice rather than the partial outcome of a specific social trajectory that makes this possibility more conceivable for some than it is for others. That this type of job depends on a broader set of arrangements that appear under duress is unquestionable (e.g., an employer that finds this work valuable and is willing to compensate for it, an audience that finds such reporting worthy of their attention). But that instability, as well as the broader transformations in democracy and capitalism, in no way alters the reproduction of inequalities that persist amid the main troubles facing the profession. This is why, to slightly rephrase Paul Willis, the most durable domination is always the domination of seemingly trivial preferences and tastes.[32]

A democratic capitalist social order is extraordinarily dynamic, and this is undoubtedly one reason for its persistence. Its very foundations generate tensions and provide opportunities through which exclusions and inequalities are sometimes addressed. The story of gender in journalism is illustrative in this regard. Historically, women's exclusion from the profession on the basis of gender was challenged on economic, social, and meritocratic grounds. Including women in the workforce ensured the production of types of news that audiences might find appealing; it promised to address social concerns that men tended to ignore or misunderstand; and it expanded the profession to more closely approximate principles of differentiation based less on status and more on skill. That women play a more prominent role in journalism today than they did in the past is undeniable. It reflects in part the adaptive capacities of a democratic capitalist social order to respond to organized struggles for inclusion.

And yet gender inequalities have hardly disappeared. As a rule, women in journalism continue to hold jobs that are less prestigious than their male counterparts. While female editors-in-chief are not unheard of, they remain a fraction of newsroom leadership in both France and the United States. What's more, these inequalities tend to assume new forms even as, and sometimes in response to, efforts to address the grievances raised. Like a phantasmagorical game of whack-a-mole, gender-based inequalities vanquished in one form often simply reappear elsewhere in another guise. Thus, if pay discrimination is decreasing, no doubt because of organized resistance to its existence, it nonetheless remains true that women face very different choices than their male counterparts in terms of their career pursuits. Whereas most men can expect to be both fathers and journalists simultaneously, for many women the choice often appears to be of the either/or variety. It is this much deeper sense of social order, premised on very old ideas regarding the gendered division of labor in society, that is reproduced through this dynamism.

By exploring socially cultivated dispositions, backgrounds, and trajectories, the sociology of journalists developed here highlights the dynamic and enduring ways that social orders are reproduced. If this complements a more established sociology of journalism, it hardly constitutes a microsociology ignorant of and uninterested in the broader forces that make some options more or less conceivable, both to individual journalists and to the profession writ large. Rather, the approach utilized here is a way of grasping analytically how a very broad set of conditions—the moment in history in which one lives, the nation-state in which one works, the social properties one brings to bear—gets crystallized in particular cases. The journalist's predicament *operates* individually and it appears as issues of personal choice and preference. However, the meanings it promises, and the dilemmas it raises, are never merely questions of individual will and volition.

For journalists, no dilemma is nowadays more basic than the struggle to secure a personally acceptable balance of rewards in a profession that is turned increasingly toward commercial concerns. In finding ways to address this concern, they are thus induced to address economic priorities first and foremost but almost never to the total exclusion of social aims. This threatens to corrode some of the aspects of journalism that have long made the profession interesting and worth pursuing: for work that is meaningful and substantive, with a lifestyle that affords some degree of status and prestige, and that provides opportunities for self-expression and self-fulfillment. But the very persistence of these attractions also points to a potential basis for professional renewal. In this regard, the predicament journalists face—its threats as well as its opportunities—is hardly unique to the profession of journalism alone.

VOCATIONS IN THE GRIP OF THE MARKET

Indeed, journalism can be seen as just one of many contemporary vocations in which individuals experience an intensified struggle to achieve a personally acceptable balance of rewards. Cultural producers, educators, healthcare professionals, humanitarian workers: these and other occupations are attractive because they promise remuneration in exchange for doing work that is perceived as being socially beneficial.[33] This sense of social purpose underwrites the lesser prioritization typically accorded in these jobs to material comforts and the correspondingly stronger emphasis placed on a sense of recognition and self-worth, and the promise of self-fulfillment derived from the perceived social contribution. While the pursuit of a contemporary vocation can be experienced subjectively as a form of selflessness, it nonetheless presents those who pursue it with a practical predicament of how to reconcile the overall rewards they attain or expect to attain from this work.

This predicament has long induced individuals to find ways to merge their chosen vocation's social functions with its commercial needs. None existed to the exclusion of economic considerations. Just as it takes money to do long-form journalism, or support the work of cultural producers more broadly, material resources are also needed to ensure that teachers can effectively educate students, that healthcare professionals can provide patients and their families with care, and that humanitarians can offer relief to populations in need. This has been and can be organized in ways that rely on market forces to greater and lesser degrees. However, contemporary vocations always exist in the tensions generated by the unstable alliance between its social functions and its commercial pursuits. In contrast to more purely autonomous fields of activity,[34] their very existence is necessarily predicated on some equilibrium between the varying functions.

The growing turn toward the market, itself part of a much broader neoliberal social project to reorganize collective goods in order to bolster economic returns, functions like a magnet that leads contemporary vocations to focus increasingly on commercial concerns.[35] The specifics vary, of course, and journalism is certainly a magnified case of this general trend due in large part to the implosion of its business model. But no contemporary vocation is untouched by this shift. Cultural producers are expected to produce content that is attractive to audiences that are themselves economically attractive; educators are increasingly tasked with teaching students practical skills and training them for jobs while also becoming more "entrepreneurial" themselves by raising funds rather than expecting public support via the tax system; healthcare professionals are expected to standardize care by eliminating inefficiencies, thus ensuring that the provision of care not overshadow the need to make money; humanitarians work increasingly for large organizations concerned about the reproduction of their organization itself, and this leads to a growing emphasis on accountability or reputation protection, sometimes to the detriment of aid provisioning.

The consequences of this turn are not uniformly negative. Inefficiencies are not socially valuable of their own accord, just as being accountable to donors and responsive to audiences is not irreconcilably opposed to doing good or providing news and any other cultural good that accords with professional definitions of excellence. Moreover, because social functions are not static, they can be adapted to and are redefined so as to better adapt them to the economic circumstances in which a vocation finds itself. Thus, if some journalists can take pride in assuming the role of being practical advisers in everyday life, some educators can also find meaning in education that is less about the cultivation of knowledge and more about the practical training for specific jobs. The fact that those who find these more commercially oriented functions attractive also tend to hold less favorable social properties only deepens the ambivalence associated with this turn of vocations toward the market.

But not all aspects of a vocation can be so easily merged with commercial incentives. Smaller class sizes really do seem to help students learn more effectively, even if they cost more on a per capita basis; longer visits with patients really do tend to bolster the quality of care they receive; slower rhythms of production really do allow journalists and cultural producers the time for reflexivity and investigation that are typically given short shrift in work environments that favor immediacy over all else. The diminishing opportunities to do exactly these types of work are one significant reason why the vocations are themselves less attractive today. The concentration of opportunities to do this work among those with the most favorable properties is also a cause for concern. Similarly, it is also why so many of those who end up in the profession find themselves managing the disappointment that stems from a disjuncture between their initial attractions and their everyday experiences.

It is tempting to register these developments as fomenting a "crisis" in contemporary vocations. The growing difficulty in attracting recruits to at least some of these vocations (e.g., teachers) is very clearly both a cause for concern and a result of the commercial turn within these lines of work; on that front, talk of crisis is in no way an exaggeration. The sense of dissatisfaction and sometimes disillusionment that follows those who pursue these vocations also creates questions about the sustainability of this commercially oriented model. The sense of work that is hollowed out and worn down by economic demands, which are themselves sometimes antithetical to social aims, is likewise real. If vocations do experience crises in both recruitment and retention, it stems in no small part from these intensifying commercial pressures.

But do the very real problems that confront contemporary vocations rise to the level of a broader crisis of these vocations? The fact that fewer people are attracted to them is hardly surprising, nor is the tendency of at least some to leave the profession. More surprising, though, is the fact that a substantial number of individuals are still attracted to these occupations in spite of these conditions. And if they are sometimes disappointed by the reality of the work, many nonetheless retain their belief that the game is "worth the candle." Even those who leave tend to question themselves and their relation to the profession and its evolutions, not the vocation's worth. The problems facing contemporary vocations are thus not strictly equivalent to crises witnessed in other vocations, like the religious orders, which are confronted with rising levels of disbelief that the work is worthy of their efforts at all. Instead, most contemporary vocations instead struggle to retain their connection to the very things that make that work attractive in the first place and in which so many still believe.

As ever, the reasons for these persistent attractions and pursuits are mixed. To see them as entirely selfless or idealistic is to miss the mixture of practical rationales and rewards that underpin these occupational trajectories. Certainly, some people remain in vocations for entirely nonprofessional reasons. A teacher can find the job boring or the conditions difficult but remain primarily because it's a job that has nice holidays and reserves the summer for one's personal pursuits. A nurse can fear that the long hours she works now might pale in comparison to the work she would have to do to approximate her earnings in a different occupation. In general, the worry that, however unpleasant a job is, it could always be worse elsewhere no doubt goes some way to explaining why at least some people do not leave jobs that are otherwise disappointing and dissatisfying. The power of inertia and the force of habit are no less strong in structuring contemporary vocational pursuits than they are in any other domain of social life.

But these diverse rationales are also a reminder that vocations are important not just for what they do but also for what they are, sociologically speaking. In the lower value that individuals in them accord to material rewards, these vocations collectively express a distance to, and in some ways a skepticism of, the market, or at least to its primacy in social life. This is clearest in the choice to pursue a job in which the salaries are expected not to rival the salaries found elsewhere. The journalist thus knows from the time she is in school that she could make more money doing public relations or advertising; the same point can be made for the humanitarian who shuns working in the corporate sector. That they do not, at least for a time, undertake this better-compensated work no doubt highlights the weight and value of these vocations' social functions. Even the preference for lesser pay as a way to protect one's family time, holidays, or personal hobbies points to some of the many things that money, strictly speaking, cannot buy. The fact that some leave labor to justify their departures and highlight the ways they can still "do good" while working in public relations or corporate communication is further evidence in this regard.

These social functions and personal reasons that serve as attractions to these vocations are neither timeless nor transversal. They do not reside in the depths of some ineffable human nature. Instead, they are part of a mode of perception and a way of being that stem from the social order in which contemporary democratic capitalist societies exist. That they have not been extinguished entirely in the most recent turn to the market is evidence of the dynamism—or tensions, or contradictions; it really does depend on one's perspective—of this very order. The putative openness of these vocations on the basis of talent and skills need not distract from the ways in which democratic societies have always been and continue to be plagued by deep social inequalities. But their tensions are also a reminder that whatever strengths a democratic capitalist system possesses, it remains fundamentally unable to deliver so many of the experiences and sources of meaning that are necessary for living a fulfilling life.

The threats that contemporary vocations, journalism very much included, nowadays face stem in large part from this turn towards the market. But the persistence of these vocational attractions can also be read as the basis for their potential renewal. Indeed, all the things that make vocations attractive are important because they are also connected to broader political, aesthetic, and moral horizons. They furnish the possibility that the work one does will not amount to "just a job" but also an effort to aid those who suffer, to fight injustice in the many forms in which it appears, to hold the powerful to account on behalf of the people, and even to develop new ways of thinking about the social world. For all their force and the more-than-occasional havoc they wreak, markets never eliminate these horizons outright. They do, however, threaten to exhaust them in their relentless focus on economic considerations. Like anything else worth preserving, vocations are therefore always social achievements, never the simple result of market forces or individual volition. As such, they are also always at risk. For journalists, as for those in other vocations, a life spent seeking to realize them is, to reprise the poetry of Stanley Kunitz once more, the "principle of being" from which they "struggle not to stray."

Epilogue

Is Journalism Dying?

Modern journalism was born in the nineteenth century with the understanding that it possessed both social and commercial functions.[1] Its social functions persist—partly, as shown in these pages, through a process of redefinition. The economic outlook, however, is for many news organizations gloomy. Because these monetary troubles for the most part beget no easy solutions, journalists' commitments to their craft can look like sandcastles built amid an incoming tide: interesting, perhaps admirable, but ultimately imperiled. What's more, the very act of redefining the profession's social functions might also be interpreted as hastening its demise. Making news quick, entertaining, and useful may or may not effectively address journalism's commercial concerns. But it also risks making news so thin and superficial that it holds even less relevance for potential audiences and makes it even less distinguishable from other sources of information. Do these economic woes, and the adjustments among journalists they induce, therefore imply that journalism is not simply changing but instead dying?

The perspective developed in this book suggests that what is imperiled is less journalism per se than the capacity of journalists to secure a personally acceptable balance of rewards from journalism. The two are no doubt connected. If no journalist could secure an acceptable balance of rewards, there would be no journalism. The reality of contemporary journalism, however, is that it retains its capacity to attract recruits—thus ensuring that journalism in some forms persists—even as its actual conditions of existence tend to frustrate those very attractions. The fact that many journalists temporarily adjust to this state of affairs, either by finding ways to manage their disappointments or by redefining the profession's social functions, does nothing to change the fact that securing an acceptable balance of rewards is an increasingly precarious ordeal for many. It is this very general uncertainty that the contemporary journalist's predicament brings into view.

The struggle to secure an acceptable balance of rewards is hastened by the growing emphasis placed by managers and owners on commercial concerns. This can be seen most clearly in the reduction of newsroom staff via layoffs and restructurings. While this cuts operating costs for organizations, it shrinks the overall number of jobs available for journalists. Just as importantly, it induces a sense of uncertainty among those who remain regarding the viability of their positions. From a different angle, this commercial emphasis is also visible in efforts to reskill journalists to do more with less. If this is a reasonable enough economic policy from the perspective of owners and managers, unsurprisingly it tends to make it difficult for many journalists to do work in which they can take pride. This pride is not merely personal; it is one of the symbolic rewards needed to underwrite a journalist's continuing commitment to the profession.

Foregrounding the journalist's predicament underscores the struggles necessary to retain this belief in a worthwhile profession. This in no way negates the very real economic woes—themselves linked to broad transformations in the production, circulation, and consumption of contemporary news and information—that threaten journalism. Rather, it shifts the analytical focus away from the metaphorical tide that threatens castles made of sand and considers why anyone would bother building sandcastles under these conditions. That belief, a sense that the game is worth the candle, underpins the activities that literally bring journalism to life. Absent such a belief, there would be no news of any sort. A tide can only destroy the castles that humans bother to build in the first place.

At some point, it's possible that the ongoing diminution of rewards might deteriorate the belief that a life in journalism is worth the candle. In some ways, this is already happening among liberal professional families that discourage journalism as a career for their children; that is one reason why university programs in some countries are seeing declining enrollments. But reduced rewards also tend to induce new patterns of social recruitment, attracting new entrants more disposed to find the rewards on offer both attractive and acceptable. Journalism school entrance exams, which increasingly emphasize individual motivation over cultural knowledge, are one setting where such shifts are instantiated. If these new patterns of social recruitment were to prove unsuccessful, then it would make sense to discuss the death of journalism as such.

At present, and for the foreseeable future, the more likely development is not disbelief in journalism per se but difficulty in making a career in journalism work. While promising an exciting lifestyle connected to broader social values, journalism delivers to many journalists something quite different: long hours, and performing tasks for which one is insufficiently trained and which often bear very little connection to the common good. If it is reasonable for audiences to sometimes find such content uninteresting, it is also eminently sensible that frustration and dissatisfaction should be a common response for so many journalists. That gap—between a profession that seems worthy and work conditions that threaten to erode that belief—is one of the most basic problems that many contemporary journalists, and thus also contemporary journalism, face.

In this regard, the journalist's predicament, while clearly particular to journalism, is analogous to the experiences observed in other vocations. Nursing and education, to take just two examples, are not usefully characterized as existing on the precipice of death; indeed, it is difficult to imagine contemporary societies without them. Nurses and educators do, however, face conditions that make it difficult for them to secure a personally acceptable balance of material and symbolic rewards from their work. It is these conditions, which are brought on in part by the growing weight of commercial forces in those professional spaces, that threaten the belief that these sorts of vocations are worthy of one's efforts.

If journalism and other vocations are valuable, then the conditions under which individuals pursue their craft are also worthy of attention. Obviously, this includes aspects of work related to material concerns: the hours worked, the nature of contracts, the salaries conferred. These conditions have clearly deteriorated for many and are one reason why some no longer find a life in journalism or other vocations to be worth the candle. But the diminution of symbolic rewards is no less threatening to any vocation's viability. Indeed, it is those rewards that so often counterbalance the lesser pay, longer hours, and financial insecurity. One is willing to work evenings and weekends because they feel the work they are doing is interesting and important, because their efforts are recognized as valuable by those whose opinions they value, and because they see their work as being connected to the common good. The dissipation of those rewards makes it difficult to rationalize such commitments.

So long as someone finds these commitments reasonable, there will be journalism. This does not mean that the news productions will themselves be memorable, or that they will necessarily accord with the various normative expectations so often ascribed to journalists. But it does serve as a reminder that threats to journalism do not only come directly from failing business models, dwindling audiences, or new competitors in the struggle for public attention. In a very basic way, what makes journalism possible is that everyday people called journalists get up and produce something that audiences recognize as journalism. Their reasons for doing so are always a mix of the personal and professional; whatever those reasons are, they sustain the belief that what they are doing is worthwhile. More than anything else, this is why journalists' conditions of existence are worthy of attention: they underpin everything else that makes journalism possible.

Toward the end of each interview conducted for this book, journalists were asked what they would desire, if they could change anything about journalism. Nearly everyone talked about having the time and resources to do work that they really liked. What interested them and what they would work on, of course, varied substantially. But the idea of doing work that was meaningful stood out as important above everything else. For a long time, those responses seemed slightly puzzling. Why wouldn't they ask for better salaries, more manageable work schedules, and greater job security? There is no reason to doubt that such material rewards would be attractive to them, and it is a sign of the profession's ongoing devaluation that so few would even bother to mention it. Yet their responses can be read as a plea that is both more basic and much more ambitious, and that is to give journalists the conditions that are necessary for producing work in which pride can be taken. In refusing to accept what they currently do as the highest mark of what they might accomplish, these journalists thought better of themselves. Such aspirations fuel the belief that one's work is worthy. Sustaining that belief requires conditions that fewer and fewer journalists are able to attain.

Appendix A:
Interviewing as Comprehension

This book utilizes semistructured interviews to explore the effect of diminishing material and symbolic rewards on a journalist's belief that the profession remains worthy of their efforts. As a technique, interviews—whether of the semistructured variety or otherwise—are regularly deployed to learn about journalists' perceptions: the types of journalism and journalists that they admire, their views on how the profession has evolved over time, their thoughts about the relationship between their work commitments and their personal lives, their understanding of the experiences that precipitate their departure from journalism, and so forth. Such data therefore provide a useful entry point for exploring our theoretical interest in the contemporary journalist's predicament. More specifically, and given our interest in understanding the struggle to secure a *personally acceptable* balance of rewards, these interviews afford the opportunity to explore the renewal, attenuation, or cessation of an individual journalist's belief that the game remains "worth the candle."

This theoretical concern required approaching each interview as an opportunity, above all else, to learn about journalists' individual desires, needs, and worries. Every effort was made to create the conditions necessary to elicit these perceptions. The research was described to prospective interviewees as being part of a project to understand how journalists made sense of their careers in light of the economic, social, and technological transformations confronting their profession. Positing a general professional transformation (rather than, say, decline) left the project framing deliberately open enough so that it could be of potential interest to journalists who saw these developments as threats as well as those who perceived them as opportunities. The emphasis on individual journalists' perceptions, moreover, explicitly invited interviewees to describe their desires, needs, and worries, whatever they may be. Finally, the interviews themselves aimed to create an atypical situation, one at least partially suspended from the usual daily constraints (e.g., of time) and thus more favorable to the production of a discourse typically submerged in everyday life—not because journalists are generally incapable of vocalizing their perceptions but because everyday conditions are not favorable to their realization.

While aiming to comprehend the subjective specificities of each journalist's predicament, we also sought to grasp the objective conditions that made particular desires, needs, and worries more and less present for individual journalists. This required not only gathering "the usual suspects" of sociological analysis like parent's occupations, educational attainment, and the like;[1] it also entailed trying to understand the social trajectories—one's movement in social space over time—that made a given person's predicament seem more or less sensible to them. Every interview therefore began with a lengthy exploration of the interviewee's experiences in journalism: not only what attracted them to the profession (an important subjective perception) but also the specific jobs they held, the tasks associated with that work, and how they moved within (and, for some, beyond) the profession over time. This exploration aimed to mitigate the false coherence and sense of inevitability sometimes accorded to biographical narratives by reconstructing, step by step, the objective moments in their careers. Just as importantly, this data helped us to grasp the position a given journalist occupied in the hierarchically ordered social space that is journalism.

Rather than conceive interviews as the mere exchange of information, which raises questions about the extent to which discourses reflect practices, this approach posits a relationship between the position one occupies and the discourses they produce. The task of the researcher is to link these two and, in doing so, to understand the social conditions that structure the perceptions that are made visible in journalists' interviews. This in no way denies the possibility that their discourses might be jumbled, and it does not deny that their perspectives will be necessarily situated and thus partial. Instead, it conceives of the interview as a social relation whose purpose is aimed, precisely and literally, at *comprehension*—i.e., grasping together, through the journalist's perceptions and the researcher's analysis of their social conditions, why a journalist feels or thinks the way that they do at a given moment in time.[2]

This approach led us to sometimes interview the same journalist multiple times, especially as their career trajectories changed (e.g., in the event of a departure from journalism). These shifts in social position were almost always accompanied by changes, which could be more or less dramatic, in the journalists' discourses. Thus, a journalist who previously declared themselves to be "born to do journalism" could also, five years later, leave the profession and declare that journalism is "really a job for the young." The seeming contradiction of these statements exists only insofar as the analysis remains at the level of discourse. This is why the power of words rarely lies in the words themselves but instead in the social conditions that produce them, and that remain invisible only insofar as the researcher neglects to render them visible.

In this regard, the demographic details reported in these pages are attempts to highlight patterned relationships in the data set between perceptions, on the one hand, and positions, on the other. The sample size is far too small to carry any predictive capacity about the relationship between any particular variables and outcomes. But prediction is not the aim of this analysis. Rather, it is to show the social properties that cluster alongside particular perceptions. Thus, the analysis in chapter 3 does not seek to predict the variables associated with those who "live off" journalism, which is an interesting question but one that would require different data and methods. Instead, it describes the social properties most commonly found among those who perceive themselves as living off journalism (which tend to be French women, and especially those with young children). It is precisely this relation—between social properties and perceptions—that forms the analytical core of this book.

The possibility of a tension between one's position and the discourses they produce are no doubt real. The journalist's predicament is necessarily a *struggle* in part because one need not fully accept one's actual conditions. Some journalists with difficult working conditions, for example, would tell us that their job was "super difficult...but" that they nonetheless "love it." The presence of the coordinating conjunction ("but") is evidence of the cognitive and emotional labor necessary for convincing oneself that their struggles remain worthy. It is when those conjunctions disappear—when the job becomes no more or less than "super difficult"—that their belief in the worthiness of their efforts comes under question. Or not, as it can also be rationalized as a total acceptance, a sense that this is the way journalism was meant to be, especially because "nobody said it would be easy." The relationship between position and discourse is therefore never a mechanical one, but an invitation to understand why some journalists can find difficult conditions acceptable while others find relatively favorable conditions unacceptable.

The descriptive labels (e.g., living for, living off) found in the empirical chapters are efforts to crystallize, in as pithy a way as possible, the products of the relationship between positions and discourses. While these are empirical findings in their own right, they are not offered as ideal types of journalistic perceptions around the world. Whether journalists in, say, South America see their best works as acts of "decoding" or "dignifying" is of less interest than trying to understand what the relationship between positions and discourses makes possible regarding best work in those settings. This is the necessarily "contextual" work associated with the style of comparison favored here.[3] Like a math problem, the mechanisms that produce the results are often of far more interest than the empirical results themselves. To the extent that cross-national similarities exist, they are most likely to appear at these levels, which are necessarily couched beneath the superficial differences that can be so readily observed.

Journalists' names are kept anonymous. The rationale for this decision was threefold. First, the book's theoretical interest is in the positions that individuals occupy rather than the individuals themselves. The trajectories associated with these positions are diverse but not infinite. By sketching out patterns between perceptions and positions, we seek to foreground these social relationships, which are the core analytical emphasis of the research. Second, anonymity allowed for journalists to state things that would otherwise risk being left out of the interviews. This was particularly true when it came to talking about frustrations and disappointments with the profession, topics that were important to many journalists but also sensitive, given the relatively small spaces the profession occupies in Toulouse and Seattle. In this regard, anonymity was utilized to establish a relation of trust with the journalists interviewed. Third, anonymity was also a tool for shedding light on the experiences of those who struggle most without revealing their individual identities. During interviews, it was freelancers in particular who worried about the revelation of their identities and its potential impact on their employability. These people often exist, in an everyday sense, without names: they are unknown to much of the public and, sometimes, to many of their peers. Anonymity in these cases is a tool for shedding light on such unknown persons without revealing their individual identities.

To minimize the risk of misunderstanding respondents' perceptions, in both cities we cultivated relationships with key informants. These informants gave feedback on our empirical labels (e.g., live for, live off; journalists' best work; conserve, challenge, accede), and we relied on this input to ensure their accuracy. They also occasionally served as intermediaries, connecting us to journalists whose perspectives they thought were absent or underplayed in our analysis. As a further test of analytical generalizability, we discussed our empirical labels and analytical framework with journalists working in other cities. At least within the United States and France, their input led us to be reasonably confident that our labels have validity beyond the two cities examined and, more importantly, so does our analytical framework.

While we rely primarily on interviews, the journalist's predicament could certainly be explored utilizing other methods. Surveys could capture the perceptions of a broader number of journalists across a wider range of social spaces. Observations could examine the specific practices associated with journalists occupying particular positions. Content analysis could explore the effects of intensifying commercial pressures on news content. If interviewing is a useful way to access perceptions that are often not visible in practice, they are certainly just one tool in the researcher's toolkit for studying transformations in journalism. Rather than claim their superiority, we instead think of them in relation to the theoretical perspective that shapes the research. Whatever insights are generated in the seemingly endless debates about methods, they usually serve most usefully as reminders that such discussions are better grasped in close relation to theoretical concerns.

Appendix B: Seattle and Toulouse as Regional Media

This book is based on a decade of research conducted among journalists in Seattle and Toulouse. For those not familiar with the media of these cities, the details here provide information to aid the reader's understanding of the specific contexts in which the journalist's predicament is studied. While these individual news organizations and journalists are by definition unique—there is just one *Seattle Times* in the world, ditto for *La Dépêche du Midi*—they also share key features with regional media found elsewhere, both within and beyond France and the United States. Therefore, empirical description of these cases is complemented by a brief discussion of the principles used to study regional media. These principles, which could be applied to cases other than those studied here, seek to grasp regional media not only as geographically delimited settings but also as social spaces structured by relations of competition and cooperation over the legitimate definition of what journalism is and should be.

In Seattle, the family-owned *Seattle Times* is the city's main daily newspaper. It employs roughly 170 journalists. While much reduced in recent years—in 2005, when it competed with another daily newspaper for audience share, the figure stood at 375—it remains by far the largest employer of journalists in the city. Three television stations (KOMO,

KING, KIRO) collectively employ about one hundred journalists; this figure has remained relatively stable despite changes in corporate ownership over the past ten years, and much shuffling of individual personnel in and out of the newsroom. The largest public radio station, KUOW, employs approximately sixty journalists; it has eliminated several positions in recent years as part of programming shakeups to recapture lost audience share. Together, these outlets not only employ the greatest number of journalists; they also, especially the *Times* and the television stations, capture the bulk of audience share in the Seattle news market.

These larger news outlets are complemented by a host of smaller organizations that employ comparatively fewer numbers of journalists. The *Seattle Daily Journal of Commerce* provides business news. *Seattle Channel*, operated by the city, provides public affairs programming on cable and online. KNKX offers a second option for public radio listeners; its staff, while small, has grown since evolving from its former identity as KPLU; as of 2022, it employs about twenty journalists. The most prominent alternative weekly newspapers, *The Stranger* and *Seattle Weekly*, have in recent years cut staff substantially, ceased print publication, and moved to online-only formats. Their full-time staff is much reduced; amid the Covid-19 pandemic, *The Stranger* laid off most of its staff and declared publicly that it was struggling to remain open. The veritable explosion of news startups in the past decade has produced few long-term survivors; among the best known are *Crosscut, West Seattle Blog, South Seattle Emerald,* and *Capitol Hill Seattle*.[1] A smattering of community publications—worthy of study in their own right—generally operate on shoestring budgets and employ few full-time journalists.

In Toulouse, the family-controlled *La Dépêche du Midi* is the city's main newspaper. With roughly eighty journalists, it is one of the city's largest employers of journalists. France 3, the region's public broadcaster, is the other major source of jobs for reporters and editors; it employs about fifty journalists in Toulouse. Together, these two organizations capture both the greatest proportion of journalists and the largest audiences. Over the past fifteen years, in these two outlets, the number of journalists has marginally declined, mostly through retirements and redundancies. During this same time, *La Dépêche* Media Group has purchased smaller regional publications, like the regional publisher *Midi Presse* and Via Occitanie, a commercial television station; it has also expanded regionally to cities as far away as Montpellier. In the case of France 3 Occitanie, the group has also risen, whereas the outlet has stagnated. These changes reflect not only an economic logic of expansion and consolidation; they were also made possible by administrative reforms that in 2016 redefined the region from Midi-Pyrénées to the more encompassing Occitanie.

These larger outlets are complemented by smaller organizations that employ comparatively smaller numbers of journalists. *ActuToulouse* is an online news site that publishes general interest news; it is held by a subsidiary of Ouest-France group, a major player in regional publishing in the country more generally. ToulÉco, another entirely online news site, provides economic news about the region. A2PRL is the main commercial radio station; it employs a small staff that provides general interest news. Several magazines—*Le Brigadier, Le Journal Toulousain, Boudu, L'Empaillé*—employ a staff of about five or six journalists. Compared to Seattle, Toulouse has seen a small number of online news startups focused explicitly on Toulouse; all have shut down. In 2018, though, one online news site dedicated to Toulouse did appear: *Mediacités Toulouse* is part of the Parisian Mediapart group.

In studying journalists in these two cities, we began with several theoretical assumptions that are likely to hold for regional media elsewhere. First, news organizations in regional media tend to be structured by relations between dominant and peripheral actors. Organizations like the *Seattle Times* and *La Dépêche du Midi* are dominant not only because they capture the largest market share or employ the greatest number of journalists. Their influence also comes from the fact that all other organizations within these spaces exist and maneuver in relation to them. Peripheral actors may compete or cooperate with the dominant; they cannot, however, ignore them. This is why alternative weeklies and online pure players so often describe their work as "filling a gap" or incorporating audiences that the dominant news media tend to exclude; the gaps they seek to fill and the audiences they hope to incorporate are made possible by the journalism that dominant news media, by design or neglect, do not do. For their part, dominant actors aim to reproduce their dominant position, in the process retaining their capacity to enforce their vision—itself never static—of what journalism in these regional spaces ought to entail.

As social spaces, regional media are also settings in which different visions of how to combine journalism's commercial and social functions coexist. If all organizations must address these dual functions, they do so not only in different ways but to differing degrees. Public television and radio like France 3 and KUOW tend to provide greater amounts of public affair news than commercial outlets like A2PRL and KIRO, which offer comparatively more coverage of crime, entertainment, and other "soft" news topics. These different topical foci represent distinctive ideas about how to simultaneously satisfy journalism's social and commercial functions. This ensures that both functions are reproduced, while also opening up empirical questions about the relative balance between the two. It is the perceived imbalance of these commercial functions that drives concern about the impacts of new owners in these settings. These concerns, real enough, also suggest a theoretical limit when analyzing regional media, as it would make little sense to speak of a socially structured regional media space in which vying visions over how to combine journalism's social and commercial functions were absent.

Regional media exist in relation to the broader national journalistic spaces in which they are embedded. As a rule, regional journalists and news organizations accrue fewer material and symbolic rewards than the best-known journalists and news organizations, which tend to be located in Paris, New York, or Washington, DC. Salaries are on average lower for journalists working in regional media spaces; journalists in these settings also tend to win fewer of the most prestigious professional prizes than their nationally dominant counterparts. While these differences appear primarily geographic, they refer in a deeper sense to a social dimension that is often hidden. A journalist can live in Seattle or Toulouse but not be part of its regional journalistic space; this is the case for the relatively few who hold jobs for the *New York Times, Washington Post, AFP*, or *Libération*. It is these nationally dominant publications, and the journalists that work at them, that tend to hold the monopoly regarding the legitimate definition of what journalism is and should be within a national context. Regional media, whether dominant or periphery, relate their own productions in relation to these larger understandings.

Finally, regional media are structured by laws and markets. While these might in principle be specific to a given regional space, much of the time the most relevant policies are found at the national level. Labor laws, to cite one example highlighted throughout this book, are set at the national level and apply equally across all regional spaces; the regulations that make it difficult to fire an established employee apply regardless of whether that person works in Toulouse or elsewhere; their absence makes such terminations more possible throughout all newsrooms in the United States, regardless of where they are located geographically. Similarly, the structure of markets—themselves shaped in important ways by national governments—affords varying levels of support to less commercially oriented news organizations; they can also do more or less to protect existing actors. By tradition, French policymakers seek to safeguard incumbent news organizations while Americans provide a far more laissez faire orientation to the matter; French media also tend to be more highly centralized in Paris. In this regard, the study of regional media follows a well-established tradition in comparative journalism scholarship by locating the most relevant policy and market influences on news organizations and journalists as existing at the national level.

In studying regional media as social spaces, our aim has been to grasp first and foremost the specific contexts in which journalists confront and manage the effect of diminishing material and symbolic rewards on their belief that the profession is worth the effort. These contexts are difficult to "standardize"—to use the language often employed in comparative projects—precisely because the empirical realities being analyzed are so disparate. Therefore, we aimed to explore the mechanisms that produce empirically observable results in both settings (e.g., managing disappointment as a mode of adjustment). Paradoxically, it is these mechanisms that can be applied and explored more generally and certainly well beyond the two cities studied in this book. In doing so, we offer comparatively minded researchers one way—hardly the only—to conduct research that aspires to be both contextually sensitive and theoretically generative.[2]

Appendix C: Tables and Data

Analysis of journalists' social properties is based on data collected in interviews. To facilitate comparison, the following categories were used: gender, education, employer, job title, and professional experience, each of which has been identified in prior research as shaping journalists' dispositions. In both country samples, journalists identified as male or female; therefore, only these two categories were used. For education, any of the *grandes écoles*, within or beyond Paris, were categorized as prestigious; in the United States, any school with an acceptance rate of 20 percent or lower was given a similar classification. In both places, any degree beyond the bachelor's was classified as advanced; with rare exceptions, these degrees were professional master's degrees, often in journalism or a related communication field.

Major news organizations were defined as those capturing the majority of the audience and employing the bulk of journalists. In Toulouse, these are *La Dépêche du Midi* and France 3; in Seattle, they are the *Seattle Times* and the local television news providers (KOMO, KING, and KIRO). While the public radio station KUOW employs a sizable number of journalists, it has a smaller audience share and also self-consciously thinks of itself as "filling a gap" in news coverage left by larger outlets; for this reason, it is not classified as a dominant outlet. Within all news organizations, job titles were classified as either "general assignment/

freelancer" or "beat reporter/editor." The former designates a collection of positions that tend to be less prestigious and often less stable. A small number of nonreporting positions (e.g., videographers) that shared a similar status were included in this category. The latter classification includes jobs that tend to be situated higher in the news hierarchy, and thus tend to enjoy more stability. Finally, professional experience was classified by decades: i.e., less than ten years, between ten and twenty years, and more than twenty years of experience, with the year of entry into the profession considered the first year.

The data for each chapter is presented here. Table 1 provides an overview of each journalist's social properties. This data also presents information regarding parents' occupations. To preserve the diversity of these job titles, while ensuring transparency in reporting the data, we describe broad patterns in parents' occupations in the descriptive summaries but do not collapse these job titles into discrete categories within the subsequent tables.

LIVING FOR—AND MAYBE OFF—JOURNALISM

Table 2 shows the distribution of journalists' expectations. As a group, those who *live for* journalism comprise nearly equal numbers of women and men holding all ranges of job titles and professional experience; they are differentiated primarily by their employment at a nondominant news outlet and, to a lesser extent, their possession of an advanced university degree. Those who *live off* journalism—a group found only in France—are overwhelmingly women holding jobs as freelancers or general assignment reporters with limited professional experience working at nonmajor news outlets. They, too, have a substantial minority with advanced university degrees. Finally, those who *live for and off* journalism are predominantly men working as beat reporters and editors, with ample professional experience working at both dominant and peripheral news outlets. More than their peers, they are likely to hold university degrees from prestigious universities and to come from liberal professional families.

At first blush, the social properties of those living for journalism appear evenly distributed. Across both cases, sixteen freelancers and general assignment reporters described themselves in this way, as did nineteen beat reporters and editors. Professional experience is likewise evenly distributed: eighteen respondents have a decade or less professional experience, seventeen have more. Gender distribution tells a similar story: nineteen women and sixteen men describe themselves as living for journalism. A diverse array of parents' occupations also appears among journalists in this category; parents with more middle- or working-class jobs, however, only appear among these journalists. Examples of these occupations are construction workers, bank employees, labor organizers, farmers, and carpenters. Journalists coming from higher social origins are not absent; qualitative interview data suggest that many are able to rely in part on those families for financial support. Clearly, then, different conditions can sometimes give rise to similar expectations, at least when looking at those who live for journalism.

Cross-national differences account for some of the apparently even distribution among those who live for journalism. In the United States, beat reporters and editors account for nearly two-thirds of the sample, compared to less than a quarter in France. In part, this reflects the wider array of news organizations in Seattle, each of which has its own staff of editors.[1] By contrast, the limited number of news organizations in Toulouse ensures that the title of editor remains restricted to a relatively smaller number of people who therefore are more likely to live off, and not just for, journalism. When looking at employer type, four times as many respondents in the Seattle sample work for peripheral news outlets as for dominant ones (twenty-one to five, respectively); in Toulouse, the ratio is two to one. Finally, the American sample is also more heavily weighted toward women, while the French sample displays the opposite tendency. Of the twenty-six respondents in the U.S. sample, sixteen are women. By contrast, males constitute a greater proportion of the French respondents who describe themselves as living for journalism (six to three, respectively).

In both countries, employers are one significant differentiator among these respondents. Just eight journalists that live for journalism work at dominant news outlets. By contrast, twenty-seven hold jobs at peripheral news outlets. This suggests the enduring attraction of a job in journalism, as well as the more specific appeal of working at a news organization that is not perceived as being part of the mainstream. Less optimistically, it also hints at the precarity associated with jobs at peripheral news outlets. Very few individuals working at them report approximating anything close to "living off" their chosen profession. Advanced degrees are another differentiator among respondents. About a third (ten of thirty-five) hold such degrees. This suggests that the inculcation of an expectation that journalism is a job to live for—if not always off—has taken hold in journalism education, especially in recent years.

The French respondents who describe themselves as living off journalism are distinguished by their gender, job titles, and professional experience. Seven of nine respondents are female; six of them hold jobs as freelancers or general assignment reporters; five of them have fewer than ten years of professional experience, while just one has greater than twenty years of experience. They tend to work for peripheral news organizations, especially commercial radio outlets. Like their peers living for journalism, a substantial minority (four of nine) holds advanced university degrees; just one, however, holds a degree from a prestigious university.

In both countries, those who live both for and off journalism evince several patterns of social stratification. Seventeen of the twenty-two respondents were beat reporters and editors; just five worked as freelancers or general assignment reporters. Eighteen had at least a decade of professional journalism experience; twelve had more than twenty years, while just four had less than ten years. These respondents were also overwhelmingly male (eighteen men, four women). Nearly half of these respondents (ten of twenty-two) held university degrees from prestigious institutions. Finally, parents' occupations tend toward liberal professions among these journalists. Examples from this group include lawyers, doctors, journalists, professors, and architects; a few are also the children of small business owners.

On the whole, the social distribution suggests that those who live both for and off of journalism tend to be men with substantial professional experience working as beat reporters or editors. By contrast, women with less professional experience working as general assignment reporters and freelancers are more likely to self-describe as either living for or, for some in France, living off of journalism. That being said, being male, having ample professional experience, and holding a more prestigious job title are not guarantees of joining the ranks of those who live for and off journalism. Plenty of respondents with these social properties are found in the "living for" label. Conversely, though, it is rare to find someone who lives both for and off of journalism who is not a man with a prestigious job title and ample professional experience, even if those properties on their own in no way guarantee that an individual will belong to that category.

AT THEIR BEST

Table 3 displays the social properties of journalists across the "best work" labels with which they are associated. Journalists whose own work most closely matches the profession's dominant ideals (i.e., discover, edify) tend to possess more, and more distinctive, social properties. The vast majority—twenty-three of twenty-six journalists—work as beat reporters or editors. University degrees from prestigious educational institutions are also most prevalent among this group, with fifteen of eighteen holding such degrees. The labels associated with these two types of best work also skew male (eighteen men, six women). Professional experience is similarly distributed in unequal fashion, with eighteen of the journalists possessing more than ten years' experience compared to eight with ten or fewer years. Finally, many of these individuals tend to be the children of liberal professional parents.

These proportions are generally reversed among journalists whose best work expresses some distance from the profession's dominant ideals. Journalists whose best work is labeled as decode or dignify tend to hold jobs as general assignment reporters or freelancers, with twenty-six of forty journalists holding such titles. Nearly all of those classified in these labels received university education from nonprestigious institutions (e.g., in the United States, these are community colleges, regional public universities, and small private liberal arts colleges; in France, these are any schools outside the elite *grandes écoles* in and beyond Paris): just three (out of forty) hold degrees from elite universities; advanced degrees are more common, though their prevalence among this group trails that of peers whose work is categorized as edifying or discovering. This likely highlights the overall increase in graduate education among journalists, and thus a slight degree of devaluation associated with such credentials. Finally, women cluster more in these labels than men (twenty-four versus sixteen, respectively), even as professional experience is evenly distributed: twenty have ten or fewer years of professional experience, twenty have more than ten years.

Cross-national differences appear in terms of where journalists with the most—and most prestigious—social properties cluster. In the United

States, such journalists are found primarily under the "discover" label: all are beat reporters or editors and all but one possesses more than a decade's worth of professional journalism experience. By contrast, in France the best-resourced journalists describe their best work as acts of edification: all but two are beat reporters or editors and hold degrees from prestigious universities, and all but three have more than ten years of professional work experience. Edify is the least common form of best work in the U.S. sample, while discovery is least common in the French sample.

By contrast, those who decode and dignify possess very similar social properties cross-nationally. They skew female as a group and tend to be general assignment reporters or freelancers with limited professional experience. Educational attainment tends to come from nonprestigious institutions: just three (of forty) hold degrees from such universities. Finally, nondominant news outlets are more commonly their employers, suggesting that such outlets likely perform some of the historically less prestigious social functions. The fact that prize-winning journalists in both cities tend to work at dominant news outlets is one additional indicator of this apparent division of labor within each city's news field.

CONSERVE, CHALLENGE, ACCEDE

Table 4 shows the social properties associated with the three responses. In both countries, those who seek to ignore economic constraints and technological constraints, and by doing so conserve the preferred ideal of journalism, tend to be men, holding jobs as beat reporters or editors at dominant news media, with ample professional experience, and moderately high volumes of cultural capital. Those who conserve comprise more than twice as many men as women (thirteen versus six); nearly all—eighteen of nineteen—hold jobs as beat reporters and editors; and fourteen of nineteen tend to work for dominant news organizations. Nearly half hold high volumes of cultural capital, as indicated by the possession of a degree from an advanced university or an advanced degree.

Those who challenge the status quo by investing in economic constraints and technological transformations tend to be both men and women, often working at peripheral news organizations, possessing less than a decade of professional experience and substantial volumes of cultural capital. Of those who challenge, ten are women and fourteen are men. Three-fourths work at nonlegacy news organizations; nearly half have less than a decade of professional experience, while just a quarter have more than two decades of experience. The prevalence of educational attainment cannot be overstated: nineteen of twenty-four hold degrees from prestigious universities or advanced degrees. Finally, those who challenge also tend to occupy intermediate positions in the field. Across all social properties, the lowest distribution of journalists for any attribute who invested is 26.1 percent (major, legacy news employees) and the highest is 52.6 percent (individuals with degrees from prestigious universities; percentages not shown in table).

Those who accede, by enduring transformations without expecting to benefit from them, include more women than men and nearly all freelancers or general assignment reporters working for peripheral news organizations with limited professional experience; they also hold moderately high volumes of cultural capital. In contrast to both the conserve and challenge strategies, which to varying degrees are majority male, women constitute the majority of those who acceded: fourteen are women, nine are men. Nearly all work for peripheral news organizations (twenty of twenty-three); and more than half have less than a decade of professional experience while just three have more than twenty years. Like those who conserve, about half of the journalists in this group hold advanced degrees or degrees from prestigious educational institutions.

The relationship between social properties and practical strategies is not mechanical. It is possible for a freelancer or general assignment reporter to ignore contemporary economic and technological transformations and in doing so seek to conserve the status quo (one did). It is also the case that journalists hailing from liberal professional families tend to be split in between conserving and challenging; this reflects both the desire among these groups to retain the profession's most-esteemed social functions as well as the perceived opportunity to benefit from their redefinition. Finally, some properties tend to be distributed fairly evenly over multiple categories. Across the whole sample, for example, the number of men who challenged (fourteen) and conserved (thirteen) was nearly equal. Relatedly, journalists with between ten and nineteen years of professional experience were distributed almost evenly across the three strategies (seven, seven, and six).

Cross-nationally, the most salient difference pertains to the overall distribution of responses. A greater number of the journalists in the American sample challenged (twenty of thirty-six, compared to four of thirty in the French sample). By contrast, almost half of all the journalists in the French sample conserved (fourteen), compared to just five in the United States. These differences, in turn, appear related to the degree to which specific social properties correspond to particular practical strategies. For example, whereas nearly all beat reporters and editors in the French sample sought to conserve (thirteen of fourteen), in the American sample sixteen of twenty-five sought to challenge. Thus, while all the people in the American sample who sought to conserve were beat reporters or editors, this particular property on its own does not seem to enable one to ignore the economic and technological transformations with which they are confronted.

LEAVING JOURNALISM

Table 5 reports on the social properties of those from the original sample who departed from journalism by January 2022. What is most striking is how evenly distributed the social properties are among those who depart, with similar numbers of women and men leaving, and no clear differences in departure linked to education, employment, job title, or professional experience. While the overall numbers are small, this suggests that departure from the profession can come from nearly anyone.

Differences appear primarily in terms of the extent to which departures are conceived as choices or necessities. Beat reporters and editors in both country samples are more likely to see departure as the former; general assignment reporters and freelancers tend toward the latter view. The slightly greater prevalence of journalists at dominant news organizations that see their departures as necessary stems from the fact that several Seattle television stations experienced new corporate management that ushered in layoffs and sometimes made conditions sufficiently unpalatable that some journalists exited rather than deal with the transformations in their work lives.

Note that, due to the small numbers of journalists in this chapter, the qualitative results in this section also turn to individuals not included in part of the original sample who had also left the profession.

TABLE 1
Journalists and Their Social Properties

Country	Gender	Job Title	Employer	Educational Background	Highest Degree	Year Entered Journalism	Parents' Occupations
U.S.	F	GA reporter	nonmajor	nonprestigious	BA	2013	civil servants
U.S.	F	GA reporter	nonmajor	nonprestigious	BA	2015	carpenter, homemaker
U.S.	F	GA reporter	nonmajor	nonprestigious	BA	2000	teachers
U.S.	F	GA reporter	major	nonprestigious	BA	2017	winemakers
U.S.	M	Beat reporter/editor	nonmajor	nonprestigious	BA	2014	farmers
U.S.	F	GA reporter	nonmajor	nonprestigious	MA	2017	personal assistant
U.S.	F	GA reporter	nonmajor	nonprestigious	BA	2005	labor organizer, teacher
U.S.	M	Beat reporter/editor	major	prestigious	BA	1981	businessman, teacher
U.S.	F	Freelance reporter	nonmajor	nonprestigious	MA	1999	house painter
U.S.	F	Beat reporter/editor	major	nonprestigious	BA	1979	lawyer, journalist
U.S.	M	Beat reporter/editor	nonmajor	nonprestigious	BA	1998	small business owner

(continued)

TABLE 1 (*continued*)

Country	Gender	Job Title	Employer	Educational Background	Highest Degree	Year Entered Journalism	Parents' Occupations
U.S.	F	Beat reporter/editor	major	prestigious	BA	2010	doctor, homemaker
U.S.	M	Beat reporter/editor	major	prestigious	BA	1995	teachers
U.S.	M	GA reporter	major	nonprestigious	BA	1980	insurance, homemaker
U.S.	M	Beat reporter/editor	major	prestigious	BA	1996	professor, homemaker
U.S.	F	Beat reporter/editor	major	prestigious	BA	1992	lawyer; real estate agent
U.S.	F	Beat reporter/editor	nonmajor	nonprestigious	BA	2008	construction, homemaker
U.S.	M	Beat reporter/editor	nonmajor	nonprestigious	MA	2004	actor, writer
U.S.	M	Beat reporter/editor	nonmajor	nonprestigious	BA	2014	lawyer
U.S.	F	Beat reporter/editor	nonmajor	nonprestigious	BA	1999	military, homemaker
U.S.	F	Beat reporter/editor	major	nonprestigious	MA	2014	accountant, teacher
U.S.	M	Beat reporter/editor	nonmajor	nonprestigious	BA	1998	unknown
U.S.	M	Beat reporter/editor	nonmajor	nonprestigious	BA	2006	pharmacist, manager

U.S.	M	Beat reporter/editor	nonmajor	prestigious	MA	2006	journalists
U.S.	F	Beat reporter/editor	nonmajor	nonprestigious	BA	2017	unknown
U.S.	M	GA reporter	major	prestigious	BA	1996	advertising
U.S.	M	Freelance reporter	nonmajor	nonprestigious	BA	2005	small business owner
U.S.	F	Beat reporter	nonmajor	nonprestigious	BA	2009	travel agent
U.S.	F	GA reporter	nonmajor	prestigious	MA	2014	documentarian, photographer
U.S.	F	GA reporter	major	nonprestigious	BA	2008	salesman, homemaker
U.S.	M	Beat reporter/editor	nonmajor	n/a	n/a	2004	unknown
U.S.	F	Beat reporter/editor	nonmajor	non-prestigious	MA	1975	unknown
U.S.	M	GA reporter	major	prestigious	MA	2009	doctor, homemaker
U.S.	F	Beat reporter/editor	nonmajor	prestigious	MA	2010	teacher, travel consultant
U.S.	F	Beat reporter/editor	nonmajor	prestigious	BA	1973	author, homemaker
U.S.	M	Beat reporter/editor	nonmajor	prestigious	MA	2006	lawyer, homemaker
U.S.	M	Beat reporter/editor	major	nonprestigious	BA	1993	businessman, homemaker

(continued)

TABLE 1 (*continued*)

Country	Gender	Job Title	Employer	Educational Background	Highest Degree	Year Entered Journalism	Parents' Occupations
U.S.	F	GA reporter	major	nonprestigious	BA	2003	salesperson
U.S.	F	GA reporter	major	nonprestigious	MA	N/A	podiatrist, homemaker
U.S.	M	Freelance reporter	nonmajor	nonprestigious	BA	1997	construction worker
U.S.	M	Beat reporter/editor	major	nonprestigious	BA	1998	unknown
FR	F	GA Reporter	nonmajor	nonprestigious	M1	2005	teachers
FR	F	GA Reporter	nonmajor	nonprestigious	M1	2005	teachers
FR	M	Beat reporter/editor	nonmajor	nonprestigious	M1	2009	employees
FR	F	freelance	nonmajor	nonprestigious	M1	1997	absent father; secretary
FR	M	freelance	nonmajor	nonprestigious	M1	1999	teachers
FR	F	GA Reporter	major	nonprestigious	M2	2012	special needs teachers
FR	M	Freelance reporter	nonmajor	prestigious	M2	2013	small bus. owner; homemaker
FR	M	GA Reporter	nonmajor	prestigious	M2	2013	workers

FR	M	Freelance reporter	major	prestigious	M2	2013	unknown
FR	F	Freelance reporter	nonmajor	nonprestigious	M1e	1998	bank employees
FR	F	Freelance reporter	nonmajor	nonprestigious	M1	1998	journalist, homemaker
FR	M	Freelance reporter	nonmajor	prestigious	M2	2008	construction, hairdresser
FR	M	GA Reporter	major	nonprestigious	Bac	1985	teacher, salesperson
FR	M	Beat reporter/editor	nonmajor	prestigious	Bac + 2	1981	army general, homemaker
FR	M	GA Reporter	major	prestigious	Bac + 2	2002	small bus. owner; secretary
FR	F	GA Reporter	major	prestigious	L3	1981	unknown
FR	M	GA Reporter	major	nonprestigious	M1	1996	civil servant; homemaker
FR	M	Beat reporter/editor	nonmajor	nonprestigious	M1	1999	small bus. owner; journalist
FR	M	GA Reporter	major	nonprestigious	M1	2001	small bus. owner; secretary
FR	F	Beat reporter/editor	nonmajor	nonprestigious	M1	2012	salesperson; secretary
FR	M	Beat reporter/editor	major	prestigious	M2	2005	manager, assistant
FR	F	Freelancer	nonmajor	prestigious	M2	1983	mining engineer, homemaker

(continued)

TABLE 1 (continued)

Country	Gender	Job Title	Employer	Educational Background	Highest Degree	Year Entered Journalism	Parents' Occupations
FR	M	GA Reporter	nonmajor	prestigious	M2	2015	executives for aerospace co.
FR	F	Beat reporter/editor	nonmajor	nonprestigious	M2	1998	university professors
FR	M	Beat reporter/editor	major	nonprestigious	M2	1990	architect, homemaker
FR	M	GA Reporter	major	prestigious	M1	1989	civil servant, secretary
FR	F	GA Reporter	major	nonprestigious	M2	1995	small bus. owner; secretary
FR	M	GA Reporter	nonmajor	prestigious	M2	1995	lawyer and real estate developer, homemaker
FR	M	GA Reporter	major	nonprestigious	L3	2009	teacher and public functionary
FR	M	GA Reporter	nonmajor	prestigious	M2	2007	bank employee, civil servant

Because of a small number of nonresponses to specific questions, the total number of journalists' responses in the descriptive tables does not all add up to seventy-one. Moreover, the proportion of social properties (e.g., gender) changes slightly between tables due to these nonresponses (e.g., tables 2 and 4 includes thirty women and thirty-six men, while table 3 has thirty-two women and thirty-four men).

TABLE 2

Distribution of Social Properties Across Career Expectations of Journalism

	Living For			Living Off			Both		
	U.S.	FR	Total	U.S.	FR	Total	U.S.	FR	Total
Gender									
Female (N = 30)	16	3	**19**	0	7	**7**	3	1	**4**
Male (N = 36)	10	6	**16**	0	2	**2**	7	11	**18**
Education									
Advanced degree (N = 21)	5	5	**10**	0	4	**4**	3	4	**7**
Prestigious university (N = 19)	4	4	**8**	0	1	**1**	5	5	**10**
Employer									
Dominant (N = 23)	5	3	**8**	0	3	**3**	6	6	**12**
Peripheral (N = 43)	21	6	**27**	0	6	**6**	4	6	**10**
Job Title									
Freelance/GA reporter (N = 27)	9	7	**16**	0	6	**6**	2	3	**5**
Beat reporter or editor (N = 39)	17	2	**19**	0	3	**3**	8	9	**17**
Experience									
≤ 10 years (N = 27)	13	5	**18**	0	5	**5**	2	2	**4**
11–19 years (N = 20)	9	2	**11**	0	3	**3**	1	5	**6**
≥ 20 years (N = 19)	4	2	**6**	0	1	**1**	7	5	**12**

FR = France; GA = General Assignment Reporter; U.S. = United States.

TABLE 3

Distribution of Social Properties Across Best Work Labels

	Decode			Dignify			Discover			Edify		
	U.S.	FR	Total	U.S.	FR	Total	U.S.	FR	Total	U.S.	FR	Total
Gender												
Female (N=32)	10	6	**16**	4	4	**8**	3	0	**3**	2	1	**3**
Male (N=34)	6	3	**9**	2	5	**7**	5	4	**9**	2	7	**9**
Education												
Prestigious university (N=18)	1	1	**2**	1	0	**1**	5	1	**6**	3	6	**9**
Advanced degree (N=21)	2	2	**4**	1	3	**4**	4	2	**6**	1	6	**7**
News Organization												
Dominant (N=25)	5	4	**9**	2	2	**4**	2	3	**5**	2	5	**7**
Peripheral (N=41)	12	5	**17**	5	7	**12**	6	1	**7**	2	3	**5**
Job Title												
Freelance/GA reporter (N=29)	9	7	**16**	4	6	**10**	0	1	**1**	0	2	**2**
Beat report/ editor (N=37)	7	2	**9**	2	3	**5**	10	3	**13**	4	6	**10**
Experience												
≤ 10 years (N=28)	8	4	**12**	3	5	**8**	1	1	**2**	3	3	**6**
11–19 yrs (N=20)	3	2	**5**	2	3	**5**	4	2	**6**	1	3	**4**
≥ 20 years (N=18)	5	3	**8**	1	1	**2**	4	1	**5**	1	2	**3**

TABLE 4
Distribution of Social Properties Across Responses

	Accede			Challenge			Conserve		
	U.S.	FR	Total	U.S.	FR	Total	U.S.	FR	Total
Gender									
* Female (N=30)	8	6	14	9	1	10	2	4	6
* Male (N=36)	3	6	9	11	3	14	3	10	13
Education									
* Advanced degree (N=21)	1	6	7	7	2	9	0	5	5
* Prestigious university (N=19)	1	4	5	8	2	10	0	4	4
Employer									
* Dominant (N=23)	2	1	3	4	2	6	5	9	14
* Peripheral (N=43)	9	11	20	16	2	18	0	5	5
Job Title									
* Freelance/GA reporter (N=27)	7	11	18	4	4	8	0	1	1
* Beat reporter or editor (N=39)	4	1	5	16	0	16	5	13	18
Experience									
* ≤ 10 years (N=27)	5	8	13	9	2	11	1	2	3
* 11–19 years (N=20)	3	4	7	7	0	7	0	6	6
* ≥ 20 years (N=19)	3	0	3	4	2	6	4	6	10

TABLE 5

Distribution of Social Properties Across Departures from Journalism

	Choice			Necessity		
	U.S.	FR	Total	U.S.	FR	Total
Gender						
* Female (N=12)	4	2	6	5	1	6
* Male (N=9)	1	2	3	4	2	6
Education						
* Advanced degree (N=12)	1	4	5	5	2	7
* Prestigious university (N=4)	2	1	3	1	0	1
Employer						
* Dominant (N=9)	2	1	3	5	1	6
* Peripheral (N=12)	3	3	6	4	2	6
Job Title						
* Freelancer/GA reporter (N=12)	0	2	2	7	3	10
* Beat reporter or editor (N=9)	5	2	7	2	0	2
Experience						
* ≤ 10 years (N=3)	1	0	1	2	0	2
* 11–19 years (N=11)	2	4	6	4	1	5
* ≥ 20 years (N=7)	2	0	2	3	2	5

Notes

INTRODUCTION

1. Stanley Kunitz, *The Collected Poems* (New York: Norton, 1978), 217.
2. Vincent Dubois, *Culture as a Vocation: Sociology of Career Choices in Cultural Management* (New York: Routledge, 2015).
3. Érik Neveu, *Sociologie du Journalisme* (Paris: La Découverte, 2019).
4. Max Weber, *Max Weber's Complete Writings on Academic and Political Vocations*, ed. John Dreijmanis, trans. Gordon C. Wells (New York: Algora, 2008), 80–97.
5. The extent of existential angst regarding the profession's viability can be glimpsed in the titles of books written by both journalists and scholars. See Bernard Poulet, *La fin des journaux et l'avenir de l'information* (Paris: Editions Gallimard, 2009); Stephen D. Reese, *The Crisis of the Institutional Press* (Cambridge: Polity, 2021); and David M. Ryfe, *Can Journalism Survive? An Inside Look at American Newsrooms* (Cambridge: Polity, 2012).
6. Pierre Bourdieu, *Pascalian Meditations* (Stanford, CA: Stanford University Press, 2000).
7. The expression, which Bourdieu regularly invokes in his discussions of *illusio*, comes from Montaigne and refers to gambling by candlelight in the sixteenth century. At that time, given the costs associated with candles, winnings were only worth the effort to the extent they matched or exceeded the candle's expense. In this sense, journalism is "worth the candle" to the extent that the

overall balance of material and symbolic rewards is acceptable to an individual journalist.
8. In drawing on Bourdieu, this book follows prior scholarship that finds his theoretical tools useful for analyzing journalism. For an introduction to this work, see Rodney Benson and Érik Neveu, eds., *Bourdieu and the Journalistic Field* (Cambridge: Polity, 2005).
9. Studies of regional journalism in France include Franck Bousquet and Pauline Amiel, *La presse quotidienne régionale* (Paris: La Découverte, 2021); Patrick Le Floch, *Économie de la presse quotidienne régionale: Déterminants et conséquences de la concentration* (Paris: L'Harmattan, 1997); Nicolas Kaciaf, "Faire rendre des comptes: Les conditions de l'investigation journalistique à l'échelle locale," *Politiques de communication* 15, no. 2 (2020): 139–66, https://doi.org/10.3917/pdc.015.0139; and Érik Neveu, "The Local Press and Farmers' Protests in Brittany: Proximity and Distance in the Local Newspaper Coverage of a Social Movement," *Journalism Studies* 3, no. 1 (2002): 53–67, https://doi.org/10.1080/14616700120107338. For a selection of regional journalism scholarship in the United States, see Penelope Muse Abernathy, *The Expanding News Desert* (Chapel Hill: Center for Innovation and Sustainability in Local Media, School of Media and Journalism, University of North Carolina, 2018), https://etaara.com/wp-content/uploads/2022/02/The-Expanding-News-Desert-10_14-Web.pdf; Danny Hayes and Jennifer L. Lawless, *News Hole: The Demise of Local Journalism and Political Engagement* (New York: Cambridge University Press, 2021); Philip M. Napoli et al., "Local Journalism and the Information Needs of Local Communities: Toward a Scalable Assessment Approach," *Journalism Practice* 13, no. 8 (2019): 1024–28, https://doi.org/10.1080/17512786.2019.1647110; and Sue Robinson, *Networked News, Racial Divides: How Power and Privilege Shape Public Discourse in Progressive Communities* (New York: Cambridge University Press, 2018). For a collection of articles on the topic, pertaining to Western Europe and North America more broadly, see Rasmus Kleis Nielsen, ed., *Local Journalism: The Decline of Newspapers and the Rise of Digital Media* (London: I. B. Tauris, 2015).
10. Rasmus Kleis Nielsen and Sarah Anne Ganter, *The Power of Platforms: Shaping Media and Society* (New York: Oxford University Press, 2022).
11. Joy Jenkins and Rasmus Kleis Nielsen, *The Digital Transition of Local News* (Oxford: Reuters Institute for the Study of Journalism, 2018), https://reutersinstitute.politics.ox.ac.uk/sites/default/files/2018-04/JenkinsNielsenDigitalTransitionLocalNews.pdf.
12. Matthew Powers and Sandra Vera-Zambrano, "Explaining the Formation of Online News Startups in France and the United States: A Field Analysis,"

Journal of Communication 66, no. 5 (2016): 857–77, https://doi.org/10.1111/jcom.12253.

13. For French media's lesser dependence on advertising, see Rodney Benson, *Shaping Immigration News: A French-American Comparison* (New York: Cambridge University Press, 2013); on magazines, see Brooke Erin Duffy, *Remake, Remodel: Women's Magazines in the Digital Age* (Champaign: University of Illinois Press, 2013); for wire services, see Zeynep Devrim Gürsel, *Image Brokers: Visualizing World News in the Age of Digital Circulation* (Oakland: University of California Press, 2016).
14. Patrick Champagne, *La double dépendance: Sur le journalisme* (Paris: Raisons d'Agir, 2016); and Victor Pickard, *Democracy Without Journalism?: Confronting the Misinformation Society* (New York: Oxford University Press, 2020).
15. These figures come from Commission de la Carte d'Identité des Journalistes Professionnels, www.ccijp.net/article-165-statistiques.html.
16. Mason Walker, "U.S. Newsroom Employment Has Fallen 26% Since 2008," *Pew Research*, July 13, 2021, www.pewresearch.org/fact-tank/2021/07/13/u-s-newsroom-employment-has-fallen-26-since-2008/.
17. Christine Leteinturier and Cégolène Frisque, *Les espaces professionnels des journalistes: Des corpus quantitatifs aux analyses qualitatives* (Paris: Éditions Panthéon-Assas, 2015).
18. This information comes from the United States Bureau of Labor Statistics, www.bls.gov/ooh/media-and-communication/reporters-correspondents-and-broadcast-news-analysts.htm; on working conditions, see Mirjam Gollmitzer, "Employment Conditions in Journalism," Oxford Research Encyclopedias, Communication, March 26, 2019, https://doi.org/10.1093/acrefore/9780190228613.013.805; and Carey L. Higgins-Dobney, "Producing in Precarity: A Focus on Freelancing in US Local Television Newsrooms," in *Newswork and Precarity*, ed. Kalyani Chadha and Linda Steiner (London: Routledge, 2022), 71–83.
19. Stephen Cushion, "Rich Media, Poor Journalists: Journalists' Salaries," *Journalism Practice* 1, no. 1 (2007): 120–29, https://doi.org/10.1080/17512780601078910.
20. These developments are not unique to France and the United States. Nicole S. Cohen, *Writers' Rights: Freelance Journalism in a Digital Age* (Montreal: McGill-Queen's University Press, 2016); and Henrik Örnebring, *Newsworkers: A European Perspective* (London: Bloomsbury, 2016).
21. Pauline Amiel, "L'identité professionnelle des localiers à l'heure des mutations économiques et numérique de la presse locale: Vers un journalisme de service?," *Les Cahiers du Numérique* 15, no. 4 (2019): 17–38, https://doi.org/10.3166/lcn.15.4.17-38; and Élise Ho-Pun-Cheung, "Concilier contraintes économiques et

indépendance: Un journalisme à la frontière de la profession," *Politiques de communication* 16, no. 1 (2021): 85–113, https://doi.org/10.3917/pdc.016.0085.
22. Dean Starkman, "The Hamster Wheel: Why Running as Fast as We Can Is Getting Us Nowhere," *Columbia Journalism Review*, September/October 2010, https://archives.cjr.org/cover_story/the_hamster_wheel.php.
23. Florence Le Cam and David Domingo, "The Tyranny of Immediacy," in *Gatekeeping in Transition*, ed. Tim Vos and François Heinderyckx (New York: Routledge, 2015), 123–40; and Zvi Reich and Yigal Godler, "A Time of Uncertainty: The Effects of Reporters' Time Schedule on Their Work," *Journalism Studies* 15, no. 5 (2014): 607–18, https://doi.org/10.1080/1461670X.2014.882484.
24. Benson, *Shaping Immigration News*, 164–69.
25. The language of ecosystems comes from C. W. Anderson, *Rebuilding the News: Metropolitan Journalism in the Digital Age* (Philadelphia, PA: Temple University Press, 2013).
26. Andrew Chadwick, *The Hybrid Media System: Politics and Power*, 2nd ed. (New York: Oxford University Press, 2017); Julien Figeac et al., "Mobile Phones in the Spread of Unreliable Information on Twitter: Evidence from the 2017 French Presidential Campaign," *Mobile Media and Communication* 9, no. 3 (2021): 441–64, https://doi.org/10.1177/2050157920972157; and Adrienne Russell, *Networked: A Contemporary History of News in Transition* (Cambridge: Polity, 2011).
27. Jeremy Tunstall, *Journalists at Work: Specialist Correspondents; Their News Organizations, News Sources and Competitor-Colleagues* (London: Constable, 1971).
28. Bruce A. Williams and Michael X. Delli Carpini, *After Broadcast News: Media Regimes, Democracy, and the New Information Environment* (New York: Cambridge University Press, 2011), 135–67.
29. David T. Z. Mindich, *Tuned Out: Why Americans Under 40 Don't Follow the News* (New York: Oxford University Press, 2005).
30. See, for example, Matt Carlson, Sue Robinson, and Seth C. Lewis, *News After Trump: Journalism's Crisis of Relevance in a Changed Media Culture* (New York: Oxford, 2021).
31. Safia Dahani, "Incorporer la contrainte, transmettre la critique, occuper les médias: Sur la médiatisation de jeunes dirigeants du Front National," *Savoir/Agir* 46, no. 4 (2018): 83–88, https://doi.org/10.3917/sava.046.0083; and Arnaud Mercier and Laura Amigo, "Insulting and Hateful Tweets Against Journalists and 'Merdias,'" *Mots: Les langages du politique* 125, no. 1 (2021): 73–91, https://doi.org/10.4000/mots.28043.
32. Silvio Waisbord, "Mob Censorship: Online Harassment of US Journalists in Times of Digital Hate and Populism," *Digital Journalism* 8, no. 8 (2020): 1030–46, https://doi.org/10.1080/21670811.2020.1818111.

33. Olivier Baisnée et al., "La 'violence' des Gilets Jaunes: Quand la fait-diversification fait diversion; Les routines journalistiques à l'épreuve des manifestations à Toulouse (novembre 2018-juin 2019)," *Sur Le Journalisme, About Journalism, Sobre Jornalismo* 10, no. 1 (2021): 28–43, https://doi.org/10.25200/SLJ.v10.n1.2021.452.
34. Todd Gitlin, *Occupy Nation: The Roots, the Spirit, and the Promise of Occupy Wall Street* (New York: Harper Collins, 2012).
35. Patrick Champagne, *Faire l'opinion: Le nouveau jeu politique*, 2nd ed. (Paris: Les Éditions de Minuit, 2015); and Jonathan M. Ladd, *Why Americans Hate the Media and How It Matters* (Princeton, NJ: Princeton University Press, 2011).
36. Natalie Jomini Stroud, *Niche News: The Politics of News Choice* (New York: Oxford University Press, 2011).
37. Michael Schudson, *The Rise of the Right to Know: Politics and the Culture of Transparency, 1945–1975* (Cambridge, MA: Harvard University Press, 2015), 135–79.
38. Pierre Bourdieu, *The Logic of Practice*, trans. Richard Nice (Stanford, CA: Stanford University Press, 1990).
39. Gérard Mauger, "Sens pratique et conditions sociales de possibilité de la pensée 'pensante,'" *Cités* 38, no. 2 (2009): 61–77.
40. Pierre Bourdieu, "The Forms of Capital," in *Handbook of Theory and Research for the Sociology of Education*, ed. John G. Richardson (Westport, CT: Greenwood, 1986), 244.
41. For a discussion of these principles, see Sandra Vera-Zambrano and Matthew Powers, "The Roots of Journalistic Perception: A Bourdieusian Approach to Media and Class," in *The Routledge Companion to Media and Class*, ed. Erika Polson, Lynn Schofield Clark, and Radhika Gajjala (London: Routledge, 2020), 157–67; and Matthew Powers and Sandra Vera-Zambrano, "What Are Journalists for Today?," in *Rethinking Media Research for Changing Societies*, ed. Matthew Powers and Adrienne Russell (Cambridge: Cambridge University Press, 2020), 65–77.
42. The lack of racial diversity in the two samples, itself a reflection of the profession's demographics in the regional press of both countries, makes any meaningful comparative analysis of this issue extremely difficult. The theoretical perspective presented here can, however, be utilized to analyze racial dynamics in other settings.
43. Albert O. Hirschman, *Shifting Involvements: Private Interest and Public Action* (Princeton, NJ: Princeton University Press, 1982).
44. Bourdieu, *Pascalian Meditations*, 227.
45. See Jeffrey C. Alexander, "The Mass News Media in Systemic, Historical and Comparative Perspective," in *Mass Media and Social Change*, ed. Elihu Katz and Tamás Szecskö (Beverly Hills: Sage, 1981), 17–51; Benson, *Shaping*

Immigration News; Benson and Neveu, *Bourdieu and the Journalistic Field*; Angèle Christin, *Metrics at Work: Journalism and the Contested Meaning of Algorithms* (Princeton, NJ: Princeton University Press, 2020); Cyril Lemieux and John Schmalzbauer, "Involvement and Detachment Among French and American Journalists: To Be or Not to Be a 'Real' Professional," in *Rethinking Comparative Cultural Sociology: Repertoires of Evaluation in France and the United States*, ed. Michèle Lamont and Laurent Thévenot (New York: Cambridge University Press, 2000), 148–69; Jean-Gustave Padioleau, *"Le Monde" et le "Washington Post": Précepteurs et mousquetaires* (Paris: Presses Universitaires de France,1985); and Sylvain Parasie, *Computing the News: Data Journalism and the Search for Objectivity* (New York: Columbia University Press, 2022).

46. Benson, *Shaping Immigration News*, 15.
47. Leteinturier and Frisque, *Les espaces professionnels des journalistes*.
48. Joshua Benton, "The Game of Concentration: The Internet Is Pushing the American News Business to New York and the Coasts," *NiemanLab*, March 25, 2016, www.niemanlab.org/2016/03/the-game-of-concentration-the-internet-is-pushing-the-american-news-business-to-new-york-and-the-coasts/.
49. For details about the news media in these two cities, as well as principles underpinning the analysis of regional media as a research object, see appendix B. An initial description of the cities is also in Matthew Powers, Sandra Vera-Zambrano, and Olivier Baisnée, "The News Crisis Compared: The Impact of the Journalism Crisis in Toulouse, France and Seattle, USA," in *Local Journalism: The Decline of Newspapers and the Rise of Digital Media*, ed. Rasmus Kleis Nielsen (London: I. B. Tauris, 2015), 31–50.
50. Other candidates might include Chicago/Lyon, which share an industrial and working-class base, and Marseille/San Francisco, which are port cities shaped in important ways by immigration. In any comparison, the aim is functional equivalence of each city *in relation to its national setting*. Therefore, it's important that Toulouse and Seattle, for instance, occupy a secondary position relative to New York and Paris rather than empirical equivalence in some substantive properties (e.g., population).
51. Dominique Marchetti, "Contribution à une sociologie des transformations du champ journalistique dans les années 80 et 90: A propos d' 'événements sida' et du 'scandale du sang contaminé'" (PhD diss., École des Hautes Études en Sciences Sociales, 1997); and Géraud Lafarge and Dominique Marchetti, "Les portes fermées du journalisme: L'espace social des étudiants des formations 'reconnues,'" *Actes de la Recherche en Sciences Sociales* 189, no. 4 (2011): 72–99, https://doi.org/10.3917/arss.189.0072.
52. Robert S. Weiss, *Learning from Strangers: The Art and Method of Qualitative Interview Studies* (New York: Free Press, 1994), 23.

53. Matthew Powers and Sandra Vera-Zambrano, "The Universal and the Contextual of Media Systems: Research Design, Epistemology, and the Production of Comparative Knowledge," *International Journal of Press/Politics* 23, no. 2 (2018): 143–60, https://doi.org/10.1177/1940161218771899.
54. For alternative approaches to comparison, which emphasize the accumulation of empirical results via standardized concepts and measurements, see Frank Esser, Jesper Strömbäck, and Claes H. de Vreese, "Reviewing Key Concepts in Research on Political News Journalism: Conceptualizations, Operationalizations and Propositions for Future Research," *Journalism* 13, no. 2 (2012): 139–43, https://doi.org/10.1177/1464884911427795; Frank Esser and Thomas Hanitzsch, "On the Why and How of Comparative Inquiry in Communication Studies," in *Handbook of Comparative Communication Research*, ed. Frank Esser and Thomas Hanitzsch (London: Routledge, 2012), 3–22; Pippa Norris, "Comparative Political Communications: Common Frameworks or Babelian Confusion?," *Government and Opposition* 44, no. 3 (2009): 321–40, https://doi.org/10.1111/j.1477-7053.2009.01290.x; and Werner Wirth and Steffen Kolb, "Securing Equivalence: Problems and Solutions," in Esser and Hanitzsch, *Handbook of Comparative Research*, 469–85. Hallin and Mancini's important work utilizes ideal types as a way to generate questions and explore cross-national variations. See Daniel C. Hallin and Paolo Mancini, *Comparing Media Systems: Three Models of Media and Politics* (New York: Cambridge University Press, 2004).
55. Michael Schudson, *The Sociology of News* (New York: Norton, 2011), 218.
56. For a discussion in social science research more generally, see Erving Goffman, "Felicity's Condition," *American Journal of Sociology* 18, no. 1 (1983): 1–53, https://doi.org/10.1086/227833. The term itself comes from J. L. Austin, *How to Do Things with Words* (New York: Oxford University Press, 1965).
57. Important prior work in the sociology of journalists, on which we draw, can be found in Mark Deuze, *Media Work* (Cambridge: Polity, 2007); Mark Deuze and Tamara Witschge, *Beyond Journalism* (Cambridge: Polity, 2020); Roger Dickinson, "Accomplishing Journalism: Towards a Revived Sociology of a Media Occupation," *Cultural Sociology* 1, no. 2 (2007): 189–208, https://doi.org/10.1177/1749975507078187; Thomas Hanitzsch et al., *Worlds of Journalism: Journalistic Cultures Around the Globe* (New York: Columbia University Press, 2019); David Hesmondhalgh and Sarah Baker, *Creative Labour: Media Work in Three Cultural Industries* (New York: Routledge, 2013); Lafarge and Marchetti, "Les portes fermées du journalisme"; Leteinturier and Frisque, *Les espaces professionnels des journalistes*; Örnebring, *Newsworkers*; Tunstall, *Journalists at Work*; and David Weaver, Lars Willnat, and G. Cleveland Wilhoit, "The American Journalist in the Digital Age: Another Look at U.S. News People," *Journalism*

and Mass Communication Quarterly 96, no. 1 (2019): 101–30, https://doi.org/10.1177/1077699018778242.

58. In the U.S. context, see Napoli et al., "Local Journalism and the Information Needs of Communities," for a statement of these functions as they pertain to regional media. For a comparative discussion of France and the United States, see Benson, *Shaping Immigration News*, 131–71.
59. Michael Schudson, *Why Democracies Need an Unlovable Press* (Cambridge: Polity, 2008).
60. Dubois, *Culture as a Vocation*, 1–4.
61. Colette Brin, Jean Charron, and Jean de Bonville, eds., *Nature et transformations du journalisme: Théorie et recherches empiriques* (Québec, Canada: Presses de l'Université Laval, 2004), 2.
62. Sophie Denave, "Les conditions individuelles et collectives des ruptures professionnelles," *Cahiers Internationaux de Sociologie* 120, no. 1 (2006): 95, https://doi.org/10.3917/cis.120.0085.

1. THE GENESIS OF THE JOURNALIST'S PREDICAMENT

1. Christian Delporte, *Les Journalistes en France, 1880–1950: Naissance et construction d'une profession* (Paris: Le Seuil, 1999); and Michael Schudson, *Discovering the News: A Social History of American Newspapers* (New York: Basic, 1978).
2. Claude Bellanger et al., eds., *Histoire générale de la presse française*, vol. 4, *de 1940 à 1958* (Paris: Presses Universitaires de France, 1975); and Charles E. Clark, *The Public Prints: The Newspaper in Anglo-American Culture, 1665–1740* (New York: Oxford University Press, 1994).
3. See Michael B. Palmer, *Des petits journaux aux grandes agences: Naissance du journalisme moderne, 1863–1914* (Paris: Aubier, 1983); and Michael Schudson, *Discovering the News*.
4. Max Weber, *Max Weber's Complete Writings on Academic and Political Vocations*, ed. John Dreijmanis, trans. Gordon C. Wells (New York: Algora, 2008), 80–97. For a discussion of Weber's approach to journalism, see Gilles Bastin, "The Press in the Light of Modern Capitalism: A Planned Survey by Max Weber on Newspapers and Journalism," *Max Weber Studies* 13, no. 2 (2013): 151–75, https://muse.jhu.edu/article/808729. For an application of Weber's principles to journalism in France and the United States, see Sandra Vera-Zambrano and Matthew Powers, "Journalistic Judgment in Comparative Perspective: A Weberian Analysis of France and the United States," *International Journal of Press/Politics* 27, no. 2 (2022): 478–96, https://journals.sagepub.com/doi/10.1177/1940161221997250.

5. Christophe Charle, *Le Siècle de la Presse (1830–1939)* (Paris: Seuil, 2009); and Marc Martin, "Journalistes parisiens et notoriété (vers 1830–1870): Pour une histoire sociale du journalisme," *Revue Historique* 266, no. 1 (539) (1981): 31–74, www.jstor.org/stable/40953576.
6. For an example of the distinction between a French "opinion-driven" and American "fact-based" model, see Jeffrey C. Alexander, "The Mass News Media in Systemic, Historical and Comparative Perspective," in *Mass Media and Social Change*, ed. Elihu Katz and Tamás Szecskö (Beverly Hills: Sage, 1981), 17–51. For warnings about the limits of this opposition, see Érik Neveu, *Sociologie du Journalisme* (Paris: La Découverte, 2019), 16; and Cyril Lemieux and John Schmalzbauer, "Involvement and Detachment Among French and American Journalists: To Be or Not to Be a 'Real' Professional," in *Rethinking Comparative Cultural Sociology: Repertoires of Evaluation in France and the United States*, ed. Michèle Lamont and Laurent Thévenot (New York: Cambridge University Press, 2000), 148–69.
7. Charle, *Le Siècle de la Presse*; and Schudson, *Discovering the News*.
8. W. A. Swanberg, *Citizen Hearst: A Biography of William Randolph Hearst* (New York: Charles Scribner's Sons, 1961); and Marc Martin, *Médias et journalistes de la République* (Paris: Editions Odile Jacob, 1997).
9. Sharon A. Boswell and Lorraine McConaghy, *Raise Hell and Sell Newspapers: Alden J. Blethen and the Seattle Times* (Pullman: Washington State University Press, 1996), 97.
10. These figures were Alcide Goût (who was also the mayor of his birth city, Calmont), Remi Couzinet, and Rémi Sans.
11. Félix Torres, *La Dépêche du Midi: Histoire d'un journal en République, 1870–2000* (Paris: Hachette Littératures, 2002).
12. Gerald J. Baldasty, *The Commercialization of News in the Nineteenth Century* (Madison: University of Wisconsin Press, 1992), 84.
13. Jonathan Paine, *Selling the Story: Transaction and Narrative Value in Balzac, Dostoevsky, and Zola* (Cambridge, MA: Harvard University Press, 2019), 188.
14. In both countries, the rise of a commercial model developed and expanded prior efforts. The American penny papers of the 1830s and 1840s "avowed their commercial ambitions and hoped that high circulation—and the advertising it would attract—would make them successful enterprises." See C. W. Anderson, Leonard Downie, and Michael Schudson, *The News Media: What Everyone Needs to Know* (New York: Oxford University Press, 2016), 17. Entrepreneurs like Émile de Girardin, who founded *La Presse* in 1836, undertook similar efforts in France. See Dominique Kalifa et al., *Histoire culturelle et littéraire de la presse française au XIXe siècle* (Paris: Nouveau Monde, 2011). The distinctiveness of the latter half of the nineteenth-century press thus lay less with any one specific

innovation, and more with its overall scale and scope, which modified the entire field by making commercial concerns a dominant priority.

15. Paul Starr, *The Creation of the Media: Political Origins of Modern Communications* (New York: Basic, 2004), 252.
16. Raymond Kuhn, *The Media in France* (London: Routledge, 1995), 17.
17. Kuhn, 18.
18. Circulation numbers for the newspapers in Toulouse and Seattle that would become dominant highlight this expansion in audience size. *La Dépêche* went from printing seven thousand copies per day in 1874 to twenty-eight thousand in 1884. See Pierre Albert, "L'Apogée de la presse française," in *Histoire générale de la presse française*, ed. Claude Bellanger et al., vol. 3, *de 1871 à 1940* (Paris, Presses Universitaires de France, 1973). The *Seattle Times* went from roughly six thousand in 1896, when Alden Blethen purchased the paper, to twenty-five thousand by 1901. See Sharon A. Boswell and Lorraine McConaghy, *Raise Hell and Sell Newspapers*, 96–122.
19. Paul Aron, "Entre journalisme et littérature, l'institution du reportage," *COnTEXTES. Revue de sociologie de la littérature*, no. 11 (2012), https://doi.org/10.4000/contextes.5355.
20. Randall Sumpter, *Before Journalism Schools: How Gilded Age Reporters Learned the Rules* (Columbia: University of Missouri Press, 2018), 11.
21. In Paris alone, Pascal Durand reports, in 1887 there were more than a hundred thousand "people of the profession and occasional writers." See Pascal Durand, "Crise de presse: Le journalisme au péril du 'reportage' (1870–1890)," *Quaderni* 24, (1994): 126, https://doi/10.3406/quad.1994.1094.
22. Martin, "Journalistes parisiens et notoriété," 37; and Marc Martin, "'La grande famille': l'Association des journalistes parisiens (1885–1939)," *Revue Historique* 275, 1 (1986): 129–57, www.jstor.org/stable/40954345.
23. Frank Luther Mott, *American Journalism: A History, 1690–1960* (New York: Macmillan, 1962); and Charle, *Le Siècle de la Presse.*
24. Schudson, *Discovering the News*, 79.
25. See Dominique Kalifa, "Les tâcherons de l'information: petits reporters et faits divers à la 'Belle Époque,'" *Revue d'histoire moderne et contemporaine* 40, no. 4 (1993): 589, https://doi.org/10.3406/rhmc.1993.1691. Kalifa goes so far as to say that the general rule of early reporting in France was "less about informing the public than keeping them in suspense."
26. Sumpter, *Before Journalism Schools*, 13; and Marie-Ève Thérenty, *Mosaïques: Être écrivain entre presse et roman (1829–1836)* (Paris: Honoré Champion, 2003).
27. In France, some of the major figures utilized journalism as an object in their early forays into fiction. Gaston Leroux, for example, detailed the adventures of an intrepid reporter in *The Mystery of the Yellow Room*, giving the image of the

new journalist as someone who is curious, possesses investigative skills similar to a detective, and maintains a commitment to using journalism to change the world for the better. Conversely, Guy de Maupassant's *Bel Ami* highlighted the opportunist, and sometimes cynical, nature of these same journalists.

28. In a provocative essay, James Carey uses the term *profession* to designate the fact that journalists came increasingly to sell their skills as brokers of information, and the messages they create need not bear any underlying relationship to their personal beliefs. This differs from partisan or literary predecessors that sought to cultivate ideas in which they were personally invested. Our emphasis utilizes different theoretical resources; however, we share an interest in moving beyond discussions about "true" professions and whether journalists fit within it and instead highlight the novel social role that developed for journalists in the nineteenth century. Our thanks to Richard Kielbowicz for calling our attention to this essay. See James W. Carey, "The Communications Revolution and the Professional Communicator," *The Sociological Review* 13, no. 1 (1965): 23–38, https://doi.org/10.1111/j.1467-954X.1965.tb03107.x.

29. Edward Caudill, "E. L. Godkin and His (Special and Influential) View of 19th Century Journalism," *Journalism Quarterly* 69, no. 4 (1992): 1039–49.

30. Schudson, *Discovering the News*, 70.

31. Delporte, *Les journalistes en France*.

32. Boswell and McConaghy, *Raise Hell and Sell Newspapers*, 121.

33. Formal journalism education also began in the 1890s in both countries. Dick May founded the first French journalism school in 1899; the first journalism classes in the United States were offered at the University of Pennsylvania business school in 1893. See Vincent Goulet, "Dick May et la première école de journalisme en France: Entre réforme sociale et professionnalisation," *Questions de communication*, no. 16 (2009): 27–44, https://doi.org/10.4000/questionsdecommunication.81; and Rodney Benson, *Shaping Immigration News: A French-American Comparison* (New York: Cambridge University Press, 2013).

34. Denis Ruellan, *Nous, journalistes: Déontologie et identité* (Grenoble: Presses universitaires de Grenoble, 2011), 65.

35. Theodore Dreiser, *A Book About Myself* (New York: Boni and Liveright, 1922), 467.

36. Schudson, *Discovering the News*, 71. For his part, Pulitzer was clear about the importance of a fact-oriented newspaper. In a memo to employees, he wrote: "The *World* . . . should have, daily, some striking development or feature . . . that will lift it away from its competitors and make it talked about. 'Did you see that in the *World*?' should be asked every day and something should be designed to cause this." George Juergens, *Joseph Pulitzer and the New York World* (Princeton, NJ: Princeton University Press, 1966), 48.

37. Schudson, *Discovering the News*, 71.
38. Hazel Dicken-Garcia, *Journalistic Standards in Nineteenth-Century America* (Madison: University of Wisconsin Press, 1989). As Richard Kaplan shows, many newspapers remained highly partisan up through the late 1800s. Rather than write on their own authority, however, journalists tended to base their stories on empirical details (i.e., facts) gathered from friendly sources. Which segments of the powerful were to be "held to account" thus varied in part on the partisan leanings of the commercially oriented newspaper for which one worked, even as the principle of using facts to inform took hold. See Richard Kaplan, *Politics and the American Press: The Rise of Objectivity (1865–1920)* (New York: Cambridge University Press, 2002).
39. Pierre Van den Dungen, "Écrivains du quotidien: Journalistes et journalisme en France au XIXème siècle," *Semen: Revue de sémio-linguistique des textes et discours* 25 (2008), https://journals.openedition.org/semen/8108.
40. Literally, "diverse facts" but also a label that suggests crime and disaster news.
41. Thomas Ferenczi, "L'éthique des journalistes au xixe siècle," *Le Temps des médias* 1, no. 1 (2003): 190, https://doi.org/10.3917/tdm.001.0190. Resistance to reporting techniques associated with the fact-based model were less pronounced in the American case, but not absent. Some congressional correspondents, who functioned in the years after the Civil War as insiders offering analysis, criticized the practice of interviewing. Benjamin Perley Poore, one of the mid-nineteenth century's best-known correspondents, saw the interview as a "dangerous method of communicating between our public men and the people because it diminished the correspondent's role from interpreter to mere scribe." See Donald Richie, *Press Gallery: Congress and the Washington Correspondents* (Cambridge, MA: Harvard University Press, 1991), 82.
42. Pascal Durand, "Le Reportage," in *La civilisation du journal: Histoire culturelle et littéraire de la presse française au XIXe siècle*, ed. Dominique Kalifa et al. (Paris: Nouveau Monde, 2011), 1011.
43. Martin, *Médias et journalistes*; and Schudson, *Discovering the News*.
44. Durand, "Crise de presse"; and Michael Schudson, "Question Authority: A History of the News Interview in American Journalism, 1860s–1930s," *Media, Culture and Society* 16, no. 4 (1994): 565–87, https://doi.org/10.1177/016344379401600403.
45. Ferenczi, "L'éthique des journalistes," 193. Summarizing French scholarship of this period, Sandrine Lévêque writes that "historians agree to situate at the turn of the century the beginning of a timid process of professionalization around the promotion of reporting and the passage of a press from opinion to a news media." Sandrine Lévêque, "Femmes, féministes et journalistes: Les rédactrices

de La Fronde à l'épreuve de la professionnalisation journalistique," *Le Temps des médias* 1, no. 12 (2009): 42, https://doi.org/10.3917/tdm.012.0041.
46. Marc Angenot, "1889: Un état du discours social," Médias 19, www.medias19.org/publications/1889-un-etat-du-discours-social/chapitre-25-genres-et-styles-du-journalisme.
47. Ted Curtis Smythe, *The Gilded Age Press, 1865–1900* (Westport, CT: Praeger, 2003).
48. Jean K. Chalaby, "Journalism as an Anglo-American Invention: A Comparison of the Development of French and Anglo-American Journalism, 1830s–1920s," *European Journal of Communication* 11, no. 3 (1996): 317, https://doi.org/10.1177/0267323196011003002.
49. Keith Gandal, *The Virtues of the Vicious: Jacob Riis, Stephen Crane, and the Spectacle of the Slum* (New York: Oxford University Press, 1997); and Jean Marie Lutes, "Into the Madhouse with Nellie Bly: Girl Stunt Reporting in Late Nineteenth-Century America," *American Quarterly* 54, no. 2 (2002): 217–53, www.jstor.org/stable/30041927.
50. Juergens, *Joseph Pulitzer*, 58.
51. François Bessire, ed., *L'écrivain éditeur*, vol. 2 (Paris: Librairie Droz, 2001), 121.
52. Kathy Roberts Forde and Katherine A. Foss, "'The Facts—the Color!—The Facts': The Idea of a Report in American Print Culture, 1885–1910," *Book History* 15 (2012): 123–51, www.jstor.org/stable/23315046.
53. Anne-Claude Ambroise-Rendu, "L'affaire Troppmann et la tentation de la fiction," *Le Temps des médias* 14, no. 1 (2010): 47–61, https://doi.org/10.3917/tdm.014.0047.
54. Swanberg, *Citizen Hearst*, 75.
55. H. Dauncey, "La Dépêche de Toulouse et le sport (1870–1913): La progressive sportivisation d'un journal politique," in *La presse régionale et le sport: Naissance de l'information sportive (années 1870–1914)*, ed. Philippe Tétart (Rennes: Presses universitaires de Rennes, 2008), 125–41; but also see Torres, *La Dépêche du Midi*.
56. Boswell and McConaghy, *Raise Hell and Sell Newspapers*, 96.
57. Swanberg, *Citizen Hearst*, 16.
58. John C. Hughes, *Pressing On: Two Family-Owned Newspapers in the 21st Century* (Olympia: Washington State Legacy Project, 2015), 18.
59. Boswell and McConaghy, *Raise Hell and Sell Newspapers*, 122.
60. Schudson, *Discovering the News*.
61. Edwin Diamond, *Behind the Times: Inside the New New York Times* (Chicago: University of Chicago Press, 1993), 41.
62. Frederick Brown, "Zola and Manet: 1866," *Hudson Review* 41, no. 1 (1988): 73, https://doi.org/10.2307/3850840.

63. Juergens, *Joseph Pulitzer*, 16.
64. Ferenczi, "L'éthique des journalistes," 192.
65. Marc Martin, *Les grands reporters: Les débuts du journalisme moderne* (Paris: Louis Audibert Editions, 2005), 45.
66. Caudill, "Godkin," 1042.
67. As Caudill writes, Godkin "didn't find fault with making money." Rather, "it was just the way it was made" that bothered him; Caudill, 1042.
68. Pierre Albert, *La presse française* (Paris: La Documentation Française, 1998).
69. The motto of *Le Figaro*—which, like its name, comes from the theater—illustrated this understanding well: "Without the freedom to criticize, there is no true praise."
70. Palmer, *Des petits journaux*, 89.
71. Ferenczi, "L'éthique des journalistes."
72. Benoît Lenoble, "L'identité médiatique du *Figaro* (1866–1914)," in *Le Figaro: Histoire d'un journal*, ed. Claire Blandin (Paris: Nouveau Monde, 2010), 62.
73. Lenoble, "L'identité médiatique du *Figaro*."
74. Beyond Paris, the owners of *La Dépêche* also had great marriages or local *grande bourgeoisie* connections and occupied political positions in the region. One cannot understand the history and importance of that newspaper without acknowledging its political position: all radicals in France had a place in a newspaper that was both politically radical and economically lucrative.
75. Schudson, *Discovering the News*.
76. Schudson, *Discovering the News*.
77. Alexandra Villard de Borchgrave and John Cullen, *Villard: The Life and Times of an American Titan* (New York: Doubleday, 2001).
78. Richard B. Kielbowicz, *News in the Mail: The Press, Post Office, and Public Information, 1770–1860s* (Westport, CT: Greenwood, 1989); and Culver H. Smith, *The Press, Politics, and Patronage: The American Government's Use of Newspapers, 1789–1875* (Athens: University of Georgia Press, 1977). In Seattle, Alden Blethen opportunistically supported or opposed specific politicians and political initiatives. As Boswell and McConaghy make clear, this opportunism was first and foremost about making the enterprise successful as an enterprise, rather than as a political actor. See Boswell and McConaghy, *Raise Hell and Sell Newspapers*.
79. Dominique Marchetti, "The Revelations of Investigative Journalism in France," *Global Media and Communication* 5, no. 3 (2009): 368–88, https://doi.org/10.1177/1742766509346610.
80. Doug Underwood, *Literary Journalism in British and American Prose: An Historical Overview* (Jefferson, NC: McFarland, 2019).
81. Schudson, *Discovering the News*; and Ferenczi, "L'éthique des journalistes."

82. Forde and Foss, "The Facts—the Color!," 134.
83. Sandrine Lévêque, *Les journalistes sociaux: Histoire et sociologie d'une spécialité journalistique* (Rennes: Presses universitaires de Rennes, 2000); and Sumpter, *Before Journalism Schools*. As Lévêque notes, some prominent women defended fact-based reporting as a way to gain access from which they had previously been excluded. Séverine—the pen name of Caroline Rémy de Guebhard—defended a "standing journalism" that she undertook against the "seated journalism" practiced by her male elders. See Lévêque, "Femmes, féministes et journalistes," 41–53.
84. Mott, *American Journalism*; and Charle, *Le Siècle de la Presse*.
85. Martin, *Les grands reporters*.
86. Sumpter, *Before Journalism Schools*, 9.
87. Sumpter, 4.
88. Lutes, "Into the Madhouse with Nellie Bly"; and Colette Cosnier, "Les reporteresses de La Fronde," in *Les représentations de l'affaire Dreyfus dans la presse en France et à l'étranger: Actes du colloque de Saint-Cyr-sur-Loire (novembre 1994)*, ed. Eric Cahm and Pierre Citti (Tours: Université François Rabelais, 1997), 73–82.
89. Baldasty, *The Commercialization of News*, 89.
90. Baldasty, 89.
91. Baldasty, 89.
92. Society reporting in Washington, DC, was also relegated to women, and not coincidentally also seen as "trivial." These same women were, moreover, excluded from congressional reporting. See Smith, *The Press, Politics, and Patronage*. More generally, a strand of academics criticized inexperienced reporters for their role in the perceived deterioration of language (e.g., by exposing audiences to grammatical errors, clichéd phrases, and unnecessary neologisms), which they referred to derisively as "newspaper English." See Sumpter, *Before Journalism Schools*, 40.
93. See Martin, *Médias et journalistes*. Also, Dominique Kalifa writes that it is "practically impossible, for want of suitable sources to better define the route of these reporters: social origin, training, professional background, cultural capital, [all] remain unknown." Kalifa, "Les tâcherons de l'information," 584.
94. Kalifa, "Les tâcherons de l'information," 595.
95. Brooke Kroeger, *Nellie Bly: Daredevil, Reporter, Feminist* (New York: Times Books, 1994).
96. Sumpter, *Before Journalism Schools*, 9.
97. Marc, *Médias et journalistes*; and Schudson, *Discovering the News*.
98. Lincoln Steffens, *The Autobiography of Lincoln Steffens* (New York: Heyday, 1931), 181.

99. Steffens, *The Autobiography of Lincoln Steffens*, 198.
100. Martin, *Médias et journalistes*.
101. Steffens, *The Autobiography of Lincoln Steffens*, 177.
102. William Salisbury, *The Career of a Journalist* (New York: BW Dodge, 1908), 521–22.
103. Max Weber, "Politics as a Vocation," in *From Max Weber: Essays in Sociology*, ed. H. H. Gerth and C. Wright Mills (New York: Oxford University Press, 1946), 98.
104. Dicken-Garcia, *Journalistic Standards in Nineteenth-Century America*.
105. Kroeger, *Nellie Bly*.
106. Weber, *Max Weber's Complete Writings*.
107. Lincoln Steffens, "The Business of a Newspaper," *Scribner's Magazine* 22, no. 4 (1897): 458.
108. Jacques Rancière, *The Names of History: On the Poetics of Knowledge*, trans. Hassan Melehy (Minneapolis: University of Minnesota Press, 1994), 45.

2. LIVING FOR—AND MAYBE OFF—JOURNALISM

1. All names have been changed to protect individual identities. For details regarding this decision, see the appendix A.
2. Interview with Seattle print journalist, July 26, 2018.
3. That said, sports journalism is an increasingly popular point of entry in both the Anglophone and Francophone journalistic spaces. See Karim Souanef, *Le journalisme sportif: Sociologie d'une spécialité dominée* (Presses universitaires de Rennes, 2019); and David Rowe, "Sports Journalism: Still the 'Toy Department' of the News Media?," *Journalism* 8, no. 4 (2007): 385–405, https://doi/10.1177/1464 884907078657.
4. Daniel Jackson, Einar Thorsen, and Sally Reardon, "Fantasy, Pragmatism and Journalistic Socialisation: UK Journalism Students' Aspirations and Motivations," *Journalism Practice* 14, no. 1 (2020): 105, https://doi.org/10.1080/175127 86.2019.1591929.
5. Renita Coleman et al., "Why Be a Journalist?: US Students' Motivations and Role Conceptions in the New Age of Journalism," *Journalism* 19, no. 6 (2016): 800–819, https://doi.org/10.1177/1464884916683554.
6. Serena Carpenter et al., "An Examination of How Academic Advancement of U.S. Journalism Students Relates to Their Degree Motivations, Values, and Technology Use," *Journalism and Mass Communication Educator* 70, no. 1 (2015): 58–74, https://doi.org/10.1177/1077695814551834; and Folker Hanusch et al., "Journalism Students' Motivations and Expectations of Their Work in Comparative Perspective," *Journalism and Mass Communication Educator* 70, no. 2 (2015): 141–60, https://doi.org/10.1177/1077695814554295.

7. In the United States, however, Bowers's study showed that even in the heyday of *All the President's Men*, most aspiring journalists were attracted to a profession that offered "interesting" and "creative work," not necessarily an opportunity to reveal political malfeasance. See Thomas A. Bowers, "Student Attitudes Toward Journalism as a Major and a Career," *Journalism Quarterly* 51, no. 2 (1974): 265–70, https://doi.org/10.1177/107769907405100210.
8. Colette Brin, Jean Charron, and Jean de Bonville, eds., *Nature et transformation du journalisme: Théorie et recherches empiriques* (Québec, Canada: Presses de l'Université Laval, 2004).
9. Émile Durkheim, *Moral Education: A Study in the Theory and Application of the Sociology of Education* (New York: Free Press of Glencoe, 1961), first published in 1922.
10. Guy Berger and Joe Foote, "Taking Stock of Contemporary Journalism Education: The End of the Classroom as We Know It," in *Global Journalism Education In the 21st Century: Challenges and Innovations*, ed. Robyn S. Goodman and Elanie Steyn (Austin: Knight Center for Journalism in the Americas, University of Texas, 2017): 245–65; and Samuel Bouron, "Les écoles de journalisme face à l'expansion du marché: Stratégies d'internationalisation et transformations des curricula," *Cahiers de la recherche sur l'éducation et les savoirs*, no. 14 (2015): 245–66, http://journals.openedition.org/cres/2835.
11. Thomas E. Patterson, *Informing the News: The Need for Knowledge-Based Journalism* (New York: Vintage, 2013).
12. Géraud Lafarge and Dominique Marchetti, "Les portes fermées du journalisme: L'espace social des étudiants des formations 'reconnues,'" *Actes de la Recherche en Sciences Sociales* 189, no. 4 (2011): 72–99, https://doi.org/10.3917/arss.189.0072; and Dominique Marchetti, "Les ajustements du marché scolaire au marché du travail journalistique," *Hermès, La Revue* 35, no. 1 (2003): 81–89, https://doi.org/10.4267/2042/9320. One of the most prestigious journalism schools in the United States, Columbia University, undertook precisely this strategy under the direction of Nicholas Lemann, who began a decade of leadership in 2003.
13. Max Besbris and Caitlin Petre, "Professionalizing Contingency: How Journalism Schools Adapt to Deprofessionalization," *Social Forces* 98, no. 4 (2020): 1524–47, https://doi.org/10.1093/sf/soz094; and Ivan Chupin, *Les écoles du journalisme: Les enjeux de la scolarisation d'une profession, 1899–2018* (Rennes: Presses universitaires de Rennes, 2018). Northwestern's Medill School—another historically prestigious American journalism school—offers one early example of this shift in curriculum. When John Lavine was named dean in 2006, he emphasized media management and marketing; his effort to reimagine journalism education stirred controversy, notably among the faculty most committed to investigative

reporting. In 2011, the school changed its name to reflect the new curricular directions instituted under his leadership as well as broader changes in the composition of the faculty that had been underway for over a decade. It is now the Medill School of Journalism, Media, and Integrated Marketing Communications.

14. On these shifting patterns of social recruitment in France, see Lafarge and Marchetti, "Les portes fermées du journalism"; as well as Géraud Lafarge, "Le champ journalistique et l'espace des écoles de journalism," *Savoir/Agir* 46, no. 4 (2018): 17–25, https://doi.org/10.3917/sava.046.0017. At the less prestigious schools, entrance exams have been reformatted to emphasize an applicant's motivation rather than writing skills or cultural knowledge. This aims explicitly to expand recruitment to students otherwise "shut out" from journalism school, especially at the newer private schools of journalism and the industry-related academies like Prisma. In the United States, only the most elite schools retain tests of general knowledge. Columbia University's Graduate School, for example, provides a test of current affairs. "There is no way to study for the exam," reads the program's website, and it explicitly examines the applicant's writing, reading, and critical thinking skills.

15. A random sample of journalism students in the United States, for example, reports that students are "still motivated to enter the profession for the same reason as yesterday's" students, and that the attraction of journalism remains the perception of it as a vehicle for personal expression. See Coleman et al., "Why Be a Journalist?" Reviewing the literature from a comparative perspective, Jackson and colleagues write that "wherever in the world the question [what attracted you to journalism?] has been asked," respondents emphasize "the appeal of journalism as an outlet for young peoples' passions . . . and talents . . . as well as the exciting, non-routine, non-conventional, and sociable nature of journalism." Jackson, Thorsen, and Reardon, "Fantasy, Pragmatism and Journalistic Socialisation."

16. Interview with Seattle freelance journalist, July 13, 2018.
17. Interview with Toulouse radio journalist, October 23, 2015.
18. Interview with Toulouse print journalist, November 24, 2015.
19. Interview with Seattle online journalist, December 2, 2015.
20. Interview with Toulouse print journalist, October 22, 2015.
21. Interview with Seattle radio journalist, July 11, 2018.
22. Interview with Seattle online journalist, October 5, 2015.
23. Interview with Seattle online journalist, February 24, 2016.
24. Barbie Zelizer and Stuart Allan, *Keywords in News and Journalism Studies* (Berkshire, UK: Open University Press, 2010).
25. Interview with Toulouse radio journalist, October 22, 2015.
26. Interview with Seattle newspaper journalist, July 10, 2018.

27. Interview with Seattle print journalist, July 12, 2018.
28. Interview with Seattle online journalist, December 2, 2015.
29. Interview with Toulouse radio journalist, October 22, 2015.
30. Interview with Seattle radio journalist, July 11, 2018.
31. Jürgen Habermas, *Between Facts and Norms: Contributions to a Discourse Theory of Law and Democracy* (Cambridge, MA: MIT Press, 1998); and Géraldine Muhlmann, *Journalism for Democracy* (Cambridge: Polity, 2010).
32. Interview with Toulouse online journalist, October 22, 2015.
33. Interview with Seattle online journalist, October 22, 2015.
34. Interview with Toulouse freelance journalist, June 25, 2015.
35. Interview with Seattle print journalist, September 15, 2015.
36. Interview with Seattle radio journalist, October 26, 2015.
37. Interview with Toulouse print journalist, November 2, 2015.
38. Interview with Seattle online journalist, December 2, 2015.
39. Interview with Seattle television journalist, October 28, 2015.
40. Interview with Seattle television journalist, October 16, 2015.
41. Robert G. Picard, *Journalists' Perceptions of the Future of Journalistic Work* (Oxford: Reuters Institute for the Study of Journalism, 2015), 1.
42. Mark Deuze, *Media Work* (Cambridge: Polity, 2007); and David Hesmondhalgh and Sarah Baker, *Creative Labour: Media Work in Three Cultural Industries* (New York: Routledge, 2013).
43. Jackson, Thorsen, and Reardon, "Fantasy, Pragmatism and Journalistic Socialisation," 118.
44. As one respondent puts it, "I can say I want to be bigger than clickbait. Still, at the end of the day, if I get offered a job and I don't have any other options, what am I going to do? I'm going to take the job wherever it is." Jackson, Thorsen, and Reardon, "Fantasy, Pragmatism and Journalistic Socialisation," 118.
45. For a longer description of these regulations, see Matthew Powers and Sandra Vera-Zambrano, "Explaining the Formation of Online News Startups in France and the United States: A Field Analysis," *Journal of Communication* 66, no. 5 (2016): 857–77, https://doi.org/10.1111/jcom.12253.
46. Mirjam Gollmitzer, "Employment Conditions in Journalism," Oxford Research Encyclopedias, Communication, March 26, 2019, https://doi.org/10.1093/acrefore/9780190228613.013.805.
47. For a comparative perspective on government support for journalism, see Rodney Benson, Matthew Powers, and Timothy Neff, "Public Media Autonomy and Accountability: Best and Worst Policy Practices in 12 Leading Democracies," *International Journal of Communication* 11 (2017): 1–22.
48. Nicole S. Cohen and Greig de Peuter, *New Media Unions: Organizing Digital Journalists* (New York: Routledge, 2020), 64.

49. Michèle Lamont, *Money, Morals, and Manners: The Culture of the French and the American Upper-Middle Class* (Chicago: University of Chicago Press, 1992); and Michèle Lamont, *The Dignity of Working Men: Morality and the Boundaries of Race, Class, and Immigration* (Cambridge, MA: Harvard University Press, 2000).
50. Interview with Seattle freelance journalist, October 5, 2015. The distinction between "living for" and "living off" comes from Max Weber's analysis of politics as a vocation. His distinction refers to the degree to which one can make politics "a permanent source of income" and thus a career that can be lived off. He contrasts this arrangement with those who lack such security and thus "live for" politics, which gives that individual's life "meaning in the service of a cause." Weber notes that the contrast is not an exclusive one but that the capacity to live off politics requires some "preconditions" to be met. See Max Weber, *Max Weber's Complete Writings on Academic and Political Vocations*, ed. John Dreijmanis, trans. Gordon C. Wells (New York: Algora, 2008).
51. Interview with Toulouse freelance journalist, October 1, 2015.
52. Interview with Seattle television journalist, October 21, 2015.
53. Interview with Toulouse online journalist, March 11, 2016.
54. Interview with Toulouse online journalist, December 19, 2013.
55. Interview with Seattle freelance journalist, October 23, 2015.
56. Interview with Toulouse freelance journalist, November 2, 2015.
57. Interview with Seattle television journalist, April 15, 2021.
58. Interview with Toulouse radio journalist, October 12, 2015.
59. Interview with Toulouse radio journalist, October 6, 2015.
60. Interview with Toulouse freelance journalist, November 23, 2015.
61. Interview with Toulouse radio journalist, October 6, 2015.
62. Interview with Toulouse radio journalist, October 23, 2015.
63. Interview with Toulouse radio journalist, October 6, 2015.
64. Interview with Toulouse freelance journalist, November 23, 2015.
65. Interview with Toulouse radio journalist, October 23, 2015.
66. Interview with Toulouse radio journalist, October 22, 2015.
67. Interview with Toulouse online journalist, October 29, 2015.
68. Interview with Toulouse freelance journalist, November 23, 2015.
69. Interview with Toulouse radio journalist, October 23, 2015.
70. Interview with Toulouse radio journalist, October 6, 2015.
71. Interview with Toulouse radio journalist, October 12, 2015.
72. Interview with Seattle radio journalist, July 11, 2018.
73. Switching metaphors, he said: "Or maybe the other analogy is the street cop. Chasing calls. Versus the detective investigating cases. The first ten years, you're so excited to just be in the car running a call. And then you're like OK, I think I'm ready to go investigate some cases."

74. Interview with Toulouse print journalist, November 5, 2015.
75. "My pleasure came not from [being on] the air but writing. . . . I take great pleasure in writing. There's some sort of perfect phrase search. . . . [I]t's like when you do a crossword. It's a writing game."
76. Interview with Seattle print journalist, December 3, 2015.
77. Interview with Toulouse print journalist, November 9, 2015.
78. Jeffrey C. Alexander, "The Mass News Media in Systemic, Historical and Comparative Perspective," in *Mass Media and Social Change*, ed. Elihu Katz and Tamás Szecskö (Beverly Hills: Sage, 1981), 17–51.
79. See also Cyril Lemieux and John Schmalzbauer, "Involvement and Detachment Among French and American Journalists: To Be or Not to Be a 'Real' Professional," in *Rethinking Comparative Cultural Sociology: Repertoires of Evaluation in France and the United States*, ed. Michèle Lamont and Laurent Thévenot (New York: Cambridge University Press, 2000), 148–69; and Érik Neveu, *Sociologie du journalism* (Paris: La Découverte, 2019).
80. Matthew Powers, Sandra Vera-Zambrano, and Olivier Baisnée, "The News Crisis Compared: The Impact of the Journalism Crisis in Toulouse, France and Seattle, USA," in *Local Journalism: The Decline of Newspapers and the Rise of Digital Media*, ed. Rasmus Kleis Nielsen (London: I. B. Tauris, 2015), 31–50.
81. Interview with Seattle print journalist, October 15, 2017.

3. AT THEIR BEST

1. On the idea of "good work," which foregrounds among others issues a sense of self-realization through one's productions, see David Hesmondhalgh and Sarah Baker, *Creative Labour: Media Work in Three Cultural Industries* (New York: Routledge, 2013).
2. David H. Weaver et al., *The American Journalist in the 21st Century: U.S. News People at the Dawn of the New Millennium* (Mahwah, NJ: Lawrence Erlbaum, 2007).
3. Thomas Hanitzsch et al., *Worlds of Journalism: Journalistic Cultures Around the Globe* (New York: Columbia University Press, 2019); and Lars Willnat, David H. Weaver, and G. Cleveland Wilhoit, *The American Journalist in the Digital Age: A Half-Century Perspective* (New York: Peter Lang, 2017).
4. Géraud Lafarge and Dominique Marchetti, "Les hiérarchies de l'information: Les légitimités 'professionnelles' des étudiants en journalisme," *Sociétés contemporaines* 106, no. 2 (2017): 21–44, https://doi.org/10.3917/soco.106.0021.
5. Pierre Albert, *La presse française* (Paris: La Documentation Française, 1998), 41.

6. John Johnstone, Edward Slawski, and William W. Bowman, *The News People: A Sociological Portrait of American Journalists and Their Work* (Urbana: University of Illinois Press, 1976).
7. David H. Weaver and G. Cleveland Wilhoit, *The American Journalist: A Portrait of U.S. News People and Their Work* (Bloomington: Indiana University Press, 1986); David H. Weaver, and G. Cleveland Wilhoit, *The American Journalist in the 1990s: U.S. News People at the End of an Era* (Mahwah, NJ: Lawrence Erlbaum, 1996); Weaver et al., *The American Journalist in the 21st Century*; and David H. Weaver, Lars Willnat, and G. Cleveland Wilhoit, "The American Journalist in the Digital Age: Another Look at U.S. News People," *Journalism and Mass Communication Quarterly* 96, no. 1 (2019): 101–30, https://doi.org/10.1177/1077699018778242.
8. The precise format of the question and the methods for analyzing the responses changed in subsequent surveys; however, both the 1992 and 2002 surveys asked journalists about their best work. See Weaver and Wilhoit, *The American Journalist in the 1990s*; and Weaver et al., *The American Journalist in the 21st Century*.
9. Weaver and colleagues report that a journalist's support of a given role only had "a modest association with the kind of story he or she chose as an exemplary work." They likewise find "no clear association" between professional roles and rationales used to explain the choice of best work." Weaver et al., *The American Journalist in the 21st Century*, 419. Other uses of the best work question are found in Randal A. Beam, "The Social Characteristics of U.S. Journalists and Their 'Best Work,'" *Journalism Practice* 2, no. 1 (2008): 1–14, https://doi.org/10.1080/17512780701768428; and Lori A. Bergen, "Testing the Relative Strength of Individual and Organizational Characteristics in Predicting Content of Journalists' Best Work" (PhD diss., Indiana University, 1991).
10. Hanitzsch et al., *Worlds of Journalism*.
11. Weaver, Willnat, and Wilhoit, *The American Journalist in the Digital Age*. Equally curious is the absence of the best work question from qualitative studies focused on meaning-making and interpretation. In neither the Anglophone nor Francophone scholarship are we aware of scholars that have utilized this question as a way to explore definitions of professional excellence.
12. In this regard, the refusal or inability to recall one's best work implies an individual with waning belief that the profession remains "worth the candle." The few respondents who could not recall such work did, in fact, depart the profession shortly after the interview. We explore this point in further detail in chapter 5.
13. Zvi Reich, "Different Practices, Similar Logic: Comparing News Reporting Across Political, Financial, and Territorial Beats," *International Journal of Press/*

Politics 17, no. 1 (2012): 76–99, https://doi.org/10.1177/1940161211420868; and David Rowe. "Sports Journalism: Still the 'Toy Department' of the News Media?," *Journalism* 8, no. 4 (2007): 385–405, https://doi.org/10.1177/1464884907078657.

14. See the contrasting views offered by W. Lance Bennett, "Toward a Theory of Press-State Relations in the United States," *Journal of Communication* 40, no. 2 (1990): 103–25, https://doi.org/10.1111/j.1460-2466.1990.tb02265.x; and Michael Schudson, *Why Democracies Need an Unlovable Press* (Cambridge: Polity, 2008).

15. Lafarge and Marchetti, "Les hiérarchies de l'information."

16. Pierre Bourdieu, "L'emprise du journalisme," *Actes de la Recherche en Sciences Sociales* 101/102, no. 1 (1994): 3–9; Patrick Champagne, *La double dépendance: Sur le journalisme* (Paris: Raisons d'Agir, 2016); James T. Hamilton, *All The News That's Fit to Sell: How the Market Transforms Information Into News* (Princeton: Princeton University Press, 2004); and Doug Underwood, *When MBAs Rule the Newsroom: How Marketers and Managers Are Reshaping Today's Media* (New York: Columbia University Press, 1993).

17. Lafarge and Marchetti, "Les hiérarchies de l'information"; Éric Lagneau, "Agencier à l'AFP: l'Éthique du métier menacée," *Hermès, la Revue* 1, no. 35 (2003): 109–18, https://doi.org/10.4267/2042/9323; and Érik Neveu, *Sociologie du journalisme* (Paris: La Découverte, 2019).

18. Lafarge and Marchetti, "Les hiérarchies de l'information."

19. Interview with Toulouse print journalist, November 5, 2015.

20. In their survey of French journalism students, Lafarge and Marchetti similarly report that "it is almost unthinkable that students not listen to the news from Radio France." Lafarge and Marchetti, "Les hiérarchies de l'information," 30.

21. Interview with Seattle online journalist, December 2, 2015.

22. Nikos Smyrnaios, "Les pure players entre innovation journalistique et contrainte économique: les cas d'Owni, Rue89 et Arrêt sur images," *Recherches en communication* 39 (2013): 133–50, https://doi.org/10.14428/rec.v39i39.49653; and Andrea Wagemans, Tamara Witschge, and Mark Deuze, "Ideology as Resource in Entrepreneurial Journalism," *Journalism Practice* 10, no. 2 (2016): 160–77, https://doi.org/10.1080/17512786.2015.1124732.

23. Rodney Benson, "Can Foundations Solve the Journalism Crisis?," *Journalism* 19, no. 8 (2018): 1059–77, https://journals.sagepub.com/doi/10.1177/1464884917924612. For example, Charles Ornstein and Tracy Weber—two prominent and early recruits—came from the *Los Angeles Times*. The importance of reputation and prestige in online pure players is also important in regional spaces; see Matthew Powers and Sandra Vera-Zambrano, "Explaining the Formation of Online News Startups in France and the United States: A Field Analysis," *Journal of Communication* 66, no. 5 (2016): 857–77, https://doi.org/10.1111/jcom.12253.

24. Magda Konieczna, *Journalism Without Profit: Making News When the Market Fails* (New York: Oxford University Press, 2018).
25. Interview with Seattle freelance journalist, July 13, 2018.
26. Interview with Seattle print journalist, November 4, 2015.
27. Interview with Toulouse radio journalist, October 23, 2015.
28. Interview with Toulouse television journalist, October 22, 2015.
29. Interview with Toulouse radio journalist, October 22, 2015.
30. Interview with Seattle print journalist, October 30, 2015.
31. Interview with Seattle radio journalist, October 16, 2015.
32. Interview with Seattle print journalist, September 15, 2015.
33. Interview with Seattle online journalist, July 13, 2018.
34. Interview with Toulouse radio journalist, October 22, 2015.
35. Interview with Seattle radio journalist, July 11, 2018.
36. Interview with Seattle online journalist, July 10, 2018.
37. Interview with Seattle online journalist, December 10, 2015.
38. Interview with Seattle online journalist, December 2, 2015.
39. Interview with Seattle online journalist, November 25, 2015.
40. Interview with Toulouse online journalist, October 29, 2015.
41. Interview with Seattle print journalist, October 30, 2015.
42. Interview with Seattle online journalist, November 23, 2015; and Seattle television journalist July 20, 2018.
43. Interview with Seattle online journalist, October 30, 2015.
44. Interview with Seattle online journalist, November 25, 2015.
45. Interview with Seattle television journalist, July 20, 2018.
46. For a description of these social characteristics, see appendix B.
47. Interview with Seattle print journalist, October 26, 2015.
48. Interview with Seattle television journalist, October 28, 2015.
49. Interview with Seattle online journalist, February 23, 2016.
50. Interview with Seattle online journalist, November 25, 2015.
51. The aerospace reporter, quoted earlier, made a similar point, noting that what he liked about his beat was the extraordinary range of sources he could call on, from blue collar union workers who "don't give a shit what management thinks" to executives who "are getting million-dollar salaries." He notes: "It is like an incredible spectrum of people, and all of them are feeding me information. And I get the information that the CEO doesn't get, because the structure of the company doesn't allow you to hear what the people at the bottom are saying. So in that way it is a fabulous beat. And it is a very fertile ground for getting information. It is unofficial but true." Interview with Seattle print journalist, October 26, 2015.
52. Interview with Toulouse print journalist, May 8, 2015.

53. Interview with Seattle radio journalist, July 11, 2018.
54. Interview with Toulouse print journalist, September 28, 2015.
55. Interview with Seattle print journalist, October 26, 2015.
56. Interview with Seattle online journalist, November 25, 2015.
57. Interview with Seattle print journalist, October 26, 2015.
58. Interview with Toulouse journalist, November 9, 2015.
59. Interview with Toulouse television journalist, November 4, 2015.
60. Interview with Seattle print journalist, October 30, 2015.
61. Interview with Seattle print journalist, December 3, 2015.
62. Interview with Toulouse television journalist, October 22, 2015.
63. Interview with Seattle print journalist, October 30, 2015.
64. Interview with Seattle print journalist, December 3, 2015.
65. Interview with Toulouse television journalist, October 5, 2015.
66. Interview with Seattle print journalist, October 30, 2015.
67. Interview with Seattle print journalist, December 10, 2015.
68. Interview with Toulouse print journalist, November 2, 2015.
69. Interview with Toulouse radio journalist, October 6, 2015.
70. Interview with Seattle online journalist, May 4, 2015.
71. Interview with Seattle online journalist, February 23, 2016.
72. Interview with Toulouse print journalist, June 25, 2015.
73. Interview with Seattle online journalist, December 2, 2015.
74. Interview with Seattle television journalist, October 7, 2015.
75. Interview with Seattle print journalist, October 30, 2015.
76. Interview with Seattle online journalist, December 2, 2015.
77. Interview with Seattle radio journalist, October 26, 2015.
78. Interview with Toulouse radio journalist, October 22, 2015.
79. Interview with Seattle print journalist, December 7, 2015.
80. For discussions of empathy in journalism, see Katherine Fink and Michael Schudson, "The Rise of Contextual Journalism, 1950s–2000s," *Journalism* 15, no. 1 (2014): 3–20, https://doi.org/10.1177/1464884913479015; and Janet D. Blank-Libra, *Pursuing an Ethic of Empathy in Journalism* (New York: Routledge, 2017).
81. Interview with Toulouse print journalist, November 24, 2015.
82. Interview with Seattle print journalist, October 5, 2015.
83. Interview with Seattle radio journalist, July 18, 2018.
84. Interview with Toulouse online journalist, March 11, 2016.
85. Interview with Seattle television journalist, October 21, 2015.
86. Interview with Seattle radio journalist, July 18, 2018.
87. Interview with Seattle print journalist, September 15, 2015.
88. Interview with Toulouse radio journalist, October 12, 2015.
89. Interview with Seattle print journalist, September 15, 2015.

90. Pierre Bourdieu, *The Logic of Practice*, trans. Richard Nice (Stanford, CA: Stanford University Press, 1990), 53.
91. Interview with Seattle television journalist, October 28, 2015.

4. CONSERVE, CHALLENGE, ACCEDE

1. For an earlier version of this argument, using different theoretical tools and research questions, see Matthew Powers and Sandra Vera-Zambrano, "Endure, Invest, Ignore: How French and American Journalists React to Economic Constraints and Technological Transformations," *Journal of Communication* 69, no. 3 (2019): 320–43, https://doi.org/10.1093/joc/jqz015.
2. Ivan Chupin, Nicolas Hubé, and Nicolas Kaciaf, *Histoire politique et économique des médias en France* (Paris: La Découverte, 2012); and Susan J. Douglas, *Inventing American Broadcasting, 1899–1922* (Baltimore, MD: Johns Hopkins University Press, 1987).
3. Jacques Siracusa, "Le montage de l'information télévisée," *Actes de la Recherche en Sciences Sociales* 131/132, no. 1 (2000): 92–106, https://doi.org/10.3917/arss.p2000.131n1.0092.
4. Patrick Champagne, *La double dépendance: Sur le journalisme* (Paris: Raisons d'Agir, 2016); and Jean-Baptiste Comby and Benjamin Ferron, "La subordination au pouvoir économique: Dépolarisation et verticalisation du champ journalistique," *Savoir/Agir* 46, no. 4 (2018): 11–15, https://doi.org/10.3917/sava.046.0011.
5. Barbie Zelizer, "Journalism's 'Last' Stand: Wirephoto and the Discourse of Resistance," *Journal of Communication* 45, no. 2 (1995): 78–92, https://doi.org/10.1111/j.1460-2466.1995.tb00729.x.
6. Robert W. McChesney, *Telecommunications, Mass Media, and Democracy: The Battle for the Control of U.S. Broadcasting, 1928–1935* (New York: Oxford University Press, 1993).
7. Pablo J. Boczkowski, *Digitizing the News: Innovation in Online Newspapers* (Cambridge, MA: MIT Press, 2004); and Matt Carlson, *Journalistic Authority: Legitimating News in the Digital Era* (New York: Columbia University Press, 2017).
8. Rasmus Kleis Nielsen and Sarah Anne Ganter, *The Power of Platforms: Shaping Media and Society* (New York: Oxford University Press, 2022); and Franck Rebillard and Nikos Smyrnaios, "Quelle 'plateformisation' de l'information? Collusion socioéconomique et dilution éditoriale entre les entreprises médiatiques et les infomédiaires de l'Internet," *Tic et Société* 13, nos. 1/2 (2019): 247–93.
9. Lucas Graves, *Deciding What's True: The Rise of Political Fact-Checking in American Journalism* (New York: Columbia University Press, 2016); and Megan

Le Masurier, "What Is Slow Journalism?," *Journalism Practice* 9, no. 2 (2015): 138–52, https://doi.org/10.1080/17512786.2014.916471.

10. Seth C. Lewis, "The Tension Between Professional Control and Open Participation," *Information, Communication and Society* 15, no. 6 (2012): 836–66, https://doi.org/10.1080/1369118X.2012.674150; Angèle Christin, *Metrics at Work: Journalism and the Contested Meaning of Algorithms* (Princeton, NJ: Princeton University Press, 2020); and Caitlin Petre, *All the News That's Fit to Click: How Metrics Are Transforming the Work of Journalists* (Princeton, NJ: Princeton University Press, 2021).
11. Interview with Toulouse freelance journalist, November 23, 2015.
12. Interview with Seattle print journalist, October 26, 2015.
13. Interview with Seattle radio journalist, October 16, 2015.
14. Interview with Seattle print journalist, October 26, 2015.
15. Interview with Seattle television journalist, October 28, 2015. Respondents also talked about how the existing audience for many news organizations was aging. Discussing the public radio audience in Seattle, one journalist noted that, demographically speaking, it has "gone into the upper fifties, which is not a forecast for success in the future." Therefore, "you really have to figure out new ways to do it" (interview with Seattle radio journalist, July 18, 2018).
16. Interview with Seattle radio journalist, July 11, 2018.
17. Colette Brin, Jean Charron, and Jean de Bonville, eds., *Nature et transformation du journalisme: Théorie et recherches empiriques* (Québec, Canada: Presses de l'Université Laval, 2004).
18. Edson C. Tandoc Jr. and Tim P. Vos, "The Journalist Is Marketing the News: Social Media in the Gatekeeping Process," *Journalism Practice* 10, no. 8 (2016): 950–66, https://doi.org/10.1080/17512786.2015.1087811.
19. Interview with Seattle radio journalist, July 11, 2018.
20. This is hardly limited to regional media. The most prestigious news offerings in both countries also contribute to this, with, for example, the *New York Times* prominently featuring themes on its homepage on wellness (the top story at the time of this writing: "Why do women sprout chin hairs as they age?") and consumer purchasing ("What is the best raincoat for April showers in the city?").
21. Nikki Usher, *Making News at the New York Times* (Ann Arbor: University of Michigan Press, 2014).
22. Usher, 121.
23. Pauline Amiel and Matthew Powers, "A Trojan Horse for Marketing?: Solutions Journalism in the French Regional Press," *European Journal of Communication* 34, no. 3 (2019): 233–47, https://doi.org/10.1177/0267323119830054.

24. Alexander L. Curry and Keith H. Hammonds, "The Power of Solutions Journalism," *Solutions Journalism Network* 7 (2014): 1–14, https://engagingnewsproject.org/wp-content/uploads/2014/06/ENP_SJN-report.pdf.
25. Érik Neveu, "News Without Journalists: Real Threat or Horror Story?," *Brazilian Journalism Research* 6, no. 1 (2010): 29–54, https://doi.org/10.25200/BJR.v6n1.2010.225.
26. A similar shift can be seen in developments like "participatory" or "engaged journalism." See David Domingo et al., "Participatory Journalism Practices in the Media and Beyond: An International Comparative Study of Initiatives in Online Newspapers," *Journalism Practice* 2, no. 3 (2008): 326–42, https://doi.org/10.1080/17512780802281065. In the latter, the role of the journalist is conceived explicitly to "actively consider and interact with [the] audience in furtherance of its journalistic and financial mission." See Jake Batsell, *Engaged Journalism: Connecting with Digitally Empowered News Audiences* (New York: Columbia University Press, 2015), 7.
27. Mark Deuze, "What Is Multimedia Journalism?," *Journalism Studies* 5, no. 2 (2004): 139–52, https://doi.org/10.1080/1461670042000211131.
28. Ana Luisa Sánchez Laws, "Can Immersive Journalism Enhance Empathy?," *Digital Journalism* 8, no. 2 (2020): 213–28, https://doi.org/10.1080/21670811.2017.1389286.
29. Jake Batsell, *Engaged Journalism: Connecting with Digitally Empowered News Audiences* (New York: Columbia University Press, 2015).
30. Tim P. Vos and Gregory P. Perreault, "The Discursive Construction of the Gamification of Journalism," *Convergence: The International Journal of Research Into New Media Technologies* 26, no. 3 (2020): 470–85, https://doi.org/10.1177/1354856520909542.
31. Max Besbris and Caitlin Petre, "Professionalizing Contingency: How Journalism Schools Adapt to Deprofessionalization," *Social Forces* 98, no. 4 (2020): 1524–47, https://doi.org/10.1093/sf/soz094; and Ivan Chupin, *Les écoles du journalisme: Les enjeux de la scolarisation d'une profession (1899–2018)* (Rennes: Presses universitaires de Rennes, 2018).
32. James T. Hamilton, *Democracy's Detectives: The Economics of Investigative Journalism* (Cambridge, MA: Harvard University Press, 2016).
33. Graves, *Deciding What's True*.
34. Érik Neveu, "On Not Going Too Fast with Slow Journalism," *Journalism Practice* 10, no. 4 (2016): 448–60, https://doi.org/10.1080/17512786.2015.1114897.
35. Neveu, "News Without Journalists."
36. Interview with Toulouse print journalist, June 1, 2015.
37. Interview with Seattle print journalist, October 26, 2015.
38. Interview with Seattle print journalist, October 30, 2015.

39. Interview with Toulouse television journalist, November 4, 2015.
40. Interview with Seattle television journalist October 28, 2015.
41. Interview with Toulouse television journalist, October 5, 2015.
42. Interview with Seattle print journalist, October 30, 2015.
43. Interview with Seattle print journalist, October 26, 2015.
44. Interview with Toulouse print journalist, November 5, 2015.
45. Interview with Toulouse print journalist, May 15, 2015.
46. Interview with Toulouse print journalist, May 8, 2015.
47. Interview with Toulouse television journalist, November 4, 2015.
48. Interview with Toulouse print journalist, June 1, 2015.
49. Interview with Seattle print journalist, September 15, 2015.
50. Interview with Toulouse print journalist, May 8, 2015.
51. Interview with Seattle print journalist, October 26, 2015.
52. Interview with Toulouse television journalist, October 30, 2015.
53. Interview with Toulouse print journalist, April 27, 2015.
54. Interview with Toulouse print journalist, October 5, 2015.
55. Interview with Toulouse print journalist, November 9, 2015.
56. Kalyani Chadna and Linda Steiner, eds., *Newswork and Precarity* (London: Routledge, 2022).
57. Interview with Seattle television journalist, October 28, 2015.
58. Interview with Seattle print journalist, September 15, 2015.
59. Interview with Seattle radio journalist, July 11, 2018.
60. For a detailed discussion of journalists' technology use in the two cities, see Matthew Powers and Sandra Vera-Zambrano, "How Journalists Use Social Media in France and the United States: Analyzing Technology Use Across Journalistic Fields," *New Media and Society* 20, no. 8 (2018): 2728–44, https://doi.org/10.1177/1461444817731566.
61. Interview with Seattle print journalist, October 2, 2015.
62. Interview with Seattle radio journalist, January 8, 2014.
63. Interview with Seattle online journalist, October 28, 2015.
64. Interview with Seattle television journalist, October 7, 2015.
65. Interview with Seattle television journalist, October 21, 2015.
66. Interview with Toulouse print journalist, October 29, 2015.
67. Interview with Seattle online journalist, February 24, 2016.
68. Interview with Toulouse print journalist, May 6, 2015.
69. Interview with Seattle radio journalist, July 11, 2018.
70. Interview with Seattle television journalist, October 7, 2015.
71. Interview with Seattle radio journalist, October 16, 2015.
72. Interview with Seattle television journalist, October 21, 2015.
73. Interview with Seattle television journalist, October 7, 2015.

74. Cited in www.yakwala.fr/content/anatomie-lancement-pure-player-local-car redinfo-%20toulouse-xavier-lalu.
75. Cited in www.lejournaltoulousain.fr/archives/points-de-vue/tribune-libre/xavier-lalu-carre-dinfo-fete-sa-premiere-annee-le-debut-dun-age-dor-du-journalisme-14765.
76. Interview with Toulouse print journalist, November 5, 2015.
77. Interview with Toulouse print journalist, November 5, 2015.
78. Interview with Toulouse freelance journalist, November 23, 2015.
79. Interview with Seattle print journalist, December 7, 2015.
80. Interview with Seattle television journalist, October 1, 2015.
81. Interview with Seattle radio journalist, October 26, 2015.
82. Interview with Toulouse radio journalist, October 6, 2015.
83. Interview with Toulouse print journalist, November 23, 2015.
84. Interview with Seattle online journalist, November 23, 2015.
85. Interview with Toulouse print journalist, November 24, 2015.
86. Interview with Seattle print journalist, December 7, 2015.
87. Matthew Powers and Sandra Vera-Zambrano, "Explaining the Formation of Online News Startups in France and the United States: A Field Analysis," *Journal of Communication* 66, no. 5 (2016): 857–77, https://doi.org/10.1111/jcom.12253.
88. Interview with Seattle print journalist, December 10, 2015.
89. Interview with Seattle print journalist, December 7, 2015.
90. Interview with Toulouse radio journalist, October 23, 2015.
91. Interview with Toulouse television journalist, November 4, 2015.
92. Interview with Toulouse radio journalist, October 23, 2015.
93. Interview with Toulouse radio journalist, October 6, 2015.
94. Interview with Toulouse radio journalist, October 6, 2015.
95. Interview with Seattle print journalist, December 10, 2015.
96. Interview with Seattle online journalist, December 2, 2015.
97. Interview with Seattle online journalist, December 2, 2015.
98. Interview with Seattle online journalist, December 2, 2015.
99. Interview with Seattle online journalist, December 2, 2015.
100. Interview with Seattle print journalist, October 5, 2015.
101. Interview with Toulouse radio journalist, October 6, 2015.
102. Interview with Toulouse radio journalist, October 23, 2015.
103. Pierre Bourdieu, *The Field of Cultural Production: Essays on Art and Literature* (New York: Columbia University Press, 1993).
104. Guy Berger and Joe Foote, "Taking Stock of Contemporary Journalism Education: The End of the Classroom as We Know It," in *Global Journalism Education In the 21st Century: Challenges and Innovations*, ed. Robyn S. Goodman

and Elanie Steyn (Austin: Knight Center for Journalism in the Americas, University of Texas, 2017), 245–65; and Chupin, *Les écoles du journalisme*.

5. LEAVING JOURNALISM

1. Christine Leteinturier, "Continuité/Discontinuité des carrières des journalistes français encartés: Étude de deux cohortes de nouveaux titulaires de la carte de presse," *Recherches en communication* 43 (2016): 27–55, https://doi.org/10.14428/rec.v43i43.48753.
2. Thomas Frank comes close to expressing this view in the American context. In a review of books that explore what he terms "the destruction of the postwar middle-class economic order," he notes that "the vast size" of the reporting compared to effect it has had ("close to nothing," in his estimation) should "perhaps call into question the utility of journalism." See Thomas Frank, "Storybook Plutocracy," *Public Books*, November 21, 2013, www.publicbooks.org/storybook-plutocracy/.
3. Sophie Denave, "Les conditions individuelles et collectives des ruptures professionnelles," *Cahiers Internationaux de Sociologie* 120, no. 1 (2006): 95, https://doi.org/10.3917/cis.120.0085.
4. Denave, 95.
5. Nicole S. Cohen, Andrea Hunter, and Penny O'Donnell, "Bearing the Burden of Corporate Restructuring: Job Loss and Precarious Employment in Canadian Journalism," *Journalism Practice* 13, no. 7 (2019): 817–33, https://doi.org/10.1080/17512786.2019.1571937; François Nel, *Laid Off: What Do UK Journalists Do Next?* (Preston: University of Central Lancashire, 2010); Timothy Marjoribanks, Lawrie Zion, and Merryn Sherwood, "Mobilising Networks After Redundancy: The Experiences of Australian Journalists," *New Technology, Work and Employment* 36, no. 3 (2021): 371–89, https://doi.org/10.1111/ntwe.12192; Penny O'Donnell, Lawrie Zion, and Merryn Sherwood, "Where Do Journalists Go After Newsroom Job Cuts?," *Journalism Practice* 10, no. 1 (2016): 35–51, https://doi.org/10.1080/17512786.2015.1017400; and Scott Reinardy, Lawrie Zion, and Annalise Baines. "'It's Like Dying but Not Being Dead': U.S. Newspaper Journalists Cope with Emotional and Physical Toll of Job Losses," *Newspaper Research Journal* 42, no. 3 (2021): 364–78, https://doi.org/10.1177/07395329211030577.
6. Nicole S. Cohen, *Writers' Rights: Freelance Journalism in a Digital Age* (Montreal: McGill-Queen's University Press, 2016).
7. Jasmine B. MacDonald et al., "Burnout in Journalists: A Systematic Literature Review," *Burnout Research* 3, no. 2 (2016): 34–44, https://doi.org/10.1016/j.burn.2016.03.001; José Matos, "'It Was Journalism That Abandoned Me': An Analysis of Journalism in Portugal," *TripleC: Communication, Capitalism and Critique*

18, no. 2 (2020): 535–55, https://doi.org/10.31269/triplec.v18i2.1148; Henrik Örnebring and Cecilia Möller, "In the Margins of Journalism," *Journalism Practice* 12, no. 8 (2018): 1051–60, https://doi.org/10.1080/17512786.2018.1497455; Linda Steiner, "Stories of Quitting: Why Did Women Journalists Leave the Newsroom?," *American Journalism* 15, no. 3 (1998): 89–116, https://doi.org/10.1080/08821127.1998.10731989; and Benno Viererbl and Thomas Koch, "Once a Journalist, Not Always a Journalist?: Causes and Consequences of Job Changes from Journalism to Public Relations," *Journalism* 22, no. 8 (2021): 1947–63, https://doi.org/10.1177/1464884919829647.

8. Roei Davidson and Oren Meyers, "Should I Stay or Should I Go? Exit, Voice and Loyalty Among Journalists," *Journalism Studies* 17, no. 5 (2016): 591, https://doi.org/10.1080/1461670X.2014.988996.

9. Manuel Goyanes and Eduardo Fco Rodríguez-Gómez, "Presentism in the Newsroom: How Uncertainty Redefines Journalists' Career Expectations," *Journalism* 22, no. 1 (2021): 52–68, https://doi.org/10.1177/1464884918767585; and Daniel Nölleke, Phoebe Maares, and Folker Hanusch, "Illusio and Disillusionment: Expectations Met or Disappointed Among Young Journalists," *Journalism* 23, no. 2 (2022): 320–36, https://doi.org/10.1177/1464884920956820.

10. Nölleke, Maares, and Hanusch, "Illusio and Disillusionment."

11. Jean-Marie Charon and Adénora Pigeolat, "Pourquoi quitter le journalisme?," *L'Observatoire des Médias*, December 7, 2020, www.observatoiredesmedias.com/2020/12/07/pourquoi-quitter-le-journalisme-etude/.

12. Örnebring and Möller, "In the Margins of Journalism," 1054.

13. Sophie Denave, *Reconstruire sa vie professionnelle: Sociologie des bifurcations biographiques* (Paris: Presses Universitaires de France, 2015).

14. Beverly Skeggs, *Formations of Class and Gender: Becoming Respectable* (London: Sage, 1997); Linda Steiner, "Failed Theories: Explaining Gender Difference in Journalism," *Review of Communication* 12, no. 3 (2012): 201–23, https://doi.org/10.1080/15358593.2012.666559; and Liesbet Van Zoonen, "One of the Girls?: The Changing Gender of Journalism," in *News, Gender and Power*, ed. Cynthia Carter, Gill Branston, and Stuart Allan (New York: Routledge,1998), 33–46.

15. Jean-Baptiste Legavre, "Figure du deuil professionnel: Du 'vrai' journalisme au journalisme d'organisation," in *Les Dimensions Émotionnelles du Politique*, ed. Isabelle Sommier and Xavier Crettiez (Rennes: Presses universitaires de Rennes, 2019), 255–72.

16. Interview with former Seattle journalist, February 25, 2021.

17. Interview with former French journalist, April 1, 2021.

18. Interview with former American journalist, April 26, 2021.

19. Interview with former French journalist, April 8, 2021.

20. Interview with former American journalist, April 22, 2021.
21. Interview with former American journalist, April 15, 2021.
22. Interview with former American journalist, April 22, 2021.
23. Interview with former American journalist, July 10, 2018. Male journalists, for their part, retrospectively described family time and personal life as something they had always missed due to their work commitments; however, these were rarely described as part of the deep questioning of their beliefs that the job was worthwhile. For example, one described a sense that he could "never have a normal life" and "be there" for his kids' games; however, these had been long-standing issues—and not fully resolved by a new job outside of journalism.
24. Interview with former American journalist, April 22, 2021.
25. Interview with former American journalist, April 19, 2021.
26. Interview with former American journalist, April 15, 2021.
27. Interview with former American journalist, April 19, 2021.
28. Interview with former American journalist, April 15, 2021.
29. Denave, "Les conditions individuelles et collectives," 95.
30. Interview with former American journalist, April 19, 2021.
31. Interview with former American journalist, April 22, 2021.
32. Interview with former French journalist, June 5, 2021.
33. Interview with former American journalist, July 10, 2018.
34. Interview with former French journalist, June 16, 2021.
35. Interview with former American journalist, April 22, 2021.
36. Interview with former American journalist, April 26, 2021.
37. Interview with former French journalist, April 1, 2021.
38. Interview with former French journalist, May 5, 2021.
39. Interview with former American journalist, April 20, 2021.
40. Interview with former American journalist, April 29, 2021.
41. Interview with former American journalist, April 26, 2021.
42. Interview with former French journalist, May 5, 2021.
43. Interview with former American journalist, April 19, 2021.
44. Interview with former American journalist, July 10, 2018.
45. Interview with former American journalist, May 1, 2021.
46. Interview with former American journalist, April 29, 2021.
47. Interview with former French journalist, June 5, 2021.
48. Interview with former American journalist, April 22, 2021.
49. Interview with former American journalist, February 25, 2021.
50. Matthew Powers, "The Direction and Demographics of Journalists' Trajectories: Evidence from One American City," *Journalism Studies* 23, no. 3 (2022): 392–411, https://doi.org/10.1080/1461670X.2022.2029541.

CONCLUSION

1. This translates in English to "The Grip of Journalism." It was published as an appendix in *On Television* under the title "The Power of Journalism." See Pierre Bourdieu, *On Television* (New York: New Press, 1998).
2. David M. Ryfe, "The Economics of News and the Practice of News Production," *Journalism Studies* 22, no. 1 (2021): 60–76, https://doi.org/10.1080/1461670X.2020.1854619.
3. Hartmut Rosa, *Social Acceleration: A New Theory of Modernity* (New York: Columbia University Press, 2013).
4. Érik Neveu, "Bourdieu's Capital(s): Sociologizing an Economic Concept," in *The Oxford Handbook of Pierre Bourdieu*, ed. Thomas Medvetz and Jeffrey J. Sallaz (New York: Oxford University Press, 2018), 347–74.
5. Vincent Dubois, *Culture as a Vocation: Sociology of Career Choices in Cultural Management* (New York: Routledge, 2015); and Charles Suaud, *La vocation: Conversion et reconversion des prêtres ruraux* (Paris: Editions de Minuit, 1978). On the "biographical illusion," see Pierre Bourdieu, "L'illusion biographique," *Actes de la Recherche en Sciences Sociales* 62/63, no. 1 (1986): 69–72.
6. Daniel C. Hallin and Paolo Mancini, *Comparing Media Systems: Three Models of Media and Politics* (New York: Cambridge University Press, 2004).
7. David Morley, *Television, Audiences and Cultural Studies* (London: Routledge, 1992), 3; and Érik Neveu, "In Hope That Scientific Nomadism May Turn Out to Be Meaningful After All," *Bulletin of Sociological Methodology/Bulletin de Méthodologie Sociologique* 151, no. 1 (2021): 38–62, https://doi.org/10.1177/07591063211019952.
8. Matthew Powers and Sandra Vera-Zambrano, "The Universal and the Contextual of Media Systems: Research Design, Epistemology, and the Production of Comparative Knowledge," *International Journal of Press/Politics* 23, no. 2 (2018): 143–60, https://doi.org/10.1177/1940161218771899.
9. For an earlier discussion on this topic, see Matthew Powers and Sandra Vera-Zambrano, "What Are Journalists For Today?," in *Rethinking Media Research for Changing Societies*, ed. Matthew Powers and Adrienne Russell (Cambridge: Cambridge University Press, 2020), 65–77.
10. Max Weber, *Max Weber's Complete Writings on Academic and Political Vocations*, ed. John Dreijmanis, trans. Gordon C. Wells (New York: Algora, 2008), 84.
11. Cyril Lemieux, *Mauvaise presse: Une sociologie compréhensive du travail journalistique et de ses critiques* (Paris: Éditions Métailié, 2000).
12. Patrick Champagne, *La double dépendance: Sur le journalisme* (Paris: Raisons d'Agir, 2016); and Victor Pickard, *Democracy Without Journalism?*:

Confronting the Misinformation Society (New York: Oxford University Press, 2020).

13. Michael Schudson, "Autonomy from What?," in *Bourdieu and the Journalistic Field*, ed. Rodney Benson and Érik Neveu (Cambridge: Polity, 2005), 214–23.
14. Pickard, *Democracy Without Journalism?*
15. Érik Neveu addresses the issue archly: "Stock market crashes, tsunamis, and revolutions are therefore invited to avoid July-August to be brought to the attention of the public." Érik Neveu, *Sociologie du Journalisme* (Paris: La Découverte, 2019), 98.
16. Nikki Usher, *News for the Rich, White, and Blue: How Place and Power Distort American Journalism* (New York: Columbia University Press, 2021).
17. Just as often, though, nonmarket forms of support can in fact serve as a form of market pressure, as foundations and donors need not necessarily be more interested in the social functions of the press but in the establishment of a business model. More funding does not necessarily bring about the expected or anticipated results on its own. See Matthew Powers and Sandra Vera-Zambrano, "Explaining the Formation of Online News Startups in France and the United States: A Field Analysis," *Journal of Communication* 66, no. 5 (2016): 857–77, https://doi.org/10.1111/jcom.12253.
18. Rodney Benson, Timothy Neff, and Mattias Hessérus, "Media Ownership and Public Service News: How Strong Are Institutional Logics?," *International Journal of Press/Politics* 23, no. 3 (2018): 275–98, https://doi.org/10.1177/1940161218782740; and Magda Konieczna, *Journalism Without Profit: Making News When the Market Fails* (New York: Oxford University Press, 2018).
19. Ivan Chupin, *Les écoles du journalisme: Les enjeux de la scolarisation d'une profession (1899–2018)* (Rennes: Presses universitaires de Rennes, 2018).
20. Max Besbris and Caitlin Petre, "Professionalizing Contingency: How Journalism Schools Adapt to Deprofessionalization," *Social Forces* 98, no. 4 (2020): 1524–47, https://doi.org/10.1093/sf/soz094.
21. Michael Schudson, *The Good Citizen: A History of American Civic Life* (New York: Simon and Schuster, 1998).
22. Michael Schudson, *The Rise of the Right to Know: Politics and the Culture of Transparency, 1945–1975* (Cambridge, MA: Harvard University Press, 2015).
23. For key overviews, see Mark Deuze, *Media Work* (Cambridge: Polity, 2007); and David Hesmondhalgh and Sarah Baker, *Creative Labour: Media Work in Three Cultural Industries* (New York: Routledge, 2013). For specific studies related to Western Europe and North America, see on television: Brigitte Le Grignou and Érik Neveu, *Sociologie de la Télévision* (Paris: La Découverte, 2017); on books: John B. Thompson, *Book Wars: The Digital Revolution in Publishing* (Cambridge: Polity, 2021); on music: David Hesmondhalgh, *Why Music Matters* (Malden, MA:

Wiley Blackwell, 2013); and on film: Janet Wasko, *Hollywood in the Information Age: Beyond the Silver Screen* (Cambridge: Polity, 2013).
24. Alexis de Tocqueville, *The Old Regime and the French Revolution* (New York: Doubleday, 1983); and Alexis de Tocqueville, *Democracy in America: The Complete and Unabridged Volumes I and II* (New York: Bantam Classics, 2000).
25. Karl Marx, *Capital: A Critique of Political Economy*, vol. 1 (New York: Penguin, 1990), first published in 1867; and Max Weber, *The Protestant Ethic and the Spirit of Capitalism* (New York: Penguin, 2002), first published in 1905.
26. Roger Chartier, *The Cultural Origins of the French Revolution* (Durham, NC: Duke University Press, 1991), 17.
27. Silvio Waisbord, "Truth Is What Happens to News: On Journalism, Fake News, and Post-Truth," *Journalism Studies* 19, no. 13 (2018): 1872, https://doi.org/10.1080/1461670X.2018.1492881.
28. Wolfgang Streeck, *How Will Capitalism End?: Essays on a Failing System* (New York: Verso, 2017).
29. State-led capitalism, with its tendency to ignore the boundaries between state and economy, is another "possible future" for capitalism. The implications for a journalism that speaks on behalf of "the people" seem ambivalent, as the extant literature on journalism in China suggests.
30. W. Lance Bennett and Steven Livingston, eds., *The Disinformation Age: Politics, Technology, and Disruptive Communication in the United States* (New York: Cambridge University Press, 2020).
31. Belief in this order persists even when journalists no longer believe the profession is worthy of their own efforts. At least in the sample presented here, journalists leave not because the profession is no longer worthy in general or because they no longer believe in the general idea of a "fourth estate." They depart because the profession no longer makes sense *for them*.
32. Paul Willis, *Profane Culture* (Princeton: Princeton University Press, 1978), 3.
33. Dubois, *Culture as a Vocation*.
34. Pierre Bourdieu, *The Field of Cultural Production: Essays on Art and Literature* (New York: Columbia University Press, 1993).
35. Wendy Brown, *Undoing the Demos: Neoliberalism's Stealth Revolution* (New York: Zone, 2015).

EPILOGUE

1. Max Weber, *Max Weber's Complete Writings on Academic and Political Vocations*, ed. John Dreijmanis, trans. Gordon C. Wells (New York: Algora, 2008), 84.

APPENDIX A

1. John Levi Martin, *Thinking Through Methods: A Social Science Primer* (Chicago: University of Chicago Press, 2017).
2. Pierre Bourdieu, "Understanding," in *The Weight of the World: Social Suffering in Contemporary Society*, by Pierre Bourdieu, Alain Accardo, Gabrielle Balazs, et al. (Stanford, CA: Stanford University Press, 1999), 607–26.
3. Matthew Powers and Sandra Vera-Zambrano, "The Universal and the Contextual of Media Systems: Research Design, Epistemology, and the Production of Comparative Knowledge," *International Journal of Press/Politics* 23, no. 2 (2018): 143–60, https://doi.org/10.1177/1940161218771899.

APPENDIX B

1. Matthew Powers and Sandra Vera-Zambrano, "Explaining the Formation of Online News Startups in France and the United States: A Field Analysis," *Journal of Communication* 66, no. 5 (2016): 857–77, https://doi.org/10.1111/jcom.12253.
2. Matthew Powers and Sandra Vera-Zambrano, "The Universal and the Contextual of Media Systems: Research Design, Epistemology, and the Production of Comparative Knowledge," *International Journal of Press/Politics* 23, no. 2 (2018): 143–60, https://doi.org/10.1177/1940161218771899.

APPENDIX C

1. Matthew Powers, Sandra Vera-Zambrano, and Olivier Baisnée, "The News Crisis Compared: The Impact of the Journalism Crisis in Toulouse, France and Seattle, USA," in *Local Journalism: The Decline of Newspapers and the Rise of Digital Media*, ed. Rasmus Kleis Nielsen (London: I. B. Tauris, 2015), 31–50.

Bibliography

Abernathy, Penelope Muse. *The Expanding News Desert*. Chapel Hill: Center for Innovation and Sustainability in Local Media, School of Media and Journalism, University of North Carolina, 2018. https://etaara.com/wp-content/uploads/2022/02/The-Expanding-News-Desert-10_14-Web.pdf.

Albert, Pierre. "L'apogée de la presse française." In *Histoire générale de la presse française (de 1871 à 1940)*, edited by Claude Bellanger, Jacques Godechot, Pierre Guiral, and Fernando Terrou, 358–69. Vol. 3 of *Histoire générale de la presse française*. Paris: Presses Universitaires de France, 1973.

———. *La presse française*. Paris: La Documentation Française, 1998.

Alexander, Jeffrey C. "The Mass News Media in Systemic, Historical and Comparative Perspective." In *Mass Media and Social Change*, edited by Elihu Katz and Tamás Szecskö, 17–51. Beverly Hills: Sage, 1981.

Ambroise-Rendu, Anne-Claude. "L'affaire Troppmann et la tentation de la fiction." *Le Temps des médias* 14, no. 1 (2010): 47–61. https://doi.org/10.3917/tdm.014.0047.

Amiel, Pauline. "L'identité professionnelle des localiers à l'heure des mutations économique et numérique de la presse locale: Vers un journalisme de service?" *Les Cahiers du Numérique* 15, no. 4 (2019): 17–38. https://doi.org/10.3166/lcn.15.4.17-38.

Amiel, Pauline, and Matthew Powers. "A Trojan Horse for Marketing? Solutions Journalism in the French Regional Press." *European Journal of Communication* 34, no. 3 (2019): 233–47. https://doi.org/10.1177/0267323119830054.

Anderson, C. W. *Rebuilding the News: Metropolitan Journalism in the Digital Age.* Philadelphia, PA: Temple University Press, 2013.

Anderson, C. W., Leonard Downie, and Michael Schudson. *The News Media: What Everyone Needs to Know.* New York: Oxford University Press, 2016.

Angenot, Marc. "Genres et styles du journalisme." Chapter 25 in *1889: Un état du discours social.* Médias 19. Last modified September 14, 2021. www.medias19.org/publications/1889-un-etat-du-discours-social/chapitre-25-genres-et-styles-du-journalisme.

Aron, Paul. "Entre journalisme et littérature, l'institution du reportage." *COnTEXTES. Revue de sociologie de la littérature,* no. 11 (2012). https://journals.openedition.org/contextes/5355.

Austin, J. L. *How to Do Things with Words.* New York: Oxford University Press, 1965.

Baisnée, Olivier, Alizé Cavé, Cyriac Gousset, and Jérémie Nollet. "La 'violence' des Gilets Jaunes: Quand la fait-diversification fait diversion; Les routines journalistiques à l'épreuve des manifestations à Toulouse (novembre 2018-juin 2019)." *Sur Le Journalisme, About Journalism, Sobre Jornalismo* 10, no. 1 (2021): 28–43.

Baldasty, Gerald J. *The Commercialization of News in the Nineteenth Century.* Madison: University of Wisconsin Press, 1992.

Bastin, Gilles. "The Press in the Light of Modern Capitalism: A Planned Survey by Max Weber on Newspapers and Journalism." *Max Weber Studies* 13, no. 2 (2013): 151–75. https://muse.jhu.edu/article/808729.

Batsell, Jake. *Engaged Journalism: Connecting with Digitally Empowered News Audiences.* New York: Columbia University Press, 2015.

Beam, Randal A. "The Social Characteristics of U.S. Journalists and Their 'Best Work.'" *Journalism Practice* 2, no. 1 (2008): 1–14. https://doi.org/10.1080/17512780701768428.

Bellanger, Claude, Jacques Godechot, Pierre Guiral, and Fernando Terrou, eds. *Histoire générale de la presse française (de 1871 à 1940).* Vol. 3 of *Histoire générale de la presse française.* Paris: Presses Universitaires de France, 1973.

Bennett, W. Lance. "Toward a Theory of Press-State Relations in the United States." *Journal of Communication* 40, no. 2 (1990): 103–25. https://doi.org/10.1111/j.1460-2466.1990.tb02265.x.

Bennett, W. Lance, and Steven Livingston, eds. *The Disinformation Age: Politics, Technology, and Disruptive Communication in the United States.* New York: Cambridge University Press, 2020.

Benson, Rodney. "Can Foundations Solve the Journalism Crisis?" *Journalism* 19, no. 8 (2018): 1059–77. https://journals.sagepub.com/doi/10.1177/1464884917724612.

———. *Shaping Immigration News: A French-American Comparison.* New York: Cambridge University Press, 2013.

Benson, Rodney, Timothy Neff, and Mattias Hessérus. "Media Ownership and Public Service News: How Strong Are Institutional Logics?" *International Journal of Press/Politics* 23, no. 3 (2018): 275–98. https://doi.org/10.1177/1940161218782740.

Benson, Rodney, and Érik Neveu, eds. *Bourdieu and the Journalistic Field*. Cambridge: Polity, 2005.

Benson, Rodney, Matthew Powers, and Timothy Neff. "Public Media Autonomy and Accountability: Best and Worst Policy Practices in 12 Leading Democracies." *International Journal of Communication* 11 (2017): 1–22.

Benton, Joshua. "The Game of Concentration: The Internet Is Pushing the American News Business to New York and the Coasts." *NiemanLab*, March 25, 2016. www.niemanlab.org/2016/03/the-game-of-concentration-the-internet-is-pushing-the-american-news-business-to-new-york-and-the-coasts/.

Bergen, Lori A. "Testing the Relative Strength of Individual and Organizational Characteristics in Predicting Content of Journalists' Best Work." PhD diss., Indiana University, 1991.

Berger, Guy, and Joe Foote. "Taking Stock of Contemporary Journalism Education: The End of the Classroom as We Know It." In *Global Journalism Education in the 21st Century: Challenges and Innovations*, edited by Robyn S. Goodman and Elanie Steyn, 245–65. Austin: Knight Center for Journalism in the Americas, University of Texas, 2017.

Besbris, Max, and Caitlin Petre. "Professionalizing Contingency: How Journalism Schools Adapt to Deprofessionalization." *Social Forces* 98, no. 4 (2020): 1524–47. https://doi.org/10.1093/sf/soz094.

Bessire, François, ed. *L'écrivain éditeur*. Vol. 2. Paris: Librairie Droz, 2001.

Blank-Libra, Janet, D. *Pursuing an Ethic of Empathy in Journalism*. New York: Routledge, 2017.

Boczkowski, Pablo J. *Digitizing the News: Innovation in Online Newspapers*. Cambridge, MA: MIT Press, 2004.

Boswell, Sharon A., and Lorraine McConaghy. *Raise Hell and Sell Newspapers: Alden J. Blethen and the Seattle Times*. Pullman: Washington State University Press, 1996.

Bourdieu, Pierre. *Distinction: A Social Critique of the Judgment of Taste*. Cambridge, MA: Harvard University Press, 1984.

———. "L'emprise du journalisme." *Actes de la Recherche en Sciences Sociales* 101/102, no. 1 (1994): 3–9. https://doi.org/10.3406/arss.1994.3078.

———. *The Field of Cultural Production: Essays on Art and Literature*. New York: Columbia University Press, 1993.

———. "The Forms of Capital." In *Handbook of Theory and Research for the Sociology of Education*, edited by John G. Richardson, 241–58. Westport, CT: Greenwood, 1986.

———. "L'illusion biographique." *Actes de la Recherche en Sciences Sociales* 62/63, no. 1 (1986): 69–72.

———. *The Logic of Practice*. Translated by Richard Nice. Stanford, CA: Stanford University Press, 1990.

———. *On Television*. New York: New Press, 1998.

———. *Pascalian Meditations*. Translated by Richard Nice. Stanford, CA: Stanford University Press, 2000.

———. *The State Nobility: Elite Schools in the Field of Power*. Translated by Lauretta C. Clough. Stanford: Stanford University Press, 1998.

———. "Understanding." In *The Weight of the World: Social Suffering in Contemporary Society*, by Pierre Bourdieu, Alain Accardo, Gabrielle Balazs, et al., 607–26. Stanford, CA: Stanford University Press, 1999.

Bouron, Samuel. "Les écoles de journalisme face à l'expansion du marché: Stratégies d'internationalisation et transformations des curricula." *Cahiers de la recherche sur l'éducation et les savoirs*, no. 14 (2015): 245–66. http://journals.openedition.org/cres/2835.

Bousquet, Franck, and Pauline Amiel. *La presse quotidienne régionale*. Paris: La Découverte, 2021.

Bowers, Thomas A. "Student Attitudes Toward Journalism as a Major and a Career." *Journalism Quarterly* 51, no. 2 (1974): 265–70. https://doi.org/10.1177/107769907405100210.

Brin, Colette, Jean Charron, and Jean de Bonville, eds. *Nature et transformation du journalisme: Théorie et recherches empiriques*. Québec, Canada: Presses de l'Université Laval, 2004.

Brown, Frederick. "Zola and Manet: 1866." *Hudson Review* 41, no. 1 (1988): 71–92. https://doi.org/10.2307/3850840.

Brown, Wendy. *Undoing the Demos: Neoliberalism's Stealth Revolution*. New York: Zone, 2015.

Carey, James W. "The Communications Revolution and the Professional Communicator." *Sociological Review* 13, no. 1, suppl (1965): 23–38. https://doi.org/10.1111/j.1467-954X.1965.tb03107.x.

Carlson, Matt. *Journalistic Authority: Legitimating News in the Digital Era*. New York: Columbia University Press, 2017.

Carlson, Matt, Sue Robinson, and Seth C. Lewis. *News After Trump: Journalism's Crisis of Relevance in a Changed Media Culture*. New York: Oxford University Press, 2021.

Carpenter, Serena, Anne Hoag, August E. Grant, and Brian J. Bowe. "An Examination of How Academic Advancement of U.S. Journalism Students Relates to Their Degree Motivations, Values, and Technology Use." *Journalism and Mass

Communication Educator 70, no. 1 (2015): 58–74. https://doi.org/10.1177/1077 695814551834.

Castells, Manuel. *Communication Power.* New York: Oxford University Press, 2013.

Caudill, Edward. "E. L. Godkin and His (Special and Influential) View of 19th Century Journalism." *Journalism Quarterly* 69, no. 4 (1992): 1039–49.

Chadna, Kalyani, and Linda Steiner, eds. *Newswork and Precarity.* London: Routledge, 2022.

Chadwick, Andrew. *The Hybrid Media System: Politics and Power.* 2nd ed. New York: Oxford University Press, 2017.

Chalaby, Jean K. "Journalism as an Anglo-American Invention: A Comparison of the Development of French and Anglo-American Journalism, 1830s–1920s." *European Journal of Communication* 11, no. 3 (1996): 303–26. https://doi.org/10 .1177/0267323196011003002.

Champagne, Patrick. *La double dépendance: Sur le journalisme.* Paris: Raisons d'Agir, 2016.

———. *Faire l'opinion: Le nouveau jeu politique.* 2nd ed. Paris: Les Éditions de Minuit, 2015.

Charle, Christophe. *Le Siècle de la Presse (1830–1939).* Paris: Seuil, 2009.

Charon, Jean-Marie, and Adénora Pigeola. "Pourquoi quitter le journalisme?" *L'Observatoire des Médias.* December 7, 2020. www.observatoiredesmedias.com /2020/12/07/pourquoi-quitter-le-journalisme-etude/.

Chartier, Roger. *The Cultural Origins of the French Revolution.* Durham, NC: Duke University Press, 1991.

Christin, Angèle. *Metrics at Work: Journalism and the Contested Meaning of Algorithms.* Princeton, NJ: Princeton University Press, 2020.

Chupin, Ivan. *Les écoles du journalisme: Les enjeux de la scolarisation d'une profession (1899–2018).* Rennes: Presses universitaires de Rennes, 2018.

Chupin, Ivan, Nicolas Hubé, and Nicolas Kaciaf. *Histoire politique et économique des médias en France.* Paris: La Découverte, 2012.

Clark, Charles E. *The Public Prints: The Newspaper in Anglo-American Culture, 1665–1740.* New York: Oxford University Press, 1994.

Cohen, Nicole S. *Writers' Rights: Freelance Journalism in a Digital Age.* Montreal: McGill-Queen's University Press, 2016.

Cohen, Nicole S., and Greig de Peuter. *New Media Unions: Organizing Digital Journalists.* New York: Routledge, 2020.

Cohen, Nicole S., Andrea Hunter, and Penny O'Donnell. "Bearing the Burden of Corporate Restructuring: Job Loss and Precarious Employment in Canadian Journalism." *Journalism Practice* 13, no. 7 (2019): 817–33. https://doi.org/10.1080 /17512786.2019.1571937.

Coleman, Renita, Joon Yea Lee, Carolyn Yaschur, Aimee Pavia Meader, and Kathleen McElroy. "Why Be a Journalist? US Students' Motivations and Role Conceptions in the New Age of Journalism." *Journalism* 19, no. 6 (2016): 800–819. https://doi.org/10.1177/1464884916683554.

Comby, Jean-Baptiste, and Benjamin Ferron. "La subordination au pouvoir économique: Dépolarisation et verticalisation du champ journalistique." *Savoir/Agir* 46, no. 4 (2018): 11–15. https://doi.org/10.3917/sava.046.0011.

Cosnier, Colette. "Les reporteresses de La Fronde." In *Les représentations de l'affaire Dreyfus dans la presse en France et à l'étranger: Actes du colloque de Saint-Cyr-sur-Loire (novembre 1994)*, edited by Eric Cahm and Pierre Citti, 73–82. Tours: Université François Rabelais, 1997.

Curry, Alexander L., and Keith H. Hammonds. "The Power of Solutions Journalism." *Solutions Journalism Network* 7 (2014): 1–14. https://engagingnewsproject.org/wp-content/uploads/2014/06/ENP_SJN-report.pdf.

Cushion, Stephen. "Rich Media, Poor Journalists: Journalists' Salaries." *Journalism Practice* 1, no. 1 (2007): 120–29. https://doi.org/10.1080/17512780601078910.

Dahani, Safia. "Incorporer la contrainte, transmettre la critique, occuper les médias: Sur la médiatisation de jeunes dirigeants du Front National." *Savoir/Agir* 46, no. 4 (2018): 83–88. https://doi.org/10.3917/sava.046.0083.

Dauncey, H. "La Dépêche de Toulouse et le sport (1870–1913): La progressive sportivisation d'un journal politique." In *La presse régionale et le sport: Naissance de l'information sportive (années 1870–1914)*, edited by Philippe Tétart, 125–41. Rennes: Presses universitaires de Rennes, 2008.

Davidson, Roei, and Oren Meyers. "Should I Stay or Should I Go? Exit, Voice and Loyalty Among Journalists." *Journalism Studies* 17, no. 5 (2016): 590–607. https://doi.org/10.1080/1461670X.2014.988996.

Delporte, Christian. *Les journalistes en France, 1880–1950: Naissance et construction d'une profession*. Paris: Le Seuil, 1999.

Denave, Sophie. "Les conditions individuelles et collectives des ruptures professionnelles." *Cahiers Internationaux de Sociologie* 120, no. 1 (2006): 85–110. https://doi.org/10.3917/cis.120.0085.

———. *Reconstruire sa vie professionnelle: Sociologie des bifurcations biographiques*. Paris: Presses Universitaires de France, 2015.

Deuze, Mark. *Media Work*. Cambridge: Polity, 2007.

———. "What Is Multimedia Journalism?" *Journalism Studies* 5, no.2 (2004): 139–52. https://doi.org/10.1080/1461670042000211131.

Deuze, Mark, and Tamara Witschge. *Beyond Journalism*. Cambridge: Polity, 2020.

Diamond, Edwin. *Behind the Times: Inside the New New York Times*. Chicago: University of Chicago Press, 1993.

Dicken-Garcia, Hazel. *Journalistic Standards in Nineteenth-Century America*. Madison: University of Wisconsin Press, 1989.
Dickinson, Roger. "Accomplishing Journalism: Towards a Revived Sociology of a Media Occupation." *Cultural Sociology* 1, no. 2 (2007): 189–208. https://doi.org /10.1177/1749975507078187.
Domingo, David, Thorsten Quandt, Ari Heinonen, Steve Paulussen, Jane B. Singer, and Marina Vujnovic. "Participatory Journalism Practices in the Media and Beyond: An International Comparative Study of Initiatives in Online Newspapers." *Journalism Practice* 2, no. 3 (2008): 326–42. https://doi.org/10.1080/175 12780802281065.
Dorr, Rheta Childe. *A Woman of Fifty*. New York: Funk and Wagnalls, 1924.
Douglas, Susan J. *Inventing American Broadcasting, 1899–1922*. Baltimore, MD: Johns Hopkins University Press, 1987.
Dreiser, Theodore. *A Book About Myself*. New York: Boni and Liveright, 1922.
Dubois, Vincent. *Culture as a Vocation: Sociology of Career Choices in Cultural Management*. New York: Routledge, 2015.
Duffy, Brooke Erin. *Remake, Remodel: Women's Magazines in the Digital Age*. Champaign: University of Illinois Press, 2013.
Durand, Pascal. "Crise de presse: Le journalisme au péril du 'reportage' (1870–1890)." *Quaderni* 24 (1994): 123–52. https://doi.org/10.3406/quad.1994.1094.
———. "Le Reportage." In *La civilisation du journal: Histoire culturelle et littéraire de la presse française au XIXe siècle*, edited by Dominique Kalifa, Philippe Régnier, Marie-Ève Thérenty, and Alain Vaillant, 1011–24. Paris: Nouveau Monde, 2011.
Durkheim, Émile. *Moral Education: A Study in the Theory and Application of the Sociology of Education*. New York: Free Press of Glencoe, 1961. First published in 1922.
Elias, Norbert. *The Civilizing Process: Sociogenetic and Psychogenetic Investigations*. Oxford: Blackwell, 2000. First published in 1939.
Esser, Frank, and Thomas Hanitzsch. "On the Why and How of Comparative Inquiry in Communication Studies." In *The Handbook of Comparative Communication Research*, edited by Frank Esser and Thomas Hanitzsch. London: Routledge, 2012.
Esser, Frank, Jesper Strömbäck, and Claes H. de Vreese. "Reviewing Key Concepts in Research on Political News Journalism: Conceptualizations, Operationalizations, and Propositions for Future Research." *Journalism* 13, no. 2 (2012): 139–43. https://doi.org/10.1177/1464884911427795.
Ferenczi, Thomas. "L'éthique des journalistes au xixe siècle." *Le Temps des médias* 1, no. 1 (2003): 190–99. https://doi.org/10.3917/tdm.001.0190.
Figeac, Julien, Pierre Ratinaud, Nikos Smyrnaios, Guillaume Cabanac, Ophélie Fraisier-Vannier, Tristan Salord, and Fanny Seffusatti. "Mobile Phones in the

Spread of Unreliable Information on Twitter: Evidence from the 2017 French Presidential Campaign." *Mobile Media and Communication* 9, no. 3 (2021): 441–64. https://doi.org/10.1177/2050157920972157.

Fink, Katherine, and Michael Schudson. "The Rise of Contextual Journalism, 1950s–2000s." *Journalism* 15, no. 1 (2014): 3–20. https://doi.org/10.1177/1464884913479015.

Gandal, Keith. *The Virtues of the Vicious: Jacob Riis, Stephen Crane, and the Spectacle of the Slum*. New York: Oxford University Press, 1997.

Gitlin, Todd. *Occupy Nation: The Roots, the Spirit, and the Promise of Occupy Wall Street*. New York: Harper Collins, 2012.

Goffman, Erving. "Felicity's Condition." *American Journal of Sociology* 89, no. 1 (1983): 1–53. https://doi.org/10.1086/227833.

Gollmitzer, Mirjam. "Employment Conditions in Journalism." Oxford Research Encyclopedias, Communication. March 26, 2019. https://doi.org/10.1093/acrefore/9780190228613.013.805.

Goulet, Vincent. "Dick May et la première école de journalisme en France: Entre réforme sociale et professionnalisation." *Questions de communication*, no. 16 (2009): 27–44. https://doi.org/10.4000/questionsdecommunication.81.

Goyanes, Manuel, and Eduardo Fco Rodríguez-Gómez. "Presentism in the Newsroom: How Uncertainty Redefines Journalists' Career Expectations." *Journalism* 22, no. 1 (2021): 52–68. https://doi.org/10.1177/1464884918767585.

Graves, Lucas. *Deciding What's True: The Rise of Political Fact-Checking in American Journalism*. New York: Columbia University Press, 2016.

Gürsel, Zeynep Devrim. *Image Brokers: Visualizing World News in the Age of Digital Circulation*. Oakland: University of California Press, 2016.

Habermas, Jürgen. *Between Facts and Norms: Contributions to a Discourse Theory of Law and Democracy*. Cambridge, MA: MIT Press, 1998.

Hallin, Daniel C., and Paolo Mancini. *Comparing Media Systems: Three Models of Media and Politics*. New York: Cambridge University Press, 2004.

Hamilton, James T. *All The News That's Fit to Sell: How the Market Transforms Information Into News*. Princeton, NJ: Princeton University Press, 2004.

———. *Democracy's Detectives: The Economics of Investigative Journalism*. Cambridge, MA: Harvard University Press, 2016.

Hanitzsch, Thomas, Folker Hanusch, Jyotika Ramaprasad, and Arnold S. de Beer, eds. *Worlds of Journalism: Journalistic Cultures Around the Globe*. New York: Columbia University Press, 2019.

Hanusch, Folker, Claudia Mellado, Priscilla Boshoff, María Luisa Humanes, Salvador de León, Fabio Pereira, Mireya Márquez Ramírez, et al. "Journalism Students' Motivations and Expectations of Their Work in Comparative Perspective."

Journalism and Mass Communication Educator 70, no. 2 (2015): 141–60. https://doi.org/10.1177/1077695814554295.

Hayes, Danny, and Jennifer L. Lawless. *News Hole: The Demise of Local Journalism and Political Engagement*. New York: Cambridge University Press, 2021.

Hesmondhalgh, David. *Why Music Matters*. Malden, MA: Wiley Blackwell, 2013.

Hesmondhalgh, David, and Sarah Baker. *Creative Labour: Media Work in Three Cultural Industries*. New York: Routledge, 2013.

Higgins-Dobney, Carey L. "Producing in Precarity: A Focus on Freelancing in US Local Television Newsrooms." In *Newswork and Precarity*, edited by Kalyani Chadha and Linda Steiner, 71–83. London: Routledge, 2022.

Hirschman, Albert O. *Shifting Involvements: Private Interest and Public Action*. Princeton, NJ: Princeton University Press, 1982.

Ho-Pun-Cheung, Élise. "Concilier contraintes économiques et indépendance: Un journalisme à la frontière de la profession." *Politiques de communication* 16, no. 1 (2021): 85–113. https://doi.org/10.3917/pdc.016.0085.

Hughes, John C. *Pressing On: Two Family-Owned Newspapers in the 21st Century*. Olympia: Washington State Legacy Project, 2015.

Jackson, Daniel, Einar Thorsen, and Sally Reardon. "Fantasy, Pragmatism and Journalistic Socialisation: UK Journalism Students' Aspirations and Motivations." *Journalism Practice* 14, no. 1 (2020): 104–24. https://doi.org/10.1080/17512786.2019.1591929.

Jenkins, Joy, and Rasmus Kleis Nielsen. *The Digital Transition of Local News*. Oxford: Reuters Institute for the Study of Journalism, 2018.

Johnstone, John W. C., Edward Slawski, and William W. Bowman. *The News People: A Sociological Portrait of American Journalists and their Work*. Urbana: University of Illinois Press, 1976.

Juergens, George. *Joseph Pulitzer and the New York World*. Princeton, NJ: Princeton University Press, 1966.

Kaciaf, Nicolas. "Faire rendre des comptes: Les conditions de l'investigation journalistique à l'échelle locale." *Politiques de communication* 15, no. 2 (2020): 139–66. https://doi.org/10.3917/pdc.015.0139.

Kalifa, Dominique. "Les tâcherons de l'information: Petits reporters et faits divers à la 'Belle Époque.'" *Revue d'histoire moderne et contemporaine (1954–)* 40, no. 4 (1993): 578–603. https://doi.org/10.3406/rhmc.1993.1691.

Kalifa, Dominique, Philippe Régnier, Marie-Ève Thérenty, and Alain Vaillant. *La Civilisation du Journal: Histoire Culturelle et Littéraire de la Presse Française au XIXe Siècle*. Paris: Nouveau Monde, 2011.

Kaplan, Richard. *Politics and the American Press: The Rise of Objectivity, 1865–1920*. New York: Cambridge University Press, 2002.

Kielbowicz, Richard B. *News in the Mail: The Press, Post Office, and Public Information, 1770–1860s*. Westport, CT: Greenwood, 1989.

Konieczna, Magda. *Journalism Without Profit: Making News When the Market Fails*. New York: Oxford University Press, 2018.

Kroeger, Brooke. *Nellie Bly: Daredevil, Reporter, Feminist*. New York: Times Books, 1994.

Kuhn, Raymond. *The Media in France*. London: Routledge, 1995.

Kunitz, Stanley. *The Collected Poems*. New York: Norton, 1978.

Ladd, Jonathan M. *Why Americans Hate the Media and How It Matters*. Princeton, NJ: Princeton University Press, 2011.

Lafarge, Géraud. "Le champ journalistique et l'espace des écoles de journalisme." *Savoir/Agir* 46, no. 4 (2018): 17–25. https://doi.org/10.3917/sava.046.0017.

Lafarge, Géraud, and Dominique Marchetti. "Les hiérarchies de l'information: Les légitimités 'professionnelles' des étudiants en journalisme." *Sociétés contemporaines* 106, no. 2 (2017): 21–44. https://doi.org/10.3917/soco.106.0021.

———. "Les portes fermées du journalisme: L'espace social des étudiants des formations 'reconnues,'" *Actes de la Recherche en Sciences Sociales* 189, no. 4 (2011): 72–99. https://doi.org/10.3917/arss.189.0072.

Lagneau, Éric. "Agencier à l'AFP: l'éthique du métier menacée." *Hermès, La Revue* 1, no. 35 (2003): 109–18. https://doi.org/10.4267/2042/9323.

Lamont, Michèle. *The Dignity of Working Men: Morality and the Boundaries of Race, Class, and Immigration*. Cambridge, MA: Harvard University Press, 2000.

———. *Money, Morals, and Manners: The Culture of the French and the American Upper-Middle Class*. Chicago: University of Chicago Press, 1992.

Le Cam, Florence, and David Domingo. "The Tyranny of Immediacy." In *Gatekeeping in Transition*, edited by Tim P. Vos and François Heinderyckx, 123–40. New York: Routledge, 2015.

Le Floch, Patrick. *Économie de la presse quotidienne régionale: Déterminants et conséquences de la concentration*. Paris: L'Harmattan, 1997.

Legavre, Jean-Baptiste. "Figure du deuil professionnel: Du 'vrai' journalisme au journalisme d'organisation." In *Les Dimensions Émotionnelles du Politique*, edited by Isabelle Sommier and Xavier Crettiez, 255–72. Rennes: Presses universitaires de Rennes, 2019.

Le Grignou, Brigitte, and Érik Neveu. *Sociologie de la Télévision*. Paris: La Découverte, 2017.

Le Masurier, Megan. "What Is Slow Journalism?" *Journalism Practice* 9, no. 2 (2015): 138–52. https://doi.org/10.1080/17512786.2014.916471.

Lemieux, Cyril. *Mauvaise presse: Une sociologie compréhensive du travail journalistique et de ses critiques*. Paris: Éditions Métailié, 2000.

Lemieux, Cyril, and John Schmalzbauer. "Involvement and Detachment Among French and American Journalists: To Be or Not to Be a 'Real' Professional." In *Rethinking Comparative Cultural Sociology: Repertoires of Evaluation in France and the United States,* edited by Michèle Lamont and Laurent Thévenot, 148–69. New York: Cambridge University Press, 2000.

Lenoble, Benoît. "L'Identité médiatique du *Figaro* (1866–1914)." In *Le Figaro: Histoire d'un journal,* edited by Claire Blandin, 47–63. Paris: Nouveau Monde, 2010.

Leteinturier, Christine. "Continuité/Discontinuité des carrières des journalistes français en cartés: Étude de deux cohortes de nouveaux titulaires de la carte de presse." *Recherches en communication* 43 (2016): 27–55. https://doi.org/10.14428/rec.v43i43.48753.

Leteinturier, Christine, and Cégolène Frisque. *Les espaces professionnels des journalistes: Des corpus quantitatifs aux analyses qualitatives.* Paris: Éditions Panthéon-Assas, 2015.

Lévêque, Sandrine. "Femmes, féministes et journalistes: Les rédactrices de La Fronde à l'épreuve de la professionnalisation journalistique." *Le Temps des médias* 1, no. 12 (2009): 41–53. https://doi.org/10.3917/tdm.012.0041.

———. *Les journalistes sociaux: Histoire et sociologie d'une spécialité journalistique.* Rennes: Presses universitaires de Rennes, 2000.

Lewis, Seth C. "The Tension Between Professional Control and Open Participation." *Information, Communication and Society* 15, no. 6 (2012): 836–66. https://doi.org/10.1080/1369118X.2012.674150.

Lutes, Jean Marie. "Into the Madhouse with Nellie Bly: Girl Stunt Reporting in Late Nineteenth-Century America." *American Quarterly* 54, no. 2 (2002): 217–53. http://www.jstor.org/stable/30041927.

MacDonald, Jasmine B., Anthony J. Saliba, Gene Hodgins, and Linda A. Ovington. "Burnout in Journalists: A Systematic Literature Review." *Burnout Research* 3, no. 2 (2016): 34–44. https://doi.org/10.1016/j.burn.2016.03.001.

Marchetti, Dominique. "Les ajustements du marché scolaire au marché du travail journalistique." *Hermès, la Revue* 35, no. 1 (2003): 81–89. https://doi.org/10.4267/2042/9320.

———. "Contribution à une sociologie des transformations du champ journalistique dans les années 80 et 90: à propos d' 'événements sida' et du 'scandale du sang contaminé.' " PhD diss., École des Hautes Études en Sciences Sociales (EHESS), 1997.

———. "The Revelations of Investigative Journalism in France." *Global Media and Communication* 5, no. 3 (2009): 368–88. https://doi.org/10.1177/1742766509346610.

Marjoribanks, Timothy, Lawrie Zion, and Merryn Sherwood. "Mobilising Networks After Redundancy: The Experiences of Australian Journalists." *New Technology, Work and Employment* 36, no. 3 (2021): 371–89. https://doi.org/10.1111/ntwe.12192.

Martin, John Levi. *Thinking Through Methods: A Social Science Primer.* Chicago: University of Chicago Press, 2017.
Martin, Marc. "'La grande famille': l'Association des journalistes parisiens (1885–1939)." *Revue Historique* 275, no. 1 (557) (1986): 129–57. www.jstor.org/stable/40954345.
———. *Les grands reporters: Les débuts du journalisme moderne.* Paris: Louis Audibert Editions, 2005.
———. "Journalistes parisiens et notoriété (vers 1830–1870): Pour une histoire sociale du journalism." *Revue Historique* 266, no. 1 (539) (1981): 31–74. www.jstor.org/stable/40953576.
———. *Médias et journalistes de la République.* Paris: Editions Odile Jacob, 1997.
Marx, Karl. *Capital: A Critique of Political Economy.* Vol. 1. New York: Penguin, 1990. First published in 1867.
Matos, José. "'It Was Journalism That Abandoned Me': An Analysis of Journalism in Portugal." *TripleC: Communication, Capitalism and Critique* 18, no. 2 (2020): 535–55. https://doi.org/10.31269/triplec.v18i2.1148.
Mauger, Gérard. "Sens pratique et conditions sociales de possibilité de la pensée 'pensante.'" *Cités* 38, no. 2 (2009): 61–77.
McChesney, Robert W. *Telecommunications, Mass Media, and Democracy: The Battle for the Control of U.S. Broadcasting, 1928–1935.* New York: Oxford University Press, 1993.
Mercier, Arnaud, and Laura Amigo. "Insulting and Hateful Tweets Against Journalists and 'Merdias.'" *Mots: Les langages du politique* 125, no. 1 (2021): 73–91. https://doi.org/10.4000/mots.28043.
Mindich, David T. Z. *Tuned Out: Why Americans Under 40 Don't Follow the News.* New York: Oxford University Press, 2005.
Morley, David. *Television, Audiences and Cultural Studies.* London: Routledge, 1992.
Mott, Frank Luther. *American Journalism: A History, 1690–1960.* New York: Macmillan, 1962.
Muhlmann, Géraldine. *Journalism for Democracy.* Cambridge: Polity, 2010.
Napoli, Philip M., Sarah Stonbely, Kathleen McCollough, and Bryce Renninger. "Local Journalism and the Information Needs of Local Communities: Toward a Scalable Assessment Approach." *Journalism Practice* 13, no. 8 (2019): 1024–28. https://doi.org/10.1080/17512786.2019.1647110.
Nel, François. *Laid Off: What Do UK Journalists Do Next?* Preston: University of Central Lancashire, 2010.
Neveu, Érik. "Bourdieu's Capital(s): Sociologizing an Economic Concept." In *The Oxford Handbook of Pierre Bourdieu,* edited by Thomas Medvetz and Jeffrey J. Sallaz, 347–74. New York: Oxford University Press, 2018.

———. "In Hope That Scientific Nomadism May Turn Out to Be Meaningful After All." *Bulletin of Sociological Methodology/Bulletin de Méthodologie Sociologique* 151, no. 1 (2021): 38–62. https://doi.org/10.1177/07591063211019952.

———. "The Local Press and Farmers' Protests in Brittany: Proximity and Distance in the Local Newspaper Coverage of a Social Movement." *Journalism Studies* 3, no. 1 (2002): 53–67. https://doi.org/10.1080/14616700120107338.

———. "News Without Journalists: Real Threat or Horror Story?" *Brazilian Journalism Research* 6, no. 1 (2010): 29–54. https://doi.org/10.25200/BJR.v6n1.2010.225.

———. "On Not Going Too Fast with Slow Journalism." *Journalism Practice* 10, no. 4 (2016): 448–60. https://doi.org/10.1080/17512786.2015.1114897.

———. *Sociologie du journalisme*. Paris: La Découverte, 2019.

Nielsen, Rasmus Kleis, ed. *Local Journalism: The Decline of Newspapers and the Rise of Digital Media*. London: I. B. Tauris, 2015.

Nielsen, Rasmus Kleis, and Sarah Anne Ganter. *The Power of Platforms: Shaping Media and Society*. New York: Oxford University Press, 2022.

Nölleke, Daniel, Phoebe Maares, and Folker Hanusch. "Illusio and Disillusionment: Expectations Met or Disappointed Among Young Journalists." *Journalism* 23, no. 2 (2022): 320–36. https://doi.org/10.1177/1464884920956820.

Norris, Pippa. "Comparative Political Communications: Common Frameworks or Babelian Confusion?" *Government and Opposition* 44, no. 3 (2009): 321–40. https://doi.org/10.1111/j.1477-7053.2009.01290.x.

O'Donnell, Penny, Lawrie Zion, and Merryn Sherwood. "Where Do Journalists Go After Newsroom Job Cuts?" *Journalism Practice* 10, no. 1 (2016): 35–51. https://doi.org/10.1080/17512786.2015.1017400.

Örnebring, Henrik. *Newsworkers: A Comparative European Perspective*. London: Bloomsbury, 2016.

Örnebring, Henrik, and Cecilia Möller. "In the Margins of Journalism." *Journalism Practice* 12, no. 8 (2018): 1051–60. https://doi.org/10.1080/17512786.2018.1497455.

Padioleau, Jean-Gustave. *"Le Monde" et le "Washington Post": Précepteurs et mousquetaires*. Paris: Presses Universitaires de France, 1985.

Paine, Jonathan. *Selling the Story: Transaction and Narrative Value in Balzac, Dostoevsky, and Zola*. Cambridge, MA: Harvard University Press, 2019.

Palmer, Michael B. *Des petits journaux aux grandes agences: Naissance du journalisme moderne, 1863–1914*. Paris: Aubier, 1983.

Parasie, Sylvain. *Computing the News: Data Journalism and the Search for Objectivity*. New York: Columbia University Press, 2022.

Patterson, Thomas E. *Informing the News: The Need for Knowledge-Based Journalism*. New York: Vintage, 2013.

Petre, Caitlin. *All the News That's Fit to Click: How Metrics Are Transforming the Work of Journalists*. Princeton, NJ: Princeton University Press, 2021.

Pettegree, Andrew. *The Invention of News: How the World Came to Know About Itself.* New Haven, CT: Yale University Press, 2014.

Picard, Robert G. *Journalists' Perceptions of the Future of Journalistic Work.* Oxford: Reuters Institute for the Study of Journalism, 2015.

Pickard, Victor. *Democracy Without Journalism? Confronting the Misinformation Society.* New York: Oxford University Press, 2020.

Poulet, Bernard. *La fin des journaux et l'avenir de l'information.* Paris: Editions Gallimard, 2009.

Powers, Matthew. "The Direction and Demographics of Journalists' Trajectories: Evidence from One American City, 2015–2021." *Journalism Studies* 23, no. 3 (2022): 392–411. https://doi.org/10.1080/1461670X.2022.2029541.

Powers, Matthew, and Sandra Vera-Zambrano. "Endure, Invest, Ignore: How French and American Journalists React to Economic Constraints and Technological Transformations." *Journal of Communication* 69, no. 3 (2019): 320–43. https://doi.org/10.1093/joc/jqz015.

———. "Explaining the Formation of Online News Startups in France and the United States: A Field Analysis." *Journal of Communication* 66, no. 5 (2016): 857–77. https://doi.org/10.1111/jcom.12253.

———. "How Journalists Use Social Media in France and the United States: Analyzing Technology Use Across Journalistic Fields." *New Media and Society* 20, no. 8 (2018): 2728–44, https://doi.org/10.1177/1461444817731566.

———. "The Universal and the Contextual of Media Systems: Research Design, Epistemology, and the Production of Comparative Knowledge." *International Journal of Press/Politics* 23, no. 2 (2018): 143–60. https://doi.org/10.1177/1940161218771899.

———. "What Are Journalists for Today?" In *Rethinking Media Research for Changing Societies*, edited by Matthew Powers and Adrienne Russell, 65–77. Cambridge: Cambridge University Press, 2020.

Powers, Matthew, Sandra Vera-Zambrano, and Olivier Baisnée. "The News Crisis Compared: The Impact of the Journalism Crisis in Toulouse, France and Seattle, USA." In *Local Journalism: The Decline of Newspapers and the Rise of Digital Media*, edited by Rasmus Kleis Nielsen, 31–50. London: I. B. Tauris, 2015.

Rancière, Jacques. *The Names of History: On the Poetics of Knowledge.* Translated by Hassan Melehy. Minneapolis: University of Minnesota Press, 1994.

Rebillard, Franck, and Nikos Smyrnaios. "Quelle 'plateformisation' de l'information? Collusion socioéconomique et dilution éditoriale entre les entreprises médiatiques et les infomédiaires de l'Internet." *Tic et Société* 13, nos. 1/2 (2019): 247–93.

Reese, Stephen D. *The Crisis of the Institutional Press.* Cambridge: Polity, 2021.

Reich, Zvi. "Different Practices, Similar Logic: Comparing News Reporting Across Political, Financial, and Territorial Beats." *International Journal of Press/Politics* 17, no. 1 (2012): 76–99. https://doi.org/10.1177/1940161211420868.

Reich, Zvi, and Yigal Godler. "A Time of Uncertainty: The Effects of Reporters' Time Schedule on Their Work." *Journalism Studies* 15, no. 5 (2014): 607–18. https://doi.org/10.1080/1461670X.2014.882484.

Reinardy, Scott, Lawrie Zion, and Annalise Baines. "'It's Like Dying but Not Being Dead': U.S. Newspaper Journalists Cope with Emotional and Physical Toll of Job Losses." *Newspaper Research Journal* 42, no. 3 (2021): 364–78. https://doi.org/10.1177/07395329211030577.

Ritchie, Donald A. *Press Gallery: Congress and the Washington Correspondents.* Cambridge, MA: Harvard University Press, 1991.

Roberts Forde, Kathy, and Katherine A. Foss. "'The Facts—the Color!—the Facts': The Idea of the Report in America Print Culture, 1885–1910." *Book History* 15 (2012): 123–51. www.jstor.org/stable/23315046.

Robinson, Sue. *Networked News, Racial Divides: How Power and Privilege Shape Public Discourse in Progressive Communities.* New York: Cambridge University Press, 2018.

Rosa, Hartmut. *Social Acceleration: A New Theory of Modernity.* New York: Columbia University Press, 2013.

Rowe, David. "Sports Journalism: Still the 'Toy Department' of the News Media?" *Journalism* 8, no. 4 (2007): 385–405. https://doi.org/10.1177/1464884907078657.

Ruellan, Denis. *Nous, journalistes: Déontologie et identité.* Grenoble. Presses universitaires de Grenoble, 2011.

Russell, Adrienne. *Networked: A Contemporary History of News in Transition.* Cambridge: Polity, 2011.

Ryfe, David M. *Can Journalism Survive? An Inside Look at American Newsrooms.* Cambridge: Polity, 2012.

———. "The Economics of News and the Practice of News Production." *Journalism Studies* 22, no. 1 (2021): 60–76. https://doi.org/10.1080/1461670X.2020.1854619.

Salisbury, William. *The Career of a Journalist.* New York: BW Dodge, 1908.

Sánchez Laws, Ana Luisa. "Can Immersive Journalism Enhance Empathy?" *Digital Journalism* 8, no. 2 (2020): 213–28. https://doi.org/10.1080/21670811.2017.1389286.

Schudson, Michael. "Autonomy from What?" In *Bourdieu and the Journalistic Field*, edited by Rodney Benson and Érik Neveu, 214–23. Cambridge: Polity, 2005.

———. *Discovering the News: A Social History of American Newspapers.* New York: Basic, 1978.

———. *The Good Citizen: A History of American Civic Life.* New York: Simon and Schuster, 1998.

———. "Question Authority: A History of the News Interview in American Journalism, 1860s–1930s." *Media, Culture and Society* 16, no. 4 (1994): 565–87. https://doi.org/10.1177/016344379401600403.

———. *The Rise of the Right to Know: Politics and the Culture of Transparency, 1945–1975*. Cambridge, MA: Harvard University Press, 2015.

———. *The Sociology of News*. New York: Norton, 2011.

———. *Why Democracies Need an Unlovable Press*. Cambridge: Polity, 2008.

———. *Why Journalism Still Matters*. Cambridge: Polity, 2018.

Siebert, Fred, Theodore Peterson, Theodore Bernard Peterson, and Wilbur Schramm. *Four Theories of the Press: The Authoritarian, Libertarian, Social Responsibility, and Soviet Communist Concepts of What the Press Should Be and Do*. Champaign-Urbana: University of Illinois Press, 1956.

Siracusa, Jacques. "Le montage de l'information télévisée." *Actes de la Recherche en Sciences Sociales* 131/132, no. 1 (2000): 92–106. https://doi.org/10.3917/arss.p2000.131n1.0092.

Skeggs, Beverly. *Formations of Class and Gender: Becoming Respectable*. London: Sage, 1997.

Smith, Culver H. *The Press, Politics, and Patronage: The American Government's Use of Newspapers, 1789–1875*. Athens, Georgia: University of Georgia Press, 1977.

Smyrnaios, Nikos. "Les pure players entre innovation journalistique et contrainte économique: les cas d'Owni, Rue89 et Arrêt sur images." *Recherches en communication* 39 (2013): 133–50. https://doi.org/10.14428/rec.v39i39.49653.

Smythe, Ted Curtis. *The Gilded Age Press, 1865–1900*. Westport, CT: Praeger, 2003.

Souanef, Karim. *Le journalisme sportif: Sociologie d'une spécialité dominée*. Presses universitaires de Rennes, 2019.

Starkman, Dean. "The Hamster Wheel: Why Running as Fast as We Can Is Getting Us Nowhere." Columbia Journalism Review. September/October 2010. https://archives.cjr.org/cover_story/the_hamster_wheel.php.

Starr, Paul. *The Creation of the Media: Political Origins of Modern Communications*. New York: Basic, 2004.

Steffens, Lincoln. *The Autobiography of Lincoln Steffens*. New York: Heyday, 1931.

———. "The Business of a Newspaper." *Scribner's Magazine* 22, no.4 (1897): 447–67.

Steiner, Linda. "Failed Theories: Explaining Gender Difference in Journalism." *Review of Communication* 12, no. 3 (2012): 201–23. https://doi.org/10.1080/15358593.2012.666559.

———. "Stories of Quitting: Why Did Women Journalists Leave the Newsroom?" *American Journalism* 15, no. 3 (1998): 89–116. https://doi.org/10.1080/08821127.1998.10731989.

Streeck, Wolfgang. *How Will Capitalism End? Essays on a Failing System*. New York: Verso, 2017.

Stroud, Natalie Jomini. *Niche News: The Politics of News Choice.* New York: Oxford University Press, 2011.

Suaud, Charles. *La vocation: Conversion et reconversion des prêtres ruraux.* Paris: Editions de Minuit, 1978.

Sumpter, Randall S. *Before Journalism Schools: How Gilded Age Reporters Learned the Rules.* Columbia: University of Missouri Press, 2018.

Swanberg, W. A. *Citizen Hearst: A Biography of William Randolph Hearst.* New York: Charles Scribner's Sons, 1961.

Tandoc, Edson C., Jr., and Tim P. Vos. "The Journalist Is Marketing the News: Social Media in the Gatekeeping Process." *Journalism Practice* 10, no. 8 (2016): 950–66. https://doi.org/10.1080/17512786.2015.1087811.

Thérenty, Marie-Ève. *La Littérature au Quotidien: Poétiques journalistiques au XIXe siècle.* Paris: Édition du Seuil, 2007.

———. *Mosaïques: Être écrivain entre presse et roman (1829–1836).* Paris: Honoré Champion, 2003.

Thompson, John B. *Book Wars: The Digital Revolution in Publishing.* Cambridge: Polity, 2021.

de Tocqueville, Alexis. *Democracy in America: The Complete and Unabridged*, volumes 1 and 2. New York: Bantam Classics, 2000.

———. *The Old Regime and the French Revolution.* New York: Doubleday, 1983.

Torres, Félix. *La Dépêche du Midi: Histoire d'un journal en République, 1870–2000.* Paris: Hachette Littératures, 2002.

Tunstall, Jeremy. *Journalists at Work: Specialist Correspondents; Their News Organizations, News Sources, and Competitor-Colleagues.* London: Constable, 1971.

Underwood, Doug. *Literary Journalism in British and American Prose: An Historical Overview.* Jefferson, NC: McFarland, 2019.

———. *When MBAs Rule the Newsroom: How Marketers and Managers Are Reshaping Today's Media.* New York: Columbia University Press, 1993.

Usher, Nikki. *Making News at the New York Times.* Ann Arbor: University of Michigan Press, 2014.

———. *News for the Rich, White, and Blue: How Place and Power Distort American Journalism.* New York: Columbia University Press, 2021.

Van den Dungen, Pierre. "Écrivains du quotidien: Journalistes et journalisme en France au XIXème siècle." *Semen: Revue de sémio-linguistique des textes et discours* 25 (2008). https://journals.openedition.org/semen/8108.

Van Zoonen, Liesbet. "One of the Girls? The Changing Gender of Journalism." In *News, Gender and Power*, edited by Cynthia Carter, Gill Branston and Stuart Allan, 33–46. New York: Routledge, 1998.

Vera-Zambrano, Sandra, and Matthew Powers. "Journalistic Judgment in Comparative Perspective: A Weberian Analysis of France and the United States."

International Journal of Press/Politics 27, no. 2 (2022): 478–96. https://journals.sagepub.com/doi/10.1177/1940161221997250.

———. "The Roots of Journalistic Perception: A Bourdieusian Approach to Media and Class." In *The Routledge Companion to Media and Class*, edited by Erika Polson, Lynn Schofield Clark, and Radhika Gajjala, 157–67. London: Routledge, 2020.

Viererbl, Benno, and Thomas Koch. "Once a Journalist, Not Always a Journalist? Causes and Consequences of Job Changes from Journalism to Public Relations." *Journalism* 22, no. 8 (2021): 1947–63. https://doi.org/10.1177/1464884919829647.

Villard de Borchgrave, Alexandra, and John Cullen. *Villard: The Life and Times of an American Titan*. New York: Doubleday, 2001.

Vos, Tim P., and Gregory P. Perreault. "The Discursive Construction of the Gamification of Journalism." *Convergence: The International Journal of Research Into New Media Technologies* 26, no. 3 (2020): 470–85. https://doi.org/10.1177/1354856520909542.

Wagemans, Andrea, Tamara Witschge, and Mark Deuze. "Ideology as Resource in Entrepreneurial Journalism." *Journalism Practice* 10, no. 2 (2016): 160–77. https://doi.org/10.1080/17512786.2015.1124732.

Waisbord, Silvio. "Mob Censorship: Online Harassment of US Journalists in Times of Digital Hate and Populism." *Digital Journalism* 8, no. 8 (2020): 1030–46. https://doi.org/10.1080/21670811.2020.1818111.

———. "Truth Is What Happens to News: On Journalism, Fake News, and Post-Truth." *Journalism Studies* 19, no. 13 (2018): 1866–78. https://doi.org/10.1080/1461670X.2018.1492881.

Walker, Mason. "U.S. Newsroom Employment Has Fallen 26% Since 2008." Pew Research Center. July 13, 2021. www.pewresearch.org/fact-tank/2021/07/13/u-s-newsroom-employment-has-fallen-26-since-2008/.

Wasko, Janet. *Hollywood in the Information Age: Beyond the Silver Screen*. Cambridge: Polity, 2013.

Weaver, David H., and G. Cleveland Wilhoit. *The American Journalist: A Portrait of U.S. News People and Their Work*. Bloomington: Indiana University Press, 1986.

———. *The American Journalist in the 1990s: U.S. News People at the End of an Era*. Mahwah, NJ: Lawrence Erlbaum, 1996.

Weaver, David H., Randal A. Beam, Bonnie J. Brownlee, Paul S. Voakes, and G. Cleveland Wilhoit. *The American Journalist in the 21st Century: U.S. News People at the Dawn of the New Millenium*. Mahwah, NJ: Lawrence Erlbaum, 2007.

Weaver, David, Lars Willnat, and G. Cleveland Wilhoit. "The American Journalist in the Digital Age: Another Look at U.S. News People." *Journalism and Mass Communication Quarterly* 96, no. 1 (2019): 101–30. https://doi.org/10.1177/1077699018778242.

Weber, Max. *Max Weber's Complete Writings on Academic and Political Vocations.* Edited by John Dreijmanis. Translated by Gordon C. Wells. New York: Algora, 2008.

———. "Politics as a Vocation." In *From Max Weber: Essays in Sociology*, edited by H. H. Gerth and C. Wright Mills, 77–128. New York: Oxford University Press, 1946.

———. *The Protestant Ethic and the Spirit of Capitalism.* New York: Penguin, 2002. First published in 1905.

Weiss, Robert S. *Learning from Strangers: The Art and Method of Qualitative Interview Studies.* New York: Free Press, 1994.

Williams, Bruce A., and Michael X. Delli Carpini. *After Broadcast News: Media Regimes, Democracy, and the New Information Environment.* New York: Cambridge University Press, 2011.

Willis, Paul. *Profane Culture.* Princeton, NJ: Princeton University Press, 1978.

Willnat, Lars, David H. Weaver, and G. Cleveland Wilhoit. *The American Journalist in the Digital Age: A Half-Century Perspective.* New York: Peter Lang, 2017.

Wirth, Werner, and Steffen Kolb. "Securing Equivalence: Problems and Solutions." In *The Handbook of Comparative Communication Research*, edited by Frank Esser and Thomas Hanitzsch, 469–85. London: Routledge, 2012.

Zelizer, Barbie. "Journalism's 'Last' Stand: Wirephoto and the Discourse of Resistance." *Journal of Communication* 45, no. 2 (1995): 78–92. https://doi.org/10.1111/j.1460-2466.1995.tb00729.x.

Zelizer, Barbie, and Stuart Allan. *Keywords in News and Journalism Studies.* Berkshire, UK: Open University Press, 2010.

Index

A2PRL (radio station), 205, 206
Abernathy, Penelope Muse, 228*n*9
acceding: balance of rewards, 115, 116, 117; economic constraints and technological status quo, 215; by going along with new technology and deteriorating work conditions, 117, 133–38, 140
ActuToulouse (online news site), 205
adjustment, modes of: with balance of rewards, 114–16; beliefs and, 5–6, 12–15, 18, 19; best work, 87, 106; as gamble, 116, 141; with journalism as polysemic profession, 55–57, 68–69, 75, 85
advertising, 2, 8, 9, 42, 181; penny papers, 235*n*14
aerospace reporter, 97, 99, 126, 250*n*51
Agence France-Presse (AFP), 206
Airbus, 17, 62
All the President's Men (Woodward and Bernstein), 243*n*7
alternative weeklies, 81–82, 204, 205

American Journalist in the Digital Age, The (Weaver, Willnat, and Wilhoit), 233*n*57, 248*n*11
American Journalist Survey, 89–90
Amiel, Pauline, 228*n*9, 229*n*21
Andrieux, Louis, 32
anonymity, 200–1, 242*n*1
"Ask A . . ." (radio program), 107–8
Association of Parisian Journalists (Association des Journalistes Parisiens), 34
Association Syndicale Professionnelle des Journalistes Républicains Français, l' (Professional Association of French Journalists), 34
audiences (readership): aging, 9, 253*n*15; class and, 23, 37–39, 40–42; competition for attention, 2, 8, 33, 121, 133, 151; as consumers, 121, 122; with distrust and antipathy, 8, 10, 11, 152; as "dutiful citizens," 179; engaged journalism and, 254*n*26; fact-based reporting and, 30–31;

audiences (readership) (*continued*)
  with high cultural capital, 179;
  Internet news and younger, 120; for
  long-form reporting, 176, 179, 180; as
  partisans, 178; technology and, 121;
  translating words of power holders
  for, 89, 103–6
audiovisual news organizations, 9, 94

balance of rewards: acceding, 115, 116,
  117; adjustment modes with, 114–16;
  challenging, 114–15, 116, 117;
  conserving, 114, 116, 117; for men, 58;
  with novel forms of journalism, 25;
  predicament of journalists with, 2,
  3, 5, 27, 191, 192, 193
Baldasty, Gerald, 45
Bandy de Nalèche, Étienne, 40–41
BBC, 65
beat reporters and editors, 114, 214; with
  best work, 96–97, 213, 214; job
  descriptions, 44; leaving journalism,
  216; living for and off journalism, 210,
  212; living for journalism, 210, 211
Before Journalism Schools (Sumpter),
  236*n*20, 241*n*83
Bel Ami (Maupassant), 43, 236*n*27
beliefs: with adjustment modes, 5–6,
  12–15, 18, 19; of journalism as "worth
  the candle," 4, 13, 142, 188, 192, 194,
  197, 227*n*7, 248*n*12; in questioning
  and leaving journalism, 26, 143,
  149–52; in worth of journalism, 3–4,
  5, 8, 11, 23, 46, 48, 49. *See also*
  leaving journalism
Benson, Rodney, 15, 245*n*47, 249*n*23
Bernstein, Carl, 59, 63, 243*n*7
best work: as data source, 87–88,
  89–92; decoding, 89, 103–6; defined,
  86; dignifying, 89, 106–9;

discovering, 88–89, 96–99;
economic pressures influencing, 91;
edifying, 88, 89, 99–102; "good" and,
86–87, 112; inability to recall,
248*n*12; of journalists, 96–109;
journalists and journalism worthy
of admiration, 92–96; journalists at
pinnacle, 109–13; labels, 213–14, 224;
ordinary and, 91; pride and, 86, 91,
97, 98, 102, 104, 107, 109;
professional excellence and, 87, 88;
surveys, 90, 248*nn*8–9; symbolic
hierarchies, 24, 86–87, 88, 91–92
Blethen, Alden, 32, 35, 38, 236*n*18,
  240*n*78
bloggers, 99, 104, 126, 127, 129
Blondin, Antoine, 94
Bloomingdale Asylum, 41
Bly, Nellie, 36, 41, 46
Boeing, 17, 97, 99
Bonville, Jean de, 59
Boswell, Sharon A., 235*n*9, 240*n*78
Boudu (magazine), 205
Bourdieu, Pierre, 4, 169, 227*n*7, 228*n*8,
  260*n*1
Bousquet, Franck, 228*n*9
Bowers, Thomas A., 243*n*7
Breslin, Jimmy, 94
Brigadier, Le (magazine), 205
Brin, Colette, 59
Buchanan, Edna, 94
Bureau of Labor Statistics, U.S., 228*n*18
business models, for news, 3, 187, 194,
  261*n*17; commercial, 31–33; new, 50,
  116, 169, 183
bylines, stories without, 45

cameraman, television news, 156, 161,
  162–63
capitalism, 181–82, 184, 262*n*29

Capitol Hill Seattle (online news site), 204
Carey, James, 237*n*28
Caudill, Edward, 240*n*67
Chalaby, Jean, 36, 239*n*48
challenging: balance of rewards, 114–15, 116, 117; economic constraints and technological status quo, 214–15, 216; by investing in technology, 117, 128–33; power holders, 88–89, 96–99, 182
Chambers, Julius, 41
Charlie Hebdo (magazine), 104
Charron, Jean, 59
children, 94, 95, 105–6, 107, 108; with journalism as career choice, 177, 193; journalists with, 115, 148, 150, 151, 153, 155–56, 159, 161–62, 164–65
chronicles, 36, 40, 47
circulation, 38–39, 104, 235*n*14, 236*n*18
class: audiences and, 23, 37–39, 40–42; elites, 10, 19, 22–23, 36, 39, 40–41, 46–48, 52; middle, 1, 12, 19, 32, 42–48, 177, 180, 211; popular, 37, 38; working, 6, 14, 211
Club de la Presse, 35
Columbia University Graduate School of Journalism, 243*n*12, 244*n*14
commentaries, 6, 40, 48
commercial function, of journalism: in schools, 122; social and, 4, 5, 6, 29–30, 50, 118, 151, 176, 191, 206; with technology and new equilibrium, 118–23
commercial model, of journalism, 31–33, 41, 51, 52, 119, 235*n*14
commercial pressures, 169, 173, 188, 201; death of journalism and, 192; immediacy and, 121; journalism schools with, 139–40; market and, 27, 175, 261*n*17; politics and, 240*n*74; symbolic rewards eroded by, 140, 193; technology and, 119–20, 121, 138–41
Commission de la Carte d'Identité des Journalistes Professionnels, 229*n*15
community, 102, 107, 157, 160, 204; college, 103, 213; engagement editor, 129; radio stations, 80; reporters, 71
Comparing Media Systems (Hallin and Mancini), 233*n*54
Complément d'enquête (television news magazine), 93
comprehension: defined, 199; interviewing as, 197–202
congressional reporting, 241*n*92
Conover, Ted, 179
conserving: balance of rewards, 114, 116–17; economic constraints and technological status quo, 214, 215, 216; by ignoring technology, 117, 123–28
contracts, 104, 163, 193–94; permanent, 9, 56, 73, 74–75, 77, 129, 144, 158, 160–61, 167
correspondents, 4, 28, 33, 36, 49, 238*n*41
Covid-19 pandemic, 204
Craigslist, 8
Crane, Stephen, 34
crime, 38–39, 46–47, 75, 93, 100, 106, 108–9
criticism, 28, 43, 50, 106, 126, 175, 176
Crosscut (online news site), 204
cultural capital, 179, 214–15, 241*n*93

Davis, Richard Harding, 34, 43
death, of journalism, 129, 191–94, 227*n*5
decoding: best work, 89, 103–6; complex topics, 179
Delporte, Christian, 34

Index 287

Denave, Sophie, 143, 146
Dépêche de Toulouse, La (newspaper), 32, 38, 132–33, 236*n*18, 240*n*74
Dépêche du Midi, La (newspaper), 127, 203–5, 209
Dépêche Media Group, *La*, 204–5
Dicken-Garcia, Hazel, 238*n*38
digital news organizations, 9, 116
digital technology, 21, 116, 119–20, 123–26, 128, 132–34, 138–39, 154
dignifying, best work, 89, 106–9
disappointment, 87, 146, 200; adjustment modes and, 5, 12–15, 18, 19; disillusionment and, 19, 48, 141; managing, 57, 84, 85, 171, 188, 192, 207
discovering, best work, 88–89, 96–99
disillusionment, 19, 48, 141, 146, 154, 188
donors, 187, 261*n*17
Dorr, Rheta Childe, 46
Dreiser, Theodore, 34, 35
Dreyfus affair, 40
"dry" information, 39, 40, 50
Durand, Pascal, 236*n*21

ecology, news, 18–19, 21, 180
economics: bankruptcy, 115, 149; capitalism and, 181–82, 184, 262*n*29; constraints with technological transformations, 25, 115, 116, 139, 140, 214–16; cost controls, 44–45, 115, 170; of digital technology, 119; elites, 19; with grim outlook, 9, 68, 182, 191; labor, 115, 170; pressures, 23, 91, 124, 125; of regional media, 23; restructuring of newsrooms, 192; revenue, 2, 8, 9, 29, 33, 40, 116–20, 130, 132, 175
Économie de la presse quotidienne régionale (Le Floch), 228*n*9

ecosystems: contemporary information, 2, 8, 10, 21, 180; language of, 230*n*25; news ecology, 18–19, 21, 180
edifying, best work, 88, 89, 99–102
editors, 46, 86, 129, 150, 153, 184–85. *See also* beat reporters and editors
education: community college, 103, 213; *grandes écoles*, 209, 213; higher, 47, 209, 212, 213; nonprestigious universities, 6, 14, 71, 103, 213, 214; prestigious universities, 6, 14, 46–47, 78, 81, 97, 129; with social properties of journalists, 209, 210, 212, 213, 214, 215; teaching, 3, 34, 46, 71, 121, 158, 189; technology and multimedia skills, 129–31, 133; work conditions, 193. *See also* schools, journalism
Edwards, Alfred, 32
elites, 10, 19, 41; with fact-based reporting, 22–23, 39, 40; *le grand reportage* and, 36, 52; jobs for men, 46–48
Empaillé, L' (magazine), 205
empirical details, news and, 22–23, 31
employers, 8, 115, 149, 209, 210, 211. *See also* publishers
employment. *See* jobs
"Employment Protection Schemes" (Plan de Sauvegarde de l'Emploi), 69
"emprise du journalisme, L'" ("The Grip of Journalism," Bourdieu), 169, 260*n*1
"enemy of the people," 10
engaged (participatory) journalism, 101, 131, 173, 254*n*26
"éthique des journalistes au xixe siècle, L'" (Ferenczi), 238*n*41, 238*n*45
exits. *See* leaving journalism

Expanding News Desert, The (Abernathy), 228*n*9
experience, professional: with social properties of journalists, 209, 210–11, 212, 213, 214, 215; women from nonprestigious universities with less, 6, 14

Facebook, 8, 104, 124, 134, 151, 182
fact-based reporting: audiences and, 30–31; divisions over, 37–42; elites with, 22–23, 39, 40; in *fait divers*, 38, 39, 52; French journalists with, 22, 29, 30, 35–36, 38, 39, 40, 52; information without, 121; journalists in U.S. with, 29, 30, 35, 40, 51; principle of, 35, 44; resistance to, 238*n*41; women with agency and, 241*n*83
fact-based storytelling, 30, 37–42, 175
"factory" work, 76, 155
"Faire rendre des comptes" (Kaciaf), 228*n*9
fait divers, 36, 38, 39, 45, 52, 75, 100, 241*n*93
families, of journalists: children, 115, 148, 150, 151, 153, 155–56, 159, 161–62, 164–65; in France, 69; liberal, professional parents, 6, 14, 81, 97, 193, 210, 212, 213, 215; with life and work balance, 148, 151, 153–55, 157–64; men with work and time away from, 154, 259*n*23; middle class, 211; occupation of parents, 210, 211, 212; working class, 211
far-right politics, in France, 10–11, 101–2
Ferenczi, Thomas, 35–36, 40, 238*n*41, 238*n*45
fiction, journalism in, 43–44, 236*n*27
Figaro, Le (newspaper), 39–41, 240*n*69
firings, jobs, 69, 127, 145
First Gulf War, 65

five-cent (*un sou*) newspapers, 32
Foss, Katherine A., 44
Foucart, Stéphane, 179
"fourth estate," 35, 181–82, 262*n*31
France: Dreyfus affair, 40; economic constraints and technological status quo, 216; far-right politics in, 10–11, 101–2; *grandes écoles*, 209, 213; journalism schools in, 11, 59–60, 73, 80, 139–40, 177, 228*n*9, 237*n*33, 249*n*20; labor laws, 23, 56, 69, 83, 127, 136, 144, 160–61, 165, 167; newspapers with publication suspended in, 176; Nuit Debout protests, 158; print runs, 33; with privatization of television, 169; radio stations, 92, 136, 205, 249*n*20; Rainbow Warrior, 91; regional media and, 24, 173, 203–7, 231*n*42, 232*n*49, 253*n*20; riots in, 100; social order, 180. *See also* journalism, in France; journalists, in France; Paris, France; Toulouse, France
France Info, 92
France 3 (public television station), 204, 206, 209
France 3 Occitanie, 205
Frank, Thomas, 257*n*2
freelancers: best work, 109–11, 213; economic constraints and technological status quo, 215; French journalists, 9, 71–72, 73–74; hours, 77, 135; job insecurity, 78; leaving journalism, 144, 153, 163, 216; living for and off journalism, 212; living for journalism, 111, 210; living off journalism, 210, 212; with long-form reporting, 15; salaries, 48, 77; with technology, 134–35; women, 6, 46, 73–74
funding, 73, 132, 261*n*17

Gallegher (Davis), 43
gamble: adjustment modes as, 116, 141; journalism as, 48–53, 59
gambling, by candlelight, 227*n*7
Gannett, 175
gender: disparities with salaries, 44; division of labor and, 148, 151, 153, 154, 158–59, 166–67, 185; inequality, 14, 103–4, 184; living for journalism and, 211; with social properties of journalists, 209, 211, 212
general assignment reporters, 6, 109–10, 135, 209, 213, 215; in France, 80, 82; leaving journalism, 144, 216; living for and off journalism, 79, 212; living for journalism, 210; living off journalism, 210, 212; with street cop analogy, 246*n*73
Giffard, Pierre, 45–46
Gilets Jaunes (Yellow Vests), 10–11
Girardin, Émile de, 235*n*14
Godkin, E. L., 34, 40, 240*n*67
"good work," 86–87, 112, 150, 247*n*1
Google, 8, 182
gossip, 41, 45, 64, 109
government advertisements, 42
grandes écoles, 209, 213
grand reportage, le, 36, 52
"Grip of Journalism, The" ("L'emprise du journalisme," Bourdieu), 169, 260*n*1
"gutter journalism," 45

Hallin, Daniel C., 233*n*54
hamster wheel model, 9–10
Hanusch, Folker, 146, 242*n*6
harassment, of journalists, 10–11
Hayes, Danny, 228*n*9
healthcare, 3, 105–6, 107, 186, 187, 189, 193
Hearst, William Randolph, 31, 38, 41, 175

hedge fund owners, 176
Hirschman, Albert O., 14
homelessness, 94, 96, 101, 102, 108
hours worked, 54, 71, 73–75, 77, 135, 149, 193–94
Huet, Sylvestre, 179

identity, professional: Commission de la Carte d'Identité des Journalistes Professionnels, 228*n*15; deprioritizing, 5, 158; leaving journalism and letting go of, 144, 155, 161, 163, 165, 166, 168; resocializing, 26, 147–49, 166
ignoring, technology, 123–28
illusio, 4, 227*n*7
immediacy, 121, 187
immersive journalism, 122
immigrants, 42, 65, 67, 107–8
individuals, giving worth to, 89, 106–9
inequalities: gender, 14, 103–4, 184; social, 8, 13–14, 22, 48, 50, 89, 92, 172, 184, 190
informants, 83, 201
information: contemporary ecosystem of, 2, 8, 10, 21, 180; "dry," 39, 40, 50; without fact checks, 121; "Local Journalism and the Information Needs of Local Communities," 228*n*9; outsourcing, 76; polysemic profession and revealing, 61, 63–64; revealing, 63–64; U.S. journalism oriented toward, 7, 15, 24, 30, 37
informing, 30, 39, 84, 121, 236*n*25; defined, 12; principle of, 3, 22–23, 29
internships, 11, 58, 73, 81, 85
interviewing, 17–18, 36, 238*n*41
interviewing, as comprehension: anonymity, 200–1; informants, 201; predicament of journalists and

objective conditions, 198, 199–200; predicament of journalists and specifics, 197; purpose of, 197–98; social conditions and positions, 198–99

investigative reporting, 72, 128, 243*n*13, 246*n*73; with discovering and best work, 88–89, 96–99; in France, 42, 59; persistence and hard work with, 64; in U.S., 37, 41, 42, 52–53, 59

investing, in technology, 128–33

Iraq war, 65

Islamophobia, 160

Jackson, Daniel, 244*n*15, 245*n*44

Jaurès, Jean, 40

jobs: advertising, 156, 161; contracts, 9, 56, 73, 74–75, 77, 129, 144, 153, 158–59, 160–61, 163, 167, 193–94; descriptions, 5, 34, 43–44, 246*n*73; for elite men, 46–48; employers, 8, 115, 149, 209, 210, 211; growth, 33–34, 43, 44, 115; hours worked, 54, 71, 73–75, 77, 135, 149, 193–94; insecurity, 3, 68, 71, 78, 135, 138, 140, 170; loss, 56, 69, 81–82, 83, 115, 127, 135, 140, 145, 150, 192, 204, 216; for middle class, 33, 43; offers, 245*n*44; opportunities, 68; protections, 44, 127, 145; reality of, 49; reduced number of, 8, 9, 68, 136, 138, 168; salaries, 1, 3, 9, 12, 19, 34, 44–45, 48–49, 69, 71–77, 80, 127, 138, 144, 153–54, 158, 160–61, 167, 193–94, 206, 250*n*51; sales, 156; stability, 2, 43, 69, 130, 159; titles, 17, 173, 209–10, 212–13, 216; vocations and market, 186–90; work conditions, 3, 8, 49, 135, 193–94. *See also* leaving journalism

Johnstone, John, 90

Journal, Le (newspaper), 33

Journal des Débats, Le (newspaper), 40–41

Journal de Toulouse, Le (newspaper), 32

journalism: balance of rewards with novel forms of, 25; belief in worth of, 3–4, 5, 8, 11, 23, 46, 48, 49; birth of modern, 22–23, 31–37; crisis reconsidered in, 142–43, 166–68; criticism, 50, 106, 175; death of, 191–95, 227*n*5; engaged or participatory, 101, 131, 173, 254*n*26; in fiction, 43–44, 236*n*27; finding place in, 42–48; as gamble, 48–53, 59; "gutter," 45; immersive, 122; legitimate, 109, 170; "L'emprise du journalisme," 169, 260*n*1; literature on, 244*n*15, 262*n*29; living for, 23–24, 69–74, 86, 111, 210, 211, 212, 246*n*50; living for and off, 23, 55–56, 78–82, 210, 212–13; living off, 23, 55, 56, 57, 69, 74–78, 83, 183–84, 210, 212, 246*n*50; *Local Journalism*, 228*n*9; men with highest positions in, 43; as professional calling, 34, 35, 36–37, 186–90; reporting and questioning utility of, 257*n*2; "slow," 81, 123; *Sociologie du Journalisme*, 261*n*15; solutions, 121–22, 170, 191; sports, 45, 54, 55, 59, 62, 94, 104, 242*n*3; "standing" and "seated," 241*n*83; *Steps Into Journalism*, 34; as storytelling, 61–63, 66, 67, 70; technology and novel forms of, 119; women in, 6, 36, 41, 44–46, 51, 61–64, 66–67, 69–71, 73–74, 76–77, 81–82, 158–60, 184–85, 241*n*83, 241*n*92; Worlds of Journalism survey, 90; as "worth the candle," 4, 13, 142, 188, 192, 194, 197, 227*n*7,

journalism (*continued*)
248*n*12. *See also* leaving journalism; polysemic profession, journalism as; schools, journalism; social function, of journalism

journalism, in France: best work, 214; birth of modern, 31, 32, 33, 34, 35–46; commercial model of, 41, 51, 52, 235*n*14; employers, 8; with ideas and opinion, 7, 15, 24, 30, 37, 41, 51; investigative reporting, 42, 59; literature and, 236*n*27; living for, 211, 212; living for and off, 212; living off, 23, 55, 56, 57, 69, 74–78, 83, 183–84, 210, 212, 246*n*50; with politics and literature, 40; prestigious, 52; with professional prizes, 93; "slow," 81; social function of, 24, 37–38, 39, 40, 41; students, 11, 73, 249*n*20; U.S. compared to, 15–18; worthy of admiration, 92–96

journalism, in U.S.: best work, 213–14; birth of modern, 31–33, 34–35, 36, 37; commercial model of, 51, 235*n*14; employers in, 8; France compared to, 15–18; with ideas and opinion, 42; "information-oriented," 7, 15, 24, 30, 37; investigative reporting, 37, 41, 42, 52–53, 59; living for, 211; living for and off, 212; prestigious, 41; social function of, 24, 37–38, 39, 40, 41; students, 11, 61, 244*n*15; worthy of admiration, 92–96

journalistes sociaux, Les (Lévêque), 241*n*83

Journalistic Standards in Nineteenth-Century America (Dicken-Garcia), 238*n*38

journalists: associations for, 34; best work of, 96–109; with commercial pressures, 140, 169, 173, 188; Commission de la Carte d'Identité des Journalistes Professionnels, 228*n*15; *La Dépêche du Midi* with number of, 204; as "enemy of the people," 10; interviewed after leaving journalism, 17–18; KNKX with number of, 204; KUOW with number of, 204; legacy of deceased, 94–95; MMJs, 64, 115, 122, 128–29, 131, 141, 151, 154, 170; with new social roles, 178–79; at pinnacle, 109–13; purpose of, 174–80; radio, 1, 78–79, 80, 115, 120–21, 134, 136, 155, 212; reasons for becoming, 1–2, 20, 54–55, 183, 243*n*7, 244*n*15, 247*n*75; regional, 5, 206; retirement of, 69, 160, 204; role of, 10, 12; *Seattle Times* with number of, 203; social conditions and, 20, 36–37, 45, 51, 89, 91, 139–41, 172; social media and harassment of, 10–11; sociology of, 18–21; solo, 131; at television stations, 78. *See also* families, of journalists; leaving journalism; predicament, of journalists; social properties, of journalists

journalists, in France: with decoding, 89; with dignifying, 89; edifying, 89; editors, 46; with engagement, 102; with fact-based reporting, 22, 29, 30, 35–36, 38, 39, 40, 52; families of, 69; freelancers, 9, 71–72, 73–74; general assignment reporters, 80, 82; living for and off journalism, 80–81; manuals for, 34; with moral crusades, 36; population of, 9, 236*n*21; radio, 1, 80, 155; with symbolic rewards, 7; working in Toulouse, 16–17; working outside

Paris, 16, 77, 150; worthy of admiration, 92–96
journalists, in U.S.: American Journalist Survey, 89–90; with decoding, 89; with dignifying, 89; discovering, 89–90; editors, 46; with empirical details, 22–23; with engagement, 102; with fact-based reporting, 29, 30, 35, 40, 51; freelancers, 9; population of, 9; radio, 1, 78–79; with symbolic rewards, 7; working in Seattle, 16–17; working outside New York or Washington, DC, 16; worthy of admiration, 92–96
Journal Politique et Littéraire de Toulouse et de la Haute-Garonne (newspaper), 32
Journal Toulousain, Le (magazine), 205

Kaciaf, Nicolas, 228n9
Kalifa, Dominique, 45, 236n25, 241n93
Kaplan, Richard, 238n38
KIRO (television station), 209
Klondike Gold Rush, 46
KNKX (public radio station), 204
KPLU (public radio station), 204
Kroeger, Brooke, 46
Kunitz, Stanley, 2, 190
KUOW (public radio station), 204, 206, 209

labor: cutting costs with MMJs, 115, 170; distribution of, 124; division of, 148, 151, 153, 154, 155–56, 158–59, 161–62, 166–67, 181, 185, 214; organizers, 67, 211; U.S. Bureau of Labor Statistics, 228n18
labor laws: France, 23, 56, 69, 83, 127, 136, 144, 160–61, 165, 167; in national and regional spaces, 206–7; U.S., 23, 56, 69, 83, 127, 144, 161, 167
Lafarge, Géraud, 249n20
language: deterioration of, 241n92; of ecosystems, 230n25
Lavine, John, 243n13
Lawless, Jennifer L., 228n9
layoffs, 56, 81–82, 115, 145, 204; candidates, 135; with French labor laws, 69, 127; managers with, 150, 192, 216; with U.S. labor laws, 83
leaving journalism: beliefs in question, 26, 143, 149–52; with crisis reconsidered, 142–43, 166–68; firings, 69, 127, 145; freelancers, 144, 153, 163, 216; inability to recall best work and, 248n12; interviewing journalists after, 17–18; job loss, 83, 140, 145; layoffs, 56, 69, 81–82, 83, 115, 127, 135, 145, 150, 192, 204, 216; organizing exits and resocializing professional identities, 147–49; professional identity and, 144, 155, 161, 163, 165, 166, 168; professional life after, 114; reasons for, 5, 145–47, 262n31; resocializing professional identities and, 26, 166; with sense of choice, 144, 156–61; with sense of necessity, 144, 161–66; social properties across departures, 216, 226; timing and, 172; trigger events, 25, 143, 146–47, 152–56, 166
Leboncoin.fr, 8
Le Floch, Patrick, 228n9
Legavre, Jean-Baptiste, 148
Lemann, Nicholas, 243n12
Leroux, Gaston, 34, 47, 236n27
Le Roux, Hugues, 36
Lévêque, Sandrine, 238n45, 241n83
Libération (newspaper), 93, 206

life: professional, 2, 3, 114, 138, 140, 148; with work balance, 148, 151, 153–55, 157–64
lifestyle, 58–59, 177
Lincoln, Abraham, 42
literature: on exits from journalism, 146; on journalism, 244*n*15, 262*n*29; journalism in fiction, 43–44, 236*n*27; literary writing, 39, 40, 42; politics and, 28–30, 32, 34, 40, 41
living for and off journalism, 23; men, 210, 212, 213; polysemic profession, 55–56, 78–82
living for journalism, 23–24, 211, 212, 246*n*50; best work and, 86; freelancers, 111, 210; polysemic profession, 55, 56, 57, 69–74
living off journalism, in France, 23, 246*n*50; general assignment reporters and freelancers, 210, 212; polysemic profession, 55, 56, 57, 69, 74–78, 83, 183–84
"Local Journalism and the Information Needs of Local Communities" (Napoli), 228*n*9
Londres, Albert, 42, 44
long-form reporting: audiences for, 176, 179, 180; edifying to broaden understanding, 99–100; freelancers with, 15; in-depth and well-composed, 5, 10, 170–71, 176; as pinnacle, 24, 71, 73, 74, 79, 95–96, 122–23; professional prizes for, 114; as rarity, 10, 26
Los Angeles Times (newspaper), 249*n*23
Lyon, France, 232*n*50

Maares, Phoebe, 146
managers, 74, 75, 115, 116, 124, 153; economic policies of, 192; with layoffs, 150, 192, 216; with modernization, 41; newsroom, 156–57
Mancini, Paolo, 233*n*54
manuals, for journalists, 34
Marchetti, Dominique, 249*n*20
market: pressures, 27, 175, 261*n*17; vocations and, 186–90
marketing, 55, 136, 142, 161, 243*n*13
Marseille, France, 232*n*50
Marshall Project (online journalism organization), 93
Martin, Marc, 33–34, 35
master's degrees, 209
material rewards, 194; diminution of, 2, 8–11, 68; symbolic and, 2, 4, 7, 12, 49, 128, 131–32, 227*n*7
Matin, Le (newspaper), 33
Maupassant, Guy de, 34, 43, 236*n*27
May, Dick, 237*n*33
McConaghy, Lorraine, 240*n*78
media, 180–86, 233*n*54, 243*n*13. *See also* regional media; social media
Mediacités Toulouse (online news site), 205
Mediapart (online news site), 93
Medill School, Northwestern University, 243*n*13
men: balance of rewards for, 58; best work, 213; economic constraints and technology status quo, 214–15; with highest positions in journalism, 43; jobs for elite, 46–48; leaving journalism, 216; from liberal professional families with degrees from prestigious universities, 6, 14, 97; living for and off journalism, 210, 212–13; living for journalism, 210, 211; with work commitments and missed family time, 154, 259*n*23

middle class, 33, 42, 177, 180, 211;
  reporters from lower, 45–46;
  reporters from upper, 46–48;
  salaries below level of, 1, 12, 19, 43, 44
Midi Presse (newspaper), 204
Midi-Pyrénées, 205
Millaud, Moïse Polydore, 31, 38
MMJs. *See* multimedia journalists
Möller, Cecilia, 146
Monde, Le (newspaper), 92, 93
Monde Diplomatique, Le (newspaper), 92
Montaigne, Michel de, 227*n*7
moral crusades, 36
Morley, David, 173–74
motto, of *Le Figaro*, 240*n*69
muckrakers, 41, 42, 47, 51, 83, 96
multimedia journalists (MMJs):
  challenging by investing in
  technology, 128–29; cutting labor
  costs with, 115, 170; with
  disillusionment, 141, 154; immersive
  journalism with, 122; with
  persistence and hard work, 64;
  professional mobility of, 115, 131; with
  stories and time constraints, 151
Murray, Ed (former mayor), 98, 99
Mystery of the Yellow Room, The
  (Leroux), 236*n*27

Napoli, Philip M., 228*n*9, 234*n*58
Nation (magazine), 34, 42
national journalistic spaces, 206–7. *See
  also* New York; Paris, France;
  Washington, DC
Neveu, Érik, 228*n*9, 235*n*6, 254*n*25,
  260*n*4, 261*n*15
news: business models for, 3, 31–33, 50,
  116, 169, 183, 187, 194, 261*n*17;
  ecology, 18–19, 21, 180; empirical
  details and, 22–23, 31; Internet, 120;

online sites, 73–74, 82, 95, 121, 129,
  132, 153–54, 204–5; organizations, 9,
  94, 116, 209, 215; startups, 140,
  204–5; television, 93, 97, 99, 114–15,
  131, 132, 152, 156, 158–59, 161, 162–64
news outlets: dominant, 73, 117, 127,
  205, 210–11, 214, 216; nondominant,
  73, 117, 210, 214; peripheral, 210, 211,
  212, 214–15
"newspaper English," 241*n*92
newspapers: alternative weeklies,
  81–82, 204, 205; five-cent, 32; penny
  papers, 32, 235*n*14; print runs, 33;
  proliferation in nineteenth century,
  33; with publication suspended, 176;
  regional, 8–9; in Seattle, 32, 38,
  203–5, 209, 236*n*18; in seventeenth
  century, 28; three cent, 32; in
  Toulouse, 127, 203–5, 209. *See also
  specific newspapers*
newsroom managers, 156–57
New York: competition for audiences,
  33; as national journalistic space,
  206; Paris and, 3, 7, 9, 16, 32, 39, 83,
  93, 232*n*50
New Yorker (magazine), 92, 95–96
New York Evening Post (newspaper), 34,
  40, 42
New York Herald (newspaper), 40
New York Journal (newspaper), 32, 41
New York Press Club, 35
New York Times (newspaper), 40, 206;
  best work at, 92, 93, 94, 96; Ochs
  and, 32, 39, 41–42
New York World (newspaper), 32, 35, 38,
  41, 51, 237*n*36
Nielsen, Rasmus Kleis, 228*n*9
Nixon, Richard, 63
"No initiative, no hassle" (Pas
  d'initiative, pas d'emmerde), 127

Index 295

Nölleke, Daniel, 146
nonreporting positions, job titles, 210
Northwestern University, 243*n*13
Nuit Debout protests (2016), 158
nursing, 3, 189, 193

Occupy movement, 11
Ochs, Adolph, 32, 39, 41–42
online news sites, 73–74, 82, 95, 121, 129, 132, 153–54, 204–5, 249*n*23
online-only formats, 93, 95, 204
online reporters, 97–98
On Television (Bourdieu), 260*n*1
Örnebring, Henrik, 146
Ornstein, Charles, 249*n*23
Ouest-France group, 205
owners, 176, 182. *See also* publishers

Paris, France, 33, 35, 77, 80, 150, 236*n*21; as national journalistic space, 206, 207; New York and, 3, 7, 9, 16, 32, 39, 83, 93, 232*n*50
Parisian *Mediapart* group, 205
participatory (engaged) journalism, 101, 131, 173, 254*n*26
partisanship, reporting and, 31, 32, 36, 42, 178, 180, 237*n*28, 238*n*38
Pas d'initiative, pas d'emmerde ("No initiative, no hassle"), 127
patronage, political, 31
pay. *See* salaries
penny papers, 32, 235*n*14
Penny Press, The (newspaper), 32
periodicals, politics and, 28
Petit Journal, Le (newspaper), 33, 38
Petit Parisien, Le (newspaper), 33
petit reportage, le, 36, 52
photographers, 128, 131, 151, 154, 156, 161, 162, 165

Plan de Sauvegarde de l'Emploi ("Employment Protection Schemes"), 69
Planet Money (radio program), 93
Plenel, Edwy, 59, 93, 94
podcasts, 120, 122, 129, 131, 155, 158
polemics, 40
politics, 28, 36, 105, 132; far-right, 10–11, 101–2; left-leaning, 32, 80, 240*n*74; literature and, 28–30, 32, 34, 40, 41; patronage, 31; reporters covering, 70, 91; as vocation and Weber, Max, 246*n*50
Politics and the American Press (Kaplan), 238*n*38
polysemic profession, journalism as: adjustment modes, 55–57, 68–69, 75, 85; attractions, 54–55, 58–61, 63, 67–82, 83; creativity, 58–59, 60; with fragile social function, 82–85; giving voice, 61, 66–67; with information revealed, 61, 63–64; less civic vision of, 23, 57, 58, 60; lifestyle, 58–59; living for, 55, 56, 57, 69–74; living for and off, 55–56, 78–82; living off, 55, 56, 57, 69, 74–78, 83, 183–84; passion and, 58–60, 67–82; schools, 59–60; social functions and prestige, 23, 60; storytelling, 61–62, 67, 70; understanding of world, 61, 64–66
Poore, Benjamin Perley, 238*n*41
popular class, 37, 38
power holders, 88–89, 96–99, 103–6, 182
"Power of Journalism, The" (Bourdieu), 260*n*1
predicament, of journalists: as analytical construct, 174; with balance of rewards, 2, 3, 5, 27, 191, 192, 193; birth of modern journalism,

22–23, 31–37; craft and, 1–2; divisions about fact-based storytelling, 37–42; finding place in journalism, 42–48; with harassment, 10–11; with journalism as gamble, 48–53; objective conditions, 198, 199–200; social and commercial functions, 29–30, 50; specifics, 197
press: birth of modern journalism, 31–37; cards, 9, 76, 77; clubs, 34–35; nineteenth-century, 15, 52, 53, 235n14, 238n38; releases, 5, 99, 106, 125–26, 162
Press Club, in Seattle, 35
Presse, La (newspaper), 235n14
prestige, 8, 11, 25, 27, 68, 115, 127, 178, 185; diminution of, 1; entrance exams at journalism schools with less, 244n14; journalism, 41, 52; with journalism as professional calling, 34, 35, 36–37; nonprestigious universities, 6, 14, 71, 103, 213, 214; professional prizes, 206; with reputation of online pure players, 249n23; social function and, 23, 60; universities, 6, 14, 78, 81, 129
pride: best work and, 86, 91, 97, 98, 102, 104, 107, 109; as invaluable, 81; symbolic rewards, 192, 195
printing contracts, 42
print runs, in France, 33
Prisma Academy, 177, 244n14
prizes, professional, 2, 42, 82, 93, 114, 172, 206, 214
Professional Association of French Journalists, The (l'Association Syndicale Professionnelle des Journalistes Républicains Français), 34

professional roles, best work choices and, 248n9
professors, 27, 67, 90, 212
Progressive Era reforms, 30, 52–53
ProPublica (online news source), 93
public radio stations, 78–79, 94, 204, 206, 209, 253n15
public service, 20, 105, 155, 157, 165
public television stations, 79, 204, 206, 209
publishers (owners), 50, 192, 240n74; with audience and class, 38, 39, 40–41, 42; with commercial model, 31–33
Pulitzer, Joseph, 31–32, 38, 39, 41, 42, 51, 237n36
Pulitzer Prize, 82, 93
pure players, online, 205, 249n23

racial diversity, in regional media, 231n42
Radio France, 249n20
radio journalists, 1, 78–80, 115, 120–21, 134, 136, 155, 212
radio programs, 93, 94, 107–8
radio stations, 67, 73, 80, 149; French, 92, 136, 205, 249n20; living off journalism at, 74–76; public, 78–79, 94, 204, 206, 209, 253n15
Rainbow Warrior, sinking of, 91
readership. *See* audiences
regional journalists, 5, 206
regional media, 5, 10, 23, 114, 171, 176; as middle- to upper-middle-class professional space, 43, 177; national journalistic spaces and, 206–7; racial diversity in, 231n42; in U.S. and France, 24, 173, 203–7, 231n42, 232n49, 253n20

regional newspapers, 8–9
Rémy de Guebhard, Caroline (Séverine), 241n83
reporters, 47, 79, 86, 98, 127, 150; aerospace, 97, 99, 126, 250n51; beat, 96–97, 114, 210, 212, 213, 214, 216; *fait divers*, 38, 39, 45, 75, 100, 241n93; freelance, 6, 9, 15, 46, 48, 71–74, 77–78, 109–11, 134–35, 144, 153, 163, 210, 212–13, 215–16; job description, 43–44; political, 70, 91; television, 97, 99, 114–15, 131, 132, 152, 156, 158–59, 161, 163–64; women, 36, 41, 45, 46, 51, 241n83, 241n92. *See also* general assignment reporters; journalists
reporting, 45, 46, 51, 94, 210, 241n92; evolution of, 238n45; investigative, 37, 41–42, 52–53, 59, 64, 72, 88–89, 96–99, 128, 243n13, 246n73; partisanship and, 31, 32, 36, 42, 178, 180, 237n28, 238n38; with utility of journalism questioned, 257n2. *See also* fact-based reporting; long-form reporting
retirement, of journalists, 69, 160, 204
revenue, 29, 33, 40, 116–20, 130, 175; advertising, 8, 9, 132; decline, 2, 8, 9
rewards. *See* balance of rewards; material rewards; symbolic rewards
Riis, Jacob, 36
riots, in French cities, 100
Roberts Forde, Kathy, 44
Robinson, Sue, 228n9
Rosa, Hartmut, 170
Rue89 (online newspaper), 93

Sacco, Joe, 179
Sainte Croix, Avril de, 36
salaries, 3, 9, 34, 45, 193, 206, 250n51; financial insecurity, 194; firings and legal compensation, 69, 127; freelancers, 48, 77; higher, 80, 161; severance packages, 144, 158, 160–61, 167; subpar, 1, 12, 19, 43, 44, 49, 71, 72, 73, 74, 75, 76, 138, 153, 154
Salisbury, William, 48
salon chroniclers, 36
schools, journalism: class and transformations in, 23; with commercial pressures, 139–40; with declining enrollments, 193; entrance exams, 177, 244n14; in France, 11, 59–60, 73, 80, 139–40, 177, 228n9, 237n33, 249n20; *Before Journalism Schools*, 241n83; number of graduates, 167–68; polysemic attractions, 59–60; with social functions, 122, 173; textbooks, 34; in UK, 68; in U.S., 11, 59–61, 139–40, 177, 237n33, 243nn12–13, 244nn14–15
Schudson, Michael, 18–19, 34, 35, 179
scoops, 28, 35, 43, 63–64, 86, 169
"seated journalism," 241n83
Seattle: with best work, 88–89, 92, 95–103, 108, 110–12; fact-based reporting and, 38; hours worked, 135; journalists and technology in, 117, 120, 121, 124, 127–29, 133, 134, 135, 137, 139, 140; journalists working in, 16–17; KUOW, 204, 206, 209; leaving journalism, 25–26, 143, 146, 149, 150, 152, 153–55, 165; living for and off journalism in, 82; living for journalism in, 55, 211; newspapers, 32, 38, 203–5, 209, 236n18; online news sites, 204; predicament of journalists in, 7;

Press Club, 35; radio stations, 149, 204, 206, 209, 253*n*15; regional media and, 203–7, 232*n*49; as technology hub, 17; television stations, 74, 203–4, 206, 216; Toulouse and, 3, 232*n*50; weekly newspapers, 204

Seattle Channel (public television station), 204

Seattle Daily Journal of Commerce (newspaper), 204

Seattle Times (newspaper), 32, 38–39, 203–5, 209, 236*n*18

Seattle Weekly (alternative weekly), 204

Secret d'Info (radio program), 93

sensationalism, 30, 39, 45, 50, 51, 169

seventeenth century, newspapers in, 28

severance packages, 144, 158, 160–61, 167

Séverine (Caroline Rémy de Guebhard), 241*n*83

sexism, 241*n*83, 241*n*92

Shuman, Edwin L., 34

Simon, Jules, 33

60 Minutes (television news magazine), 93

"slow" journalism, 81, 123

social conditions: interviewing as comprehension and, 198–99; journalists and, 20, 36–37, 45, 51, 89, 91, 139–41, 172

social function, of journalism: commercial and, 4, 5, 6, 29–30, 50, 118, 151, 176, 191, 206; defined, 19, 36; fragility of, 82–85; in France and U.S., 24, 37–38, 39, 40, 41; in nineteenth century, 35; prestige and, 23, 60; professional prizes with, 42; redefining, 26–27, 171, 177, 179, 191, 192; in schools, 122, 173; with technology and new equilibrium, 118–23

social justice, 67, 160

social media, 8, 104, 136, 151, 182; journalists harassed on, 10–11; refreshing, 5; technologies, 114, 124–25, 126, 133, 134, 138, 150

social order, media and, 180–86

social properties, of journalists: adjustment modes with, 13–15; best work, 213–14, 224; career expectations, 210–13, 223; categories used for analysis of, 209, 210, 217–22; departures from journalism, 216, 226; job titles, 209–10, 212; less favorable, 23–24, 56; most favorable, 23, 56; occupations of parents, 210, 211, 212; across responses, 214–16, 225; technology and, 127

social recruitment, 24, 44, 57, 60, 91, 177, 193, 244*n*14

social utility, of regional media, 23

society reporting, in Washington, DC, 241*n*92

Sociologie du Journalisme (Neveu), 261*n*15

sociology, of journalists, 18–21

solo journalists, 131

solutions journalism, 121–22, 170, 191

"sou, un" (five-cent) newspapers, 32

South Seattle Emerald (online news site), 204

sports journalism, 45, 54, 55, 59, 62, 94, 104, 242*n*3

Standard Oil exposé, 41

"standing journalism," 241*n*83

Starkman, Dean, 9–10

Starr, Paul, 33

startups, news, 140, 204–5

statehouse reporters, 79

Steffens, Lincoln, 41, 46–48, 52
Steiger, Paul, 93
Steps Into Journalism (Shuman), 34
"Storybook Plutocracy" (Frank), 257*n*2
storytelling, 94, 125, 170, 177; fact-based, 30, 37–42, 175; journalism as, 61–63, 66, 67, 70; long-form, 163
Stranger, The (alternative weekly), 204
students, journalism, 11, 61, 68, 73, 244*n*15, 249*n*20
stunt reporting, women with, 45, 46, 51
Sumpter, Randall S., 33, 44–45, 241*n*83
symbolic hierarchies, 22, 24, 48, 86–87, 88, 91–92
symbolic rewards: commercial pressures eroding, 140, 193; diminution of, 2, 8–11, 68; material and, 2, 4, 7, 12, 49, 128, 131–32, 227*n*7; in national journalistic spaces, 206; pride, 192, 195; for regional media, 206

Tarbell, Ida, 41
teaching, 3, 34, 46, 71, 121, 158, 189
technology: acceding by going along with, 117, 133–38, 140; audiences and, 121; challenging and investing in, 117, 128–33; with commercial and social functions of journalism, 118–23; commercial pressures and, 119–20, 121, 138–41; conserving by ignoring, 117, 123–28; digital, 21, 116, 119–20, 123–26, 128, 132–34, 138–39, 154; hubs, 17; MMJs and, 64, 115, 122, 128–29, 131, 141, 154, 170; multimedia skills, 129–31, 133; social media, 114, 124–25, 126, 133, 134, 138, 150; social properties of journalists and, 127; transformations with economic constraints, 25, 115, 116, 139, 140, 214–16
television news: magazines, 93; reporters, 97, 99, 114–15, 131, 132, 152, 156, 158–59, 161, 163–64
television stations, 72, 74, 78–79, 169, 203–4, 206, 209, 216
"theory travels best," 173–74
This American Life (public radio program), 94
"three cent papers," 32
Tocqueville, Alexis de, 42
ToulÉco (online news site), 205
Toulouse, France: with best work, 88–89, 92, 95–98, 100–104, 107–8, 110–12; *La Dépêche du Midi*, 127, 203–5, 209; fact-based reporting and, 38; France 3, 204, 206, 209; journalists working in, 16–17; *Le Journal de Toulouse*, 32; *Journal Politique et Littéraire de Toulouse et de la Haute-Garonne*, 32; leaving journalism, 25–26, 143, 146, 149–52, 153, 154, 158, 160, 163; living for journalism in, 211; living off journalism in, 55; newspapers, 127, 203–5, 209; online news site, 132, 205; predicament of journalists, 7; public television stations, 204, 206, 209; radio stations, 136, 205; regional media and, 203–7, 232*n*49; rewards balance, 117; Seattle and, 3, 232*n*50; with technology, 120, 123–25, 127, 129, 133, 134, 136–41; as technology hub, 17
trade publications, 33, 44
trigger events, leaving journalism, 25, 143, 146–47, 152–56, 166

Troppman, Jean-Baptiste, 38
"true crime," 93
Twitter, 104, 124, 125, 126, 133, 134, 151

United Kingdom (UK), 68
United States (U.S.): Bureau of Labor Statistics, 228*n*18; economic constraints and technology status quo, 216; higher education in, 209; journalism schools in, 11, 59–61, 139–40, 177, 237*n*33, 243*nn*12–13, 244*nn*14–15; labor laws, 23, 56, 69, 83, 127, 144, 161, 167; regional media and, 24, 173, 203–7, 231*n*42, 232*n*49, 253*n*20; social order, 180. *See also* journalism, in U.S.; journalists, in U.S.; New York; Seattle
University of Pennsylvania, 237*n*33
urban corruption, 41
U.S.. *See* United States

Vauréal, Henri de (Count), 41
Veterans Administration, 97, 99
Via Occitanie (television station), 204
Villard, Henry, 42
Villemessant, Hippolyte de, 39, 40
vocations, market and, 186–90
voice, giving, 61, 66–67

Waisbord, Silvio, 182
Wall Street Journal (newspaper), 93
war reporting, 42, 94
Washington, DC, 16, 38, 206, 241*n*92
Washington Correspondents' Club, 34–35
Washington Post (newspaper), 92, 206
watchdog, 58, 89, 96, 97, 111
Watergate, 83, 91
Weaver, David, 90, 248*n*11, 248*nn*8–9
Weber, Max, 48–49, 59, 175, 246*n*50

Weber, Tracy, 249*n*23
websites, 71, 73, 84, 122, 132, 179, 244*n*14; production work, 137; refreshing, 5, 121, 134; social media, 136
wellness, in *New York Times*, 253*n*20
West Seattle Blog (online news site), 204
White, Horace, 42
Wilhoit, G. Cleveland, 90, 248*n*11
Willis, Paul, 184
Willnat, Lars, 90, 248*n*11
wit, literary, 28
women: best work, 213, 214; economic constraints, 214–15; in journalism, 6, 36, 41, 44–46, 51, 61–64, 66–67, 69–71, 73–74, 76–77, 81–82, 158–60, 184–85, 241*n*83, 241*n*92; leaving journalism, 216; living for journalism, 210, 211, 212; living off journalism, 210, 212; working-class, 14
Woodward, Bob, 59, 63, 243*n*7
work: balance and division of labor with families, 148, 151, 153, 154, 155–56, 158–60, 161–64; commitments and missed family time, 154, 259*n*23; conditions, 3, 8, 49, 135, 193–94; "factory," 76, 155; "good," 86–87, 112, 150, 247*n*1; with life balance, 148, 151, 153–55, 157–64; persistence and hard, 64; rarity of long-form, in-depth, well-composed, 5, 10, 171, 176; website production, 137. *See also* best work; jobs
working class, 6, 14, 211
Worlds of Journalism survey, 90
"worth the candle," journalism as, 4, 13, 142, 188, 192, 194, 197, 227*n*7, 248*n*12

Index 301

writing: by bloggers, 99; creative, 58, 95; exams, 162, 177, 244*n*14; fiction and journalism, 43–44, 236*n*27; joy of, 54, 59, 61, 62, 70, 80, 81, 126, 247*n*75; literary, 39, 40, 42; popular class and accessible, 37, 38. *See also* literature

Xau, Fernand, 32

yellow press, 38, 39, 50

Yellow Vests (*Gilets Jaunes*), 10–11

Zola, Émile, 34, 39, 40, 83

GPSR Authorized Representative: Easy Access System Europe, Mustamäe tee
50, 10621 Tallinn, Estonia, gpsr.requests@easproject.com

www.ingramcontent.com/pod-product-compliance
Lightning Source LLC
Chambersburg PA
CBHW031234290426
44109CB00012B/289